Speaking of Sex

SPEAKING OF SEX

The Denial of Gender Inequality

DEBORAH L. RHODE

HARVARD UNIVERSITY PRESS
Cambridge, Massachusetts
London, England

First Harvard University Press paperback edition, 1999

Portions of Chapter 4 originally appeared, in
different form, in *Signs,* copyright © 1995 by
The University of Chicago, all rights reserved.
Portions of Chapters 5, 6, and 7 originally appeared,
in different form, in *The National Law Journal,*
copyright © (1995, 1996) The New York Law
Publishing Company.

Library of Congress Cataloging-in-Publication Data

Rhode, Deborah L.
Speaking of sex: the denial of gender inequality/
Deborah L. Rhode.
p.   cm.
Includes bibliographical references and index.
ISBN 0–674–83177–2 (cloth)
ISBN 0–674–83178–0 (pbk.)
1. Sex discrimination against women—United States.
2. Sex role in the work environment—United States.
3. Work and family—United States.
4. Equal pay for equal work—United States.
5. Sex discrimination in education—United States.
I. Title.
HQ1237.5.U6R48   1997
305.42´0973—dc21   94–49905

For
Barbara Allen Babcock
and
Lawrence M. Friedman

Preface

Speaking of sex is sexy; speaking of sexual inequality is not. That point came home to me again shortly after starting this book. After settling on its title, I stumbled across an advertisement for a video of the same name. This other version of *Speaking of Sex* promised explicit demonstrations of how to improve "lovemaking skills" and gain "deeper intimacy," as well as answers to such complicated questions as "Am I normal?" All this was within reach at the "special" price of $29.95, with immediate delivery in plain, unmarked packaging. Seized with anxiety over the theft of my title, I taped the ad to the refrigerator door with a note to my sleeping husband: "What should I do about *my* book?" His response came back the following morning in a plain, unmarked envelope: "Forget the book. Buy the tape."

I took his point, if not his advice. Sexual inequality is not sexy. To many men, the topic seems tedious, threatening, or both. For women who live and work with men, it can be equally problematic.

Yet the "woman problem" is too pervasive to overlook. So it makes periodic public appearances, most notably when some exceptional event captures public attention, like the murder of Nicole Brown Simpson or the Anita Hill / Clarence Thomas hearings. But such episodes have not resulted in the social changes that are necessary to prevent similar incidents. Sex-based inequality and sex-based violence remain with us in our daily lives—in our homes, our workplaces, our schools, and our streets.

This book explores the cultural forces that perpetuate these problems. After almost fifteen years of working on issues of gender inequality at the legal level, I have become convinced of the need for broader reform strategies. On many of these issues, we have bumped up against the limits of current law, not because we lack insights about appropriate directions for change but because we lack a political consensus about their necessity.

A large part of the problem is the denial by most Americans that gender inequality *is* a serious problem or that it is one they have a responsibility to address. This book traces the foundations of denial across a wide range of cultural contexts. It begins with an overview of the strategies that enable us to discount the significance of inequality and our own role in perpetuating it. Discussion then focuses on the societal forces that institutionalize gender differences and gender disadvantages in our schools, families, workplaces, laws, and media. The analysis draws not only on the most reliable recent research, but also on narrative accounts and social satires that illumine broader themes.

What emerges from this account is the need for fundamental change in our public policies and cultural practices. During the 1930s, Alva Myrdal, a prominent Swedish leader, concluded in *Family and State* that "the entire female sex has grown into a social problem." Over half a century later, we are just beginning to understand the sense in which she was correct. What most women seek is not simply equal access to opportunities traditionally reserved for men, but equal recognition of the concerns and values traditionally associated with women.

To achieve equality on these terms will require sustained efforts in virtually all spheres of life: in the ways we raise our children, structure our workplaces, divide our family responsibilities, respond to media images, and frame our laws. Our challenges are substantial, and a necessary first step is to recognize the distance we have yet to travel.

Contents

1

The "No Problem" Problem

Almost two decades have passed since I arrived at Stanford Law School as the second woman on a faculty of some thirty-five men. When I expressed interest in teaching a course on sex discrimination, my colleagues were mainly amused. "Do our students really need a class in that?" "Don't most people manage to discriminate naturally, without formal instruction?" The dean, however, was appalled at the prospect. Not only was it a field he diplomatically described as "mush," it also would "brand me as a woman." "Well," I responded with what I hoped was faint irony, "that probably won't come as a surprise to most of the world. And what, after all, is my alternative?" But to the dean, the issue was academic credibility. And to establish that, I needed a "real" subject; he suggested commercial transactions.

In the years that followed, much changed. But much remained the same. American women no longer confront a deafening silence about gender inequality—what Betty Friedan once labeled a "problem that has no name." But although we have named many problems, we have solved few. Topics such as sexual harassment, the glass ceiling, and date rape have entered our conversations. And women increasingly have entered occupations once reserved for men. Yet ironically enough, this progress has created its own obstacles to further change. Women's growing opportunities are taken as evidence that the "woman problem" has been solved.[1]

This perception has itself become a central problem. The "no problem" problem prevents Americans from noticing that on every major measure of wealth, power, and status, women still are significantly worse off than men. More than 95 percent of corporate executives and 85 percent of elected officeholders are male; more than two-thirds of poor adults are female. For too many women, too many problems are not getting better. Sexual violence, occupational inequalities, and the feminization of poverty remain pervasive, and reproductive freedom is available only to those who can afford it. While we have made considerable progress in encouraging women to pursue traditional male roles, we have been less effective in encouraging men to assume traditional female ones. Women continue to shoulder the vast majority of responsibilities in the home, a burden that limits their opportunities in the world outside it.[2]

Yet despite these patterns, most Americans do not perceive gender inequality as a serious problem. The topic is an unwelcome intruder in most conversations. When speaking of sex, we like to discuss sexual relationships, sexual deviance, and sexual difference; we prefer to avoid sexual inequality and the patterns that sustain it. Even those who share the basic goals of the women's movement fail to give them priority personally, politically, or financially. Few Americans make substantial contributions to candidates or groups focusing on women's issues. Only about a quarter of women say they are very concerned about gender inequality and only about 7 percent of women belong to any organization dedicated to advancing women's interests. The largest of such groups, the National Organization for Women, enrolls only 250,000 of the nation's approximately 90 million adult women.[3]

What accounts for this mismatch between Americans' daily experience and social priorities on gender-related issues? Why do so many individuals fail to see women's inequality as a serious problem? And why do so many fail to see it at all?

Those are the questions that structure this book. Its point is to increase our understanding of denial—of all the ways that we resist acknowledging gender inequalities, as well as our own capacity to address them. Much of our resistance is neither intentional nor overt. Rather, it rests on selective perception, stereotypical assumptions, and unconscious bias.

The dynamics of denial fall into three basic patterns. The first involves denials of gender inequality: many individuals fail to recognize the extent of problems facing women. The second dynamic involves denials of injustice: people often rationalize women's inequality as the result of women's own choices and capabilities. The final pattern involves denials of responsibility: individuals frequently believe that whatever inequality exists, they personally are neither part of the problem nor part of the solution.

Denials of Inequality

Americans' most common response to gender inequality is to deny its dimensions. A widespread perception is that once upon a time, women suffered serious discrimination, but those days are over. Barriers have been coming down, women have been moving up, and full equality is just around the corner. If anything, many men believe that women are now getting undeserved advantages. In a series of recent articles with titles like "The Decline and Fall of the White Male," commentators air their view that "merit is out," "special privileges" are in, and the only group that can't claim equal protection under law is white men. "Pale males eat it again," announces a character in Michael Crichton's popular film *Disclosure*. This perspective is widely shared. According to recent polls, close to half of all men think that they are subject to unfair penalties for advantages that others had in the past. Two-thirds of men and three-quarters of male business leaders do not believe that women encounter significant discrimination for top positions in business, professions, or government.[4]

Such views are difficult to square with the facts. White males account for about 40 percent of the population but about 95 percent of senior managers, 90 percent of newspaper editors, 80 percent of the *Forbes* list of richest Americans, and 80 percent of congressional legislators. Significant sex-based disparities in employment salaries and status persist, even when researchers control for objective factors such as education, experience, and hours worked. As *Newsweek's* article "White Male Paranoia" points out, the pale male certainly appears to be "holding his own (and most of everybody else's) in the world of hard facts"; it's only in the "world of images and ideas . . . [that] he's taking a clobbering."[5]

What explains this gap between popular perceptions and concrete data on gender inequality? Part of the explanation lies with selective perception. Men often deny bias because they fail to recognize it. They usually don't need to; it does not significantly affect their lives. As with race, part of the privilege of dominance is the privilege of accepting without noticing its benefits.

The legal profession provides a representative example. Until the late 1960s, men constituted 95 percent of all practicing attorneys. Few thought this odd, and most never thought about it at all. Sol Linowitz, a prominent Washington lawyer, recalls that there were only two women in his law school class. Neither he nor most of his male classmates questioned the skewed ratio, although they did feel somewhat uncomfortable when their two female colleagues were around. And, he now acknowledges, "it never occurred to us to wonder whether *they* felt uncomfortable."[6]

Over the last two decades, sensitivity to sex discrimination has greatly increased. However, as a report by the American Bar Association's Commission on the Status of Women tactfully puts it, their agenda remains "unfinished." Three-quarters of female attorneys report experiencing gender bias, while only one-third of men report observing it. The vast majority of male judges are equally unaware of such discrimination, and some cannot recall a single example. Even men who acknowledge bias as a problem often discount its significance. In one recent survey, a Texas attorney summarized widespread views: "Of all the problems we have as lawyers," he noted, "gender discrimination is low on the list of important ones."[7]

To him, perhaps. But not to the female litigators who have to cope with client preferences for male attorneys, or with questions such as, "Do you really understand all the economics involved in this [antitrust] case?" Women of color and lesbian attorneys encounter bias on two fronts. In one telling instance, an African American partner in a major Chicago law firm recently reported that she had been mistaken for a stenographer at every pretrial deposition she had ever attended. Lesbians are routinely hazed, isolated, and denied employment opportunities. They, like Linowitz's classmates, often make others feel "uncomfortable"—and this is viewed as *their* problem, not their colleagues'.[8]

To men who have not been on the receiving end of such discrimination or challenges to their professional competence, this conduct often appears trivial and rarely remains memorable; it seems an isolated incident, not a representative illustration of a broader pattern. By contrast, men are far more likely to notice, recall, and resent bias against their own sex and to invest these incidents with both personal and societal significance. Columbia law professor Patricia Williams describes a typical example. "Nobody's hiring white guys anymore," was the unchallenged conclusion of one participant at a meeting of commercial lawyers. Williams surveyed the room of several hundred attorneys. She spotted one other black woman, no black men, no Hispanics, about ten Asians, and a "modest sprinkling" of white women. "So who is being hired if not white guys?" she wonders. "And if white guys aren't being hired, what on earth makes them think anyone else is?"[9]

Recent data on employment opportunities are more consistent with Williams' perception than with that of her male colleagues. Female lawyers are hired, but not promoted to the most economically rewarding and professionally prestigious positions. Two surveys involving thousands of lawyers with similar backgrounds and work experience found that men were twice as likely as women to have achieved partnership status. The obstacles are even greater for women of color.[10]

Similar patterns of denial are apparent in other employment contexts. One representative survey found that almost two-thirds of men either saw no discrimination against women or believed that it was of minor proportions. In another study, only 2 percent of male supervisors believed that their female subordinates faced any resistance or hostility based on sex; two-thirds of women reported such experiences. What female employees see as demeaning or harassing, their male colleagues often chalk up to "misplaced gallantry" or "harmless flirtation." "I have never been harassed," one male executive informed *Harvard Business Review* researchers, "but I would welcome the opportunity." For many men, it takes some first-hand experience, some observation of a wife or daughter's difficulties, or some exposure to systematic evidence before the cumulative impact of subtle discrimination becomes apparent. In commenting on his own attitude change, a male judge who co-chaired California's Gender Bias Task Force noted, "Until I was on this . . . Task Force, there was never any bias in my court."[11]

For obvious reasons, women are more sensitive to gender inequality than men are, but some perceptual blinders persist among both sexes. Not all women encounter all forms of bias, and those who lack personal experience sometimes fail to appreciate collective problems. What sociologists label the "Queen Bee Syndrome" is common among some professionally successful women. Their attitude is, "I managed, why can't you?"[12]

Many women also are unable to see patterns of discrimination because important parts of the picture are missing or murky. Salary, hiring, and promotion data that compare similarly qualified men and women are hard to come by, and the most overt sexism has gone underground. As a 1989 Supreme Court case revealed, male employers may still penalize a woman who they think needs courses in "charm school." But that is no longer what they say in mixed company or in personnel records. Moreover, gender is only one of the characteristics, and not always the most important one, that disadvantages women. Race, ethnicity, class, disability, and sexual orientation often overshadow or interact with gender.[13]

A wide array of research underscores the difficulties for both men and women in perceiving discrimination when the evidence comes in piecemeal fashion. In one study headed by psychologist Faye Crosby, individuals received information about a hypothetical company in which men earned higher salaries than women with comparable credentials. When participants in the study received information about the company's entire employment history, broken down by gender, they saw discrimination. But when participants looked at the same information case by case, they noticed no bias; each individual decision looked reasonably fair.[14]

The absence of data on collective patterns helps explain why even people who believe that gender bias is a significant problem usually fail to see it in their own workplace settings. As Crosby and her colleagues concluded, "The perception of sex discrimination reminds one of fireflies; one can always see the glow from some distance, but bagging the little critters [individually is far more difficult]."[15]

Self-interest complicates the process. For some men, the increasing unacceptability of sexism, coupled with the inconvenience of eliminating it, encourages various strategies of self-deception. These techniques frequently surface on issues of household work. Employed men, who average only half as much time as employed women on family tasks, generally manage not to notice the disparity. In one recent poll, over two-thirds of surveyed husbands reported that they shared childrearing duties equally with their wives, an assessment wildly inconsistent with that of most wives and virtually all reported research.[16]

Moreover, even men who acknowledge disparities often view women's extra tasks as matters of personal choice, not joint responsibility. Rather than accept an equal division of cleaning, cooking, or childcare obligations, some men redefine their share as unnecessary; they don't mind a little mess or a fast-food dinner, and their infants will do just fine with extra time among their "friends" at daycare. Other men seem not to notice when some of their assigned tasks need doing, or else mismanage key parts of the job. Rather than broadcast constant reminders or complaints, many women simply pick up pieces that their partners don't even realize have been dropped. As one wife wearily noted, "I do my half, I do half of [my husband's half], and the rest doesn't get done."[17]

A related strategy is to divide responsibilities "equally" without noticing that some shares are more equal than others. Surveys consistently find that men have a disproportionate number of the most enjoyable or conveniently scheduled tasks (reading to toddlers, rather than changing their diapers). Part of women's extra burden is invisible but unending "worry work." In the vast majority of households, men "help out," but also opt out of family tasks; women are the planners, the pinch hitters, and the persons ultimately responsible. When difficulties arise, the psychological division of labor remains skewed in ways that many men do not fully appreciate. Standing safely at the sidelines of a domestic crisis, fathers in sociologist Arlie Hochschild's study see themselves as involved and supportive: "Handle it the best way you can, honey, I'm 100 percent behind you." Former congresswoman Pat Schroeder recalls a telling instance of how easily men substitute emotional for actual support. Shortly after her first election, her husband explained in a *Redbook* profile that in the future he would be the one taking the children to the pediatrician. On reading his account, Schroeder immediately telephoned her husband and asked, "For $500, what is the name of the children's pediatrician?" He responded, somewhat sheepishly, that what he had meant was that he would be willing to take the children if she asked.[18]

Schroeder's story, and variations on its theme, often prompt further denials. Many men resist seeing any similarity between such accounts and their own situation. They can name *their* children's pediatrician, and so can every other father that they know. But discomfort sets in if they are pressed for details such as who takes time off from work for emergency visits. Recent research indicates that when children are ill, mothers stay home about 70 percent of the time. In many of the remaining circumstances, women make alternative childcare arrangements that will not disrupt their husbands' schedules. And when couples divorce, the vast majority of fathers assume few of the daily responsibilities of parenting. Within several years after separation, three-quarters of noncustodial fathers do not have even weekly contact with their children. To be sure, men tend to be more involved in childrearing today than when Schroeder began in Congress. But progress is not parity, and a wide gap persists between fathers' theoretical commitments to shared parenting and the time they actually devote to it.[19]

Part of what keeps men, and often women, from recognizing that gap is their choice of reference groups. Where gender appears to be a relevant characteristic, most individuals compare themselves to members of their own sex. In assessing domestic burdens, husbands look to other husbands or their own fathers rather than to wives. From this perspective, unequal divisions of labor become easy to rationalize because they remain the norm rather than the exception.[20]

Women also tend to compare their family burdens to those of members of their own sex. As a result, many wives deny that their husbands do less than their "fair share" around the home, even when responsibilities are grossly unequal. Cultural attitudes reinforce such perceptions. As Anna Quindlen notes, "When men do the dishes it's called helping. When women do dishes, that's called life." Most women are not fully aware of how much time they or their partners spend on family work and generally believe that their arrangements are far more equal than they truly are.[21]

This is not to imply that women totally fail to notice gender inequalities in household burdens. How much help they receive (or don't receive) from their male partners shows up in opinion surveys as one of the greatest sources of resentment. Yet even women who are most resentful often do not expect an equal division of household work. It is only their partner's refusal to help with particular jobs or his inability to justify refusing, that triggers conflict. And for many women, avoiding conflict is more important than achieving equality. They, like their male counterparts, use selective perception as a form of self-protection.[22]

Similar patterns operate in other contexts. According to workplace surveys, even when women recognize gender discrimination as a problem or where objective evidence points to that conclusion, most individuals still do not believe that they personally have been targets. Although many critics denounce feminism for encouraging women to exaggerate their own victimization, recent research finds that individuals generally are reluctant to see themselves in that light. Acknowledging vulnerability carries a cost: it erodes individuals' sense of control and self-esteem, and involves the unpleasantness of identifying a perpetrator. Many women understandably are unwilling to alienate men whose approval is important personally and professionally.[23]

Although some individuals enjoy nursing grievances and claiming the moral leverage of victim status, most do not. As Hillary Clinton once noted, "Who wants to walk around constantly with clenched fists?" Particularly where women feel powerless to avoid inequality, they are likely to avoid acknowledging it.[24]

Denials of Injustice

A second way of denying inequality as a social problem is to deny that gender disparities reflect social injustice. This strategy builds on broader psychological tendencies. Most people share what social science researchers label "a belief in a just world." We generally want to believe that life follows orderly, predictable, and equitable patterns in which individuals get what they deserve and deserve what they get. To hold on to this view, people often blame women's conduct and women's choices for the problems women experience.[25]

Popular explanations of workplace patterns are a case in point. Despite three decades of equal-opportunity legislation, the employment status of women and that of men remain far from equal. American workplaces are still gender-segregated and gender-stratified, with women of color at the bottom of the occupational hierarchy. Full-time female employees earn less than 75 cents for every dollar earned by men. Hispanic female college graduates average lower salaries than white male high school dropouts. Yet many individuals deny that these gender disparities reflect gender discrimination.[26]

Rather, a common view is that women's choices and capabilities explain women's disadvantages. Differences in biology are often held responsible for differences in status. Many women are thought to lack the technical competence and competitive personality that carry the greatest workplace rewards. Female workers also supposedly choose less demanding and lower-paying jobs in order to accommodate family obligations or noneconomic preferences, such as the desire to work in "touchy-feely" service occupations rather than technical positions.[27]

It is true that women as a group do make workplace choices that are somewhat different from those of men. However, those choices are in part a consequence as well as a cause of gender inequalities. Many researchers find that measurable differences in occupation, education, experience, and hours fail to explain even half of the existing wage gap. The remaining disparity is at least partly attributable to unconscious gender biases and the devaluation of "women's work."[28]

Historical, cross-cultural, and clinical research makes clear that jobs done by women often are undervalued *because* they are done by women. In controlled studies, individuals give lower ratings to the same résumés, scholarly articles, or artistic works when they carry a female rather than a male name. So too, when women are asked how much pay they deserve for performing a certain task, they select lower amounts than men. Gender disparities in salary structures reflect this undervaluation of women's work. Contrary to popular assumptions, many pay scales are impossible to square with merit principles. When childcare attendants earn less than parking-lot attendants, the gap speaks volumes about not only gender inequality but also its distortion of our social priorities.[29]

Assumptions about women's responsibility for "women's problems" are just as apparent in discussions about sexual violence. Although the frequency of rape and domestic assault is difficult to pin down with precision, the seriousness of the problem is not in doubt. America has the highest rate of reported rapes among Western industrialized nations; between a quarter and a half of all women will experience rape or attempted rape. A similar percentage will be assaulted by a spouse or partner. Domestic violence is the leading cause of injury to adult women and cuts across lines of race, class, ethnicity, and sexual orientation.[30]

Yet many Americans are convinced that women both exaggerate and perpetuate the brutality that they experience. According to front-page stories and widely quoted "experts" like Katie Roiphe (a graduate student in English), feminist fanatics use "ludicrously" broad definitions of sexual abuse and discount women's own responsibility for putting themselves at risk. Such perceptions are widely shared. Almost three-quarters of Americans do not view forced sex between acquaintances as rape, even when it falls within statutory prohibitions.[31]

Our desire to hold women accountable for such assaults has deeper cultural roots. For many individuals, sexual abuse appears less threatening if victims are responsible for provoking or inviting it. For women, blaming the victim is a way to deny their own vulnerability and to distance themselves from the problem. For men, such a reallocation of responsibility is a way to minimize their sense of collective culpability and to shift the moral high ground of debate. If feminists have encouraged unreasonable definitions of abuse, then men too can claim to be oppressed.[32]

Our tendency to fault women is apparent in virtually every systematic study of rape. For example, in research giving participants written or filmed accounts of sexual assault, many individuals inaccurately recall that victims behaved provocatively, a strategy that appears preferable to believing that an innocent person has suffered. Similarly, judges and juries often blame rape on women's seductive clothing or reckless conduct. Some courts have even managed to blame children under twelve: in one such case, the trial judge referred to the child as an "unusually promiscuous young lady."[33]

Victims of sexual assault are often victimized twice—first by the abuse and then by the blame that accompanies it. An apt illustration involves the Los Angeles "spur posse," a group of high school students who competed with each other for sexual "conquests." When some of the teens eventually faced criminal charges ranging from sexual molestation to rape, many parents rose to their sons' defense. "Nothing my boy did was anything any red-blooded American boy wouldn't do at his age," explained one father. "What can you do?" asked one boy's mother. "It's a testosterone thing." And another parent noted, "Those girls were trash."[34]

Law enforcement officials often hold similar views. The likelihood that a formal rape complaint will result in conviction and incarceration is only 10 percent. Contrary to critics' assertions about "rape hysteria," underreporting, not overreacting, is women's most common response to sexual assaults. Fear, humiliation, and lack of confidence that their case will be treated fairly deter an estimated four-fifths of victims from filing criminal charges.[35]

Many Americans similarly hold battered women responsible for their own abuse—for provoking, tolerating, or declining to prosecute assaults. One judge summarized prevailing sentiments: "Why don't [women] just get up and leave? All they have to do is get out of the house." What people too seldom ask is whether women have somewhere safe to go, and whether they will be able to support themselves and their children. In most cases of family violence, the answers are scarcely reassuring. Nearly three-quarters of all reported assaults, half of all interspousal homicides, and most serious injuries occur after the abused woman tries to "just get up and leave."[36]

Most individuals at risk of violence are entitled to protective orders, but these orders are routinely violated and violations are rarely prosecuted. In some jurisdictions, protective mandates are not even available for same-sex partners. Despite recent improvements, domestic-violence programs still come nowhere close to meeting crucial needs for housing, child care, employment assistance, and related social services. America has more than twice as many shelters for animals as for battered women.[37]

Nicole Brown Simpson's experience was all too typical, except in the amount of publicity that it belatedly attracted. Despite her repeated calls for help, those in positions of power denied the seriousness of her injuries. "This is just a family matter," O. J. Simpson informed the police, who finally arrested him for an obviously brutal assault. "Why are you making a big deal of it?" In fact, the police didn't. Neither did the Hertz Corporation, which continued to employ him as a spokesperson. Nor did the judge, who imposed a sentence requiring no jail time—only community service, together with counseling sessions that could be completed by telephone.[38]

Such tendencies to forgive and forget are by no means unusual. Fewer than 10 percent of domestic abuse cases result in significant sanctions. Most are dismissed, dropped to misdemeanor status, or diverted to counseling and mediation programs that often trivialize the offense. This nation pays an appalling price for its attitudes toward family violence. The American Medical Association, hardly a captive of feminist fanatics, estimates the cost at between $5 billion and $10 billion a year in health care, workplace absences, litigation, and incarceration. The irrationality of our current priorities emerged clearly in a Massachusetts case where a woman sought a protective order after suffering repeated assaults. The presiding judge declared that if she and her husband wanted to "gnaw" at each other, "fine," but they "shouldn't do it at taxpayers' expense." A year later the woman was dead and the husband was on trial for murder, also at taxpayers' expense.[39]

Denials of Responsibility

A final way that we avoid confronting gender inequality as a problem is to relocate responsibility for finding solutions. Our most common strategy is to individualize the issues. Whatever the cause of such inequality, we make individual women responsible for the remedy. Alternatively, even in contexts where we recognize the need for societal responses, we overstate our progress in achieving them and understate the gap between formal rights and actual practices. And when all else fails, we fall back on biological excuses for sex-based inequalities. Since men and women just *are* different, we cannot expect society to equalize their status.

Our insistence on personal solutions for societal problems reflects broader cultural values. The American ethic exalts individual achievement, not collective action. Influential bestsellers offer cautionary tales of both success and failure, but their underlying message is much the same. Their topic could be the "managerial mother" and how she manages, the rules for catching "Mr. Right" and keeping him caught, or "women who can't say no and the men who control them," but the moral is similar: most solutions for women's problems lie with individual women. It is a matter of choosing the right man, cosmetics, career sequence, or time-budgeting techniques. Women's liberation appears more a matter of self-transformation than of political struggle.[40]

By the same token, increasing numbers of middle- and upper-income women assume that they can "purchase an exit visa" from problems stemming from inadequate public policies and unequal family roles. So, for example, individuals who can afford to hire domestic help can afford to tolerate the lack of government support for childcare and the lack of husbands' willingness to evenly share childcaring responsibilities. For many women, the feminist rallying cry of the 1970s—"the personal is political"—has been reversed. The political is personal and *only* personal.[41]

This individualist ethic emerges clearly in sociologist Ruth Sidel's study of young, unmarried women. Cutting across boundaries of race, class, and ethnicity is a shared assumption that they can "have it all" without the support of government, communities, or an extended family. The "all" is not a modest vision. Nor for most of these women is it a remotely realistic one. What they typically expect is a successful career, a happy marriage, well-adjusted children, and plenty of money; what they lack is any appreciation of the broader cultural changes that such a vision would require.[42]

Women with more life experience are more likely to recognize the inadequacy of individual solutions to shared problems. But what they fail to see—often with good reason—is any way to secure an effective response. Women working a double shift at home and on the job are generally reluctant to take time for political action. And female employees in unsympathetic workplaces may feel too vulnerable to raise gender-related concerns. In Susan Gordon's representative study, almost none of the women who talked about such issues privately were willing to do so publicly. Many were wary of jeopardizing their own situation. Others had found prior efforts at workplace organizing to be futile; male employees were entrenched in their positions and female colleagues were unwilling to make waves. As a result, many women found "no place to go on record with either [their] sympathies or complaints." So too, in Sherrye Henry's and Roberta Siegel's recent surveys, most working women saw unequal opportunity as a problem, but were "not aroused enough or economically secure enough to combat it personally . . . Discrimination was like bad weather. You endured it because you couldn't change it."[43]

In some sense, the American women's movement is a victim of its own success. Its accomplishments have undercut the urgency of further struggle. Feminism's insistence on equal opportunity is widely shared, but its call to common action is widely resisted. The women's movement has created aspirations to gender equality but not the collective commitment necessary to realize them.

What also stands in the way is the failure even to recognize certain problems as problems. An example involves the constraints of femininity. The difficulty here is that many traits traditionally valued in women also perpetuate women's inequality. These traits include sensitivity, warmth, self-sacrifice, nurturance, and physical attractiveness. Most Americans believe that women *should* exhibit those qualities, and a majority of women view "being feminine" as central to how they define themselves. Yet few individuals realize how often these expectations restrict women's opportunities for self-fulfillment and for making their own decisions about what they find fulfilling.[44]

Our recent progress in expanding women's choices has magnified these constraints. We increasingly expect women to achieve in multiple arenas with conflicting demands. Personal qualities that attract workplace rewards—drive, competitiveness, and self-promotion—are at odds with the characteristics that men most value in women, and that many women value in themselves. Female employees are caught in a double bind. They are vulnerable to criticism for being "too feminine" or "not feminine enough"; what is assertive in a man may seem abrasive in a woman. Moreover, the time and effort required for success in the workplace compete with the time and effort necessary for satisfaction in the home and for meeting standards of sexual attractiveness in the culture generally. Yet as long as we insist that these tradeoffs involve matters of individual choice, we divert attention from the social conditions that restrict the choices available. As a result, too many women too much of the time end up with unsatisfying compromises. Wherever they are putting their energy, they worry that it should be going somewhere else.

Physical appearance is an issue that we seldom link to inequality. Because women enjoy many activities associated with maintaining a feminine image, they often discount the personal costs that societal expectations impose. And men who don't pay that price are even less conscious of its magnitude. But in subtle ways, our prevailing double standards institutionalize inequality. Our ideals of attractiveness are much more demanding for women than for men, and we punish women's deviations much more severely. Recent studies consistently find that females are far less satisfied with their appearance than males, as well as far less concerned about their partner's appearance. As Gloria Steinem has noted, it seems that "men are almost always okay no matter how they look, while women are rarely okay no matter how they look, and thus feel constantly in need of 'fixing.'" Women spend over $50 billion a year in efforts to slim down and measure up through diets, cosmetics, and "corrective" surgery. Virtually every part of the female body, from eyebrows to toenails, is a target of opportunity and therefore of potential anxiety.[45]

We punish women not only for failing to meet cultural expectations, but sometimes just for trying. That double bind was apparent at a recent meeting of several hundred public utility executives. When one of the few women in the group missed a session, a male colleague speculated audibly that "there must be a sale at Saks." Yet even harsher judgments await the executive who does not look as if she shopped, and shopped well, at Saks.

Hillary Clinton has been in similar no-win situations. Often mocked for looking "frumpy," she has done no better attempting to look glamorous. Her constantly changing hairstyles, fashion-conscious press releases, and seductively posed magazine profiles earn widespread ridicule. As one commentator put it, "She might as well be selling moisturizing cream." For many women, the middle ground between trying too hard and not hard enough seems always out of reach.[46]

Among those committed to women's rights, the entire question of appearance is deeply problematic. We worry about how we look and we worry about worrying. Appearance is an important source of women's self-expression as well as subordination. How to value one without perpetuating the other is by no means self-evident. In one of Nicole Hollander's cartoons, the main character fantasizes about what the world would be like without men: "No crime and lots of happy, fat women." We need other ways to advance in that general direction.

Of course, on some issues of inequality, Americans generally recognize that responsibility cannot lie entirely with individual women. In the past quarter-century America has adopted an increasing array of legal decisions, public policies, and employer initiatives that seek to ensure equal opportunity. But this progress carries a double edge. Once we pass a law or institute a policy, we often believe that we've done our bit for women and move on to other issues. The result is that we settle for equality in form rather than equality in fact. Alternatively, even when we acknowledge that some gender inequalities remain unsolved, we often put responsibility for addressing them anywhere and everywhere else.

Our willingness to accept partial policies or symbolic victories is not, of course, unique to gender-related issues. Yet this tendency creates particular problems for women, who are a diffuse and divided constituency. Their mobilization becomes increasingly difficult once policymakers have addressed the most obvious needs.

A recent illustration involves family and medical leave. After a decade of struggle, the women's movement finally won federal legislation guaranteeing twelve weeks of unpaid leave after childbirth or adoption. However, the statute provides least for those who need help most. It exempts small businesses and recently hired or part-time employees, leaving about half of American workers unprotected. Moreover, unpaid time-off benefits only those who can afford to take it, and twelve weeks falls far short of what virtually all child development experts consider appropriate. Childbirth leave is also just one part of what Americans need in order to juggle work and family responsibilities. A majority of employees lack opportunities for flexible schedules, decent part-time positions, and quality child care. The costs of these policy failures are greatest for low-income women, who are disproportionately women of color. Yet even those who acknowledge such policy limitations often duck any responsibility for filling the gaps. Male government leaders look to employers, employers look to government, and both look to families. Within those families, husbands look to wives, and wives too often simply stop looking.[47]

Managers would like to help their workforce balance job and family responsibilities, but . . . There is usually a long list of buts. From the perspective of employers, flexible schedules or reduced hours appear impractical for most jobs. Managers assume that colleagues, clients, and customers won't tolerate the inconvenience, or that the work requires total commitment. Extended family leave appears equally infeasible. It seems a largely pointless gesture for men, who rarely take advantage of even the limited policies available. Women, on the other hand, supposedly grab as much as they can, which makes such options prohibitively expensive. Yet missing from this balance sheet are the less visible costs of failing to accommodate work/family conflicts: lower morale and higher stress, absenteeism, and job turnover.[48]

Although most husbands observe such problems, many resist contributing to the solution. From their vantage point, any major shift in *their* worklife is simply not an option. After all, a demanding job is a demanding job. Yet missing from this world view is any acknowledgment of the inequalities that result when men take their own aspirations and constraints as given, while assuming that women's are negotiable.[49]

So too, on many other gender-related issues, we overstate our partial progress and overlook the problems that remain. Reproductive choice is an obvious example of how readily we deny the gap between formal rights and daily experience. Prevailing Supreme Court decisions hold that individuals have a constitutional right to end a pregnancy without "undue burdens" by the State. Yet that standard has permitted a wide range of restrictions, including extended waiting periods, expensive testing, and prohibitions on the use of public funds or facilities. Such limitations, together with inadequate responses to "pro-life" terrorism, curtail the number of abortion providers and increase the risks and costs associated with the procedure. More than four-fifths of all U.S. counties have no facility offering abortions, and clinics providing such services run constant risks of harassment, arson, and assault.[50]

Such limitations on access have the greatest impact on low-income, minority, and adolescent women—those who are least able to bear the costs of an unwanted child. The result, as feminist law professor Catharine MacKinnon notes, is that only "women with privileges get rights." Constitutional rulings may guarantee reproductive choice, but our law enforcement and health care systems do not.[51]

A final way of denying responsibility is to assume that sex-based disparities reflect sex-based differences that we cannot or should not alter. Many Americans believe that certain inequalities are biologically rooted. Even more believe that gender stereotypes may contribute to gender differences, but that the responsibility for perpetuating those stereotypes lies somewhere else. As columnist Dave Barry observes, "Any parent will tell you that girl babies will generally display a wide-eyed curiosity about the world, whereas boy babies will generally try to destroy it." The reason, we suppose, lies with hormones, brain structures, and other influences beyond our control. Parents blame schools, toys, television, and other children. Media leaders blame families, and teachers blame everyone but themselves.[52]

In fact, there is plenty of responsibility to go around, and biology should by no means bear most of it. Children absorb traditional images of masculinity and femininity at early ages. Our culture encourages gender roles that are separate and, in important respects, unequal. We now have unisex books with titles like *Maybe You Should Fly a Jet, Maybe You Should Be a Vet,* but we still give girls dolls and boys planes. And we still have a society in which about 95 percent of licensed pilots are men, and a similar proportion of childcare workers are women. When toys talk, their messages, both literal and symbolic, reaffirm traditional gender roles. That point came through clearly in a recent hoax by a group calling itself the Barbie Liberation Organization. Group members bought several hundred Barbie and GI Joe dolls and switched their voice boxes. The result was a mutant colony of Barbies that roared, "Vengeance is mine!" and a battalion of Joes that twittered, "Will we ever have enough clothes?"[53]

The point of the hoax was to encourage parents to challenge traditional sex-based stereotypes. But even adults who join that effort may be unconscious of their own roles in perpetuating traditional gender messages. One mother who insisted on supplying her daughter with tools rather than dolls finally gave up when she discovered the child undressing a hammer and singing it to sleep. "It must be hormonal," was the mother's explanation. At least until someone asked who had been putting her daughter to bed.

Whatever their biological predispositions, children receive strong cultural signals about sex-appropriate tasks and behaviors. Much of their learning comes from unintended or indirect messages. If, as is still the case, most men don't make the beds they sleep in and parents assign more homemaking chores to daughters than to sons, children will learn what is "women's work."[54]

The Unfinished Agenda

Achieving true equality between the sexes will require fundamental changes in what we hold responsible for our distance from that goal. We need to recast the gender roles that children learn in homes, schools, and the media. We must also address the social policies, workplace structures, and family patterns that obscure and institutionalize injustice.

Of course, not all Americans have the same vision of what full equality would look like. Should our destination be a society where sexual identity has little relevance and where neither women nor men dominate particular social roles? Or do we want a world where sex continues to matter, but where men and women have genuinely equal opportunities, and their roles assume truly equal value?

On these questions, our society offers no simple or single answers. But we need not reach consensus in order to make substantial progress. Although we may not agree about what gender would mean in an ideal society, we know more than enough about what it would not mean. No just society could tolerate the inequalities that women now experience in status, income, power, and physical security.

The challenge remaining is to make those inequalities visible and to translate our personal aspirations into political commitments. A half-century ago, William Allen White counseled women to "raise more hell and less dahlias."[55] This book suggests why and how.

2

The Ideology and Biology of Gender Difference

"Is it a boy or a girl?" This is usually the first question we ask at the birth of a child. And the answer remains of crucial importance throughout the child's life. In every known society, gender differences structure human identity and social relationships. Yet biology by no means dictates the form that those differences assume. The roles and characteristics that we associate with males and females vary considerably across time and culture. Still, one similarity remains striking. As anthropologist Margaret Mead once noted, there are cultures in which men weave and women fish, and ones in which women weave and men fish. But in either case, the work that women perform is valued less.[1]

What accounts for both the variations and the universalities in sex-linked differences? This is one of the central paradoxes of gender. If biology does not explain the inequalities in men's and women's social positions, why are those inequalities so pervasive and persistent? Alternatively, if biology is the central force in determining male and female identity, why do societies differ so widely in the tasks and traits that are associated with each sex?

Over the past several decades, both the similarities and variations in gender roles have become increasingly apparent. In the West, women's opportunities and employment patterns have changed considerably, but traditional gender stereotypes remain much the same. Despite some variation across class, race, ethnicity, and sexual orientation, the characteristics that American and European societies associate with men and women have changed little from the ones Aristotle described more than two thousand years ago. Masculine traits still include strength, courage, independence, competitiveness, ambition, and aggression. Feminine qualities still include emotional sensitivity, patience, caution, nurturance, passivity, and dependence. Men are taught to place higher value on power, and women to place higher value on interpersonal relationships.[2]

Challenging these gender stereotypes and expanding opportunities for both sexes has been a primary objective of the women's movement. But this objective points to another central paradox. In an important sense, feminism rests on the very differences that it challenges. Those concerned with gender equality seek to prevent traditional gender roles from limiting individuals' aspirations and achievements. Yet by definition, the women's movement also requires some sense of group identity and interests. In effect, feminism assumes the very shared experience that it seeks in part to eliminate.

This tension has pushed the campaign for sexual equality in multiple directions. The American women's movement has long struggled both to challenge and to celebrate gender difference. For many contemporary feminists, the dilemma is how to affirm the value of women's traditional role without perpetuating its constraints. A related concern is how to build on "women's experience" without losing sight of its diversity across time, culture, class, race, ethnicity, and sexual orientation. Progress on both fronts requires rethinking conventional views about the "inherent" nature of women's nature.

The Biology of Difference

The biological basis of sex-linked differences is complicated, contested, and confused. It is also increasingly irrelevant. Even those who believe that masculine and feminine traits have a physiological basis acknowledge that society can prevent these differences from translating into social disadvantages or from unnecessarily limiting individual opportunities.

However, assumptions about biology still affect assumptions about fairness—about the appropriateness of current gender roles and the possibilities for change. Popular accounts, such as Robert Wright's "Feminists Meet Mr. Darwin" and Ann Moir and David Jessel's bestselling book *Brain Sex*, warn us that "there are some biological facts of life that, with the best and most sexually liberated will in the world, we just cannot buck." Many Americans agree. In one representative poll, 40 percent believed that biology was as important as or more important than culture in creating masculine and feminine attributes. Such perceptions account for many individuals' failure to perceive gender inequality as a significant problem. In their view, as a 1995 ABC-TV documentary suggested, "perhaps instead of suing about difference we should honor it."[3]

Given these assumptions, most debates about sexual equality sooner or later bump up against beliefs about sexual physiology. So it makes sense to start out where we almost always seem to end up: What do we know and what do we only think we know about sex-based difference?

Even to speak of "knowledge" on this subject requires considerable poetic license. "Scientific" wisdom concerning gender traditionally has rested more on ideology than on biology. Until quite recently, the prevailing assumption was that women's nature was to nurture, and that the sexes' distinctive social roles reflected physiological imperatives. Innumerable theories of female incapacity emerged. Leading medical authorities identified a deadly brain-womb conflict. Women had limited "vital forces," and those who concentrated on intellectual rather than reproductive pursuits risked chronic disabilities and permanent sterility.[4]

Many contemporary assertions about sex-based differences bear an equally dubious relationship to the evidence. The differences that figure most prominently in explanations for sex-based inequality deserve particularly close attention. They include reproductive capacity, brain structure, hormonal drives, and physical size and strength.

Differences in reproductive capability provide the central biological basis for distinguishing between the sexes, though even this distinction sometimes blurs. Normally, sexual identity is determined at conception. Each cell has chromosomal pairs that carry genes. In females, one of these pairs has two XX chromosomes; in males, one of the pairs has an XY chromosome. This difference typically results in sex-specific reproductive organs, which in turn create sex-specific hormonal levels. Occasionally Mother Nature messes up by mismatching genetic codes or the hormonal environment in the womb. In extreme cases, individuals are born with some of the reproductive organs of both sexes or without any functional sexual organs. The standard response is corrective surgery, hormonal treatments, and "sex appropriate" socialization (skirts and dolls for girls; guns and pants for boys). We want individuals to fit neatly into our dual sexual categories, not to straddle the borders. Yet these abnormalities point to a threshold problem with conventional assumptions about sexual identity. How can masculinity and femininity be biologically based when some well-adjusted individuals have biological characteristics of both sexes?[5]

Despite these difficulties, the traditional "scientific" explanation for sex-based inequality has rested on sex-based differences in reproductive physiology. Sociobiologists offer the most elaborate rationale. In essence, their theories assume that male dominance and female nurturance are universal traits in humans and in most biologically similar animals. From this vantage, the pervasiveness of these sex-linked traits demonstrates their "adaptiveness" and their genetic basis. Individuals who exhibit adaptive traits leave behind more offspring, and over long cycles of evolution only their genes survive.

Under leading sociobiological accounts, the genetic grounding for sexual differences lies in the structure of sex cells. The female's egg is relatively large because it contains the yolk that nourishes the embryo during early development. By contrast, the male's sperm is small, mobile, and easily replicated. Men can make millions of sperm and therefore have the capacity to spread their genes through promiscuous sex. Women perpetuate their genes by prolonged nurturance of each embryo. In the view of prominent sociobiologists such as Edward Wilson and Richard Dawkins, "female exploitation begins here." Under the primitive subsistence conditions that prevailed throughout most human evolution, women depended on men during periods of pregnancy and breast feeding. Males supposedly were the hunters, while females were the gatherers and nurturers, and each sex developed traits adaptive to those roles. Natural selection thus favored characteristics that encouraged sexual hierarchy: physical strength, aggression, and promiscuity in men; caretaking and fidelity among women.[6]

According to sociobiologists, discriminatory patterns like the double standard of sexual morality rest on this biological foundation. Before the arrival of reliable contraceptives, men best ensured survival of their genes by sleeping around, but not settling down with a woman who did the same. Although recent birth control developments may have "short circuited this [evolutionary] logic, we're still stuck with the minds the logic created."[7]

Popular accounts of sexual difference often reach similar conclusions through simpler routes. To many individuals, it seems obvious that women's capacity for childbirth and breast feeding has encouraged nurturing instincts and priorities that account for contemporary gender roles. As one recent survey participant put it, "Just like in the animal kingdom, the mother takes care of the kids—it's instinctive." Fathers can learn to do certain tasks, "but a man cannot be a mother."[8]

Moreover, according to many commentators, the rigid gender linkages that the women's movement deplores are a result not only of biological differences but also of women's responses to those differences. Sociobiologists often argue that male drives for power and control of resources are partly the result of female preferences for successful, ambitious mates. These preferences, operating repeatedly over thousands of generations, are to blame for traits that now perpetuate gender inequality. This leads to the somewhat "startling" conclusion that women are in important respects responsible for their own subordination, as well as for male casualties in the competitive struggle; shorter life spans and higher homicide rates are just "the tip of the iceberg of the cost of competition to men."[9]

From this perspective, because the root of gender roles is biological, society's attempts at interference are costly and futile. If the sexes have not come out equal in the process, no one is to blame. The problem, as sociobiologists see it, is simply that "Mother Nature is a sexist." Women are both products and prisoners of their reproductive history.[10]

Yet a careful review of the evidence suggests that the problem lies elsewhere, as does the sexism. It is not nature but what we make of her endowments that accounts for gender inequalities. Recent anthropological evidence casts doubt both on the universality of sex-linked traits and on our inheritance of rigid gender role divisions from early hunter-gatherer societies. Contrary to many sociobiologists' assertions, it does not appear that men in these societies were the only major providers while women were constantly preoccupied with childrearing. Rather, birthrates were relatively low and the sexes shared breadwinning responsibilities.[11]

Sociobiologists' frequent reliance on other primates for evidence of universal male and female traits is equally suspect. Popular articles like "Sexual Harassment: Why Even Bees Do It" provide an amusing read but an inadequate foundation for sweeping generalizations. The animal kingdom is large enough to provide both examples and counterexamples of most gendered behaviors, and of environmental influences on prevailing patterns. Instances of female dominance and male nurturance are readily available. For example, among ruffled lemurs and South American night monkeys, males tend infants while females forage.[12]

Variations are also apparent among human patterns of male aggression and female nurturing. Mothers have not always assumed primary childcare responsibilities. Upper-class European women once relied heavily on wetnurses, governesses, tutors, and male boarding school teachers. Men in some nonindustrial cultures also have shared power and parenting tasks. So too, in contemporary American society, fathers who become primary caretakers (even involuntarily because of a wife's death) do not display any less nurturing capacity than mothers. Nor is there an adequate biological explanation for why other men, when they take on childrearing tasks, generally end up with the most enjoyable ones—playing with infants, not changing their diapers.[13]

Yet rather than addressing these counterarguments, many sociobiologists simply ignore or categorically dismiss their critics. In a telling passage, exceptional only in its candor, Robert Wright announces that "there is not a single well-known feminist who has learned enough about modern Darwinism to pass judgment on it." Yet, as the endnotes to this chapter suggest, there may not be a single prominent sociobiologist who has learned enough about modern feminist critiques to pass judgment on *them*. Those critiques rest on a vast array of scientific research that casts doubt on physiological explanations for gender hierarchies. Summarizing this evidence, Harvard biologist Ruth Hubbard reminds us that stereotypical patterns of male dominance and female nurturance "do not characterize all human societies and there is no reason to believe that our biology determines the ways we construct them."[14]

Related assumptions about women's intellectual incapacities reflect similar problems and a similarly troubled history. Nineteenth-century experts (mis)measured women's brains and declared them smaller, lighter, and therefore inferior. It later turned out that women did not have smaller brains relative to their body size. Nor did the size of the brain determine intellectual capacity, as should have been apparent from even casual comparisons of intelligence among certain large and small animals. But no matter. When scientists did not find the anatomical difference they were seeking, they often simply shifted the location of their search and their methods for measurement. For example, experts originally considered the left hemisphere of the brain to be the source of intellect and reason and the right to be the site of passion and irrationality. Not coincidentally, these scientists also believed that men had greater brain capacity on the left, and that women had greater capacity on the right. In the 1960s and 1970s, when experts began to suspect that the right hemisphere was the source of genius and creative inspiration, male superiority in brain function promptly migrated. So, too, in the 1920s, after women scored higher on the first IQ tests, authors changed the questions.[15]

Despite this undistinguished legacy, the search for sex differences in the brain doggedly continues. Over the last two decades, innumerable theories have come and gone. One prominent current hypothesis is that hormonal factors cause the left and right hemispheres to develop differently in males and females, and that the area connecting the hemispheres also varies. On this view, males process visual and spatial information predominantly with the right side, while females use both sides equally. This right-side dominance is a common explanation for men's superiority in areas such as mathematics and visual-spatial ability, and for female superiority in certain verbal activities and interpersonal skills.[16]

According to some commentators, these sex differences in brain structure also account for sex differences in occupational roles, status, and achievement. Women's destiny is to assemble watches but not to design them, to play chess but not to become grand masters. Echoing the claims about reproductive biology, these commentators acknowledge that men can nurture but insist that they don't do so "naturally"; fathers lack "the right equipment—perceptual, cognitive, emotional . . ." Missing from such accounts are the social penalties that discourage caretaking, "effeminate" behavior among men. To the authors of *Brain Sex*, there are obvious limits to what "apostles of sexual sameness" can do about prevailing gender patterns. "Infants are not blank slates . . . They have quite literally made up their minds in the womb, safe from the legions of social engineers who impatiently await them."[17]

This preference for biological rather than cultural explanations is reminiscent of accounts once offered for the rarity of great female scientists. To experts around the turn of the century, an "innate sexual disqualification" rather than "social prejudice" was obviously to blame. Neither the exclusion of female students from many of the finest universities nor sex-segregated tracks in secondary schools apparently counted as "prejudice."[18]

Similar, if more subtle, cultural blinders remain. Much of the research and even more of the media coverage concerning "real differences" present contested findings as established facts. Bestsellers announce that "the nature and cause of brain differences are now known beyond speculation, beyond prejudice, and beyond reasonable doubt." More careful overviews make poor copy. The mainstream media trumpet findings of sexual differences, no matter how small. When researchers find that men have a slight statistical advantage in imagining how objects look rotated, the caption announces "A New Turn in Gender Wars." Studies that find no significant gender disparities are much less likely to be reported or read. When *Time* and *Newsweek* run stories, the themes are why men and women *are* different, not what we still don't know about the origins of difference.[19]

ABC's recent report "Men, Women, and the Sex Difference" provides a textbook case of media spin. In an apparent attempt to seem evenhanded, reporter John Stossell presented "experts" on both sides of the debate. Feminists, he claimed, argue that sex-based differences reflect the "wicked influences of a sexist society." Supporting soundbites came from interviews with Gloria Steinem and Bella Abzug, whose excerpted comments reflected no command of the relevant research. But, continued Stossel, "from the world of science there are other voices. 'The difference is real,' say the scientists. 'It starts in the womb.'" Defending this position were lab-coated researchers, most of them female, who sounded informed and objective. The debate as it then appeared was between feminist ideology and hard facts. No hint of controversy within the scientific community ever emerged.[20]

Yet the point on which there is greatest scholarly consensus is that experts have reached no consensus on these issues. Researchers have not produced consistent findings on sex-based differences in brain structure. Nor is there agreement on the way that this structure affects cognitive functions and interacts with environmental influences. Moreover, the inequalities that supposedly result from brain structure are extremely small and unstable, a fact that the popular media usually obscure. Gender accounts for a very small part of the reported variations among individuals in math, verbal, and visual/spatial skills, usually between 1 and 5 percent. Such small disparities scarcely support sociobiologists' sweeping assertions about natural differences in the sexes' occupations, interests, and capacities.[21]

These gender disparities also are highly variable over time and across cultures. Research on some European and African societies finds no sex-based differences in verbal abilities. In the United States, gender differences in math scores have declined dramatically over the past quarter-century, as educational opportunities for girls have improved. A recent analysis of some one hundred studies in math performance involving almost four million American students found significant advantages for males only among a small sample of highly intelligent children. It is by no means clear whether this advantage reflects any innate ability. Many studies of gender differences in math performance have not taken account of even obvious influences such as the number of courses taken. Nor has any research been able to eliminate all of the gender-linked environmental factors that affect performance, such as teacher interaction, parental support, social stereotypes, and informal math instruction through games and hobbies. We can scarcely assess innate talents when guidance counselors are still acknowledging that they do not encourage girls in math because most of them "wouldn't be good at it, and in any case, what would they do with it?"[22]

Although there is much we still do not know about sex-based differences in math capabilities, there is much we do know about differences in math education. And as Chapter 3 indicates, until we address biases in our instructional approaches, we cannot begin to disentangle genetic and cultural influences.

The same is true for theories about hormonal influences. A quarter-century ago, the physician for former Vice-President Hubert Humphrey gained national prominence by alerting the nation to certain "scientific truths"—namely, the "physical and psychological . . . [limits on] a female's potential." A woman president subject to the "mental aberrations" of menopause would endanger the country in stressful situations like the Cuban Missile Crisis. As another expert similarly noted, an investor in a bank wouldn't want its president making a loan decision under the "raging hormonal influences" that can accompany menstruation.[23]

Although such extreme comments are no longer frequent in mixed company, Americans often view women's anger and assertiveness as part of their "monthly menace." My last public lecture touching on this issue prompted a question from the audience: "What's the difference between a pit bull and a woman with Premenstrual Syndrome?" The answer that eluded me was "lip gloss." Ironically enough, in an era that has produced male leaders like Adolph Hitler and Idi Amin, and in which males account for over 90 percent of violent crime, it is female instability that draws attention. Undaunted by the lack of data, some experts recently have asserted that Premenstrual Syndrome (PMS) is an epidemic problem—one that supposedly costs employers as much as $5 billion annually in absenteeism alone.[24]

By contrast, other commentators see "female potential" as limited less by hormonal hurricanes than by the wrong kind of hormones. Women have lower levels of testosterone than men, and this supposedly accounts for their lower levels of aggressiveness, drive, and achievement. Despite female soldiers' increasing role in the armed forces, key military leaders remain convinced that actual "fighting is a man's job." In the mid-1990s, several initiatives to reduce gender-based exclusions prompted opposition by leading defense experts who insisted that female soldiers are "psychologically unfit" for combat. Women supposedly see their "targets as people" and have difficulty in "killing impersonally." According to House Speaker Newt Gingrich, males who have been "biologically driven to go out and hunt giraffes" will have an obvious advantage in direct combat.[25]

Similarly, in nonmilitary settings, men's "natural" assertiveness often is viewed as a crucial credential for leadership positions. "When push comes to shove," claims Minnesota gubernatorial candidate Allen Quist, "the higher level of political authority . . . should be in the hands of the husband. There's a genetic predisposition." Many Americans find the "hard evidence" of biological difference to be "overwhelming": men simply *are* more "aggressive, competitive, risk taking, and combative than women."[26]

Much, of course, depends on what one counts as evidence. Popular assumptions about hormonal imbalance are highly exaggerated. Despite a cottage industry of commentary, Premenstrual Syndrome is a problem in search of a coherent definition, cause, and treatment. The number of women who suffer from PMS is estimated at anywhere from 5 percent to 95 percent, and as many as 150 symptoms have been identified. There is no consensus on its dynamics, in part because researchers have been unable to separate cultural from biological influences. Although some women clearly suffer physical problems in connection with menopause and menstruation, evidence of "emotional disturbances" is inconsistent and inconclusive. Societal expectations influence individual experience, and American women's reports of emotional effects do not correspond to other less subjective measures of mood changes. Nor do hormonal changes associated with menstrual conditions have any demonstrable adverse effects on cognitive tasks or work performance.[27]

Treating women as "naturally abnormal" in response to hormonal levels can mask the importance of other explanations. Much of the depression or irritability that Americans often attribute to women's "time of life" or "time of the month" may have much more to do with stressful external conditions than with internal hormonal changes. Stereotyping women as imbalanced may simply add to the stress. Such stereotyping seems especially dubious in light of recent research suggesting that men also experience hormone-related fluctuations in mood and behavior.[28]

Assumptions about a hormonal basis for male dominance and aggression require similar qualification. Sociobiological and popular discussion often assumes that male aggression is a "fact of life" (although not beyond modest "cultural improvement") and that woman's less assertive nature has "sealed her fate for millions of years." Such discussion frequently lumps together widely disparate behaviors—everything from rape to reckless driving, rough-and-tumble play, and political ambition. Yet it does not seem likely that the same hormonal drives explain all of these behaviors, particularly since they vary so widely across cultures. In some societies rape is almost unknown; in others, such as ours, it is all too common.[29]

Moreover, in most cultures, certain forms of female aggression are unexceptional. American women generally have been no less supportive than men of wartime efforts and no less effective in military, police, and prison security work. Nor is the relationship of hormones to aggression well established. Many studies find no correlation between levels of testosterone and violence, hostility, or aggression.[30]

This is not to discount the significance of sex-based differences in many aggressive behaviors or to suggest that biology plays no part in explaining them. As Chapter 3 indicates, there are ways in which "boys will be boys" despite their parents' best efforts. It may also be significant that girls with sex-related abnormalities, such as high exposure to testosterone during prenatal development, reportedly display increased aggression and preferences for "male" toys.[31]

Yet it by no means follows that the extent of current gender differences in aggression is physiologically determined or that we can separate biological from cultural influences. Recent research finds that gender accounts for only about 5 percent of the variation among individuals in aggressive behavior, and that both parents and peers are more tolerant of such behavior in males than in females. Even the best human behavior studies cannot view nature in the raw. The adults who reported masculine tendencies in girls with abnormal hormonal exposure knew of those abnormalities. Parents' and teachers' expectations about the effects of testosterone may have influenced how they interpreted and reacted to the girls' behaviors.[32]

Like other cultures, America encourages and values aggression more in males than in females. What often looks appropriately assertive in men appears abrasive in women. Games, sports, media images, parental attitudes, and peer pressures all amplify gender differences. As is clear from the evidence reviewed in subsequent chapters, violence is, in large measure, learned behavior. Whatever their biological predispositions, males acquire models for aggression from family and societal settings. As social critic Barbara Ehrenreich notes, "However science eventually defines it, 'la différence' can be amplified or minimized by human cultural arrangements. The choice is up to us, and not to our genes."[33]

A final cluster of "real differences" between the sexes involves size and strength. For centuries, men's physical advantages have served to enforce and justify their cultural dominance. These advantages in certain military, athletic, and employment contexts help rationalize other inequalities. The use or threat of physical coercion also discourages women's resistance. Of course, in any advanced industrial nation, technology has dramatically reduced the importance of gender differences in size and strength. Yet the circumstances in which such disparities seem to matter are still of interest. They underscore how culture influences the biological distinctions that it appears merely to acknowledge.

Men are, on average, taller, heavier, faster, and stronger than women. These differences appear natural because they have persisted over time and across cultures. At least in a few contexts, they also seem relevant to differences in opportunities and rewards. Military service is an obvious example. Opponents of the proposed Equal Rights Amendment to the Constitution warned that its requirements of "unisex" treatment could not accommodate genuine differences. The result would be female soldiers whose "inadequate hip structure" and "tender feet" would "hamstring the infantry." Defenders of the current ban on women in combat make comparable claims. To Barbara Bush, female soldiers just "are not physically strong enough." House Speaker Newt Gingrich similarly explains that women lack upper body strength and have "biological problems staying in a ditch for thirty days because they get infections." The relatively small number of combat jobs that might involve extended time in ditches and the possibility of establishing combat exclusions based on strength rather than gender are details not worth discussing. Nor are many Americans prepared to acknowledge, as does legal expert Richard Posner, that "we live in an age of push-button warfare. Women can push buttons as well as men." To policy-makers like Gingrich, the crucial point is that biological differences between the sexes are "very real."[34]

Opposition to gender equity in athletics rests on analogous assumptions. Given men's greater interest and demonstrated superiority in almost all sports, why should women get comparable funding, coaching, and facilities? Many Americans justify unequal athletic opportunities on biological grounds: women do not deserve "equal reward for unequal talent."[35]

The first thing to note about such arguments is the contexts in which they are and—more to the point—are not invoked. Concerns about women's physical limitations generally have surfaced only about certain women in certain circumstances, and not necessarily those posing the greatest physical demands. For example, throughout the nineteenth century, opponents of equal voting rights and equal access to the professions invoked visions of female delicacy and fragility. Women would be unable to withstand the "forensic strife" of law, the "keen pace" of business, and the psychological stress of medicine. Such concerns were highly selective and notably absent in discussions of women's far more grueling labor in farm and domestic settings. So, too, sex-based protective labor legislation that prevailed throughout the first half of the twentieth century frequently "protected" female employees out of jobs desirable to males. Occupations "inappropriate" for women included everything from shoeshining to public office. By contrast, many of the least desirable jobs, such as agricultural positions filled by women of color, were exempt from statutory protections. In those contexts, female frailties went largely unnoticed and onerous working conditions remained largely unregulated.[36]

Contemporary arguments about women's physical limitations reflect similar problems. A representative example involves the ABC broadcast on sex difference noted earlier. It attacked "elaborate and expensive government policies based on the fiction that men and women are interchangeable." Support for this claim included clips from a firefighters' training film. They show women falling down or struggling unsuccessfully to maneuver heavy equipment. Television viewers were then invited to consider: "How is America better off if the real physical demands of the job are watered down to accommodate women?"[37]

That question appears rhetorical only because others are never asked. How many male trainees might look incompetent if the film editor had wanted to illustrate *their* deficiencies? How often have women been excluded from jobs like firefighting because of arbitrary height, weight, and strength requirements that are not job related? How possible is it to redesign equipment to minimize such gender-based exclusions? These are some of the questions that sex discrimination law finally has brought into focus. Where "elaborate and expensive" litigation occurs, the reason usually has much to do with male resistance to gender integration, a point that media accounts like ABC's diplomatically overlook. The end result of such lawsuits has almost always been to increase equal opportunity, not by "watering down job requirements" but by making modest changes in work environments, such as adjustments in equipment or allocation of tasks.[38]

Moreover, sex-based disparities in height and weight, like other ostensibly innate differences, vary considerably in response to cultural influences. In societies where neither men nor women perform much physical labor, the gender gap in body sizes is considerably smaller. And in America, sex-based differences in speed and strength have narrowed as opportunities for women have broadened. Increased support for female athletes has enabled them to improve their performance in many sports at rates much greater than those of men. Given current patterns, sex disparities in some events may disappear altogether in the next half-century.[39]

Of course, certain physical differences related to reproductive physiology are likely to endure. But we are not yet in a position to identify which gender gaps will persist. As Ruth Hubbard explains:

> If a society puts half its children into short skirts and warns them not to move in ways that reveal their panties, while putting the other half into jeans and overalls and encouraging them to climb trees, play ball, and participate in other vigorous outdoor games; if later, during adolescence, the children who have been wearing trousers are urged to "eat like growing boys," while the children in skirts are warned to watch their weight and not get fat; if the half in jeans runs around in sneakers or boots, while the half in skirts totters about on spike heels, then these two groups of people will be biologically as well as socially different.[40]

So too, our culture chooses what social differences matter. We decide how much to value football over gymnastics, and how much to encourage female interest in cheerleading over shot put. We also choose to celebrate body images that are difficult to reconcile with leading sociobiological theories. America's abnormally slender, hourglass ideals for women are maladaptive in evolutionary terms. Females who lose 10 to 15 percent of their normal body fat can often become infertile, and the eating disorders associated with obsessive dieting pose significant health risks. Our cult of thinness for women and strong, full-figured body types for men contributes to the gender gap in size and to unhealthy behaviors that perpetuate it. To a significant and probably unknowable extent, the sex-based differences we encounter are those that we encourage.[41]

Although there is much about those differences that we have yet to understand, one general point seems clear. Mind, body, and culture interact in ways that scientific research cannot wholly disentangle. And while we cannot definitively resolve the nature/nurture debate, we can look more critically beneath and beyond it. John Dewey once noted that progress often occurs not when we solve questions but when "we get over them." If equality between the sexes is our ultimate goal, we need to care less about the biological origins of difference and more about its social consequences.[42]

The Culture of Difference

To challenge the biological foundations of gender differences is not to discount the importance of those differences in shaping individual identity. The organizing premise of this book is that gender matters in profound ways. Men and women differ in virtually every aspect of their life experience, including power, physical security, work, reproduction, sexuality, and family roles. The problem is not that we exaggerate the importance of gender. It is rather that we do so selectively and simplistically in ways that disadvantage women.

For those writing about gender-related issues, "'difference' is where the action is," notes columnist Katha Pollitt. For those concerned with gender inequality, this focus is a mixed blessing. Emphasizing women's distinctive contributions can serve as a useful counterweight to traditional biases. But the cost is to overstate the difference in sex-linked traits, and to overlook the disadvantages that follow from it.[43]

The strengths and limitations of difference-oriented frameworks are apparent in an increasing body of gender-related analysis. One cluster of work is largely descriptive. For example, some feminist and pop-psychological accounts of conversational patterns aim to increase understanding without passing judgment on males' and females' distinctive styles. Other works are explicitly evaluative. From their perspective, women are not just different but, in important respects, better: more caring, compassionate, and cooperative. On this view, the greater involvement of women may help transform our professional and political life.[44]

Unlike sociobiological accounts, these analyses generally do not assume that gender differences are biologically rooted. Nor do adherents agree about the causes of such differences. Some feminists believe that women's experience of mothering, or of being expected to perform nurturing roles, accounts for a wide range of sex-specific traits and values. Other theorists emphasize more general processes of socialization and subordination. Their frameworks stress the cultural pressures on women to gain status and approval by conforming to traditional feminine standards.[45]

What unites these diverse analyses is their tendency to make broad generalizations about sex-linked characteristics. Theorists such as Deborah Tannen chart the differences in male and female conversation. In their view, men are more likely to use language to maintain status, establish control, attract attention, solve problems, and exhibit knowledge. Women are more likely to use language to establish connection, give support, and reach consensus. Philosophers and psychologists like Carol Gilligan argue that women tend to reason in a "different voice." According to these theorists, men attach greater priority to abstract analysis, formal rights, and competitive structures; women give greater value to social context, caring relationships, and cooperative interaction.[46]

Building on such frameworks, feminists in a wide range of disciplines offer women's perspective as a way of reorienting professional roles and social priorities. Some theorists claim that female managers have different, more connective leadership styles, female lawyers prefer less adversarial approaches, and female doctors are more interested in patient relationships and public service work. Women's nurturing values also have provided the organizing principle for grassroots political movements on issues ranging from nuclear disarmament to drunk driving.[47]

At their best, such difference-oriented approaches can be both illuminating and empowering. To take an obvious example, a better understanding of sex-linked conversational patterns may sometimes enable women and men to avoid talking past each other. For couples who have fought for decades over whether to ask directions when they're lost or whether to figure it out from the map, some insight into the subtext of the struggle may be welcome. At the very least, stranded travelers who have read Deborah Tannen can argue from a more sophisticated script. In my own marriage, I can now aspire to a much more civilized exchange:

Me: "Darling, could you assert your need for male mastery in some other way that won't make us two hours late?"

Him: "Darling, if you want to establish intimate connections with every pedestrian who might have heard of West Fourth Street, could you wait until after I've figured out from the map whether we should be going north or south when we find it?"[48]

Difference-oriented frameworks can provide not just insight but also affirmation. They insist that values traditionally associated with women be *valued,* and that we focus on transforming institutions, not simply absorbing women within them. By affirming women's distinctive interests and perspectives, such approaches also can encourage greater political cohesiveness. If, as recent research suggests, most women have positive feelings about their gender, then analyses building on that sense of pride may be effective mobilizing strategies.[49]

Yet the affirmation of difference raises its own set of problems. As a threshold matter, "women's voice" is by no means as different or as unified as some feminist and many popular accounts imply. Much of this commentary overlooks variations over time, culture, class, race, ethnicity, age, and sexual orientation. For example, Gilligan's data draw on small unrepresentative samples of upper-middle-class whites, and most other studies of moral reasoning do not disclose significant gender distinctions. Nor does prominent work on gender differences in language adequately consider the effects of power. Men may be more likely to use speech patterns to establish control because they are more likely to occupy positions where they are *in* control. Studies that take power relationships into account generally find that language styles depend less on the sex than on the social roles and status of the speakers.[50]

So, too, related research on altruistic, political, and organizational behavior often fails to reveal the strong sex-linked virtues that some feminists claim. Although women are more likely to describe themselves as caring, they do not necessarily behave more altruistically in experimental or real-life settings outside the family. They are not, for example, more likely to help a stranger in a medical emergency. Although recent elections reflect significant gender gaps in American political behavior, over time the similarities between male and female voters have been far stronger than the differences. Even on issues where sex-linked variations often occur, such as social welfare and defense policies, gender is less critical in predicting attitudes than other factors like education, race, and employment status.[51]

In many organizational settings, comparisons of women and men reveal little or no difference in managerial styles. Male and female employees who confront similar occupational pressures tend to respond in similar ways. In general, researchers find very few psychological characteristics on which the sexes consistently differ. Even for these few characteristics, gender typically accounts for only 5 to 10 percent of the variation between individuals. This is not, of course, the picture that emerges in many pop-psychological accounts. John Gray's bestseller *Men Are from Mars, Women Are from Venus* paints the entire universe in pinks and blues. In his portrait, men and women differ in all areas of their lives. "Not only do [they] . . . communicate differently, but they think, feel, perceive, react, respond, love, need, and appreciate differently." Men value "power, competency, efficiency and achievement." Women value "love, communication, beauty and relationships." If this appears a bit simplistic, millions of book purchasers don't seem to mind.[52]

But more informed readers are beginning to wonder, "Haven't we been here before?" Yes indeed. For more than a century, the American women's movement has struggled with the dilemma of difference, looking for ways to reaffirm positive qualities traditionally associated with women without reinforcing negative or confining stereotypes. The nineteenth-century suffrage campaign tried to have it both ways. To the extent women were the same as men, the argument went, they should have the same opportunities. To the extent that women were different, their special qualities should be represented. According to some suffragists, the introduction of feminine nurturing values would "purify" politics.[53]

It didn't happen then, and it is no more likely to happen now. By oversimplifying and overclaiming the role of gender difference, many contemporary accounts divert attention from more critical factors. All too often, sex-based stereotypes become an easy out. Men and women having trouble communicating can chalk it up to gender without confronting other possibilities: "they don't like listening; they're stressed, tired or in a hurry; they don't believe that they *need* to be nice to a spouse or a subordinate." Many men are particularly pleased to discover claims of difference coming from a woman scholar. This entitles them to conclude that "it's not *my* fault we can't communicate . . . We don't speak the same language. And it's not men saying that, by the way, it's women. Women Ph.D.'s."[54]

In the insistently apolitical universe of many pop psychologists like John Gray, if a woman is dissatisfied with a man's unresponsiveness, the solution lies with her, not him. Gray's advice to female readers is that "a man needs to be accepted regardless of imperfections. Give up trying change him . . . Trust him to grow on his own . . . Practice doing things yourself and not depending on him to make you happy." In other words, just change the diapers and stop whining about it. After all, you're the ones who are supposed to be nurturing.[55]

In effect, gender difference can serve as an all-purpose rationalization for gender roles and gender hierarchies. Emphasizing male needs for achievement and female concerns with nurturance reinforces longstanding stereotypes that subordinate women and restrict opportunities for both sexes. Difference is the point at which some feminists risk an unhealthy alliance with religious conservatives. The message from both groups is often loud, clear, and strikingly similar: "In the name of liberation from male domination, women must not appropriate to themselves male characteristics contrary to their feminine originality . . . Parenthood, although it belongs to both—is realized more fully in the woman. Motherhood involves a special communion with the mystery of life . . . which profoundly marks the woman's personality." The author of this passage is Pope John Paul II, but the quotation could just as readily have come from a leading feminist theorist.[56]

The danger in this alliance is that feminist reasoning can be hijacked to support distinctly nonfeminist objectives. For example, administrators of prestigious state-supported colleges like the Citadel and the Virginia Military Institute have invoked Carol Gilligan's work to justify excluding women. To these administrators, and the lower courts that initially (though ultimately unsuccessfully) upheld the exclusions, women's different needs and values offered a rationale for separate but by no means equal programs. Similarly, many employers use women's "different goals and priorities" in the workplace to explain their absence from upper-level positions. Instead of policies that could help workers of both sexes accommodate family responsibilities, many workplaces settle for separate, slower "mommy tracks." These then become mommy traps, leaving daddies free to run the world.[57]

Given all the problems, both substantive and strategic, with difference-oriented approaches, what accounts for their persistent popularity? Katha Pollitt suggests that both sexes can end up "marooned on Gilligan's island" but for somewhat different reasons.

For women, the vision of themselves as carers and sharers is tempting in [several ways] . . . By arguing that the traditional qualities, tasks and ways of life of women are as important, valuable and serious as those of men (if not more so), Carol Gilligan and others let women feel that nothing needs to change, except the social valuation accorded to what they are already doing. It's a burst of grateful applause, which is why women like it. Men keep the power but since power is bad, so much the worse for them . . . [This is also why men like it. Childrearing remains] women's glory and joy and opportunity for self-transcendence, while Dad naps on the couch.

But this is a bargain that more and more women are reconsidering, especially in the rising number of single-parent households where napping dads and their paychecks are nowhere to be found.[58]

A quarter-century ago, in *Man's World, Woman's Place,* Elizabeth Janeway referred to stereotypes about male achievers and female nurturers as an idea whose time won't go. Our renewed fixation on difference confirms her point. We have not yet found ways to acknowledge sex-linked qualities without perpetuating their constraints. When the subject is gender, we may never entirely escape this dilemma of difference. But we can at least refocus our inquiry. Our universe of pinks and blues could acquire a more complicated color scheme. We should focus less on the quest for inherent differences and more on the inequality they create.

We also need a clearer understanding of the limits of gender in structuring our analysis. To divide the world solely by sex is to ignore the ways in which biological status is experienced differently by different groups in different contexts. There is no "generic woman," and more attention must center on variations in culture, class, race, ethnicity, age, and sexual orientation. We must become equally sensitive to the contextual forces that lead the same women to vary in the feminine characteristics that they express in different social circumstances.[59]

This focus on context offers a way around the dilemmas of difference that have long plagued the women's movement. Such a framework can acknowledge the qualities traditionally associated with women without exaggerating their extent or assuming that they are biologically determined. As an increasing body of research makes clear, changes in social expectations and in the gender composition of a particular setting significantly affect women's willingness to express gender-related traits.[60]

Our daily experiences bear this out. I have noticed the shift in my own willingness to raise "women's issues" in workplace settings now that I have ten female colleagues rather than one. Women's "different voice" speaks in more than one register; and the same is true for men. Boys may be boys, but they express that identity differently in fraternity parties than in job interviews with a female manager.

The advantage of focusing on context is that we can acknowledge gender differences but resist dichotomies. We can avoid sweeping assertions about women's and men's essential natures while noting the importance of sex-linked experiences. Whatever our biological predispositions, we shape gender differences through a complex set of forces. Much depends on childhood socialization and structural constraints such as status, wealth, and power. A better understanding of all our differences also permits a better understanding of our similarities—of women's and men's common needs, aspirations, and capacities for change.

3

Beginning at Birth

A 1918 trade journal on children's wear confidently reported that despite previous "diversity of opinion on the subject," a clear popular consensus had emerged: the "accepted rule is pink for the boy and blue for the girl." Pink suggested manliness and blue signaled delicacy. A quarter-century later, consensus was still clear, but masculinity and femininity had shifted colors.[1]

Many contemporary commentators are similarly confident that "we will not change the essential boyness of boys or girlness of girls." This perspective is widely shared, in part because so many efforts at change have yet to produce it. Despite substantial shifts in sex-based roles over the past several decades, children still display traditional sex-typed attitudes and behaviors at very early ages.[2]

The origin of this strong sense of gender identity is a matter of considerable dispute, but most adults deny that they are responsible. Frustrated parents, beleaguered teachers, and defensive media representatives are sure that the basic causes of sex stereotyping are beyond their control. This perception is part of what makes biological explanations so attractive, however wobbly their foundations. If there is, after all, some "doll gene" that explains toy preferences, this would let a lot of folks off the hook.

Yet most recent research makes clear that whatever their biological predispositions, children receive strong cultural messages about sex-appropriate traits, tasks, and behaviors. These messages often involve unconscious, subtle, or indirect signals, rather than intentional instruction. Until adults become more aware of their role in the gender socialization process, we cannot reverse its most damaging effects.

A threshold challenge lies in convincing the public that there is any significant problem to address. On this point, Americans are ambivalent. At least in principle, the vast majority of parents and educators support equality between the sexes and want children to develop their full potential. Yet most adults are uncomfortable with the prospect of a world without significant gender differences and are not preparing their children to live in one.[3]

Nor are many adults aware of the systematic gender inequalities that begin at early ages. Several recent studies documenting such inequalities have triggered waves of denial. Conservative commentators have had a field day with "the facts." Why should self-appointed "sex equity bureaucrats" be whining when girls get better grades, earn more high school degrees, and have lower rates of adolescent suicide, delinquency, and drug abuse? Yet such patterns are hardly an endorsement of current childrearing. Rather, they make clear that prevailing practices carry costs for both sexes. Moreover, too many Americans discount the disproportionate price that girls eventually pay for gender stereotypes. As Chapter 1 indicates, on almost all dimensions of power, status, income, and physical security, women end up worse off than men. And as the remainder of this chapter makes clear, those inequalities build on roles learned in childhood.[4]

Indeed, children themselves are aware of gender hierarchies, well before any bureaucrats bombard them with the relevant statistics. When 1,100 Michigan elementary students were asked to describe what life would be like if they were the opposite sex, over 40 percent of the girls saw advantages to being male; they would have better jobs, higher incomes, and more respect. Ninety-five percent of the boys saw no advantage to being female, and a substantial number thought suicide would be preferable. If we want to alter such gender hierarchies, we need a better understanding of how and where they start.[5]

Gender Identity and Gender Roles

Sandra Bem, a leading expert on sex stereotypes, describes the efforts she made to free her son from traditional assumptions. At every opportunity, she emphasized that the only "real" differences between the sexes were anatomical and also encouraged his interests in "feminine" toys and activities. The difficulty of her task became clear the day that he decided to wear a barrette to nursery school. His appearance provoked an immediate argument with a classmate who insisted that "boys don't wear barrettes." Bem's son responded with a lecture on real differences, which he illustrated by dropping his trousers and displaying the evidence. His fellow four-year-old was unpersuaded. "Everybody has a penis," he insisted, "only girls wear barrettes."[6]

Such dialogues highlight the cultural underpinnings of sex-based roles. Children develop a strong sense of gender identity many years before they associate it with anatomical differences. By age two, toddlers have sex-linked toy preferences; by age three they can identify certain occupations as more appropriate for each sex; and between ages four and six they separate into same-sex groups with distinctive play patterns and rigid assumptions about appropriate male and female behavior.[7]

Throughout childhood, gender segregation serves to reinforce gender stereotypes. Boys' activities celebrate heroism and involve rough-and-tumble activities; they reward dominance, competitiveness, and aggression. Girls' activities make romance and domesticity a far more common theme, and their play is more attentive to relationships and personal appearance. In these contexts, the most vigilant policing of sex stereotypes comes from other children. Boys are particularly intolerant of any perceived deviance, and the scorn they direct at "fags" and "sissies" reinforces conventional norms of masculinity and persistent patterns of homophobia.[8]

The causes of such rigid gender stereotyping remain unclear. Some researchers believe that physiological differences in hormonal levels, in spatial and perceptual capacities, and in verbal development patterns help explain sex-linked styles of play. Other contemporary experts offer psychoanalytic explanations, although typically not the classical Freudian accounts of penis envy and castration complexes. For example, feminist theorists such as Nancy Chodorow and Dorothy Dinnerstein stress children's relation to their primary caretaker as the foundation for gender identity. Because these caretakers generally are women, girls learn to see themselves as similar and fundamentally connected to others, while boys learn to see themselves as separate and different. Under this view, such developmental processes encourage nurturing and interpersonal skills in girls and assertiveness and independence in boys.[9]

Still other theorists stress cognitive and social learning. Their emphasis is on the strategies of imitation, observation, and reinforcement that underpin gender identity. For individuals concerned with gender inequality, these generally are the processes of greatest interest. Compared with psychoanalytic and sociobiological frameworks, social-learning theories are more responsive to context and therefore more able to account for variations over time, culture, class, race, and ethnicity. A focus on social learning also highlights the cultural forces that are most open to change.

Even theorists wedded to biological and psychoanalytic explanations acknowledge that social learning plays a crucial role in shaping sex-linked behaviors. Whatever children's predispositions, they also receive frequent signals from parents, peers, teachers, and the media. In countless ways, our culture encourages boys to be assertive, competitive, and independent—to make things work and happen. We tell girls to be nice, caring, and dependent—to worry about how they look and what others feel. Females learn how to get along; males learn how to get ahead. And children of both sexes learn, above all, that gender matters. Toys, clothing, occupations, household tasks, even pronouns differ according to sex. The cues are everywhere, and children pick up many messages that we neither notice nor intend.[10]

Recent research overwhelmingly indicates that parents still encourage conformity to sex-based stereotypes but generally are unaware of doing so. Although the direct measurable effects of such parental influence are small, family signals remain important in reinforcing other cultural messages.[11]

Those signals begin at birth. Parents hold, dress, and interact with sons and daughters differently. Boys get more rough-and-tumble play, more attention from fathers, more tolerance for aggressive action, less restrictive clothing, and far fewer domestic chores than their sisters. Girls get more concern about physical appearance. Adults obsessed with weight sometimes place even preschoolers on diets that are physically and psychologically counterproductive.[12]

Parents also interpret and monitor their children's behavior in ways that reinforce gender stereotypes. To many adults, similar crying behavior looks like anger in boys but fear in girls, and problem-solving successes seem to reflect skill in sons but luck or hard work in daughters. Although over four-fifths of surveyed parents say that it is important for children to play with toys of all kinds, they provide more approval for "sex-appropriate" choices. Pressures for conformity to traditional gender stereotypes come more from fathers than from mothers and are stronger for boys than for girls. Partly because masculine activities have higher status than feminine ones, we have greater tolerance for daughters who are tomboys than for sons who are "sissies."[13]

Whether such childrearing practices vary significantly across racial and ethnic groups has received relatively little attention. However, certain patterns appear common, particularly those that reinforce daughters' nurturing values. Almost no parents, even those who deny that they treat boys and girls differently, have the same reaction to a son's and daughter's interest in dolls or nail polish. M. G. Lord's *Forever Barbie* offers a telling example. One mother, on discovering her son's Barbie collection, informed him: "I've given those dolls to an orphanage. And we're not going to tell your father."[14]

Children also learn gender roles through observation. As long as most men don't wash the socks they wear, their sons will tend to label laundry as "women's work." Daughters who watch their mother's beauty rituals and household labor pick up similar messages. Even if parents model nontraditional roles, the price they pay isn't lost on their children. Recent research on gifted junior high students found that girls with professional mothers often had doubts about making such career choices themselves. Several daughters expressed reservations about seeking advanced degrees because their mothers were always tired or had too little time for family activities. Boys saw similar patterns and drew even stronger conclusions; two-thirds thought that mothers shouldn't work.[15]

Of course, many parents do not consciously encourage sex-based stereotypes but simply accept the ones their children acquire from other sources. For example, daughters may end up with more domestic tasks in part because they are more willing to perform them when asked; by very early ages, boys may resist anything that doesn't appear to be "man's work." Parents who deliberately try to counter sex stereotypes often bump up against stronger cultural forces. One mother who insisted on giving her son dolls finally gave up when she found them serving as airborne missiles.[16]

This is not to suggest that parents should abandon their efforts. Encouraging children to recognize stereotypical images and to cross gender boundaries can help them develop their full potential. Parental support is, for example, a key factor in enabling girls to succeed in math and science. But parents cannot do it alone. If what they say about gender roles is inconsistent with what children see in books, television, and daily life, it is not surprising which messages stick.[17]

For those who worry about gender stereotypes, gender disadvantages, and the link between the two, a stroll through toyland offers sobering reminders of progress we have not yet made. Boys' options are different and, in important ways, better. They get more toys, they have more varieties to choose from, and their choices more often teach cognitive and spatial skills. The male market includes complex models, electronic gadgets, and chemistry sets. The female market offers primarily dolls, with distant runner-ups such as stuffed animals, makeup kits, and board games like "Sealed with a Kiss."[18]

Toy manufacturers of course, deny that this is *their* fault. They are just responding to what kids want and parents buy. After "extensive" research, company leaders claim that to make their board games "interesting to girls they have to focus on one element: boys." But manufacturers of products like "Dream Phone" also offer a positive spin. The object of that game is for young girls to discover, from electronic telephone clues, which boy is their "secret admirer." This requires girls to "check into all the details" and identify places where the admirer might hang out. So, according to one company representative, "it's really a game of deductive logic."[19]

A Cathy Guisewite cartoon captures the frustration of parents who want better alternatives. In the educational section of a toy store, a woman responds to a question about whether she is shopping for a "little boy or little girl" by insisting that her gift is for a "little unisex person." The salesperson probes further. Is this "a little unisex person who'd like a depth charger attack missile . . . or a little unisex person who'd like a makeup set?" The customer persists in her desire for a "non-sex-stereotyped, non-role-specific gift," and eventually settles on a dinosaur. In ringing up the purchase, the salesperson has a final question: "Did you want the dinosaur in the maniac demolisher combat outfit, or the dinosaur in the ballerina bridesmaid outfit?"[20]

Another by-product of these gender stereotypes is their reinforce-

ment of behaviors that ultimately injure both sexes. The boys' departments of many toy stores glorify male aggression: their arsenals offer
ever more brutal selections. The female market celebrates unrealistic
and unhealthy standards of femininity. For many girls, "toys aren't us";
the dolls available are overwhelmingly geared to white consumers, and
the most popular models offer images of wildly implausible lifestyles
and body proportions.[21]

Barbies are the clearest example. Over the past thirty-five years Barbie
may have been promoted from candy striper to astronaut, but she still
comes in the same hourglass proportions and she still needs an extensive—and expensive—wardrobe for the awards ceremonies following
her flight. Commenting on the outfits for Dr. Barbie, comedian Rita
Rudner notes that the doll has "a little stethoscope and little bag. But
she also has her short tight skirt and nine-inch heels. So she's a doctor.
And a prostitute on the side." Similar curiosities emerge in Mattel's
"Dolls of the World" collection. For example, a Jamaican doll looks to
informed collectors like an "anorexic Aunt Jemima."[22]

Related criticisms focus on the way Barbies affect girls' aspirations
and anxieties. After public outcry, the manufacturer discontinued Teen
Talk Barbie's complaint that "math class is tough." However, many of
the remaining messages concerning boys and shopping leave much to
be desired. What we really need, as cartoonist Nicole Hollander suggests, is a talking Barbie with messages like "Science is cool," and
"Albert Einstein's first wife, Mileva Maric, did the work, but he got the
Nobel Prize."[23]

Such scripts do not appear imminent, particularly in light of the
company's rejection of far more modest and more pressing proposals.
Health professionals have long urged Mattel to give the doll more
realistic proportions than those that, in a woman of average height,
work out to 31–17–28. An adult with these measurements would not
have sufficient body fat to sustain normal patterns of menstruation and
pregnancy. Once again, toy manufacturers deny that this is their fault
or some "weirdly misogynistic plot." Rather, the proportions are "dic-
tated by the mechanics of clothing construction." Dolls' apparel uses
fabric scaled for people, which creates extra thick waistbands on small
garments. In this clothing, a Barbie with more normal proportions
would not have such an attractive hourglass figure. This explanation
does not, however, account for the doll's disproportionately large

breasts, which are further amplified by thick fabric. Nor is Mattel's reasoning apparent to millions of young girls, who do not grasp the mechanics of clothing design, but simply view Barbie's measurements as the feminine beauty ideal. Which is fine, if, as Dave Barry notes, your concept of an attractive woman is "someone weighing fifty-two pounds, thirty-seven of which are in the bust area."[24]

For girls whose curves emerge in less desirable locations, obsessive diets and eating disorders are an increasingly common solution. In one study of suburban eight-year-olds, four-fifths reported efforts at weight control. Another survey of some 33,000 females found that three-quarters considered themselves too fat, even though a third were underweight and less than a quarter were overweight by standard measures. Although Barbie is only one of many cultural images contributing to those perceptions, most experts believe that she and her spinoffs are an important influence.[25]

Complaints about Barbie have not, however, hurt sales; she remains by far the world's most popular toy. Millions of purchasers deny that there is a problem and dismiss feminist protests as mindlessly fanatical. The flap over Barbie's math anxieties and body image earns "feminazis" no end of ridicule. "Get a life!" is a common response. As one indignant reader of the *New York Times* complained: "Anna Quindlen's [1994] column on Barbie's thirty-fifth birthday blames [the doll] for young girls' poor self-image, anorexia and the popularity of silicone breast implants. As one who consumed Barbie in large doses during my 'formative' years, let me come to the doll's defense . . . I owned more than twenty Barbie dolls in my youth and grew up, nevertheless, to attend Yale Law School and work as a litigator on Wall Street."[26]

Well, if we're going to be autobiographical, I, too, had Barbies. And I, too, went to Yale Law School. That scarcely proves or disproves any causal relationships. Most women professionals, like most other American women, presumably survived Barbie without dramatic damage. But the issue is whether we, or our daughters, are well served by building our fantasies along such unrealistic, unhealthy, and sex-stereotyped dimensions. In a culture where 10 to 20 percent of female adolescents suffer serious eating disorders, we should be making major efforts to combat negative body images. Barbie is hardly the only cause of the problem, but she certainly is not part of the solution.[27]

Children's literature presents similar challenges. A quarter-century ago, a widely publicized study, *Dick and Jane as Victims*, surveyed some 2,700 stories. It found only three featuring an employed mother. When girls appeared as major characters, it was largely in passive roles; they lost kittens that boys found. Such studies, together with increasing demands from parents, have brought substantial improvements in children's books, but many female characters remain stuck in traditional scripts. Girls are still busy creating problems that boys solve. In recent surveys, male characters come up with solutions five to eight times as often as females, and females care for children eight times as often as males. A representative pair of 1993 books, *I Can* and *Me Too*, features a male lead and his younger sister. Every other page illustrates what he can do, and the facing page shows what she cannot. At a time when a majority of women with young children are in the workforce, only one of sixty surveyed books portrayed an employed mother.[28]

For young boys, the most popular stories feature male heroes like Robin Hood, Superman, and James Bond. In most of these plots, men are central, women are marginal, and violence remains the preferred method of solving problems. For young girls, the most popular stories are romances featuring traditional heroines like the Little Mermaid, Sleeping Beauty, Cinderella, and their modern analogues. In these narratives, women's happiness depends on men, and physically unattractive characters are doomed to roles like wicked witches and evil stepmothers. So too, for teen readers, the most popular series include titles like *Stacy's Big Crush* and *Too Many Boys*. Publisher guidelines for such books, like the guidelines for adult romances, demand heroes who are masterful, rich, and successful, and heroines who are innocent and beautiful, with outfits and appearance "described in detail." No dark sides of domesticity ever surface. Readers get no clues that in real life, for every "knight in shining armor, there's a castle waiting to be cleaned."[29]

Nor does children's literature present a representative cast of characters. The heroes and heroines of mainstream publications are almost exclusively white, middle-class, and heterosexual. When people of color enter the story, it is usually in stereotypical roles. One popular account of a Puritan child in seventeenth-century New England refers to "Indians" as "little brown mice" running across the fields in loincloths.[30]

Although parents who look hard enough can come up with alternatives from small specialty publishers, these books generally do not make it into the shopping malls and school libraries. Nor do all parents support efforts to broaden curricular offerings. In one exceptionally bitter dispute, Citizens Organized for Better Schools sued a Tennessee school board for adopting a first-grade text that consciously challenged gender stereotypes; one of its objectionable pictures showed a boy cooking instead of a girl.[31]

Cultural lag is equally apparent in other children's entertainment. Video games and comic books offer a constant dose of male violence. Ninety percent of the top forty-some video games portray no women. When female characters do play a role, the dominant theme of damsel in distress now includes ever more brutal innovations. In "stalker" games, players win by torturing or terrorizing, not rescuing, women. In the comic book market aimed at boys, female characters are still on the sidelines of men's adventures. Their principal role is the bosomy and endangered bimbo.[32]

In the market aimed at girls, however, males are the central focus of concern. Attracting boys' attention and approval is the dominant theme in ads, video games, and magazine features. The challenge in a popular Barbie computer game is for players to discover "fashion treasures" for a Fantasy Ball or to find their way out of a shopping mall to meet Ken for a date. Judging from the content of girls' magazines, life's pressing problems involve bushy eyebrows, busy boyfriends, and "thigh anxiety."[33]

The centrality of beauty and fashion in publications like *Seventeen* suggests that how the reader looks is more important than what she thinks. And the look that the mass media promote is neither realistic nor healthy. Models are almost always white, and almost never have a normal body weight. Although the readership of magazines like *Vogue, Seventeen,* and *Mademoiselle* is 12 to 14 percent African American, only around 2 percent of their ads feature blacks. Yet editors deny that this underrepresentation is their fault; in their view, models of color simply "don't sell magazines." Nor, apparently, do women of normal body size. The average fashion model weighs one-fourth less than the average woman but has breasts considerably larger than average, a feat that nature almost never achieves unassisted.[34]

The link between waif-like models and adolescent eating disorders has been well documented, and it has not escaped the attention of magazine editors or commercial sponsors. Women's health organizations have launched frequent protests against "anorexic chic," including a widely publicized campaign to place "Feed Me" stickers under billboard photos of emaciated bodies. Such images are, of course, a problem for adults as well as adolescents. Yet the typical reaction by media leaders is to deny their own contribution to the problem for either group. According to fashion editors, "people were dieting long before newsstands were invented." Moreover, clothes just "look better on those small-size girls," and "this is what [readers] want." "We live in a society that likes to glamorize the body in a thin kind of way," explains one advertising executive. "This is not the Italian Renaissance." Heavier models just look "unhealthy," and that isn't the fault of corporate America.[35]

With no apparent sense of irony, Calvin Klein similarly defends his popularization of waif models like Kate Moss on grounds of health. She, at least, is "naturally" thin. By contrast, Klein notes, so many other models have "distorted their bodies by implants . . . I mean you just cannot imagine . . . what women have been doing to themselves." If people respond in "unnatural" ways to his use of waif images, or to his pornographic posing of teen models, why is he to blame?[36]

Yet as recent accounts of the modeling industry make clear, what young women "have been doing to themselves" is related to the images that a male-dominated fashion, advertising, and publishing industry wants to promote. Those images are, in turn, connected to the eating disorders that girls who are not "naturally" thin impose on themselves. Even magazines that run an occasional story on those problems generally surround it with underweight models and features like "The Fastest Firmers for Buns and Thighs." The dominant message isn't lost on readers. After Seventeen ran an article about girls' unhealthy obsession with weight, readers mailed in angry letters linking their own concerns to advertising images from the magazine's own pages.[37]

Gender biases also shape children's television. Males dominate in such programming because, according to industry representatives, girls will watch programs with male leads but boys will not view shows with female leads. In mixed audiences, boys' preferences prevail. Fewer than 5 percent of characters on children's programs are people of color, and white women's primary roles are in commercials for food and household products. Even an educational program like Sesame Street often has had almost exclusively male casts. "We're working on it," was the explanation an executive producer provided for the absence of any female muppets in the early 1990s. Columnist Katha Pollitt was, of course, understanding. "After all, the show has only been on the air for a quarter-century; these things take time."[38]

Another area in which we're still working—with equally limited success—involves media entertainment that glorifies male aggression. Heavy-metal and rap lyrics are becoming increasingly brutal and misogynistic. On Saturday morning children's shows, the networks average about twenty-five acts of violence per hour, and about 90 percent of cartoons include violent material. Between one-half and two-thirds of surveyed programs show some violence, and experts rate about 40 percent of network television movies as inappropriately violent. By the time of graduation from high school, the average teen has spent more hours in front of television than in school and has witnessed over 250,000 violent acts. Although media leaders acknowledge that violence is a social problem, they insist that television should not be a scapegoat; after all, "no TV has killed a kid." However, three decades of research confirm the linkage between glorification of male aggression in the media and male aggression in daily life.[39]

Yet despite growing recognition of the problem, many Americans deny that they have primary responsibility to address it. Media leaders want parents to supervise their children's choices and to discuss the negative affects of violence. But the industry long fought federal legislation requiring television sets to include "V-chip" technology, which enables parents to block out violent programs. Although that legislation finally went into effect in 1996, most parents are understandably unwilling to accept sole responsibility for protecting children. V-chips are not a total solution. It will be some time before all sets have them and adequate violence-rating systems become available. Moreover, if television ratings mirror those governing motion pictures, brutality may remain pervasive. Under current regulations, if a man touches a woman's breast the movie gets an "R," but if he cuts off the breast with a chain saw the rating is "PG-13."[40]

Experts also worry that older children will find sets without V-chip blocking mechanisms or will learn to counteract them, and that industry leaders will settle for warning viewers about violence instead of trying to reduce it. Even the most vigilant working parents will have difficulty policing all of their sons' and daughters' viewing opportunities. Yet television executives are reluctant to make that task easier. In a rare moment of candor, a CBS vice-president once acknowledged: "I'm not interested in culture. I'm not interested in pro-social values. I have only one interest. That's whether people watch the program." Those of us with different priorities need to make them heard.[41]

Improving children's media will require less denial and more effort from all constituencies—parents, government, and industry leaders. We need more public and commercial television programming aimed at reducing stereotypes and preventing violence. Consumers need to increase pressure on manufacturers and commercial producers through boycotts of sexist products or items advertised on highly violent shows. Broadcasters should make greater efforts to reduce gratuitous brutality—particularly portrayals that divorce such conduct from the consequences it has in real life. Broader educational campaigns are necessary to build critical viewing skills and to promote nonstereotypical toys, games, and publications.[42]

For a culture hooked on male violence and female appearance, there are no easy solutions. But there are multiple opportunities for adults to vote with their feet, their dollars, and their ballots. Violence may be a fact of life but we need not raise our children to condone and celebrate it. Heroism, adventure, and danger are available in many fantasy forms that do not involve aggression; constructive opportunities can grow out of rescue missions, space exploration, wilderness experiences, and so forth. While anxiety about appearance is part of human experience, we need not surround young girls with images that exaggerate its importance and jeopardize their health.

Gender Bias in the Schools

At a ceremony marking his daughter's 1994 graduation from kindergarten, one New Jersey parent noticed something about the class awards that apparently had not bothered anyone else:

Boys' Awards	Girls' Awards
Very Best Thinker	All-Around Sweetheart
Most Eager Learner	Sweetest Personality
Most Imaginative	Cutest Personality
Mr. Personality	Best Manners
Hardest Worker	Best Helper[43]

This is not an isolated incident. Comprehensive recent studies find pervasive patterns of gender bias in education. What schools teach and tolerate reinforces inequalities that persist well beyond childhood. For most Americans, however, such bias is a tedious topic. The general public views it as a "once upon a time" problem that politically correct educators have largely solved. Funding of gender equity programs has declined sharply, and no federal agency is active in enforcing prohibitions against sex-based discrimination in elementary and secondary education. Of all the difficulties plaguing public schools—poverty, racism, drugs, violence—gender bias seems relatively low in the pecking order. At least until our own child bumps up against it in some particularly noticeable way. And this now happens less frequently because sexism has become more subtle. It has not, however, lost its influence on children's educational experience.[44]

A quarter-century ago, analysis of bestselling school history books revealed a biological oddity: a nation with only founding fathers. Material on women constituted less than 1 percent of the total. In a leading text, the development of the six-shooter received more space than the women's suffrage movement. Before college, I never learned that there *was* such a movement. And at my university, a basic American history course covered this seventy-five-year struggle in a single sentence. My professor mentioned in passing that a few suffragette protesters had chained themselves to the White House fence, and that women had won the right to vote soon after.[45]

The curriculum has improved, but, as one overview concludes, not nearly enough. In many standard texts, women are noticeable largely in their absence. Elementary school readers present females less often and in far fewer roles than males; men are missing only in domestic settings. Of the ten texts most frequently assigned in high school English classes, only one is by a woman and none are by people of color. Many coursebooks remain hostage to "great man" historical frameworks. These texts, as Jane Austen once described them, offer "quarrels of popes and kings, with wars or pestilences, in every page; the men all so good for nothing, and hardly any women at all—it is very tiresome." Prominent history books now discuss women as individuals or groups mainly in separate sections that constitute only 2 to 3 percent of the total material. Few explore the forces that have restricted and reinforced traditional gender roles. Such treatment undermines its own objective: women appear as an afterthought, not as part of the main story.[46]

Efforts to promote better coverage have had limited success. Although the law prohibits sex discrimination by schools that accept federal funding, curricular materials are explicitly exempt from coverage. Attempts to remedy gender bias often have fallen victim to conservative crusades against "political correctness," "filler feminism," and the "devaluing" of "the traditional family structure." A common assumption, as one disgruntled educator expressed it, is that most teachers are women and they include gender-related material "whether we want them to or not."[47]

The accuracy of that perception is open to doubt. On average, elementary school children cannot name more than four or five famous women from the past or present, excluding sports and entertainment figures. Only a few students can come close to meeting a request for ten, and even then it takes some ingenious strategies. "Think about the presidents" one fourth grader advised his classmate. "There are no lady presidents," his friend responded. "Of course not," the first boy acknowledged. "There's a law against it. But all you gotta do is take the presidents' names and put Mrs. in front of them."[48]

Gender bias is also present in vocational tracks and classroom dynamics. Girls are overrepresented in home economics and boys in technical and industrial training. Male voices get greater attention in most school settings, for reasons once suggested by Garry Trudeau in a *Doonesbury* cartoon. It begins with a mother's effort to find out how her daughter is doing in nursery school. "Okay, I guess," the child reports, "except I never get to say anything. The dorky boys get all the attention." "Maybe I should have a little talk with [the teacher]," proposes her mother. Her daughter is doubtful. "Mom, she'll never call on you! Send Daddy."[49]

It's not a bad strategy. As a recent report by the American Association of University Women (AAUW) concluded, whether "one is looking at preschool classrooms or university lecture halls . . . research spanning the past twenty years consistently reveals that males receive more teacher attention than do females." In part, this is because boys *demand* more attention, but teachers also are more likely to invite, praise, and follow up male responses. Racial and ethnic bias takes similar forms.[50]

What compounds the problem is the still widespread denial of its existence. More than 40 percent of surveyed women don't believe that girls encounter subtle discrimination in the schools. Teachers usually are unaware of gender bias in their own classroom until they see it on training-session videotapes. And if, as many observers note, boys seem to "need" more discipline and girls manage to do better in school despite less teacher attention, why worry?[51]

One reason for concern is that, in fact, girls do not do better on certain measures that matter, including test scores, self-esteem, and problem-solving ability. Their lower performance on most college entrance and national merit exams restricts admission and scholarship opportunities. So too, although the extent and importance of sex-based differences in self-esteem provoke controversy, most evidence finds a significant gap between the self-confidence of white male students and that of female students, and a related gap in problem-solving abilities. While black girls score relatively well on self-esteem, they may do so by distancing themselves from conventional performance measures like grades—a coping strategy that carries obvious costs.[52]

A related concern is that male dominance in classroom interactions and technical programs sets the stage for later patterns. Men talk more, interrupt more, and are viewed as more effective in workplace communication. They also dominate technical occupations, which offer higher pay, greater prestige, and more promotion opportunities than the positions generally targeted in predominantly female vocational programs.[53]

We cannot expect to eliminate employment inequality among adults unless we address its foundations among children. That is unlikely to occur without significant changes in educational leadership and priorities. Although nearly three-quarters of elementary and secondary school teachers are women, they hold only 10 percent of superintendent positions. Women need greater decisionmaking opportunities, and school districts need more gender bias education for teachers and students, curricular integration projects that push beyond tokenism, and development of learning environments that respond to the particular needs of girls.[54]

All too often, schools have achieved such learning environments only in all-female schools or classrooms. Many female students, of course, have benefited from gender-segregated education. Indeed, the Supreme Court recently recognized as much. In its decision invalidating an all-male admissions policy at Virginia Military Institute, the Court acknowledged that some all-female policies could stand on different footing because they serve a compensatory purpose; their goal often is to challenge, not perpetuate, gender stereotypes.[55]

In the long run, however, sex segregation is not the best solution. The all-female math and science classes that are becoming increasingly popular in public schools are way stations on the path to equality, but they should not become the final destination. Such classes highlight the importance of cooperative learning techniques, supportive teacher responses, and elimination of peer ridicule. Yet the cost of gender segregation is to reinforce the adverse stereotypes and male behavioral patterns that perpetuate the problem. The implicit message is that girls need "special" help to perform equally, not that boys' dominance and disruption must stop. By contrast, coeducational classrooms that use strategies common in all-female learning environments have proven equally successful; girls' math and science performance in these classrooms matches that of boys without the costs of segregation. If we want to eliminate gender bias, our goal should be to fix, not bypass, the problems in coeducational settings.[56]

We also need a broader definition of what those problems are. "The evaded curriculum" is a term that the AAUW report uses to describe matters that are central to the lives of students but that get inadequate attention in most schools. One significant evasion involves the sexual responsibility and birth control issues described in Chapter 7. Another concerns sexual harassment.[57]

Although harassment in the schools is attracting increasing attention, many responses have done more to caricature than to address the problem. Recent surveys document widespread abuse, but also trigger widespread denial. In a comprehensive AAUW study, four-fifths of students reported being targets of harassment. Although almost as many boys as girls had experienced such problems, girls were far more likely to suffer serious abuse, and to stay out of school or cut classes as a consequence.[58]

Conservative commentators chortled at the report and the reform initiatives that it inspired. To John Leo, the message of school codes is that males are "predatory," that "chit-chat about sex can get you brought up on charges," and that the friends who might snitch to authorities should not be trusted. "Better to talk about the weather."

Similarly, in the puritanical "hypersensitive" environment that Katie Roiphe describes, charges can seem to "materialize out of thin air" and even ogling will alert the feminist fanatics now patrolling school corridors. Columnist Debbie Price wonders whether we should really be addressing the problem of restroom graffiti in federal lawsuits: "Are we turning girls into sniveling emotional cripples who see themselves as victims?"[59]

This seems unlikely. Many parents and educators still assume that harassment is usually harmless and that "boys will be boys." As one elementary school principal puts it, "Children are going to bother each other, tease each other and make each other feel bad. But that is the story of man. That's part of growing up. I really think that calling it sexual harassment is too far out." Yet such responses compound the problem they dismiss. Surely the "story of man" could use a better subplot than the persecution of girls. Cases now reaching education administrators and legal authorities rarely involve just idle chit-chat. They generally feature serious repeated abuse. Girls are not just taunted, but also threatened and mauled. To be sure, administrators occasionally overreact to trivial incidents, like the one that left a North Carolina six-year-old "suspended for a smooch." But most complaints result in retaliation by classmates, not draconian penalties from irate administrators. And even in the widely publicized and justly criticized North Carolina case, the "sex criminal" was simply placed on in-school suspension for a day: he missed coloring and an ice cream party.[60]

A society seriously committed to reducing sexual harassment must start at early ages. We need mandatory policies and preventive educational programs that are realistic but not fatalistic. Children can be cruel in many ways, and we are not going to transform educational institutions into Sunnybrook Farms. But many model initiatives are now available that target serious abuses, establish reasonable sanctioning procedures, and offer effective instructional materials. Discouraging harassment among children is one of the better ways to prevent it among adults.

Athletics

Athletics is one of the most powerful sources of gender socialization. An estimated thirty million young people participate in sports, and current programs institutionalize inequality. These programs offer fewer opportunities to female athletes than to males and promote damaging stereotypes of masculinity and femininity. Yet, ironically, our recent progress obscures the problems that remain. Opportunities for women athletes have improved so dramatically that we no longer notice what chances they are still missing.[61]

Over the past quarter-century, the passage of antidiscrimination legislation, together with broader cultural changes in gender roles, has transformed women's sports. The number of female athletes in high school interscholastic competition increased from 300,000 (7 percent of all participants) in the early 1970s to over two million (38 percent) in the early 1990s. Girls who, in earlier eras, would have made do with gym classes in ring toss and rhythmic hula hooping now have options ranging from ice hockey to boxing. Women's field hockey teams that once practiced in parking lots can sometimes fill stadiums. Not always large stadiums; but as the 1996 Olympics demonstrated, at least some female athletic events rival their male counterparts in popular appeal.[62]

Yet this striking progress masks equally striking inequalities. In high school, boys still receive disproportionate resources and have greater choices of sports. Girls have finally gotten "a foot in the door" of the gym, but often this happens only when boys aren't using it. At surveyed colleges where women constitute more than half the student body, they account for only a third of the athletes, a fourth of athletic dollars, and less than a fifth of recruiting expenditures. Women coach fewer than half of women's teams and about 1 percent of men's teams, and almost never head athletic programs. Women of color are even more sparsely represented at all coaching and administrative levels. By the mid-1990s, only one of some 600 institutions met the standard of gender equity established by the National Collegiate Athletic Association (NCAA): "fair and equitable distribution of overall athletic opportunities, benefits, and resources," and an absence of gender-based discrimination against athletes, coaches, and administrators.[63]

What accounts for persistent inequalities is a matter of dispute. To many men, the disparities in opportunity simply reflect disparities in interest. From the perspective of most male athletic directors, further efforts to even out resources are unjust and ineffective, and jeopardize important revenue-producing programs like football and basketball. As one commentator puts it, "Equality of interest can never be legislated or enforced." Until society "undergoes a radical transformation," gender disparities will remain "a fact of American life."[64]

Of course, this is the very claim that opponents of antidiscrimination guarantees have been making for the last two decades. Had that argument prevailed in legislative arenas, many female athletes would still be stuck with hula hoops. Until more proportionate opportunities are in place, we cannot really gauge male and female interest levels. Moreover, contrary to popular assumptions, men's football and basketball do not generate significant profits in the vast majority of athletic programs. Although successful male teams may increase revenue indirectly, by building community and alumni support, a school's competitive status is unlikely to suffer if *all* institutions attempt to narrow gender inequalities.[65]

These inequalities involve more than resources. Many athletic programs indirectly compound gender bias in other ways, by giving female teams derivative and stereotypical names and by placing exaggerated importance on cheerleading. Female sporting events often feature zoologically bizarre competitions between beaverettes, lady panthers, and teddy bears. In most schools, these athletes receive less recognition than their cheerleading classmates. The number of cheerleaders continues to rise: in the mid-1990s it increased 20 percent, to well over three million. Although their routines have grown more athletic, their role remains derivative. Cheerleading is still an add-on to the main event. It involves girls applauding boys, and it rewards appearance as much as ability.[66]

The resilience of traditional feminine stereotypes is equally apparent in our rankings of women's sports. It is hardly coincidental that the most popular female competitors are in areas like skating and gymnastics, which emphasize grace and beauty rather than power and aggression. These stereotypical preferences carry a cost. Spectators' preferences for pixie-like female gymnasts have placed those competitors at substantial physical risk. Because the sport now rewards extremely agile, lightweight athletes, girls begin intense training at young ages while their bodies are still developing. The result is a high incidence of injury, often with permanently debilitating consequences. The need to maintain abnormally low weights has also encouraged almost two-thirds of female gymnasts to develop eating disorders. By contrast, men's gymnastics, which rewards strength as well as agility, permits older competitors of normal weight, and carries far fewer risks.[67]

Our preferences for stereotypically feminine athletes also impose substantial costs on lesbian athletes, coaches, and administrators. It is not surprising that rumors of lesbianism can severely damage athletic careers. What is striking, however, is the effort that often goes into avoiding such rumors. Some lesbian coaches have acquired husbands, and some female athletes have cultivated ludicrously seductive images. In one memorable example, college basketball players cast themselves as Playboy Bunnies, and posed in uniforms with floppy ears and rabbit tails. Widespread worries about sexual "deviance" prevent many athletes from expressing their sexual orientation—a fundamental aspect of human identity. And lesbian labels, whether accurate or not, often serve to punish as well as deter gender equity activists.[68]

Yet while current athletic programs are still hostage to traditional understandings of femininity, they have at least loosened its constraints. Many girls now grow up with a sense of physical power and a taste for competition that undermines conventional stereotypes. Boys, however, receive no similarly mixed messages. Male athletics often exalts the worst aspects of traditional masculine stereotypes; it rewards aggression, brutality, and conquest.

From very early ages, most boys feel strong pressure to excel at sports. By adolescence, athletic achievement is the most crucial factor in determining status among classmates. We expect this experience to build character, foster teamwork, and promote health. We discount the ways that competition frequently ritualizes and rewards violence. In sports like football, boxing, and hockey, brutal body contact is an inherent part of the game. In many others, "borderline" violence is a common occurrence. Penalties for gratuitous aggression often are not severe enough to prevent it, particularly when fans enjoy the spectacle. There is more than a little truth to the clichés about hockey fans who go to see the fights and are slightly disappointed when a hockey game breaks out.[69]

Media commentators and athletic coaches compound the problem. Dwelling on the "hits" and "hurts" is a common practice among sports reporters. A *New York Times Magazine* cover story recently increased the celebrity of Ulf Samuelson, the "most hated man in hockey." His achievements, which include permanently disabling several competitors, have resulted in a $2 million salary and no lack of professional opportunities. According to a senior league official, "There are twenty-six team managers, and twenty-five complain about him. And all twenty-five would take him in a heartbeat." If coaches prefer "winning ugly" to losing gracefully, many players feel pressure to oblige. Others enjoy the excuse to express their "manhood." As one professional hockey player puts it, "If you take the fighting out, what comes next . . .? Pretty soon we will all be out there in dresses and skirts."[70]

Such views help explain the frequency of physical injuries, homophobic attitudes, and misogynistic assumptions among male athletes. More than one-third of high school football players suffer serious injuries, and three-fourths of those who go on to professional leagues end up with permanent disabilities. Males who are reluctant to play through pain or who fail to show "appropriate" aggressiveness risk ridicule as "fags," "queers," "sissies," and "pussies." Telling a player that he "throws like a girl" or leaving sanitary napkins in his locker sends obvious messages about both the meaning of masculinity and the inferiority of women.[71]

Given these messages, it is scarcely surprising that male athletes are disproportionately involved in sexual violence. In one representative study, college athletes were 40 percent more likely to be reported for rape than the average male student. Assaultive behavior receives ample encouragement from celebrities like Mike Tyson, who acknowledged: "I like to hurt women when I make love to them." Even athletes who don't endorse violence often contribute to attitudes that underlie it. When role models like Magic Johnson claim to have "accommodated as many floozies as I could," and Wilt Chamberlain reports scoring with "20,000 different ladies," these players reinforce prevailing views that women, like trophies, are objects for conquest.[72]

Yet despite the systematic studies and the celebrated cases of athletes involved in sexual abuse, many men deny the problem. To competitors like professional football player Dan Wilkensen who face prosecution on such charges, these are "private matters," unworthy of public attention and unrelated to more systematic patterns. According to NCAA spokesmen, "it's unfair to single out athletes" for blame because only a small number are involved in reported offenses, and women who date high-profile sports "studs" should know what to expect. From the perspective of male coaches, it is equally unfair to blame sports for problems that have deeper cultural roots. As one National Football

League administrator summarized prevailing views: "An athlete's attitude toward women comes not from his sport but from his life." But for players whose lives are bound up in sports, locker room values inevitably spill over to other settings. And reported offenses reflect only a small part of the problem. Most victims see no point in bringing charges of harassment or date rape that more often result in humiliation and retaliation against the complainant than in serious sanctions against the athlete.[73]

To make significant changes in sports culture is no insignificant task. But there are some obvious places to start. Promoting greater equality in athletic opportunities will require stronger enforcement of Title IX of the Civil Rights Act, which prohibits sex-based discrimination by schools receiving federal funds. Reducing violence and sexual abuse will require increased penalties. Serious violations should result in serious sanctions, such as forfeitures of games, removal of players, and significant monetary fines. What counts as a "serious" abuse also needs to change. A penalty structure that imposes higher fines for abusing equipment than for sexually harassing female reporters contributes more to the problem than to the solution. Sports leaders should also encourage and participate in the growing number of programs aimed at reducing sexual violence, gender bias, and homophobia among athletes. Finally, more attention, both positive and negative, should center on conduct apart from winning. Coaches and players who engage in abusive behavior should not be rewarded with raises, commercial endorsements, and recognition in sporting halls of fame.[74]

Eliminating gender bias in athletics means not just equalizing opportunities but also transforming them—and developing less combative and commercial alternatives. More athletes need to see sportsmanship as a core value, not a corny anachronism invoked at banquets and ignored in dugouts. If we want to change our cultural definitions of masculinity and femininity, we need also to change our cultural values in sports.

4

Media Images

To most audiences, the role of women in the media seems like a problem long since solved. Gone are the days when situation comedies were unblushingly titled *Father Knows Best* and female newscasters were seen only as weather girls. To the average American, women's roles now appear equal and ever present. They interview presidents, outsmart felons, and rule galaxies.

But a closer look at media images reveals only partial progress. And that progress itself obscures the more subtle biases that remain: the silences, subtexts, and stereotypes that still construct our images of women and reinforce traditional gender roles. Any adequate challenge to sex-based inequality requires a better understanding of the media influences that sustain it.

Out of Sight, Out of Mind

In Americans' standard story about women and the media, a happy ending is already at hand. Female journalists have escaped the "women's page," with stories confined to food, fashion, and society "do's and doings." On billboards and soap operas, heroines have been promoted. No longer do three-quarters of the television commercials featuring women involve laundry and bathroom products. Nor do cheerful mammies announce, "Lawsee, folks sho' whoops with joy over Aunt Jemima pancakes." Because women have escaped these constraints and now *seem* to be everywhere, we lose sight of where they are missing.[1]

Their absences are in predictable places, notably those positions of greatest status and authority. Hollywood may be a town of tinsel, but its ceilings are of glass. Men hold 90 percent of upper-level executive positions and play over two-thirds of the leads in prime-time television and feature films. An event like the 1996 Olympics might push women's athletics toward center stage, but 90 percent of day-to-day television sports coverage is of male events. In the news media, women account for over two-thirds of journalism school graduates but only one-third of front-page bylines, one-fifth of television news reporters, and fewer than a tenth of editors-in-chief.[2]

We also have re-created old patterns of gender inequality in new forms. On daytime talk shows, women dominate, but the focus stays personal not political. By contrast, on talk radio and television round-tables, the focus is political but women remain peripheral. Male commentators like Rush Limbaugh and Howard Stern command some 25 million listeners for their tirades against "feminazis," "pansies," and "foreigners."[3]

Just as women are absent in presenting the news, so often are women's perspectives. In recent surveys, men account for over four-fifths of newspaper quotes or references and for three-quarters of television interviewees. Female voices are missing even on topics like single motherhood and breast implants. The result is much as Kirk Anderson portrays it in his cartoon of a talk show anchor previewing his program: "In the next half-hour, my wealthy white conservative male friends and I will discuss the annoyingly persistent black underclass, and why women get so emotional about abortion."[4]

The problem is not only *that* women are missing, but also *which* women are missing. Here again, the gaps are all too predictable. Those most often out of sight are older, lesbian, disabled, and nonwhite women. That they appear at all is, of course, a major achievement. An earlier generation would never have encountered a lesbian kiss on prime time, a situation comedy with a female Korean American lead, or an African American celebrity like Oprah Winfrey. But these exceptions define the rule. Statistically speaking, women are still far from equal representation.

News and entertainment media rarely exceed what is commonly

described as a "sprinkling of minorities." Women of color fill only 3 percent of press managerial positions, file only 2 percent of broadcast stories, and rarely receive leading roles in film and television productions. Even in daytime soap operas, where at least a quarter of viewers are women of color, nonwhite characters are dramatically underrepresented.[5]

As a modest compensatory gesture, these characters often receive exceptionally distinguished roles. If Americans received their information about the criminal justice system solely from soaps and series like *LA Law*, they might believe that a majority of judges were women of color. This, of course, is an improvement from all the decades in which these women ran vacuum cleaners, not courtrooms. But real progress would require acknowledging a more complicated reality, in which women of color do not just administer justice but often fail to receive it.[6]

Such world views elude most news and entertainment media. Realistic glimpses of mothers on welfare are few and far between. When these women do attract attention, the focus usually is on case histories that confirm popular prejudices. Front-page stories feature unemployed Hispanic or African American mothers like Claribel Ventura, who reportedly sold food stamps for drugs and sent some of her six children begging. Missing from coverage are the far more typical cases, involving women with one or two children—mothers who are struggling to stretch inadequate benefits and part-time wages into something approaching a subsistence income and a decent home environment. Welfare fraud gets banner headlines; white-collar fraud gets large yawns and small print.[7]

Similar biases are apparent in media representations of other "deviant" women, such as lesbians. The good news is that these women are increasingly visible and that coverage is increasingly positive. Leading magazines now feature cover stories like *New York*'s "Lesbian Chic," profiling celebrities whose sexual orientation has not proved career threatening. But as recent studies make clear, such "new and improved" images have not entirely displaced the "cruddy old dykes of yore." Nor are celebrity profiles a substitute for what is still missing. Rarely do we see nonstereotypical portraits acknowledging the full impact of homophobic attitudes or presenting same-sex relationships with depth and dignity.[8]

All too often, the presence of a few successful women both on and off the screen encourages media decisionmakers to deny a problem. In journalism, demands for more equal representation bump up against what former columnist Anna Quindlen describes as the "quota of one." In explaining their unwillingness to carry a column by a woman who sometimes writes about women, editors will note that they "already have one." This somehow turns out not to be a problem for columns by and about white men.[9]

Gender inequalities in the media partly reflect the same unconscious stereotypes and work/family conflicts that affect most employment settings, and that are described more fully in Chapter 6. But two forms of bias assume particular importance in media contexts: our discomfort with female authority and our preoccupation with female appearance. Many Americans have limited tolerance for women who pontificate in public or who depart too far from accepted aesthetic standards. As former news anchor Christine Craft learned the hard way, viewers tune out someone "too old, too ugly, and not deferential to men."[10]

In Madison Avenue's mythical universe, women are almost never "overweight, poor, struggling, or disabled." Women "of a certain age" are almost entirely absent, although they watch more television and control more discretionary income than other demographic groups. Even products designed for older consumers feature young models. An ad for *Longevity* magazine runs the caption "She's Seventy," with a photo of a female in her thirties lifting weights.[11]

Among men, age may lend a certain distinction; among women, it usually brings early retirement. We don't mind elder statesmen with Walter Cronkite's wrinkles. Nor are we unwilling to accept romances between aging heroes and young heroines. But such scripts don't work with gender roles reversed, which helps explain why most middle-aged actresses fade from the scene except in limited "character" parts.

Our restrictive standards of female attractiveness carry special costs for women of color. In some contexts, like beauty and fashion advertising, segregation remains the rule, with nonwhite models reserved primarily for exotic accents or "special" ethnic spreads. Yet the most obvious cause for these patterns is the one decisionmakers are at pains to deny. The problem, as they describe it, is not racism but aesthetics. Black women aren't "right" for fall colors. It's just not an "ethnic moment." Or the women of color available just lack that something "special . . . a kind of . . . je ne sais quoi."[12]

Occasionally, however, a bit of candor will seep through. Someone will acknowledge the racial biases underpinning "aesthetic" preferences. But with such confessions comes avoidance. Responsibility always lies anywhere and everywhere else. According to the executive director of a leading fashion designers' organization, Seventh on Sixth, we should not be "looking to fashion to solve all the world's problems." But surely it need not compound them. The excuses now offered for excluding certain women are the same as those once offered for excluding women altogether. Media leaders and marketing experts were long convinced that people simply wouldn't accept women in certain roles. Our progress over the past two decades should make clear that the public's tolerance is by no means as limited as its leaders once assumed. What people see affects what they accept, and the media bear some responsibility for promoting gender equality, not just reflecting it.[13]

The public, for its part, can pay closer attention to who is missing in action. Americans can also do more to register their concerns in letters, boycotts, awards, purchases, and viewing decisions. "Dream Girls," a recent traveling exhibit from the American Advertising Museum, collects the kind of commercials that women consumers and women's groups could help reward or punish. High points include a recent ad for Saturn cars in which the proverbial satisfied customer is a disabled African American woman who works as a military operations researcher. Her pitch carries special resonance: "When you've tackled everything else life has thrown your way, a little traffic isn't going to stop you."[14]

Gender Roles and Gender Stereotypes

For those who care about gender equality, the issue is not just *whether* women are represented in the media but also *how* they are represented. Virginia Slims' celebrated cigarette slogan, "You've Come a Long Way Baby," reminds us of the distance we have yet to travel. No longer do airline advertisements feature flight attendants announcing "I'm Cheryl, fly me." But women are still called "baby" on as well as off the screen, and the patterns in our real and fictional worlds are related.[15]

The signposts of partial progress surround us, and romance novels are a case in point. These publications, which claim between a quarter and a third of all American women as readers, now feature not just breathless virgins and dashing aristocrats, but also female stockbrokers and sensitive New Age guys. As one *Wall Street Journal* article advises,

"If the Damsel Is in Distress, Be Sure It's Career-Related." Romance novels' new heroines also have more realistic concerns than their predecessors: female characters now occasionally worry about domestic violence and even—gasp—contraceptives. But they still worry more about their clothes. Fashion, food, and furnishings are common preoccupations as heroines wait for the hero's next move. Unlike male adventure fantasies, which rarely cast women in central roles, the bestselling female fantasies revolve around men. According to publishers' guidelines, although the heroine should be "actively involved in a glamorous career or lifestyle . . . this should not overshadow her romantic involvement."[16]

Most mainstream media also reinforce traditional understandings of masculinity, femininity, and gender roles. We do, of course, see greater diversity than ever before. Prime time television will now allow a single mother to have a baby despite vice-presidential objections, at least if she is, like Murphy Brown, white and economically well off. But the standard script in films, television, and women's magazines still favors stereotypical roles. Commercials featuring parents with children show mothers four times as often as fathers. Occasionally some enlightened copywriter will grab our attention with a sex role reversal: daddy does diapers. But by and large, happy homemaking is reserved for women. Rarely do we see men obsessed with laundry fresheners. Industry attitudes are well captured in a *Marketing Magazine* cartoon in which a male advertising executive explains why he is rejecting a female copywriter's proposed layout. "Destereotyping the housewife can't be done overnight, Angela. Be a good kid and let her sing to her mop in this one, and I promise next time she can do something else with it."[17]

For men in media images, work and family seldom conflict: John Wayne never made meat loaf. Alternatively, when males' domestic burdens are not ignored, they are usually trivialized or romanticized. In films like *Three Men and a Baby*, *Mr. Mom*, and *Mrs. Doubtfire*, or in situation comedies like *Full House* and *Coach*, single men manage just fine despite a few comic confrontations and minor culinary crises. Almost never do male characters confront the career-versus-parenting dilemmas that women seldom escape either on or off the screen.[18]

Although the media are paying more attention to such dilemmas, the usual resolutions perpetuate the problem. Because working-class women are grossly underrepresented in major film and network television productions, viewers rarely see the most painful tradeoffs between work and family. With a few prominent exceptions like *Roseanne,* most female leads are upper-class professionals who have options that most women do not; prime-time series feature nineteen lawyers for every two schoolteachers, and secretaries with childcare difficulties are nowhere in sight. Similarly, "as the world turns" on daytime television, few scripts confront the real-world forces that most constrain women's lives: poverty, racism, dead-end jobs, and household drudgery. Indeed, except in commercials, where women still fret about bathroom odors, the dreary side of domesticity is politely overlooked.[19]

Of course, most television is entertainment, and many viewers watch in order to escape reality, not confront it. But it scarcely follows that they would be unreceptive to portraits that acknowledged the existence of gender-related problems at the political rather than personal level. All too often, the media portray issues like work/family conflicts as individual dilemmas rather than societal problems. And in screenplays, as in life, women who put their professions first usually suffer for that decision. Typical television sagas feature a neglectful mother who sees her career collapse or her son turn into a rapist. Hollywood heroines rarely get to have it all, and although they cannot be too rich or too thin, they can easily be too ambitious. In films like *Waiting to Exhale,* black professional women can neither find a decent man, nor contemplate a decent life without one. The popularity of such productions tells us less about the appeal of their world view than about the hunger for any mainstream release that casts women of color in leading and accomplished roles. So too, for women lawyers in celluloid, winning a case always ends up being less important than winning a man (*Legal Eagles, A Few Good Men,* and *The Big Easy*). Many self-centered heroines belatedly discover that their biological clock has stopped ticking *(Immediate Family),* that sexual liberation carries a price *(Forrest Gump),* or that career-driven executives finish last *(Working Girl).* Happy endings generally are reserved for characters who discover their maternal instincts in the nick of time *(Baby Boom, Parenthood).*[20]

Rarely does a mainstream release offer any realistic portrait of the downside of such domestic choices. Even films that make some effort, like *First Wives Club,* mask the true risks for women of unequal family roles. In the world that Hollywood presents, the first wives get the last laugh. Middle-aged heroines jilted for younger women come out just fine in the end. In the world that many divorced homemakers actually inhabit, the result is far less rosy.

The news media also reinforce gender roles and gender hierarchies by failing to cast women as fully independent agents, apart from their relation to men or families. This symbolic subordination is especially apparent in descriptions of politicians. The *Washington Post*'s coverage of a Texas governor's race presented Ann Richards as a "fifty-seven-year-old white-haired grandmother," and her rival, Clayton Williams, as a "West Texas oil man." In 1992, the "Year of the Woman," Lynn Yeakel appeared as "an unlikely standard bearer, a former full-time mother," and Carol Mosley Braun was a "den-mother with a cheerleader's smile." Not until the twenty-second paragraph of a campaign story on Braun did persistent readers learn that she was also a lawyer, former prosecutor, and veteran state senator. The implicit value hierarchies are aptly captured in a recent Cath Jackson cartoon. It features a male editor lecturing a female staffer on the obvious problems with an article titled "Wheelchair Woman Climbs Mt. Everest": "You've missed the main points: WHO is her husband? WHAT does he do? WHERE would she be without him and WHY isn't she at home looking after the kids?"[21]

A related tendency is to present accomplished women in sexually freighted terms. In coverage of Olympic gymnasts, commentators described one gold medalist as a "calculating coquette," and another competitor as "looking like she would sooner fall off the balance beam than neglect her eye makeup." Ethnic bias compounds the problem. *Newsweek* makes its aesthetic preferences explicit in comparing two world-champion figure skaters: Kristi Yamaguchi, with her "Betty Boop mouth" and "petite" figure, "represents the stylish Western ideal that the stout little Midori [Ito] is so envious of."[22]

The more prominent the woman, the more inviting the target. Hillary Clinton has generated a cottage industry of criticism, not only for failing to satisfy accepted standards but also just for trying. "Fashion stayed home" was the consensus after one mid-1990s European venture. However, the First Lady also earned ridicule for trying to bring it along. Not only was she denounced for wearing "absurdly" styled accessories, she was mocked for acquiescing in press releases that sounded like fashion promotions: "Mrs. Clinton wore a two-piece fuchsia Noviello Bloom suit of a linen blend . . . [with bone] shoes and a matching purse . . ."[23]

To many Americans, both in and outside the media, this constant attention to women's physical appearance seems a trivial issue. After all, prominent men are not immune from scrutiny. Bill Clinton's midriff bulge and jockey shorts also have become fair game. So what if women are more often on the receiving end of such banter? If Marcia Clark got more comments on her legs than Johnny Cochran, there was, after all, a reason: hers were better. Not only better but "great," according to the widely quoted description by opposing counsel Robert Shapiro.[24]

Yet to trivialize the problem is to miss its deeper roots and broader implications. By presenting powerful women as sexual objects, media coverage both undermines their credibility and marginalizes their contributions. The targets of such accounts can do little without compounding the problem. That double bind emerges clearly in one parody of a TV newscaster offering a campaign update: "When asked her dress size, the president lost her womanly virtues and became stern, even hectoring."[25]

For feminist leaders, the media's preoccupation with appearance imposes special costs. Activists who defy cultural standards of femininity are subject to ridicule, and their cause acquires guilt by association. The women's movement seems like the last refuge of homely harpies, and confirms claims like Rush Limbaugh's: "Feminism was established to allow unattractive women access to mainstream society." Commentator Christina Hoff Sommers doesn't go that far, but she does point out that "there are a lot of homely women in women's studies."[26]

Yet feminists who take pains to look attractive are equally vulnerable: they risk seeming vain, petty, or hypocritical for pandering to sexist values. The media have long delighted in catching activists in such seeming contradictions. When describing the first mass rally for equal rights by the contemporary women's movement, the *New York Times* chose as its headline "Leading Feminist Puts Hairdo before Strike." Betty Friedan reportedly had been delayed by her hairdresser. Conservatives claim that Gloria Steinem exploits her attractiveness and "promotes her agenda by means she affects to despise." And Naomi Wolf, author of the celebrated indictment of America's "beauty myth," is said to spend "hours having makeup applied" before she goes on television.[27]

The problem is not only the media's fixation on female appearance, but also the unrelentingly unrealistic standards that result. The average American bumps up against 1,500 advertisements daily, which are selling not only products but values, images, and ideals. The dominant vision of femininity that emerges is a slender young white woman with a flawless complexion and never a bad hair day. The message comes through clearly to women who deviate: "You're ugly, buy something."

We do; but for many of us (and, after a certain age, all of us), the prevailing cultural ideal is nowhere close to attainable. That is particularly true for women of color, who seldom figure among the celebrated images. Even in magazines like *Essence,* the editorial material affirming African American women's racial identity runs parallel to advertisements with the opposite subtext—ads featuring products like hair straightener and black models who resemble whites. Moreover, no woman, despite "phenomenal" advances in cosmetic "science," will ever manage what products like Fashion Fair Fabulous Special Beauty Creme promise: "Put your age on hold." "But so what?" is the response among many audiences. Men, in particular, often have difficulty seeing these media ideals as a problem involving gender inequality—or even as a problem at all. Isn't appearance something women *choose* to emphasize, and don't many enjoy the process? Of course the media offer an unrealistic vision, but isn't that what viewers want? Wrinkles, bags, and bulges they can see at home.[28]

A sampling of these attitudes emerged during the frenzy over whether the 1995 Miss America pageant should keep its swimsuit competition. In celebration of the pageant's seventy-fifth anniversary, viewers were able to phone in ballots, and media pundits were able to ponder the "Meaning of It All." Battle lines formed along not entirely predictable lines. Leonard Horn, the pageant's CEO, pronounced himself unable to "rationalize putting a young college woman in a swimsuit and high-heeled shoes to win a scholarship or to become Miss America." Most media commentators disagreed, as did about four-fifths of the voters. Liberal *New York Times* columnist Frank Rich cast his ballot "for flesh": better his young sons should watch "pinups" in swimsuits than "pedophiles on-line." Sam Donaldson on *This Week with David*

Brinkley saw "nothing wrong with [women] appearing in a . . . full bathing suit, not a skimpy one." And in a burst of gallantry, he informed co-panelist Cokie Roberts that "I would like to see you in a swimsuit."[29]

Although most pageant contestants justified the competition as a measure of "physical fitness," most commentators opted for candor. Many wished the pageant would just drop the pretense that it was searching for something other than "cheesecake." As columnist George Will noted, forty million viewers are not tuning in to see a "convention of Phi Beta Kappas." Nor are most Americans deeply interested in hearing contestants' "social platforms"—all those stirring commitments to clean environments and world peace. If women are "wearing causes like jewelry," asked one commentator, can't they "just stick to wearing swimsuits"?[30]

But why should these be the only choices? Our preoccupation with female attractiveness is by no means as harmless as many Americans assume. The media's unending celebration of unattainable ideals imposes substantial personal costs. Women pay the price in multiple currencies: money, time, energy, physical health, and psychological well-being. Americans spend $33 billion per year on diets, $30 billion on cosmetics, and $1.5 billion on cosmetic surgery. Between 80 and 90 percent of these consumers are women, and much of their investment is unproductive.[31]

Many beauty strategies that advertisers and advice columns peddle are as implausible as the ideal they foster. In the never-never land of Madison Avenue, dieting is an effortless enterprise: "Lose up to five pounds in five minutes," "Lose weight while you sleep," "Become too thin." Yet in the real world of yo-yo dieters and distorted body images, almost no one sees herself as too thin, and few women approach that state without chronic deprivation and serious eating disorders. Ninety-five percent of dieters regain all lost weight within five years, and many high-priced beauty aids are what dermatologists consider ineffective "cosmetic hoo-ha." For some women, fashion ideals appear attainable only through surgery that "corrects" ethnic features and often involves significant pain and physical risks. Age-old clichés that "beauty hurts" assume new force in an era of stomach stapling, jaw wiring, and breast implants. Yet as commentator Wendy Kaminer notes, "not until women stop suffering for beauty will they stop suffering, too, for the lack of it."[32]

The worst aspect of this societal pressure is its ability to enlist women in their own oppression. Obesity is often viewed as failure of self-control and competence, rather than a complex disorder with genetic and physiological as well as psychological causes. Few individuals can avoid internalizing standards that are so relentlessly present. Women who stray too far from accepted norms risk social isolation, public ridicule, and employer discrimination. Women who fear those consequences live in a constant struggle against excess pounds, encroaching wrinkles, unwelcome odors, unruly hair, and fashion blunders. The failure—real or imagined—to meet cultural expectations is often a profound source of anxiety, depression, guilt, and self-denial. In one representative poll of more than a thousand women, body image emerged as women's greatest source of dissatisfaction. In another survey, over 90 percent of formerly obese individuals reported that they would rather become blind than regain their weight.[33]

Of course, all Americans should be concerned about the adverse health consequences of being significantly overweight. But health is not what most media images are peddling, and chronic yo-yo dieting may create more risks than moderate weight gain. Women's magazines, however, aren't focusing on the relative risks. These publications are pushing "thin thighs in thirty days." Often the health-conscious reader gets a perverse combination of messages. Endless versions of the "last-chance diet" run back to back with advice on "new ways to sin," such as the latest "scoop" on tempting high-fat ice creams.[34]

Most magazine editors, however, deny any problem with their priorities. Media leaders are quick to point out that such publications have improved considerably over the past decade. Discussion of "women's issues" has moved well beyond the traditional topics of food, fashion, figure, and furnishings. But the new substantive content is typically sparse and superficial. A representative sidebar in *Glamour* notes that "the Equal Rights Amendment was introduced in Congress in 1923 . . . Isn't it about time it got passed?" Nothing is said about why it hasn't. More extended coverage is reserved for topics such the hottest tips on hair texture, "The Fine Art of Flirting" or "How to Keep Your Man." With few exceptions, most obviously *Ms.* and *Essence,* the ratio of fluff to substance is extremely high.[35]

Readers of mainstream magazines also get a steady stream of advice about how to make it in a man's world—how to be a successful manager and a supermom while battling flabby fannies and chipped nails. But absent from many accounts is any acknowledgment of the societal obstacles to individual fulfillment or of the need for common action. As the discussion below notes, the women's movement makes only cameo appearances in these publications. When feminism does surface, it looks less like a movement than what social critic Barbara Ehrenreich describes as a "self-improvement program for the upwardly mobile woman." Such messages encourage readers to believe that they can meet all challenges individually—by choosing the right degree of assertiveness, the right time-management skills, and of course the right products.[36]

Making Sexual Inequality Sexy

A related problem is the way the news and entertainment media cover sexual abuse. That they discuss these issues at all does, of course, reflect progress. Until quite recently, domestic violence and sexual harassment were notable for their absence, and acquaintance rape was ignored or romanticized.

Yet coverage remains highly selective and largely oblivious to the links between these issues and broader patterns of gender inequality. For example, despite the enormous volume of commentary attempting to account for the gang rape of a white investment banker in Central Park, the most obvious gender-related explanations rarely surfaced. Almost all the coverage centered on race and poverty, and many editors defended that selective focus. According to one *Newsday* editor, attempts to analyze rape as a sex crime are "thumbsucking journalism." In explaining his paper's inattention to gender issues, the metropolitan editor of the *New York Times* acknowledged: "I can't imagine the range of reaction to the sexual aspect of the crime would be very strong. I may be wrong but I can't think right off what questions one ought to ask about that."[37]

Another issue missing from coverage was the disproportionate frequency of sexual abuse targeting women of color and the media's lack of interest in those crimes. During the week of the Central Park assault, twenty-eight other women in New York also reported rapes. Nearly all of these assaults involved women of color, and the attacks, including at least one of comparable brutality, received almost no press attention.[38]

These patterns are, however, beginning to change. Sexual violence and harassment are starting to receive more in-depth analysis, and this coverage has made a substantial difference in public attitudes. The Anita Hill–Clarence Thomas hearings were one such turning point. Many journalists' follow-up coverage on the general problem of sexual harassment triggered extraordinary collective consciousness raising. Women have long been harassed, but only *their* livelihoods have been at risk. Now men realize that *their* future may be affected as well.

Moreover, the way in which the media stereotyped and silenced black women during the Hill-Thomas hearings did not pass unnoticed, as it might have during earlier decades. After a black sociologist's editorial in the Sunday *New York Times* attempted to legitimize Thomas' actions as a form of "down-home courtin'" among Southern blacks, a coalition of African American women formed to publish their protest. Fifteen hundred women signed a statement, which ran as an advertisement in the *Times* and received coverage in other newspapers.[39]

Similarly, the initial press treatment of the murder of Nicole Brown Simpson and Ron Goldman marked a watershed concerning domestic violence. Although it took an extraordinarily dramatic script with a celebrity star to gain media attention, the first wave of reporting was thorough and thoughtful. Such accounts left in their wake significant positive results: a new body of legislation; a heightened sense of judicial, prosecutorial, and police accountability; and an increased demand for prevention and support programs.

Equally significant was the media's coverage of their own coverage. The press questioned its prior silence about battering, its lionization of athletes, and its focus on the "tragedy of O. J. Simpson" rather than on his murdered wife and her friend. Nor did mainstream publications let pass unnoticed that it took a white victim and a black batterer to catapult issues of domestic violence to center stage.[40]

Yet the extraordinary coverage of celebrated cases blinds us to enduring biases. The media's continued desire to make sexual abuse "sexy" leads to substantial distortions, both in journalistic and entertainment contexts. With coverage of the Simpson case came countless "alternative" angles—the inaccurate or misleading assertions that women "hit men more often than men hit women" and that domestic violence is a "dance of mutual destructiveness" for which both sexes are equally responsible. Press accounts often painted Nicole Simpson as a promiscuous gold digger who provoked her own abuse. Many Americans eagerly accepted this view. "Poor Nicole," wrote one irritated reader to the editor of *People* magazine. "I'm tired of hearing it. She chose to remain a player in a high-stakes game and lost big time." Some publications' glancing coverage of domestic violence appeared little more than protective coloration for more titillating material. As with the "thought pieces" in *Playboy,* reporters and their audiences could reassure themselves that they were not really interested in lurid details but only in "this Very Important Issue."[41]

Moreover, after the initial blitz on family violence, attention turned elsewhere and the public got as much follow-up coverage on prosecutor Marcia Clark's skirts (too short) as on battered women's programs (too few). Postverdict postmortems focused largely on race. In explaining the lack of sustained coverage concerning domestic-violence issues, one newspaper editor told a National Public Radio interviewer that there's no "new angle" on that topic. Only the same old ones: inadequate sanctions, shelters, support services, and prevention programs. And millions of women are brutalized annually as a result.

On other issues of sexual abuse, the media's desire for "new" takes and sexy soundbites similarly misdescribes the problem and miscasts the solution. The mid-1990s "rape hype" controversy offers a representative case. Beginning with Katie Roiphe's highly publicized polemics on campus rape, the media have served up endless accounts of feminist "exaggerations" of sexual assault. Much of this coverage of "rape hype" has itself been hype. Even when reporters attempt to present both sides, the captions for their stories often undercut any pretense to objectivity. Most titles raise a doubting eyebrow: "Date Rape Hysteria," "Rape Hype Betrays Feminism," "Crying Rape," "Stop Whining," "Women, Sex and Rape: Have Some Feminists Exaggerated the Problem?"[42]

The debate, such as it is, appears defined largely by Catharine MacKinnon or Andrea Dworkin (cast as the radical feminists) and Katie Roiphe or Camille Paglia (as the radical skeptics). Common quotes taken out of context from MacKinnon include: "Compare victims' reports of rape with women's reports of sex. They look a lot alike." A selective soundbite from Dworkin reads: "The hurting of women is . . . basic to the sexual pleasure of men." That these caricatures are not exactly mainstream feminist positions is rarely acknowledged, and then only as an afterthought. At the other end of the spectrum, Roiphe's largely fact-free efforts to debunk rape statistics are paraded as facts. All too often, the media fail to note that respected research supports claims that she dismisses. Instead of careful scrutiny, the press delights in loaded characterizations. In covering Roiphe's claims, *Newsweek* solicited views not from experts but from media personalities like English professor Camille Paglia. The caption under the *Newsweek* photo read "Roiphe condemns feminist hysteria."[43]

The news media's soundbites on prostitution are equally selective. On the rare occasions when the press toys with the issue, almost all the coverage goes to celebrity cases. Hugh Grant's 1995 escapade with a Hollywood hooker is a prominent example. Grant's arrest became newsworthy not because an unmarried actor having sex on the side is a novel event. Rather, the case attracted attention because he violated Hollywood's conventional strategies for sexual exploitation, which usually involve seducing starlets for free. As Chicago columnist Mike Royko noted, Grant did what "many less-fortunate members of the working class do." He shopped, and the result seemed inexplicably shabby—"as if he had been caught buying his clothes at Walmart." This, of course, was what astounded so many Americans. One admirer captured widespread views with a placard reading: "I would have paid you, Hugh."[44]

As Hollywood scripts go, this one had considerable sex appeal and a surprisingly happy ending. Here, the proverbial "hooker with a heart of gold" ended up with a substantial pot of it as well. Streetwalker Divine Brown earned retirement by selling her story to a British tabloid. Even Hugh Grant found that lack of virtue is sometimes its own reward. His instant notoriety was, as one film studio spokesman put it, "in a sick way, incredibly helpful." In a single month, Grant became the subject of some 2,800 press stories and pulled some of the highest ratings in talk show history.[45]

Yet missing from almost all of this coverage was the issue that should be the most significant for women. The relevant question is not the one Jay Leno put to Grant: "What the hell were you thinking?" It is rather what we as a society are thinking when we choose to invest scarce law enforcement resources in futile, dehumanizing, and gender-biased responses to prostitution.[46]

Many of the commentators who rose to Grant's defense denied or ignored this broader problem. Some falsely portrayed prostitution as a totally victimless crime. After all, as one of his directors noted, it was not as if Grant had "violated children" or committed "unacceptable" violence. But other customers do. And American society does little to prevent it. Two-thirds to three-fourths of streetwalkers are raped and beaten an average of four to fifteen times a year. Substance abuse, sexually transmitted diseases, severe depression, and suicide also are common.[47]

For the men involved in commercial sex, adverse consequences are far less likely. Over any five-year period, an estimated one in six men has employed a prostitute. Rarely do these customers face significant penalties, a fact that almost never surfaces in media coverage of cases like Grant's. Nor do press accounts acknowledge the intersecting gender and racial inequalities of law enforcement. Women account for about 90 percent of all prostitution arrests. Eighty-five percent of those who serve jail time are women of color.[48]

When prostitution grabs mainstream media attention, it is usually because of an unusual fact: respected men are somehow involved. The exposé of Democratic campaign adviser Dick Morris and the prosecution of Hollywood madam Heidi Fleiss are cases in point: a woman's willingness to kiss and tell can keep a story on the front pages. But in more common cases, men bear few of the costs of our anti-vice efforts. The United States spends upward of $10 million annually on prostitution arrests that seldom include the main profiteers: men who are pimps or who operate brothels, massage parlors, and escort services. It costs over $2,000 to prosecute a single offender like Divine Brown, who typically returns almost immediately to the streets. Once women get arrest records for prostitution, the stigma often forecloses other employment options. Yet Harvard Law School professor Alan Dershowitz was almost alone in connecting the Grant incident to broader policy issues. As Dershowitz noted, "My God, the [Los Angeles police] must have better things to do."[49]

The real sex scandal in West Hollywood should not have been about Hugh Grant. It should have been about neighborhood residents who opposed a facility for local prostitutes that would provide food, HIV testing, and drug counseling. The money we currently devote to futile criminal strategies could much more profitably be spent on services for prostitutes, such as education, employment, health care, and drug treatment programs, as well as more protection from coercion and abuse. So too, the stories the press highlights on prostitution are not the ones

Americans most need to hear. The main questions we should be asking are not why celebrities buy sex, but why the law offers such an ineffectual and inhumane response to sexual sales. And why do so many women find it more profitable to sell their bodies than anything else?[50]

The biases in media treatment of sexual exploitation are not limited to journalistic coverage. Still greater distortions emerge in the entertainment media. One longstanding practice is to present women solely as sexual objects, to be rescued, vanquished, terrorized, or simply ogled. In most adventure dramas, men act and women appear, usually with few lines but lots of cleavage. Other common plots involve sex for sale. In box office hits like *Pretty Woman, Indecent Proposal,* and *Honeymoon in Vegas,* men buy women for prices ranging from $3,000 to $1 million per evening. The heroines don't much mind being bought, presumably because the purchasers are rich, attractive hunks like Robert Redford or Richard Gere. By contrast, in the world as we know it, "such deals are made by men who look like Aristotle Onassis and smell like death." As Betty Friedan notes, women are ill-served by Hollywood illusions that the road to success is not hard work or college degrees, but silicone implants and lonely millionaires.[51]

Both sexes are also ill-served by media presentations of sexual harassment as a harmless or welcome occurrence. In one survey of television situation comedies, over one-third of sexual exchanges were found to meet the legal definition of harassment. Women are propositioned, grabbed, or fondled on a routine basis. Canned laughter usually accompanies such incidents, and the characters rarely object. Yet most television executives deny that these messages are at all troubling. According to one producer, as "far as sexual harassment goes, we do it knowingly. We don't say, uh-oh, is this insulting to women? We know it is. That's what makes it funny . . . If people want to model themselves after a [harassing] loser, so be it."[52]

Popular culture romanticizes other forms of sexual exploitation. One all-time favorite script features tasteful ravishment by an ultimately irresistible male. In the most cloying versions, like the often-imitated marital assault scene in *Gone with the Wind,* a Clark Gable clone sweeps the protesting heroine literally as well as figuratively off her feet. And the next thing we know, she's cooing contentedly the following morning.

In more contemporary screenplays like *The Piano,* a mid-Victorian matron is forced to trade adulterous sex for the return of her beloved instrument. What begins as a coercive bargain ends as a mutually erotic experience. Her husband, on discovering his wife's affair, flies into a rage, chops off her finger with an ax, and delivers it to her lover. But as feminist critic bell hooks notes, "The outcome of [all] of this violence is positive." The husband repents, the heroine settles down with her seducer, and they all may "live happily ever after."[53]

Sexual abuse often looks equally sexy in television scripts. Michael Paul reassures viewers that an upcoming episode on *Houston Knights* is not going to present "a violent rape, where the guy rapes and kills her. It's going to be a friendly rape." In the popular soap opera *General Hospital*, a rapist ends up marrying his victim, and they fondly remember the initial assault as "the first time we made love." A television movie of the week, loosely modeled on one of the nation's infrequent prosecutions for marital rape, presents the battered victim as a pawn of feminist activists. The screenplay ends with the husband's acquittal on assault charges and the couple's reconciliation. In a minor concession to reality, a postscript notes that, in the real case, the parties permanently separated. Tastefully omitted is discussion of the husband's further history of domestic violence.[54]

Sexy but coercive sex is also a central theme in romance fiction. Although these novels include an increasingly diverse and egalitarian range of plots, one time-honored favorite involves a "dominant and forceful hero," an ultimately "yielding" heroine, and an uplifting finale in which love conquers all. But many erotic mishaps may occur along the way: female characters often say no when they mean yes and say yes when they apparently should mean no. A classic version appears in Ann Mather's *Born Out of Love:*

> "No, Logan," she breathed, but he [pressed on] . . . "No?" he probed with gentle mockery, his mouth seeking the pointed fullness of her breasts now exposed to his gaze. "Why not? It's what we both want, don't deny it."
>
> Somehow Charlotte struggled up from the depth of a sexually induced lethargy. It wasn't easy, when her whole body threatened to betray her . . . "Why am I leaving him? *I want him!*" But not on his terms, the still small voice of sanity reminded her . . .[55]

The possibility that not all readers find coercive sex erotic is, however, attracting increased attention. Publication guidelines for some series indicate that "love at first rape is expressly forbidden." Other publishers are more tolerant, and their defenders often argue that the persistent popularity of such scenes indicates that not all female readers find them disempowering. Some women reportedly identify with the hero. Others enjoy the subversion of conventional power hierarchies. By the end of these novels, the "woman always wins." And her victory may seem sweeter when her love has conquered an especially forceful man.[56]

Such conventions have an extended history. The stereotype of women as a civilizing influence on male brutes has been a staple of romance for centuries. But these updated versions of medieval courtship narratives carry an unsettling subtext. Only in romances do women uniformly escape the most common real-world consequences of male coercion: physical injuries and psychological trauma, complete with debilitating fear and lasting humiliation. As *How to Write Romance Novels That Sell* explains, readers should not feel "disgusted" by a "bodice-ripping" scene. This is easier if the heroine is "readily able to put a past rape from her mind and [to] approach the future in high spirits." In most romance fiction, there is no bad sex. Or at least none with lasting consequences.[57]

The sexiness of sexism is even more pervasive in advertising images, but it is also so common that we rarely notice. We are so accustomed to seeing half-naked women sell everything from automobiles to shaving cream that more is necessary to attract our attention. What works, it seems, is "tasteful" pornography. Mainstream fashion layouts show women bound and chained, while Newport tobacco ads illustrate the slogan "Alive with Pleasure" by having two male hunters carry off a woman hung on a pole like a fallen deer. Often the product itself is barely noticeable. A common layout for Guess Jeans features a submissive, well-endowed model who isn't wearing any. In the world as advertisers see it, men pursue, women submit, and resistance is always temporary. Seagram's Gin can "change a 'maybe' into . . . 'again,'" and Van Cleef and Arpels diamonds are just the thing for the "first woman who refused to take your phone calls." As long as "no" does not necessarily mean "no" in media images, we can scarcely expect real life to be different.[58]

Feminism and Feminists in Media Makeovers

For those concerned with gender equality, one of the most troubling aspects of media coverage is how it constructs, constrains, and often coopts the women's movement. Here again the story is one of partial progress. Much has changed since the 1960s and 1970s, when press reactions generally alternated between indifference and contempt. The *Washington Post* ran no story on the formation of the National Organization for Women (NOW), and the *New York Times* placed its brief account beneath recipes for a traditional Thanksgiving. Gloria Steinem recalls that colleagues warned her against writing about feminism: "You've worked so hard to be taken seriously, Gloria. You must not get involved with those crazy women." After an initial cover story or television news profile, many media leaders felt that they had done their bit. The directive of one male editor captured widespread attitudes: "Find an authority who'll say this is all a crock of shit." Such instructions turned into self-fulfilling prophecies. The frequent refusal to present feminists as anything other than "braless bubbleheads" justified decisionmakers' refusal to present them at all.[59]

Whatever media leaders' reluctance to chronicle the rebirth of feminism in the 1960s and early 1970s, they had no such hesitation in reporting its demise. Beginning in the early 1970s, before many media outlets had turned any serious attention to the women's movement, others were declaring it dead, dying, or permanently disabled. Despite periodic reprieves, press postmortems have continued with stunning regularity. "The women's movement is over," announced a 1981 cover story in the *New York Times Magazine*. Anyone who missed that obituary did not lack for further opportunities to mourn. Indeed, as Ellen Goodman observes, the death and resurrection of feminism has become a "media staple like the monthly makeover in fashion magazines."[60]

In these autopsies of the movement, most authors come to bury their subject, not to praise it. The diagnoses vary slightly, but movement leaders are almost always to blame. Column titles from the early 1980s to mid-1990s summarized prevailing wisdom: "Feminists Have Killed Feminism." Yet by blaming activists for the current stalemate on many women's issues, these media accounts deflect attention from the deeper causes.[61]

Part of what drives such critiques is the lure of captivating catfights. One of the simpler ways to snag media attention is for a sister to trash the sisterhood. As theorist Catharine Stimpson puts it, "If you are a man, bite a dog. If you are a woman, bite a feminist." This works best if the targets appear as "unsexed" harpies and unfeminine "frumps" with no grasp of "real" women's values. The media have long given disproportionate airtime to these grievances, partly for reasons that are not unique to feminism. The "radical fringes" of social movements often receive undue attention; they play to the press's perennial search for dramatic events, startling soundbites, and "good visuals." But the women's movement is particularly vulnerable to such treatment, because what gains attention for feminist issues often runs counter to what passes as appropriate feminine behavior.[62]

For decades the press has contributed to the extremist images that it delights in denouncing. A celebrated example is "bra burning," a term one journalist coined to describe feminists' protest at the 1968 Miss America Pageant. No undergarments were in fact charred; they were ceremoniously deposited in a trash receptacle. But among many Americans, the lingerie bonfire has moved from fiction to fact, leaving unpleasant associations behind. A recent example surfaced in a National Public Radio interview, when a middle-aged woman linked her distaste for feminism to an earlier protest. She could still remember when some movement leader "took off her bra and burned it downtown . . . in public." And as this interviewee made clear, "I'm not burning my bra. I'm keeping [it] on."[63]

Time magazine's coverage of feminism during the 1970s offers a representative sample of common media characterizations: "strident," "humorless," "extremist," "lesbian," and of course "hairy-legged." Then, more than a decade later, a cover story on women facing the 1990s reported that "hairy legs haunt the feminist movement as do images of being strident and lesbian." Do tell.[64]

Contemporary critics have a similar but equally long list of grievances, many of them wildly inconsistent. Opponents find the women's movement too inclusive or not inclusive enough. Commentators from the right see it as captive to fringe groups—lesbians, neo-Puritans, and elitist ivory tower ideologues. Observers from the left see it as dominated by straight middle-class whites who don't want to rock the boat now that they are beginning to find seats on board. As Chapter 8 indicates, to some critics mainstream feminists look dowdy and dull; to others they seem shrill and outlandish. The theoretical wing of the movement is condemned as too intellectual or not intellectual enough—too interested in arid esoteric tangents, or too driven by activist ideological agendas. The organizational wing of the movement is lambasted for a leadership that hates men or wants to be just like them.[65]

There is something for everyone in these critiques, and supporting examples are always ready to hand. Few commentators feel any need to document or quantify the extent of the problem they describe. Indeed, some critics simply pronounce their judgments as self-evident truths. "Aggressive" lesbians have "taken over" women's studies programs on college campuses, announces Irving Kristol in a *Wall Street Journal* editorial. Self-proclaimed feminists like Christina Hoff Sommers and Camille Paglia receive endless coverage of their claims that extremist factions have alienated both women and men.[66]

Media coverage of the link between feminists and lesbians has proven especially problematic, not only because it trades on homophobic stereotypes but also because it legitimates them. Following public disclosures that NOW president Patricia Ireland had both a husband and a female companion, Sally Quinn summarized a common view: "What kind of standards is she espousing? It is impossible to read the Ireland declaration and argue that the movement she leads is in touch with the majority of women." Despite strong protest by movement leaders, other columnists took a similar position, and Quinn herself added the following justification for her statement: "The perception that NOW is a lesbian-dominated organization is the reason why we have a backlash against feminism. Most women are turned off by having a lesbian presence in the movement. That's not my feeling. I'm just reporting on it. I agree with everything that gay rights supporters think. I'm just saying you should keep it to yourself, if you're a lesbian."[67]

It is also impossible to read this statement and conclude that media spokespersons such as Quinn are "in touch" with the real interests of American women. As Chapters 7 and 8 make clear, prejudice against "effeminate" gays and "unfeminine" lesbians builds on the same gender stereotypes that restrict opportunities for all individuals, whatever their sexual orientation. Fear of the lesbian label also discourages activism on women's issues. For leaders like Ireland, staying in the closet is not a solution; it is part of the problem. By condemning those who are open about their sexual orientation, commentators like Quinn compound the prejudice that they claim merely to describe.

Even when the press attempts a more positive tone in feminist profiles, its compliments often are backhanded. A typical description appears in the *New York Times Magazine*'s 1994 story on Shannon Faulkner, the woman who challenged her exclusion from an all-male military college: "She is not a crusader, activist, earthshaker, cantankerous man-hater, lesbian, or ugly duckling out to find a mate." So too, a mid-1990s *Boston Globe* profile of Clare Dalton, a professor who sued Harvard Law School for sex discrimination, reports with evident relief that she does not sound like some "crazed feminist spouting anti-male . . . jargon."[68]

Hillary Clinton's experience graphically demonstrates the risks facing "uppity women" who become associated with feminism. First ladies are frequent targets of media criticism, but only Clinton has elicited publications with titles like *Big Sister Is Watching You: Hillary Clinton and the White House Feminists Who Now Control America—and Tell the President What To Do,* or "Boy Clinton's Big Mama—The Lady Mac-Beth of Little Rock." In an effort to combat media characterizations as a "bossy, humorless, radical feminist," Clinton kept her distance from the "f-word." When pressed during the 1992 presidential campaign, Clinton responded that she believed in equality but rejected some of what the term feminism has "come to mean today"; she did not wish to dismiss "maternal values" or "cease caring about the men in my life."[69]

When polls suggested that about 70 percent of the American public preferred a "traditional first lady," Clinton made greater efforts to project that image. She got a kinder, gentler hairdo, more mother-child photo ops, and lower-profile appearances, often standing by her man but not opening her mouth. "Feminism," her press secretary doggedly insisted, "is a misplaced angle. It's not an accurate theme for [Clinton]. She represents today's modern woman," who, by (press) definition, is not an f-type.[70]

Yet despite these repeated denials, Clinton has remained unable to escape demonization as an "overbearing yuppie wife from hell." Of course, part of the problem is of her own making. As Clinton herself concedes, she has made "lots of mistakes" concerning her public image, and well-documented press profiles also raise significant character concerns on matters like Whitewater. The point here, however, is that media leaders have contributed to Clinton's difficulties while often denying the gender biases that their coverage reflects and reinforces.[71]

Indeed, some journalists even refuse to believe that the First Lady's problems "have anything to do with gender relations." To commentators like Peggy Noonan, it is "infuriating" when Clinton supporters invoke sexism; their concern seems mainly a way of "trying to divert attention from the real problem, which is who she is and what she's doing." But at least part of what irritates many Americans about what Hillary Clinton *is* doing involves cultural conflicts about the role of women. Her difficulties speak volumes about the dilemmas for women who want it both ways—who want a feminist life and a "feminine" image. As columnist Joan Lester notes, without power, many women are victimized; when they get it they're vilified.[72]

These difficulties emerged clearly in a culinary confrontation during the 1992 presidential race. Clinton backed into a bake-off with Barbara Bush following an ill-considered press comment. In response to repeated questions about conflicts of interest in her legal career while her husband was governor, Clinton observed that the problem was hardly avoidable, unless perhaps she had "stayed home, baked cookies, and had teas." The media coverage that followed lambasted Clinton from all points on the political spectrum. Moderate and conservative commentators accused her of devaluing a role that society as a whole also had undervalued. Critics from the left pointed out that Clinton herself was able to escape baking only because she could hire less privileged women to do it for her. These were, of course, fair points. What wasn't fair was how some commentators continued to use Clinton's statement out of context despite her attempts at clarification and public apology. What she intended as an explanation of conflicts of interests ended up looking like an assault on homemaking.[73]

Worse still was the media coverage Clinton received after *Family Circle* invited her and Barbara Bush to submit their favorite chocolate chip cookies for competition. In expiation for her prior sins, Clinton apparently had to enter the fray, but her gesture did little to appease media critics. "What next?" wondered one *New York Times* columnist. "Eleanor Roosevelt fudge?" Here was an accomplished professional who had "already changed her name, her hair, her clothes, and her comments . . . [now] reduced to hawking her chocolate chip cookie entry." In many press accounts, the not-so-subtle subtext was that this is a woman who willingly trades principles for political gain. As one commentator put it: "If she thought it would help get Bill elected,

[Hillary] would show up at the next rally in four-inch heels and a peek-a-boo bra."[74]

After the 1992 election, Clinton's attempts to project a more traditional feminine image prompted no less criticism. As controversy persisted over her policy role and Whitewater involvement, her public profile shifted to ever "safer" subjects: decorating the White House at Christmas; encouraging older women to have mammograms; allowing women to stay longer in hospitals following childbirth; and meeting children's needs through stronger families and communities. This makeover had little of its intended effect in many media circles. "Earth Mother Meets Mommie Dearest," was Maureen Dowd's assessment.[75]

What is, however, often missing in press criticism is any acknowledgment of the double bind confronting women like Clinton. Given the public's strong preference for "traditional" First Ladies, she could hardly abandon the effort to resemble one. Yet once the debate was framed in terms of policymaking versus cookie baking, feminine versus feminist, she could not avoid alienating some substantial constituency, whatever her response. On this terrain, professional women are at a decided disadvantage. But neither can they refuse to compete. What Clinton most needed was not a different image but a different debate, which was less about personal style and more about political substance.[76]

Women's Rights in the Wrong Roles

Uppity women seldom do better in the entertainment media. Unhappy endings are the norm for women who most directly challenge traditional gender hierarchies. Psychobabes ranging from the career-driven vamp in *Fatal Attraction* to the comic-book Catwoman in *Batman Returns* terrorize men and meet grisly fates. In *Thelma and Louise*, not even the forced double suicide of two renegade heroines was retribution enough to satisfy many male viewers. These are, after all, women who assault men and appear to enjoy it. Although the victims are not particularly sympathetic (the one who dies is an attempted rapist), some male viewers could not stomach vengeance by "killer bimbos." Critics who had expressed no distaste for slasher films that brutalized women suddenly became outraged by the "male bashing," "apocalyptic craziness," and "toxic feminism" of *Thelma and Louise.* In fact, the film is not particularly violent compared with standard screenplays involving male fugitives; it was the gender role reversal, not the degree of brutality, that many Americans found unsettling.[77]

If network television and standard Hollywood releases are any indication, it doesn't take much feminism to look like too much. Mainstream film and prime-time television producers are leery about direct engagement with "women's issues," and some treatment that does occur is stridently unsympathetic. It is, in part, a comment on Hollywood's power politics that the first major movie focusing on sexual harassment, *Disclosure,* featured a pattern that accounts for only about 1 percent of real-world complaints: women demanding sexual favors from men. In this, as in other dramatic accounts of sexual harassment such as *Oleanna,* women are either lying or loony.

So too, in *Cagney and Lacey,* one of the rare television series to feature explicitly feminist leads and themes, the feminism became increasingly muted as the struggle for ratings escalated. The original image of detective Cagney struck network executives as not "sufficiently feminine" and too "harshly women's lib." She got a midstream makeover—a new actress, softer hairdo, upscale wardrobe, and less aggressive style. Story lines on issues like abortion provoked long lists of "thou shalt nots" from the network. The suggestion that Gloria Steinem might play a cameo role met with the same degree of enthusiasm that Son of Sam might have prompted.[78]

We should not, of course, underestimate the progress that has occurred. Some feminism at least has entered prime time. A decade ago, major networks did not feature statements like the one in *Designing Women* after the Hill-Thomas hearings: "Listen, I don't mean to be strident and overbearing; I used to be nice, but quite frankly, nice doesn't cut it. We want to be treated equally and with respect. Is that too much to ask?"[79]

Yet such views are still in short supply on network television. If we wish to see greater support for women's interests, we need to make our preferences matter—in angry letters, box office receipts, TV ratings, and public broadcast contributions. In 1993, the annual Academy Awards ceremony celebrated the "Year of the Woman in Film." The festivities began with a sequence of "great moments" in motion pictures. These generally involved actresses in highly stereotypical roles: sex kitten, psychotic killer, and idealized mother. After an opening chorus of "Someday My Prince Will Come" and a harem scene featuring bikini-clad dancers, the show closed to the tune of "Thank Heaven for Little Girls." Women deserve better, but a real celebration will need to wait until there is more to celebrate.[80]

A related problem involves the repackaging of the women's movement in advertisements. By appropriating the language of liberation for product endorsements, commercial copywriters trivialize and transform the feminist impulse.

In the view from Madison Avenue, "Freedom Now" is available through feminine hygiene spray, and the answer to work/family conflicts is Hamburger Helper. "Is your face paying the price of success?" Nivea advertisements wonder. "You work hard at work. You work hard at home . . . eventually it begins to show on your face, hair . . . a little less resilience, a few more lines." The answer, of course, is not to reduce the price of success but rather to buy the product. "Who says you can't have it all?" is the lead-in for Michelob's narrative about a full-time model and part-time business student. She studies until two in the morning, has a photo shoot three hours later, and finds time for a beer in between. If this woman thinks she's having it all, she needs more than a drink.[81]

In this coopted and commodified form, feminists' rallying cry is reversed: "the political becomes the personal" and only personal. By suggesting that women can solve complex social problems through individual consumption, advertising undermines incentives for political change. We are left with a kind of "feminism lite" that fosters denial of the problems remaining.

By demanding that women's magazines provide articles "compatible" with commercial messages, advertisers also preempt challenges to their own priorities. The experience of *Ms.* magazine is instructive. Corporate sponsors objected to editorials with "negative" tones, stories on chemicals used in hair dyes, ads for lesbian poetry journals, and a cover photo of prominent Soviet authors wearing no makeup. Like other cosmetic companies, Estee Lauder refused to advertise in *Ms.* because executives believed that its readers were "not our women." In the view of Estee Lauder's president, his company was selling a "kept woman" message. When *Ms.* editor Gloria Steinem pointed out that 70 percent of American women were now salaried workers, the company's president was unmoved. After all, "they would like to be kept women." After fifteen years of trying to convince potential advertisers that "liberated" women also used cars, cosmetics, and computers, *Ms.* finally gave up. It eliminated commercial sponsors entirely and paid the price in higher costs, less frequent issues, and fewer subscribers.[82]

Not all magazines are prepared to go that route. And even in the "best circles," when content clashes with commerce, content sometimes folds first. During the mid-1990s, the *New York Times Magazine* planned to run as a cover story a debate between antipornography activist Catharine MacKinnon and First Amendment attorney Floyd Abrams. At the last minute, editors discovered that the cover folded out to a four-page ad for Express Jeans, featuring a model not wearing any, or much of anything else. When changing the ad proved "impractical," the *Times* switched the cover to a safer photo of an Afghan terrorist.[83]

The good news, such as it is, is that people noticed. The story about "the story" ran in other leading magazines. So too, even *Advertising Age* has offered some unkind words about the scantily clad party girls in beer commercials. By the 1990s, the magazine's editorialists noted, it might be time for "brewers and their agencies to wake up and join the rest of America in realizing that sexism, sexual harassment, and the cultural portrayal of women in advertising are inextricably linked." Well, perhaps some advertisers are snoozing, but the majority are probably just indifferent. From their perspective, if sexism sells, who cares if a few feminists are miffed?[84]

To change that view, more wake-up calls from broader audiences are needed. As a 1996 survey made clear, American women are still unhappy with the way that they appear in advertising. From their perspective, commercials too often present women as sex objects and too seldom portray their changing roles in work and family. These views need to be communicated more forcefully, not just in polls but in letters, boycotts, and educational initiatives. On the relatively infrequent occasions when political organizations or a critical mass of consumers have mobilized against a specific advertising campaign, their complaints have not passed unnoticed. Ads have been pulled and public sensitivity has increased.[85] If women are truly interested in "having it all," they need political action, not Hamburger Helper.

5

Sex and Violence

"A bit nutty, and a bit slutty." That was journalist David Brock's description of Anita Hill after her Senate testimony regarding harassment by Supreme Court nominee Clarence Thomas. Such characterizations, somewhat more tactfully expressed, are common in cases involving sexual abuse. When the issue is harassment, acquaintance rape, or domestic violence, it is often the victim whose conduct is on trial.[1]

Matters could, of course, be worse. And have been. For most of this nation's history, most sexual abuse went unnamed, unreported, unchallenged, and unchanged. Until the last quarter-century, America had no legal term or conceptual cubbyhole for sexual harassment. There also were no rape crisis policies or battered-women's shelters, no studies on the frequency of acquaintance rape or spousal abuse, and no discussion of the link between pornography and sexual violence. All this has changed. Yet longstanding patterns of denial remain much the same. Many men and a depressingly large number of women still discount the problem, victimize the victims, and resist the most plausible solutions.

Moreover, even those who acknowledge that sexual abuse is a serious problem often fail to see its connection to broader patterns of sexual inequality. Many Americans perceive sexual harassment, acquaintance rape, and nonviolent pornography as issues of sex, or perhaps bad sex, but not of subordination. By contrast, serious domestic assaults, stranger rapes, and slasher porn are viewed as examples of violence, not sex. What falls through the cracks are issues of power. We fail to see sexual abuse as a strategy of dominance, exclusion, control, and retaliation—as a way to keep women in their place and out of men's. Until we acknowledge the true dynamics of sexualized violence, we cannot adequately address its consequences.

Sexual Harassment

Shortly after the Hill-Thomas Senate hearings, a celebrated cartoon featured a puzzled woman questioning her male coworker. "Why don't men get it? I mean how would you like it if I made lewd remarks, described scenes from porn movies or patted your behind?" He responded: "How much for all three?" This gap between men's perceptions and women's experience emerged clearly during Clarence Thomas' confirmation proceedings. Hearing Hill, and hearing her not being heard, was a unique occasion for collective consciousness raising.[2]

Yet the outpouring of personal narratives and legal complaints that followed Hill's testimony also revealed a countercurrent of denial. This resistance centers around a few basic themes:

denial that a serious problem of harassment exists ("It doesn't happen much, or it doesn't happen here");

denial that women are seriously injured ("So what if it happened?");

denial that men are responsible for women's injuries ("She provoked, enjoyed, accepted, or asked for it");

denial that legal sanctions are the answer ("You can't legislate morality," and trying to do so squelches free speech, office romances, and decent working relationships).

A closer look at these responses reveals both our progress and its limits. For centuries, women experienced harassment, but only *they* suffered the consequences: now men who harass bear some of the costs. Those in positions of power—politicians, employers, coworkers—must increasingly listen to injured women. The problem is that too many Americans still don't hear what is being said.

The insistence that "real" harassment rarely happens is a recent variation on traditional views that it didn't happen at all. The term "sexual harassment" did not even surface until the 1970s, when courts and the Equal Employment Opportunity Commission first recognized such abuse as prohibited discrimination. American law now bans two forms of conduct: "quid pro quo" harassment, which involves unwelcome sexual advances or demands, and work environment harassment, which involves conduct that creates an intimidating, hostile, or offensive workplace. In the classic quid pro quo case, a supervisor denies a promotion to a subordinate who rejects sexual overtures. In hostile-environment claims, individuals experience everything from physical assaults to pervasive verbal degradation. Both forms of harassment involve an abuse of power, but its motivations, perpetrators, and occupational contexts differ. Quid pro cases arise when individuals feel entitled to use their superior economic and social status to impose a sexual relationship. By contrast, hostile-environment cases often reflect a desire to exclude individuals from certain positions and to remind them of their subordinate status. Women as well as men engage in such conduct, but the vast majority—over 90 percent—of reported cases involve males harassing females.[3]

Although recent highly publicized incidents have made such harassment hard to overlook, many Americans believe that it is widely exaggerated. Goaded on by "overzealous," "hypersensitive," and "neo-Puritan" "neurotics," women reportedly are flooding the courts with frivolous complaints. In harassment cases, "you can sue anybody about anything," announces talk show host John McLaughlin. And "there's a rush to judgment . . . against the male." Men are being held "liable for a look." "Unwelcome gazing," "friendly banter," harmless "horseplay," a dirty joke, or one open display of *Playboy* supposedly will bring hordes of mincing moralists down upon unwitting culprits. According to conservative commentators like John Leo and Christina Hoff Sommers, "corporate McCarthyism" and "witch trials," are the result, while feminist "PC paranoia" is to blame.[4]

Yet if the charge is exaggeration, critics, not complainants, are the worst offenders. In sifting through thousands of pages of judicial opinions and recent research, I have yet to discover the hapless individual defending himself for a look or a single tasteless joke. What emerge instead are innumerable judicial and arbitration proceedings in which decisionmakers deny relief because the harassment was insufficiently "malicious" or "brutal." In many judges' view, sex discrimination law is not meant to redress the "petty slights of the hypersensitive" or to "bring about a magical transformation in the social mores of American workplaces." In order to establish liability, plaintiffs must prove severe and pervasive conduct that was unwelcome and injurious, and that a reasonable person in their situation would have found offensive. One unusually candid judge expressed the attitude that many men bring to harassment claims: "So, we will have to hear [this complaint], but the Court doesn't think too much of it."[5]

Of course, borderline cases do exist, and recent changes in cultural norms have created some genuine confusion about where the boundaries are. There have also been occasional examples of overreaction—women who are offended by photographs of a bikini-clad wife, copies of *Playboy,* a Goya portrait of a nude, or classroom lectures using sexist metaphors. But these incidents almost never result in findings of harassment, and for every one of such aberrant yet oft-cited cases, there are countless illustrations of the converse problem. Male employers and judges frequently deny relief for conduct that they find isolated or trivial but that most women would not. Examples include:

a woman whose coworker masturbated in front of her and requested that she engage in sado-masochistic acts;

a woman who, after fielding repeated sexual propositions and slaps on the buttocks, requested help from her supervisor and was asked, "What will I get for it?";

an employee whose coworkers regularly referred to women as "whore," "cunt," "pussy," and "tits," who plastered the workplace with posters of naked women, who called the plaintiff a "fat ass," and who claimed that all she needed was "a good lay";

a woman who was maced, taunted, handcuffed to a toilet, and had her head pushed underwater.

Federal judges denied all of these claims. In their view, the conduct was not sufficiently pervasive, the claimant's injuries were not sufficiently serious, or her own conduct was not sufficiently blameless.[6]

Nor are these isolated examples. Although commentators like Phyllis Schlafly insist that for the "virtuous woman," sex harassment is not a problem, the most comprehensive research consistently indicates otherwise. Over half of all women experience harassment during their academic or working lives. That figure has changed little over the last decade, despite a substantial increase in formal remedies. Lesbians and women of color are targets of particularly virulent conduct, and suspicion of homosexual behavior increases the risk of physical assault. Immigrants are also especially vulnerable, given their unfamiliarity with American legal norms and their fear of reprisals if they submit formal complaints. Harassing conduct is frequent even by lawyers who might be expected to know what is unlawful; some 60 percent of surveyed female attorneys report experiencing such abuse. And in branches of the military that claim "zero tolerance" for harassment, 90 percent of female personnel under age fifty indicate that they have endured it—more than half in the preceding year.[7]

For the vast majority of sex harassment complaints, underreporting, not overreaction, is the norm. Only 5 to 10 percent of women experiencing abuse make formal complaints and fewer still can afford the financial and psychological costs of litigation. In the rare successful lawsuit, damages are usually quite small, averaging only about three thousand dollars. Conservative critics who worry about legal hypochondria and who advise women to "just lighten up" should look at the data and take their own advice.[8]

Many individuals' failure to see sexual harassment as a serious problem results partly from the failure to understand its consequences. The traditional "boys will be boys" response frequently reveals the gap between men's assumptions and women's experiences. "At least you weren't raped," has been some judges' and arbitrators' response to workplace abuse. From this perspective, women like Anita Hill are at fault for trying to turn a simple flirtation into a federal case. After all, "he never touched her." If her career didn't suffer, why should his?[9]

Variations on this theme play out in men's defenses to formal sex harassment charges. "Who can tell," they complain, "where courtship stops and coercion starts?" Defenders of Senator Robert Packwood were incensed that "gender avengers" pressured the Senate Ethics Committee into punishing "crude" but innocent "office gropings." As Packwood himself put it, "I don't know how you decide ahead of time what is going to be offensive . . . If you don't try, how do you know?"[10]

Men in genuine doubt could consult any of the countless publications or training programs that report what leading research confirms:

about two-thirds of surveyed women, but fewer than 15 percent of surveyed men, would find an unsolicited invitation for sex offensive. Women are also far more likely than men to object to sexist jokes and repeated requests for dates. But it should not require formal training to recognize that the conduct triggering harassment complaints rarely qualifies as harmless seduction. For example, in Packwood's case, the Senate Ethics Committee found at least eighteen instances of abuse not easily dismissed as "flirtation." As law professor Stephen Gillers observes, "Grabbing someone by surprise . . . pushing your tongue into her mouth, and putting your hands on her buttocks is not ambiguous conduct. Penal codes have names for these acts: they're called sexual assault."[11]

So too, in a highly publicized 1994 case against Baker McKenzie, a leading San Francisco law firm, defense counsel insisted that the harassment at issue reflected current "uncertainty" about "what is OK and what is not OK in the workplace." The "ambiguous" conduct reported by ten women over a six-year period involved a partner who put his hand down secretaries' blouses and grabbed their breasts. Although the firm's leaders were aware of complaints, they failed to impose serious sanctions; the lawyer was a powerful partner who brought in highly profitable work and the complainants were clerical staff and junior associates who appeared far more expendable. Missing from that calculation was any consideration of the costs—to women in general or to the firm's employees in particular—of tolerating such abuse. As it turned out, the firm's "so what" attitude was so obvious and so offensive that jurors decided to answer the question. In an all too rare occurrence, they delivered legal education through a multimillion-dollar punitive-damage award.[12]

The trivialization of injuries that led to the San Francisco lawsuit is by no means atypical. For more than a quarter-century, Astra pharmaceutical company ignored or quietly settled egregious sexual harassment complaints until a *Business Week* cover story forced its parent company to investigate. When Mitsubishi Motors was served with a complaint by the Equal Employment Opportunity Commission (EEOC) involving some 300 to 500 women, the company responded with categorical denials and clumsily orchestrated resistance. Women who had been grabbed in the breast or crotch, or sexually assaulted with factory equipment, suddenly learned that the company had "zero tolerance for harassment." Managers warned workers that the litigation might force a plant closing and bused some 2,500 employees to a "spontaneous" protest at EEOC offices.[13]

The price that women pay for such harassment is by no means as trivial as many managers appear to assume. For individual victims, harassment often results in economic and psychological injuries, including job dismissals, transfers, coworker hostility, anxiety, depression, and other stress-related conditions. For women as a group, harassment perpetuates sexist stereotypes and discourages gender integration of male-dominated workplaces. For employers and society as a whole, the price includes decreased productivity and increased job turnover. The estimated cost of harassment for a Fortune 500 company averages $8 million a year.[14]

This fact has not been lost on many employers, as the recent development of harassment policies and prevention programs suggests. But the point still has not registered fully in many educational and workplace settings. Policies that look good on paper often are ineffective in practice, partly because male decisionmakers tend to sympathize with male perpetrators except in egregious cases. Even in those cases, the costs of full-blown proceedings usually encourage informal resolution and mild sanctions.[15]

The harassment charges against the U.S. Navy are a case in point. At the 1991 Tailhook Convention, over 200 naval and marine officers engaged in sexual misconduct, including a gauntlet in which they stripped, mauled, and assaulted women. A majority of those officers received no sanctions, and only a few ended up with more than letters of caution. In another well-publicized 1995 case, the chief executive officer of W. R. Grace was able to resign with a $20 million severance package despite findings that he had harassed at least five female employees. The infrequency of serious sanctions is a major reason for women's reluctance to report abuse. They believe, quite rationally, that complaining will have little practical effect on their harassers and could make their own situations worse.[16]

Another major deterrent to harassment complaints is America's common tendency to victimize victims. A widespread assumption is that women are often responsible for sexual abuse—that they provoke, invite, tolerate, or should expect such conduct. This attitude is especially common when women enter nontraditional occupations. California jurors who denied damages to a female deputy sheriff reasoned that she had "asked for" problems by "taking a man's job." In the recent cases involving Mitsubishi and Jacksonville Shipyards, employees viewed automobile plants and shipyards as "a man's world," where abusive language and pornographic pinups were "a natural thing." So too, female sports reporters have received frequent reminders that they are in a "macho" occupation and if they mind being propositioned or labeled a "fucking cunt," they "won't survive." Many male athletes have ostracized anyone who complains. In their view, if a journalist like Lisa Owens can't deal with football players' locker room taunts, "she shouldn't get into the business." Better she should "cover tea dances."[17]

Harvard law professor Alan Dershowitz takes a similar view. From his perspective, a female candidate in a union election had no right to complain about composite photographs placing her face on nude pictures from *Hustler* and *Penthouse*. His advice: "If you can't take the heat, get out of the kitchen." By targeting women as the culprits, these commentators convey a not-so-subtle subtext: "You wanted equality? I'm giving it to you with a vengeance."[18]

Legal procedures also assume that women often invite or condone their own abuse. This view underpins provisions requiring a plaintiff to prove that sexual conduct is "unwelcome," and allowing a defendant to introduce evidence of the victim's "promiscuous" appearance and behavior. Although recent reforms seek to restrict disclosures of a complainant's prior sexual experiences, such evidence is still admissible at trial if the judge decides that its value to a defendant substantially outweighs harm to the complainant. Moreover, in pretrial proceedings, attorneys have greater freedom to ask intimate questions, and can often grill victims about their sex lives, birth control practices, and counseling histories. If a plaintiff alleges physical or psychological damage resulting from harassment, opposing attorneys can explore possible alternative causes for her distress—everything from closeted lesbian experiences to intimate marital difficulties. As a result, defendants' lawyers can discredit or deter a harassment complaint with harassing tactics of their own. Less-than-perfect plaintiffs routinely lose contested cases. Women who are too "abrasive," "antagonistic," "aggressive," "seductive," or "flirtatious," "get what they deserve," which generally does not include damage awards.[19]

The higher the stakes for the defendant, the greater the risks for the complainant. For example, in the Baker McKenzie litigation, despite numerous complaints against the same individual, the firm's lawyers attempted to paint the plaintiff as a "bounty hunter" who "irrationally misunderstood" assaultive behavior that others found "perfectly normal." Such victim bashing reached new heights in the Tailhook scandal. The assaults women endured at the convention were bad enough, but some military leaders' initial responses managed to make the situation worse. According to one vice-admiral in charge of naval operations, "Women would not have gone down the hall [where the gauntlet was] if they did not like it." Paula Coughlin, the lieutenant who exposed the scandal, appeared in graffiti and an underground newsletter as a greedy, "manhating" "party animal."[20]

The media and Senate's treatment of Anita Hill offers a textbook case in similar tactics. Here was a woman with a relatively pristine past, other corroborating witnesses, and no obvious motive to lie. Yet she emerged in conservative accounts as a "sleazy," "hysterical" feminist launching a "pit bull" attack that reinforced racist stereotypes. "Basically," as one political aide noted, "we went about the business of making [her] life a living hell."[21]

For Hill, the humiliation ultimately had a silver lining, at least as measured in speaker fees and book contracts. But the same is seldom true in garden variety harassment cases. Relatively few women can afford substantial legal costs. And relatively few lawyers will pursue harassment claims without a large fee up front, except in the rare circumstances involving clear liability and potentially large damage awards. As a result, most complainants depend on state and federal enforcement agencies, which lack resources to investigate and litigate the vast majority of cases.[22]

Even when the victim wins in court, she often loses in life. The minimal remedies usually available may not compensate for risks of retaliation, such as transfers, demotion, informal blacklisting, physical threats, and vandalism. In a survey of women who filed harassment complaints, a third felt that complaining made things worse, and only a fifth believed that such complaints were handled fairly. As one summary of such studies concludes, an "assertive" response to harassment generally results in "negative outcomes" for complainants. Many of these individuals confront a no-win situation. Those who complain promptly are "whiners," or "troublemakers." Those who wait until the situation becomes unbearable are no longer credible. If the harassment was really bad, why didn't they say so sooner? Even substantial damage awards may fail to compensate for the stress, humiliation, and career suicide involved in a lawsuit. As one "successful" litigant put it, "I wouldn't really recommend this to anybody."[23]

A further reason sexual harassment remains common is that many Americans deny the need to strengthen legal responses. Conservatives frequently see harassment law as one more ineffective and intrusive form of government regulation. Liberals often are troubled by the free speech implications of monitoring offensive expression. And individuals of all political persuasions worry about expanding opportunities for vindictive litigation. While these are all legitimate concerns, critics tend to exaggerate one set of problems at the expense of ignoring others.

Skepticism about the law is increasingly in vogue, and many people believe that legal regulation is especially inapt for issues like sexual harassment. As federal judge Alex Kozinski puts it: "Lawsuits are clumsy tools for shaping human behavior"; they "tend to enrich lawyers far more often than they satisfy the parties." A preferable alternative is education. To critics like Kozinski, harassment "is a problem far too important and delicate to be handed over to the lawyers."[24]

Well, yes and no. Conservative critics certainly are right that the law is too expensive and intrusive a chaperon for most workplace relationships. Surely the Senate Ethics Committee should not have had to produce a ten-volume record of Packwood's serial "gropings," complete with exchanges such as "Where did he pat you? . . . Do you remember if he patted you on your knee or on top of your skirt? . . . And do you remember how long the pats lasted?"[25]

However, without the realistic threat of legal sanctions, women's voices too often go unheard or unheeded. Until recently, the prevailing view was that sexual harassment was indeed a problem "too delicate" for the law. Women did not fare well under that system. When I was in college, students experienced harassment but it had neither a label nor a remedy. We spoke of having a "problem" with our professors, and the problem was always ours, never theirs. Law has changed that landscape. Contrary to critics' assertions, sexual harassment is one of the areas in which we unquestionably have legislated morality. The kind of conduct that surfaced in the Tailhook and Packwood cases now strikes most people as wrong as well as illegal.

Of course, we also have paid a price. And in the view of many, usually male critics, it is far too high; vindictive claims and threats to free expression have become all too common. As these commentators note, when men become overly cautious about sexual harassment claims, women lose out as well. Male professors may be reluctant to mentor female students and "male employees may find it prudent to avoid [socializing] . . . with female coworkers." In a society where people increasingly find their partners at work, everyone suffers from claims that "drive men from the dance floor." And that reportedly happens if "when it works we call it courtship [and] when it doesn't we call it a lawsuit."[26]

These are not groundless concerns. But they are exaggerated. And sometimes pretextual. Men who now claim that they fear socializing with females often had other reasons to avoid it in the past. While some harassment complaints may be false or frivolous, the problem appears no greater than with other legal claims. In the only reported study to date, surveyed institutions had found fewer than 1 percent of formal complaints to be demonstrably false. Moreover, where important First Amendment values are at stake, courts have not been reluctant to provide appropriate safeguards. Nor have advocates of women's rights failed to speak out when the motive or effect of harassment claims seems itself harassing, as in Paula Jones's recent lawsuit against President Clinton.[27]

Legal proceedings are not, of course, the ideal way to cope with sex at work. But they are an inevitable byproduct of cultural change. Creating rights necessarily creates opportunities for abuse of rights, and it takes time to establish clear boundaries for sexual conduct. As even skeptics sometimes concede, "more litigation today [could] . . . lead to less litigation tomorrow" by encouraging preventive educational measures and informal complaint procedures. To assist such progress, we need both to strengthen current law and to recognize its limitations.[28]

One useful first step would be to evaluate harassment from the standpoint of the reasonable person in the victim's circumstances. This is not, however, to imply that where the victim is a woman, the answer is a "reasonable woman" standard, as some courts and commentators have suggested. Such a framework is neither a complete nor a costless solution. One danger is that courts can pay only lip service to the concept and construct the reasonable woman from a man's vantage point. According to the trial judge in a case involving workers who looked up the plaintiff's skirt with a flashlight, the "reasonable woman" would view the conduct as "childish," not harassing. The fact that it might be both apparently escaped notice. A further concern is that courts will either entrench sexist stereotypes or homogenize female experience. An explicit gender-based double standard may suggest that women are incapable of functioning in "a man's world" without special protection. Such an approach could also unduly universalize women's experience by obscuring other differences based on class, race, sexual orientation, and so forth.[29]

We can, however, reduce such risks with a gender-neutral formulation, such as one that the EEOC has considered. That standard focuses on reasonable persons in the situation of the victim, but also considers characteristics like gender, race, and sexual orientation in assessing the reasonableness of the victim's claims. For example, a leading federal appellate ruling, *Ellison v. Brady,* suggests the need for such a contextual approach. The case involved an employer's failure to respond adequately to a situation in which a worker made intrusive sexual advances and wrote "disturbing" letters to a female colleague. Applying a "reasonable woman" standard, the court appropriately took into account women's disproportionate risk of violent sexual assault. Given that experience, the appellate judges found that the conduct at issue constituted a threatening and harassing work environment. The court could, however, have reached the same result through a "reasonable person" formulation that was sensitive to context. Under the EEOC's proposed approach, the issue would have been how someone in the complainant's situation might rationally have viewed the conduct in question. Co-workers who are genuinely unsure of the answers can always ask. Or they can imagine the environment that they would like for their mothers, wives, and daughters.[30]

Other law reform measures are equally important. When men harass, it should not be women's character and career that are on trial and at risk. Trial judges should do more to prevent intrusive inquiries into the victim's own background. They could also eliminate humiliating inquiries about whether the victim "welcomed" conduct that reasonable employees would find offensive. Regulation is needed for new sites of harassment, such as computer networks where women have been physically threatened as well as humiliated by sexually explicit mass mailings.

Remedies also should be available for harassment on the basis of sexual orientation. Many courts' failure to prohibit such abuse both encourages homophobia and ignores its link with other forms of sex discrimination. Harassment of "effeminate" men and "unfeminine" women builds on the same stereotypes that underpin other gender inequalities.[31]

Even with a significantly improved legal process, however, most victims are unlikely to file claims, because of the expense, embarrassment, and evidentiary hurdles. More efforts should focus on other strategies, such as clear workplace policies, well-designed educational programs, adequate legal representation, informal but unbiased complaint channels, and effective sanctions by employers.

Yet in the long run, we cannot respond adequately to sexual harassment without also responding to the institutional structures that perpetuate it. If we want to change the conditions that make women vulnerable to such abuse, we need to focus on job training, glass ceilings, affirmative action, pay equity, parental and childcare policies, and sex-role stereotypes. We also must see harassing conduct as a symptom as well as a cause of broader patterns of gender inequality. The dynamics of male entitlement, dominance, and control that foster harassment also contribute to more serious forms of abuse, such as domestic violence and rape. Only by acknowledging these connections are we likely to deal with the cultural forces that make sexual coercion seem sexy.

Domestic Violence

> The reason I don't believe [you need a protective order] is because I don't believe that anything like this could happen to me. If I was you and someone had threatened me with a gun, there is no way that I would . . . take that kind of abuse from them. Therefore, since I would not let that happen to me, I can't believe that it happened to you.
>
> Maryland trial judge[32]

For many Americans, the O. J. Simpson case challenged deeply ingrained patterns of denial. When the story broke about Nicole Simpson's nine desperate and ultimately ineffectual telephone calls to the police, the public finally heard how battered women are in fact not heard. What for centuries had been a largely private matter at last surfaced as a major public issue.

The statistics are sobering. Domestic violence is the leading cause of injury to women and claims an estimated four million victims each year. Between one-third and one-half of all women are assaulted by a spouse or partner at some point during their lifetime. One-third of all female homicide victims are killed by a husband or boyfriend. The American Medical Association estimates that the cost of domestic violence totals somewhere between $5 billion and $10 billion per year in health care, absences, lost wages, litigation, and incarceration.[33]

These patterns continue because we deny their dimensions, causes, and policy implications. Despite recent improvements, the individuals most responsible for the persistence of domestic violence—batterers and law enforcement officials—still tend to minimize its significance, blame victims for its frequency, and discount their role in its solution. Although initial coverage of the Simpson case did much to focus attention on issues relating to battered women, many Americans tuned out before they ever really tuned in.

The media's recent deluge of data on family violence has set off a countercurrent of cranky denial. Skeptics like Cathy Young, Katherine Dunn, and Christina Hoff Sommers have received widespread coverage for their claims that, once again, "feminist advocacy researchers" are exaggerating the problem. "For starters," critics assert, domestic violence is "nowhere near as extensive" as alarmists maintain. The evidence for this assertion is research indicating that most families are not violent and that much violence is relatively minor. This is a bit like arguing that poverty is nothing to worry about because most of us are not poor and few poor people actually starve. Critics also fail to acknowledge that evidence of the seriousness of domestic abuse comes not just from the feminist fringe. Reports by the American Medical Association, the U.S. surgeon general, and the Department of Justice all document that family violence is the greatest danger to this nation's women.[34]

Yet the "woman" part of the problem is what many commentators are most anxious to deny. Every now and then, another claim emerges suggesting that domestic violence against men is as bad as or worse than violence against women; it's just that battered males don't report abuse or aren't taken seriously when they do. Some of these claims—for example, that "equal" numbers of males and females are killed by a spouse, or that women's violence is more "destructive" than men's—are simply inconsistent with reputable research.[35]

Another common argument, that husbands and wives commit a comparable number of assaults, relies on a widely discredited survey technique. This approach involves asking family members whether they have engaged in particular aggressive acts over the past year. The acts range from pushing to shooting. Yet such surveys conspicuously omit certain abuses that wives almost never commit, such as sexual abuse or stalking. This methodology also excludes inquiries about context and consequences. If you rely only on this approach, you can report that women acknowledge committing about the same number of assaults as men acknowledge committing. However, by even the most conservative estimates, women are about six times more likely than men to suffer serious injuries, and are far more likely to act in self-defense. In cases reaching the criminal justice system, women account for 90 to 95 percent of those brutalized by a partner.[36]

Despite these increasingly well-publicized facts, many Americans still underestimate the seriousness of violence against women. Denial is pervasive among the two groups most responsible for the problem: men who batter and the law enforcement officials who fail to deter it. Virtually every study of male batterers finds that they discount women's injuries even as they describe them:

"I never beat my wife. I responded physically to her."

"Maybe I'd whack her once or twice but I wasn't going to kill her."

"She bruises easily."

"I only pushed her. She just happened to be at the top of the stairs at the time."[37]

Such trivialization of women's injuries was all too apparent in the *Simpson* proceedings. A familiar series of euphemisms surfaced to describe the defendant's history of violence. Simpson himself described his brutal marital assaults as "get[ting] physical." His lawyer, Johnnie Cochran, referred to the beating that led to Simpson's earlier conviction as an "unfortunate incident" and noted that "nobody's perfect." A dismissed juror, Michael Knox, was equally forgiving of the same assault, which he saw as part of the normal "ups and downs with spouses and girlfriends."[38]

Judges often share these views. One consistent finding of some two dozen reports on gender bias in the courts involves the denial and devaluation of domestic violence. In a representative California survey, a majority of male judges agreed that women's allegations of domestic abuse were often exaggerated. Three-fourths of the female judges disagreed. Male judges use many of the same euphemisms as male batterers: the beating was just a "whack"; the woman wasn't really "bruised"; things couldn't have been "as bad as she claims, or she would have left." Even when the severity of the violence is undeniable, such as when the victim is dead, some judges still give a "domestic discount" in sentencing for the crime. From their perspective, abusers look like otherwise normal and upstanding citizens with "unblemished" records, apart from the "unfortunate" or "tragic" incidents at issue. Crimes that in other contexts appear brutal and inhumane seem to matter less when they are "family matters."[39]

Part of the problem is that many male decisionmakers find it easier to identify with a male defendant than with the woman he abuses. Of course, these judges are seldom as candid about their biases as Ronald Kunz. He presided over four separate complaints by Kaina Clark against her former husband, but took action only on the fourth occasion. He then sentenced the defendant to an eight-hour class in anger management. On the day Clark completed the program, he killed himself and his former wife. Judge Kunz stood by his earlier decision and said he would continue to sentence batterers to anger management programs when "appropriate." In a 1995 television interview, the judge explained that he, too, had been through a painful divorce and could sympathize with the husband's hostility and alienation. What Kunz apparently lacked was any ability to sympathize with a battered wife's pain and terror.[40]

Female infidelity also arouses male empathy. In a 1993 New Hampshire case, a husband who brutally assaulted his estranged wife after discovering her with another man received a sentence of twenty-eight days. In a similar decision that same year, an Ohio man with a prior record of murder and rape was sentenced to seven months for battering his wife and daughter with a crowbar. To the New Hampshire judge, the defendant's conduct seemed understandable for an "average man."

To the Ohio court, the defendant's reaction looked natural "if he's any kind of man."[41]

Even when the charge is murder, judges have been known to take the same view. Following one publicized 1994 homicide, the court imposed only an eighteen-month sentence, on the grounds that the husband's reaction was normal and his conduct was unlikely to recur: "I seriously wonder," said the judge, "how many married men . . . would have the strength to walk away without inflicting some corporal punishment . . . I have no question in my mind that no judge of the circuit will ever see [this defendant] again." What every other judge *will* continue to see, however, are similar offenders: men who view their own violence as equally understandable and unlikely to result in serious sanctions.[42]

Underlying all these decisions is a callousness that compounds women's injuries. State commissions on gender bias cite countless examples, such as the Florida judge who heard testimony about a wife doused with lighter fluid and set on fire. This account moved the judge to sing "you light up my wife," to the tune of "You Light Up My Life."[43]

In an article aptly titled "There's No Accounting for Judges," Lynn Schafran of the NOW Legal Defense Fund points out that accountability is lacking in two senses. First, some judicial conduct just seems inexplicably insensitive. Second, formal sanctions for such judicial conduct are extremely rare. In the exceptional case that attracts public notice, some Americans react with outrage and call for the judge's resignation. But seldom are they successful. Moreover, our tendency is to view such proceedings as aberrant and idiosyncratic, rather than reflective of broader institutional failures.[44]

For example, in a highly publicized 1996 case involving New York judge Lorin Duckman, leading politicians demanded not structural reform but impeachment. At issue was Duckman's bail reduction for a man who had assaulted and threatened his former girlfriend, Galina Komar, and then killed her after his release from prison. What ensured the case's notoriety was the judge's prior history of callousness toward domestic-violence victims in general, and Komar in particular. As Duckman emphasized, she had severe bruises but "no broken bones" and no permanent "disfigurement." Yet the problem was not simply this judge's insensitivity; it was the statutory scheme that prevented prosecuting domestic violence as a felony in the absence of such severe injuries. New York, like many states, treats these assaults as misdemeanors, even when coupled with an abuser's threats of murder and prior felony record. For defendants facing such charges, minimal bail is the rule, not the exception. To prevent tragedies like Komar's, we need to reform the statutory structure, not simply remove a single judge.[45]

Other law enforcement practices also need to change. Despite recent improvements, too many police officers and prosecutors still see domestic "incidents" as diversions from their "real" criminal work. Violence against women of color, particularly those in poor communities, often remains a low priority. Even officials who would like to invest more resources in domestic violence see little point when others in the system are unwilling to do the same. Police blame prosecutors, prosecutors blame judges, and everyone blames battered women. Why should an officer make an arrest in a case that won't be pursued? Why should prosecutors go forward with complaints when the judge won't impose a significant sanction or the woman may not testify? And why should women risk the physical retaliation and financial hardship of filing a complaint if no one is taking them seriously?[46]

The result of this self-perpetuating cycle is that an estimated 90 percent of domestic assaults and a majority of domestic-violence arrests never result in prosecution. Two-thirds of battering complaints are classified as simple misdemeanors, even though most involve serious injuries. In recently surveyed cities, fewer than 10 percent of men arrested for domestic assault serve any jail time.[47]

This trivialization of women's injuries is not lost on women themselves, who often have other reasons to discount abuse. Many of these individuals depend on their batterers for economic support, social identity, and emotional attachment. According to some recent estimates, women who leave an abusive relationship have a 50 percent likelihood of some period of poverty, and account for half of all homeless women. Even where severe economic hardship is not an issue, many individuals have difficulty acknowledging the violence in their relationships, especially in cases where the man later appears loving and promises to change.[48]

Certain stereotypes associated with battered women—passivity, helplessness, and disfiguring injuries—also encourage individuals to deny or discount their own vulnerability. Many women who actively resist violence also resist labeling themselves as victims and their partners as batterers. The pressures for denial are particularly great for certain groups. Some racial and ethnic communities have ties to cultures where private violence is rarely a matter for public intervention. Immigrant women often lack information and language skills, fear contact with American governmental agencies, and risk shame, isolation, and retaliation if they make formal complaints. Many elderly and disabled women are physically as well as emotionally and economically dependent on an abusive caregiver, and their batterers' awareness of that vulnerability increases the risk of assault. So too, lesbians often are reluctant to risk the homophobia and the lack of gay-community support that may follow disclosure of a violent same-sex relationship. Such concerns help account for the gross underreporting of domestic assault; most surveys estimate that well over 90 percent of battering incidents never reach police attention.[49]

Not only do many Americans deny the seriousness of domestic violence; they also discount males' responsibility for causing it. Sometimes these denials vanish in the subtleties of syntax. The passive voice keeps abusive men out of sight and out of mind. Women are victimized by "cycles of violence," threatened by "aggressive behavior," and trapped in "dysfunctional families." In emergency-room records, female patients are ambushed by abstraction. They are "hit on the left wrist by a jackhammer," or are "beaten in the face with a fist." In one representative survey, four-fifths of medical case files suggesting risks of abuse included no information about the assailant.[50]

Batterers are especially likely to relocate responsibility for their violence. Abusive men blame alcohol, drugs, and most often their victims. Husbands claim that they don't "want to get violent." It's just that "booze" causes their "temporary insanity," or that wives "provoke" assaults with their "lousy meals," "rotten sex," constant "nagging," or interest in other men. As one aggrieved batterer explained, "I was just trying to motivate her. And she didn't seem too motivated." O. J. Simpson's *I Want to Tell You: My Response to Your Letters, Your Messages* offers a representative sampling of the "mental abuse" and "tortures" that allegedly provoke physical responses by long-suffering men.[51]

Of course, male batterers are not the only people who blame battered women. So do police, prosecutors, judges, and the rest of us. While we agree in principle that it is wrong for men to beat women, we make allowances in practice for men who do. Common descriptions of battered women include "cold," "emasculating," "provocative," "self-destructive," and "dependent." To many Americans, Nicole Simpson was a spoiled "rich bitch" who chose an "easy life" but didn't want to pay for it. Battering relationships are "sadomasochistic on *both* sides" announces Camille Paglia, without benefit of supporting authority.[52]

Such attitudes persist in part because they allow most Americans to distance themselves from the problem and to maintain their belief in a just world. If battered women share responsibility for their abuse, then the rest of us don't have to worry. Women can assume that "this won't happen to me"; men can assume that "it isn't our fault." It is also simpler to blame women than to question the conflicting signals that women receive. Friends, family, clergy, and the media remind us that marriages require work, that good men are hard to find, that children need a father, that welfare dependency reflects personal failure, and that "for better or worse" means what it says. We tell wives to stay married and then damn them for trying. As one African American woman notes, "I put up with violence all those years trying *not* to be the welfare mother white folks hate, and then those same white folks . . . tell me I should have left my husband." Other women caught in similar double binds blame only themselves. Our questions become their questions. Why can't they avoid provoking the violence? Why don't they just leave?[53]

The way we frame these questions is itself part of the problem. If we want to know why more women don't leave, we should first ask whether they have somewhere safe to go. The answers are not encouraging. Half of all interspousal homicides and most serious injuries occur after the victim does in fact leave. As experts like Martha Mahoney note, men's fear of abandonment is one of the most common motivations for violence. Although individuals at risk of abuse are entitled to protective orders, most of these mandates are violated and violators are seldom prosecuted. In some states, such safeguards are not even available for same-sex partners.[54]

Moreover, shelters and related social services for battered women are chronically underfunded. Despite recent progress, including modest federal subsidies authorized in the 1994 Violence Against Women Act, we are nowhere close to providing adequate assistance. About half of all counties have no formal resources for battered women. This nation provides only a small part of necessary housing, childcare, legal aid, and related assistance. We offer least to those who need help most: low-income, poor, nonwhite, elderly, disabled, and immigrant women.[55]

What traps many women in violent relationships is not only the inadequacy of law enforcement and societal assistance but also their own adaptations to abuse. Since the 1970s, a growing body of research has developed to explain this "battered-women syndrome." According to prominent theorists like Lenore Walker, victims often internalize blame for violence that they cannot prevent. After cycles of these beatings, many women come to perceive themselves as helpless. The perceptions ultimately "become reality and [victims] become passive, submissive, and helpless."[56]

Reliance on this "learned helplessness" model has, however, been of mixed value. The greatest beneficiaries have been women accused of killing an abusive partner. In these cases, expert testimony sometimes helps establish claims of self-defense by explaining the factors that prevent women from escaping abusive relationships and that justify their use of force. Such explanations also have educated judges, police officers, and the public more generally about the disabling effects of domestic violence.

Yet these gains have come at considerable cost. Part of their price is to fuel claims that women want a double standard. According to men's-rights advocates, feminists argue that "'there's never an excuse for violence against women.' Now they [are] saying 'but there's always an excuse for violence against men.'" The battered-women's syndrome reportedly turns a "dangerous personality pattern into a legal defense." It "enables a woman to kill her sleeping husband and claim self-defense because she felt helpless." In fact, however, only a tiny fraction of abused women—fewer than one in 100,000—kill their abuser, and those who do frequently face an imminent threat. Even these women seldom escape punishment; most simply receive somewhat reduced charges or sentences. But the view persists that women killers are not treated as killers.[57]

A further problem with the battered-woman defense is that it excludes those who do not fit its narrow model of helplessness. Because the prevailing stereotype of African American women does not conform to an image of passivity, they often do not benefit from this defense. So too, the suggestion that the "normal" response to abuse is a dysfunctional, passive one obscures the strategies of resistance and survival that most women adopt. Large-scale studies find, for example, that a majority of abused women do seek protection. Almost half are able to prevent further violence without ending the relationship. When other women stay with abusive partners, it is generally because they lack an alternative. They doubt their ability to support themselves and their children, and they fear retaliation against themselves or other family members.[58]

"Learned helplessness" is a term less descriptive of the typical battered woman than of the "helping" professions that have responded so inadequately to her needs. Professionals in law, medicine, politics, and social services have directed too much attention to *her* responses, not *his* abuses; to *her* psychological "dysfunction," not *our* societal failures.

Even those who avoid blaming victims also avoid blaming themselves. Implicitly if not explicitly, most Americans deny that they bear any responsibility for society's failures in addressing domestic violence. Such denials emerge most clearly when law enforcement officials explain why women who have "done the right thing" still end up in the wrong place—battered or dead. Recent research documents hundreds of cases in which a woman "did call the police, did get an order of protection . . ., did leave home," and did not survive.[59]

Yet law enforcement officials typically present these cases as inevitable tragedies, not preventable homicides. One notorious example involves Pam Guenther, whose husband repeatedly assaulted, stalked, and threatened her after she left him. He was arrested following one incident in which he held her hostage for five hours. He said he was sorry, and the investigating officer believed him. As it turns out, Guenther wasn't. His primary project after release on bail was to murder his wife. But those involved in the criminal justice process denied that they were at all responsible. The district attorney, who had neither charged the husband with a serious offense nor protested his release, stated: "I didn't feel the system let Pam Guenther down. I'm not sure any domestic-violence policy would have prevented her death."[60]

In similar cases, including the New York bail decision by Judge Duckman, leaders of the bench and bar let one another off the hook. "There's just no way of foreseeing the outcome" or "predicting a tragedy," they assured us. And the criminal justice system simply "may not be the best place to resolve marital problems of this sort." But for many women, it's all they've got. Unless we take the view, recently expressed by a National Rifle Association member on a National Public Radio talk show, that self-help is the answer: "Wimpy women should stop whining about abuse and instead just blow the guy away and save taxpayers a pile of money."[61]

A reasonable alternative is for the State to do more to safeguard victims and deter abuse. Criminal sanctions for battering need to be far more certain and severe. Mandatory arrest for domestic violence can be part of the answer, but only if coupled with other measures to assist victims. About half of all states now require police officers to arrest offenders in at least some category of domestic-violence cases, irrespective of the victim's preferences or the officers' own assessments. Although research on the effectiveness of such requirements is mixed and incomplete, most evidence suggests that a mandatory policy reduces further assaults among some offenders: those who are white, employed, married, and high school graduates. However, arrest policies that are not coupled with other protective measures and support services for victims may escalate abuse among other batterers, such as unemployed high school dropouts who have less to fear from a criminal record. Related problems are that officers arrest women who act in self-defense, and that women's fear of shame and retaliation following arrest discourages them from calling the police in the first instance.[62]

On balance, however, most advocates for battered women believe that the response to these problems is to improve, not restrict, law enforcement efforts. Mandatory arrest should be part of a coordinated community strategy that also provides more shelters, support services, legal aid, and physical protection for battered women.[63]

We also need better ways to deal with abusive men, as well as more research on what strategies of prevention, treatment, and sanctions are most effective. For some offenders, whose aggression is relatively minor and infrequent, extended prison sentences are more costly and less useful than alternatives that will deal with underlying problems. For this group, the threat of incarceration can supply the necessary incentive to complete marital counseling, mental health treatment, or substance abuse programs. Men batter because it works. At least in the short run, it enables them to get their way. Well-designed treatment and a meaningful threat of sanctions can reverse those incentives; it can make clear that domestic abuse is an unacceptable means of venting frustration or exercising control.[64]

Among other offenders, domestic abuse is part of a longer and more serious pattern of violence, and extended incarceration should play a larger part in our response. Many of these individuals have prior records of assaultive behavior outside as well as within the family, and some have psychopathic personalities. Diversion of these offenders into counseling programs generally has proven ineffective. It can also be dangerous for victims, who are led to believe that they are safe and that their partners will change.[65]

Our criminal justice system needs policies that better distinguish between these categories of offenders. It must also become more effective in evaluating diversion programs, imposing significant sanctions for repeated abuse, and withholding bail in circumstances presenting a high risk of violence. To that end, education at more than token levels is essential for judges, prosecutors, and law enforcement agents.[66]

Further education is also necessary for health, counseling, and social work professionals, as well as for the general public. Schools at all levels should incorporate antiviolence materials into their curricula. Professionals who will most often encounter family violence need better training in how to recognize and respond to abusive patterns. Additional outreach efforts and expert staff are also crucial for those with distinctive needs, such as lesbian, disabled, and immigrant women.[67]

Most important, we need greater oversight and accountability. Our most pressing challenges are not with the substance of law but with its enforcement. Arrest policies that are mandatory in form are often undermined in practice by police officers who resist compliance, or courts that grant immediate bail even to repeat offenders. Protective orders that are available in theory often become ineffectual in fact because women lack adequate legal or police assistance. Penalty provisions that look adequate on paper are circumvented in practice by judges and prosecutors who do not take family violence seriously. G. K. Chesterton once suggested that the problem with many enforcement officials is not that they are "wicked" or "stupid," but just that they have "gotten used to it." To change such attitudes, we need more effective monitoring strategies.[68]

Some women's organizations, for example, have established Court Watch programs to evaluate trial judges' responses to domestic abuse. The Violence Against Women Act authorizes modest federal funding for model community projects that develop, coordinate, and evaluate violence intervention strategies. Although these are useful first steps, the real test is whether we will demand and pay for progress on the scale that is truly necessary.[69]

Over the past quarter-century, America has made considerable strides in responding to domestic violence. We have turned a social problem into a social movement. We are finally starting to see the extent of women's injuries. But many of us still are denying our responsibility to prevent them.

Rape

By even the most conservative estimates, the United States has the highest rate of reported rape in the Western industrial world. According to government and crime center research, between two-thirds and four-fifths of these rapes involve acquaintances. But the problem of "date rape" is commonly dismissed as the "mass psychosis" of feminist fanatics. Well-publicized books and leading media accounts condemn "rape hype" and "rape hysteria." And child sexual abuse, which experts estimate affects 13 to 23 percent of American girls, evokes equally widespread disbelief.[70]

With no apparent sense of irony, critics often caricature antirape activists in far more extremist rhetoric than that used by the activists themselves. To commentators like Katie Roiphe, Camille Paglia, Mary Matalin, John Leo, and Neil Gilbert, "delusional" "yuppie feminist[s]" with "simpering prom-queen" sensibilities and "neopuritan preoccupation[s]" are determined to "transform the act of seduction into the crime of rape." In the process, these antirape activists supposedly exaggerate dangers, entrench sexist stereotypes, trivialize real rape, and erode female responsibility. By casting all women as "powerless, innocent victims" and all men as "overpowering, sex-crazed barbarians," feminists reportedly are resurrecting mid-Victorian prejudices that work against gender equality.[71]

What is most telling about the 1990s rape hype controversy is not that it offers new and persuasive insights, but rather that it builds so successfully on old and unfounded prejudices. Traditional understandings of rape reflect a pronounced sexual schizophrenia. For centuries, one form of assault—intercourse forced by a stranger on a chaste white woman—has been treated as the archetypal antisocial crime. By contrast, coercive sex that has departed from this paradigm frequently has been denied or discounted. The attitude, well captured by a popular army slogan, has been that "it never happened, and what's more [she] deserved it." Despite two decades of educational and law reform efforts, these attitudes remain resilient. As legal scholar Susan Estrich notes, most Americans continue to believe the standard stories about what "real rape" is and isn't. These beliefs, as they play out in bedrooms, locker rooms, and courtrooms, account for much of America's difficulty in combating sexual assault. Our principal problem is not that we exaggerate the problem and demonize men, but that we so often deny the problem and blame women.[72]

The most common strategy of denial starts from the common assumption that "normal" men don't rape; "barbarians" do. "Nice girls" aren't assaulted; "loose" and "careless" women are. Much, however, depends on how we define "normal" and what we consider an assault.[73]

Under most criminal statutes, rape involves sexual penetration against a person's consent through the use of force or threat of bodily harm, or through incapacitation. By that definition, the most comprehensive studies find that between 12 and 25 percent of women have experienced rape and another 12 to 20 percent have experienced attempted rape. The vast majority of these assaults, including over 85 percent of completed rapes, are not reported to the police. Women of color are most likely to be victimized, and least likely to make a formal complaint.[74]

Contrary to popular assumptions, most rapes do not involve strangers, weapons, or sexually deviant offenders. Moreover, virtually every study of "normal" college-age men has found that substantial numbers, typically around one-third, acknowledge that they would commit rape if they could be sure of not being caught. About half would force a woman to have sex if they could get away with it, although apparently they do not consider this rape. A majority of surveyed men report engaging in some sexually coercive behaviors, and 10 to 15 percent admit having forced sex on a date.[75]

The point is not what critics caricature as *the* feminist position—that "all men are rapists." It is rather that many Americans view some degree of sexual coercion as "normal" and that many "normal" individuals find it erotic. This perception helps account for the unwillingness on the part of both men and women (80 percent and 75 percent in one representative survey) to label forced sex between acquaintances as rape.[76]

To alter those attitudes, we need to address both the individual motivations and societal structures that encourage rape. Profiles of rapists indicate that many are primarily attracted to power; they want the feeling of domination, adventure, and self-esteem that comes from coercive sex. Other men emphasize anger; rape is a means to punish or avenge some wrong by a particular woman, women in general, or another adversary. Most rapists blame their victims, and some stress situational influences such as peer pressure or drug and alcohol abuse. Exposure to family violence during childhood increases the likelihood that men will engage in sexually violent activities as adults.[77]

Of course, these explanations provide only part of the story. An equally critical question is why so many men in America, but not in all societies, channel their desires for power, revenge, and peer approval into sexual assaults. The answer has much to do with the longstanding family, media, and law enforcement influences that reinforce or fail to restrain male aggression.[78]

Such influences underpin many Americans' refusal to hold men accountable for coercive sex in dating contexts. In celebrated cases like the Los Angeles Spur Posse, where male high school students were awarded points for sexual conquests, voluntary or not, parents defended their sons as "all men" and "virile specimens." Similarly, in a gang rape case in Glen Ridge, New Jersey, the defense attorney shrugged off evidence indicating that the defendants had sexually assaulted a retarded girl with a baseball bat. According to the lawyer, the defendants were just "pranksters" responding to "basic boyish needs." And after all, "boys will be boys."[79]

Judges and juries frequently share these views, together with the assumption that attractive males don't need to rape. The trial of William Kennedy Smith highlighted attitudes that leading prosecutors like Linda Fairstein repeatedly encounter. After Smith's acquittal, juror Lea Haller told the media: "I think he's too charming and too good-looking to have to resort to violence for a night out." In fact, research on rapists consistently shows that few men "need" to rape. The vast majority are involved in consensual intimate relationships and are more sexually active than the average male. Rape is not about sexual deprivation; it is about domination.[80]

A further way of denying the problem is to discount the injuries that follow from it. A common, although not always explicit, assumption is that forced sex is not all that harmful if the parties know each other and if no other injuries result. Some male politicians and athletic coaches have captured widespread views with the quip that "if rape is inevitable," women should just "relax and enjoy it." According to one Missouri mayor, "the only difference between rape and seduction is salesmanship." Referring to conduct that a jury later found to be rape, Michael Tyson defended himself by saying that, after all, "I didn't hurt anyone—no black eyes, no broken bones."[81]

The Tyson case was, however, exceptional. Prosecutors usually are unwilling to file date rape charges in the absence of other physical injury; they assume (with good reason) that to most juries, if "there aren't bruises . . . then it isn't rape." In one representative case, the lawyer for three college basketball players successfully rebutted gang rape charges on the grounds that the woman had no other injuries; indeed, her "hair was not [even] messed up." Many judges hold similar views. In explaining his light sentence for a rapist, a Massachusetts trial court noted, "It's not like [the victim] was tortured or chopped up." And in the case of a man convicted of forcibly sodomizing a retarded woman, a Manhattan judge justified leniency "on the ground that there was no violence here."[82]

Such attitudes help explain the relatively light penalties that follow most complaints of sexual assault. Eighty-five percent of reported rapes end up with no convictions, and almost 90 percent result in no incarceration. About half of convicted rapists receive probation or jail sentences of less than one year. In theory, our criminal justice system treats rape as one of the most serious offenses. In practice, we reserve such treatment for a small category of "real rapes," usually those involving violence, strangers, and white complainants. A Texas study illustrates the extent of racial biases. It found that the median sentence for a black man who raped a white woman was nineteen years; for a white man who raped a white woman, it was five years.[83]

Cases involving youthful offenders and acquaintances, even gang rapes, seldom result in serious sanctions. In one 1993 case, defendants convicted of "sexual misconduct" for raping a woman who had passed out in a bar were sentenced to pay a $750 fine and complete 250 hours of community service. Yet when law enforcement officials treat criminal conduct as "youthful indiscretions," they discourage victim reports and perpetuate the attitudes that perpetuate the problem. In the brutal Glen Ridge rape of a retarded girl, many trial observers and jurors expressed shock that the convicted defendants would serve less than two years in juvenile facilities. But as some experts noted, what *should* shock people is that such sentences are close to the national average.[84]

The trivialization of women's injuries in these cases rests on deep-seated cultural attitudes. To many Americans, date rape is little more than bad sex. As Camille Paglia puts it, when feminist "rape ranters" are unable to distinguish the "drunken fraternity brother from the homicidal maniac, women are in trouble." When critics like Paglia document these legions of "ranters," we should start to worry. Until then, we should share the concern of virtually all respected researchers in the field. They find that fraternity rape is a serious problem and that it often involves brutal premeditated assaults, not sexual "miscommunication" or consensual intimacy that goes "a little too far."[85]

Of course, many women do experience what another critic derisively labels "icky sex"; it happens when their partner was "clumsy," they let him "get carried away," they wanted to "avoid a hassle," and so forth. But critics' further claims that these women "feel that they have been raped" runs counter to virtually all recent research. Although there may be some ambiguity at the boundaries, few individuals appear unable to distinguish between a bad choice and no choice at all. The vast majority of surveyed women are reluctant to label forced sex rape if it involves acquaintances, even when it meets the statutory definition.[86]

The common assumption that date rapes or "nonviolent" rapes do not involve serious injury is similarly inconsistent with the evidence. Research from the Department of Justice and the National Crime Center indicates that although most rapes do not involve physical injury apart from the assault itself, they often produce debilitating and enduring psychological trauma. Rape by an acquaintance is no less harmful than other assaults, because it calls into question a woman's behavior, judgment, and sense of trust in ways that random acts by strangers do not.[87]

Many individuals also overlook the way that fear of rape reinforces broader structures of inequality. According to Roiphe, "considering how many things there are to be afraid of and how many are not fair, being frightened to walk around [a college campus] . . . late at night does not seem like one of God's greatest injustices." If the comparison is battle sites in Bosnia or gang warfare zones in urban ghettos, she is undoubtedly right. But why should these be the relevant comparisons? Why are we so judgmental about the women who want to feel safe, instead of about the men who make it impossible? Golda Meir made a similar point when, during her term as Israeli prime minister, a cabinet official proposed a curfew for women. Meir responded, "But it's the men who are attacking . . . If there's to be a curfew, let the men stay home, not the women."[88]

It is fair to complain, as do other critics, that a disproportionate amount of tax dollars for rape services go to college campuses, rather than to low-income communities with more assaults. But it does not follow that the solution is less money and less concern about the campuses. Among American women under thirty-five, rape provokes more fear than any other crime, including murder or robbery. That was true long before any alleged feminist fanaticism set in. Sexual assault is unique in its capacity for terror, degradation, shame, and recurring trauma. Until this registers more fully in the national consciousness, boys will go on being boys, and girls will pay the price.[89]

Part of that price is to be victimized twice—first by an assault and then by the disbelief, blame, and stigma that usually come when the victim reports it. In rape, as in cases of sexual harassment, one enduring public fantasy is that many rape charges are themselves fantasies—that "women do lie." Many individuals share John Leo's view that complainants' guilt, vindictiveness, or desire for retaliation lead to the "retroactive labeling of an unhappy sexual encounter as rape." "Hell hath no fury like a woman scorned," was one juror's explanation for acquitting three St. John's fraternity brothers after a widely publicized gang rape prosecution.[90]

How often such fury inclines women to undergo the humiliation of a rape trial is another matter. Peggy Sanday's in-depth account of evidence in the St. John case, including confessions and eyewitness testimony by some participants, leaves little doubt of who was lying. Even commentators most skeptical of date rape claims had difficulties with the St. John's result, which involved acquittals for three defendants and probation and community service for the other two. As John Leo asks, "How likely is it that a conservative, middle-class woman, virtually allergic to alcohol, disdainful of premarital sex and facing an important exam the next morning, would voluntarily get drunk and enjoy several hours of oral sex with five or six strangers?"[91]

Americans' skepticism about rape complaints, reflected in verdicts like St. John's, is fueled by a small number of highly publicized and admittedly horrendous incidents. In these cases, either the complainant publicly recants, or other evidence reveals that her claim was fabricated. Southern lynch mob proceedings against black men accused of raping white women are the most abhorrent examples. In contemporary American society, however, such demonstrably fraudulent claims are rare, despite their continued popularity on television serials.

To conclude that rape complainants often lie requires a further leap of faith, like the one that Harvard Law professor Alan Dershowitz makes in *The Abuse Excuse*. He claims that rape is not only the most underreported but also "the most overreported serious crime in America." According to Dershowitz, FBI crime statistics show that "8.4 percent of all reported rapes turn out to be 'unfounded.' That percentage translates into more than 8,000 false rape reports each year."[92]

There are two problems with such arguments. First, "unfounded" does not mean "false"; it means that police or prosecutors believe that they lack sufficient evidence to file charges. For intimate acts like rape, which generally do not occur in the presence of witnesses, problems of proof often appear insurmountable even for meritorious claims. That is particularly the case when police and prosecutors are skeptical of complaints brought by acquaintances. Second, Dershowitz provides no support for his assertion about crime statistics. Yet the overwhelming consensus in other research relying on government data is that false reports account for only about 2 percent of rape complaints, which is no higher than for other offenses.[93]

Nor do profiles of rape complainants find substantial incentives to lie. The psychological costs of prosecuting a case are usually quite high, given Americans' tendency to hold complainants responsible for their own assaults. The "tight skirt, loose morals" defense is often effective with jurors, judges, and the general public. Conviction rates in acquaintance rape cases are disproportionately low; some studies find that defendants who claim consent are three or four times as likely to be acquitted as those raising other defenses to sexual assault. As such studies also indicate, jurors' perception of the "moral character" of the complainant is more important than any other factor in determining outcomes.[94]

What the public considers relevant in assessing morality is also part of the problem. If "rape hype" critics are concerned about "neo-Puritan" attitudes, their focus should be less on feminists and more on the 30 to 50 percent of surveyed Americans who believe that women are to blame for rape if they dress provocatively. To many judges and jurors, women who go braless or wear a miniskirt may have "asked for it." They are "advertising for sex."[95]

Women also "ask for it" by "leading men on." Here again, what constitutes such behavior is quite expansive. Examples in reported cases include going to a singles bar, accompanying a man to his home, hotel, or dormitory room, engaging in "sexually provocative" behavior earlier in the day, or kissing a man in an automobile. As Ann Landers has been warning readers for years, "a woman who puts out and doesn't want to complete the sex act is asking for trouble and she will probably get it." That view helps explain the infrequency of rape reports and convictions in cases involving acquaintances. Victims can anticipate reactions like that of a Maryland Supreme Court justice in a leading case: "When an adult woman goes to a man's room, [she] certainly ha[s] to realize that they [are] not going upstairs to play Scrabble." But what more judges also have to realize is that Scrabble and rape are not the only alternatives.[96]

We have, of course, made some recent progress on this front. Rape shield statutes now protect women from routine grilling in open court about all their sexual history. But such evidence still is sometimes admissible under statutory exceptions, such as where it might show a pattern of conduct or where a judge determines that it is more probative than prejudicial. As one district attorney put it, "'Trash the victim' is the only real form of defense in a rape trial, no matter what the law says."[97]

Moreover, even when courts exclude explicit testimony about complainants' sexual history from trial proceedings, such information can sneak in by implication, or leak out to the wider public through press reports and pretrial records. Followers of the William Kennedy Smith prosecution did not lack for details about the woman who unsuccessfully charged him with rape. Her name, her traffic violations, her out-of-wedlock child, her mother's social climbing, her mediocre high school grades, and her reputation as having a "wild streak" all received widespread coverage. At trial, defense counsel was able to raise questions about the complainant's morality through indirect methods. Jurors got to pass around her Victoria's Secret underwear, ostensibly to check for tears. They also got to hear how she abandoned her child to go bar hopping. What jurors didn't get to hear was the testimony of three other women who also reported that Smith had assaulted or raped them on dates. This evidence was "too prejudicial" for admission.[98]

Women of color have been particularly victimized by rape proceedings. Their complaints are statistically less likely than a white woman's to result in prosecution, conviction, or serious sentences. They also run special risks when their assailant is a prominent man of color—a politician, athlete, entertainer, or community leader. Desiree Washington, the complainant in the Tyson case, was painted as a gold digger who needlessly destroyed a revered role model for sexual conduct that she had invited. More than two-thirds of African Americans believed that Tyson had been unfairly convicted. Similarly, a black woman who unsuccessfully brought charges against popular black college basketball players was lambasted as a "frisky" lesbian whose charges inflamed racist stereotypes.[99]

Complainants' conduct or reputation can also affect the defendant's sentence. Examples are endless. A Baltimore man who raped his employee after she passed out from drinking got probation on the theory that her unconscious condition "facilitated the rape." And the Manhattan defendant who sodomized a retarded woman got a reduced sentence because she had been raped before and the court assumed that the impact of the defendant's assault therefore was "considerably less" severe.[100]

Such decisions speak volumes not only about judges' insensitivity, but also about their ignorance concerning sexual abuse. Experts in the field know that women who are victimized more than once have the most pain and the most difficulty recovering. Contrary to courts' views, a second assault usually has greater impact than the first because victims often relive earlier rapes and end up with an even greater sense of guilt and vulnerability. In sexual-assault cases involving drugs or alcohol, judges' double standards are hard to miss: intoxication makes men seem less culpable and women more so.[101]

As with other forms of sexual abuse, our tendency to demean and devalue complainants serves deeper needs. By assuming victims are at fault, "nice" women can minimize their own fears. So can "normal" men, since the chance that any sexual assaults will end in a formal complaint, let alone conviction, remains quite low. But the price of reducing our fears is to perpetuate the problem that creates them.

What ultimately is most troubling about recent rape debates is their highly selective focus. In the mainstream media, we hear mostly about how women cause, exaggerate, or fail to prevent the problem. Many discussions seem to lose sight of the fact that it is overwhelmingly men who rape and men who need to stop. Only by addressing these broader cultural patterns are we likely to make life safer for women.

For that effort to be successful, we must start much sooner. At early ages, children begin absorbing society's traditional assumptions about the legitimacy of male aggression and the illegitimacy of female sexual expression. By ages twelve to fourteen, large percentages of both boys and girls agree that forced sex is legitimate under certain circumstances, such as:

when the boy spends a lot of money on the girl (39 percent of males and 12 percent of females);

when a couple has dated a long time (43 percent of males and 32 percent of females);

when the girl leads the boy on (54 percent of males and 31 percent of females).[102]

Older adolescents have similar views, as well as double standards for evaluating males' and females' sexual conduct. The traditional labeling of boys as "studs" and girls as "sluts" not only inhibits female sexuality, but also encourages sexual miscommunication. In one study, almost a third of college women admitted having said no when they didn't mean it, in part because they didn't want to appear promiscuous. As long as women feel pressure to fake resistance, men will feel entitled to disregard it, and the dangers of unjust accusations and coercive sex will persist.[103]

To change these patterns, educational programs should begin in elementary school and continue throughout college. Special initiatives also should target groups that account for a disproportionate number of assaults, such as college athletes and fraternity members. We also need more research on what programs are most effective. It is scarcely an affirmation of current approaches when interviewed students are clueless about realistic strategies for reducing their risk of rape. Recent suggestions include "never be alone with a boy"; "bring a gun on a date."[104]

Changes in our criminal justice system are equally critical. For example, although states have removed requirements that the complainant physically resist her assailant in order to prove nonconsent, prosecutors, judges, and juries continue to demand such evidence. Rape shield statutes have reduced intrusive questioning of complainants, but have been compromised by insensitive judicial interpretations and media reports. Heightened penalty provisions have made no difference where prosecutors and judges are unwilling to invoke them. Legal reform requires not simply doctrinal changes, but also education of law enforcement officials and sustained monitoring of their decisionmaking.[105]

Substantial progress will also require more substantial resource commitments. We urgently need increased funding for rape crisis programs and research on treatment and prevention. Community outreach efforts must also target racial and ethnic minorities who have been especially ill-served by the criminal justice system. The stakes in this agenda are considerable, not only for the appalling numbers of American women who experience rape, but for the still greater number who fear it and who structure their lives to avoid it.[106]

Pornography: Sex, Censorship, and Subordination

Americans face no shortage of speech about sex, especially pornographic sex. Although we may not have the world's largest pornography industry, we undoubtedly have the largest concentration of people talking about pornography regulation. Yet like other issues of gender inequality, there remains widespread denial about both the extent of the problem and the complex tradeoffs involved in regulating it.

A threshold controversy concerns whether we even have a problem and whether "pornography" is a meaningful term to describe it. Under conventional dictionary definitions, pornography is sexual expression that is designed to cause arousal. Under contemporary feminists' definitions, the term usually refers to sexually explicit material that subordinates women. To some of these feminists, such material is a primary cause of gender inequality and should be a primary target of regulatory initiatives. By contrast, other feminists, as well as civil liberties leaders, view both definitions of pornography as far too ambiguous and inclusive to serve as the basis for government regulation. From their perspective, censoring material that some women might find subordinating would compound a sexist double standard of morality that the women's movement should be attempting to eliminate.

Beginning in the 1980s, this controversy among feminists became increasingly personal and polemical. By substituting invective for analysis, many activists ended up talking past one another, as well as past an increasingly confused public. In a debate where participants caricature opponents as "hysterical" neo-Puritans or as porn "collaborators," less strident voices can scarcely be heard. And now that the warring factions are typed as antisex and pro-porn, most Americans understandably are reluctant to join either battalion. The result is policy paralysis and political fragmentation.[107]

Underlying this rhetorical crossfire are deep-seated cultural conflicts. Pornography brings out tensions between competing commitments to free speech, "family values," and gender equality. Moreover, of all the contemporary women's-rights issues, sexual expression is the sexiest: descriptions of the pornography "problem" can be almost as titillating as pornography itself. Activists like Andrea Dworkin and Catherine MacKinnon discuss gender inequality in the context of women being "bound, battered, tortured, humiliated . . . hung from a meat hook . . . penetrated by eels and rats and knives and pistols . . . [or] merely taken through every available orifice." This clearly beats discussions of sex discrimination in pension plans. But what gets lost in debates of sexism by soundbite are more complicated questions about the relationships between acts and images, power and pleasure, law and culture.[108]

Our current controversy builds on longstanding difficulties in legal doctrine. Until quite recently, "pornography" was not a term that figured in American law. Legal standards have referred to "obscenity," and they have been vaguely defined and idiosyncratically enforced. At the height of censorship, government authorities prosecuted everything from nudity on playing cards to classics by Tolstoy. Contemporary

Supreme Court doctrine holds that the government can ban material if, under contemporary community standards, the work as a whole appeals to the "prurient interest," depicts sex in a "patently offensive" way, and lacks serious literary, artistic, political, or scientific value.[109]

This obscenity standard is problematic both in theory and in practice. A threshold difficulty is the odd psychological state that judges and juries must reach in order to find a work legally obscene. They must admit that the material is both sexually arousing *and* patently offensive. In effect, decisionmakers must be "turned on and grossed out" at the same time. Since this is a state that few individuals are happy to admit, the threshold standard for censorship is rarely met. Even when it is, the material often is exempt from regulation based on its socially redeeming value.[110]

Moreover, the cost of item-by-item enforcement is far too great to contain a mushrooming industry. Once sexually degrading materials begin to saturate a local market, it becomes increasingly difficult to prove that they are offensive under contemporary community standards. As a consequence, American pornography suppliers have become solidly entrenched, with estimated annual profits exceeding $10 billion. Consumers rent more than 400 million X-rated videos each year, and computer technology is expanding opportunities for interactive sadism. In one of the most popular current games, a female image invites viewers to take off her clothes, gag or shackle her, force her to perform sex with another woman, and have her make noises suggesting sexual pleasure. Bulletin board systems on the Internet also are competing to be "the nastiest place on earth," complete with images of parents forcing children to have sex with animals.[111]

Not only is current obscenity law unable to stem industry growth; it also cannot prevent harassing prosecutions. Law enforcement officials often bring charges that have little chance of prevailing, particularly against works by gay, lesbian, and minority artists. Among the most highly publicized examples have been the prosecutions of Two Live Crew for offensive song lyrics and of the Cleveland Art Museum for showing homoerotic photographs by Robert Mapplethorpe. Many schools, libraries, and arts organizations also have banned or denied funding for "dirty" materials. Frequently suppressed "smut" includes books by William Faulkner, J. D. Salinger, and Alice Walker.[112]

Yet obscenity law misses what many feminists see as the main harm of pornography: the way it portrays women. These feminists focus on misogyny rather than morality; their target is subordination, not prurience. Efforts to push obscenity law in this direction began in the 1980s, when several cities enacted prohibitions that federal courts later ruled unconstitutional. For example, an Indianapolis ordinance defined pornography as the "sexually explicit subordination of women, graphically depicted in words or pictures" that debased women in particular ways. Among the contexts specified were women enjoying pain, rape, or humiliation; women serving as sexual objects for "domination, conquest, exploitation and passion"; and women "appearing in positions of servility or submission." Under this ordinance, private citizens could sue those who trafficked in pornography or coerced participation in its preparation or use. After courts found that such ordinances violated the First Amendment, the battle shifted to Congress. During the early 1990s, debate dealt mainly with statutory regulations governing sex on the Internet and with proposed legislation authorizing damages for individuals who could prove that they were victims of crimes traceable to pornography.[113]

Defenders of free expression, including many feminists, have opposed such legislation, and the controversy has become increasingly polemical. Opponents of pornography often tend to overstate its harms and understate the risks of government regulation. Opponents of such regulation frequently fall into the opposite patterns. And those who acknowledge complexities or propose alternative reform possibilities rarely attract media spotlights.

One central controversy involves the harms associated with pornography. Prevailing views span a broad range:

"Pornography is the theory and rape the practice." (Antipornography slogan popularized by Robin Morgan, feminist author and activist)

"There are many factors that play a causal role in [rape] . . . but . . . the overwhelming evidence [is] that pornography is a major one of them." (Diana Russell, sociologist; author of prominent studies on rape)

"Numerous academic and governmental surveys [have] . . . rejected the purported link between sexual expression and aggression." (Nadine Strossen, law professor and president of the American Civil Liberties Union)

"The only thing pornography is known to cause directly is the solitary act of masturbation. As for corruption, the only immediate victim is English prose." (Gore Vidal, author)[114]

The harms that feminists associate with pornography are not the ones that lawmakers traditionally associate with obscenity: the corruption of morals, the offense to public sensibilities, and the erosion of family values. Rather, what many feminists stress are injuries to women both as individuals and as a group. According to these feminists, pornography eroticizes inequality. It degrades, dehumanizes, and objectifies women, legitimates men's brutality, and perpetuates racist stereotypes.

The most obvious harms involve models who are coerced and abused in the creation of pornographic material. In theory, these individuals have remedies under existing criminal and civil law; in practice, such remedies are almost never available. Rarely do women want to compound their injuries by initiating litigation that usually involves considerable financial costs, personal humiliation, fear of retaliation, and difficulties of proof. Yet while it is clear that some models have experienced barbaric treatment, it is less clear how often this happens, and what would effectively prevent it. We lack any systematic research on the frequency of exploitation, and many sex workers claim that it is not a widespread problem. Nor is it obvious that bans on pornography would lessen the risk. As America's history with alcohol prohibition indicates, forcing a highly profitable industry underground is unlikely to protect participants. Even with laws like the Indianapolis ordinance, victims would confront most of the same deterrents to reporting abuse that make current legal provisions so ineffectual.[115]

A second category of harms involves the use of pornography as a blueprint for sexual violence and degradation. The testimony of injured victims, particularly when coupled with police reports and psychiatric records, leaves no doubt about the brutality that pornographic materials sometimes inspire. But again, the difficulty is that we have no gauge of frequency. Nor do we know whether pornography actually *causes* abuse, or only influences its form. Even if we could link sexual violence to certain pornographic works, suppression would not necessarily be an appropriate response. "Copycat" crimes are common, and pornography is by no means the only or even the most common source of inspiration. Dramatizations of *The Brothers Karamazov, Roots, The Ten Command-*

ments, and *The Burning Bed* (a feminist account of domestic violence) are among the culprits. Comprehensive research also finds that no literary work equals the Bible as a reported factor in inspiring and justifying sexual abuse.[116]

A more indirect harm, but in many feminists' view the most pervasive one, involves pornography's effects on attitudes toward sexual violence and sexual subordination. Most boys first learn about sex through pornography, and the messages it sends scarcely encourage relationships of mutual respect, caring, and intimacy. Selections like "Cheerleader Gang Bang," "Black Bitch," "Teen Twits and Twats," and "Jap Sadists' Virgin Slave" link sexual pleasure with female degradation and racial domination. Because such messages work at the noncognitive level, the usual remedy for offensive speech—more speech—may not be effective. As the federal court noted in the Indianapolis case, pornography "does not persuade people so much as change them."[117]

Two decades of laboratory research provide concrete evidence of harmful effects. Studies have consistently found that exposure to sexually violent material increases viewers' expressed willingness to commit rape and decreases their sensitivity to its damage. Yet such research cannot adequately demonstrate the duration or degree of pornography's effect on behavior in the outside world. Most experts believe that the change in viewers' attitudes following laboratory experience with pornography reflects the violence more than the sex. Although this distinction can be difficult to draw, many experts estimate that violent materials account for well under 10 percent of the pornography market. Sex offenders do not differ significantly from other individuals in their exposure or response to pornography. These offenders are more likely to be readers of *Field and Stream* than of sexually explicit material.[118]

Other efforts to measure the harms of pornography by comparing changes over time or across cultures have been even more inconclusive. Although reported rapes have increased in some countries when pornography laws have grown more liberal, reported crimes are a highly imperfect index of sexual violence. Moreover, correlation does not prove causation. Other factors may account for the increase both in pornography and in reported assaults, and not all studies even find such correlations. Cross-cultural research also raises doubts about direct causal relationships. Some countries with high pornography consumption have low rates of reported violence against women. Other countries that heavily censor sexual expression are scarcely feminist meccas; middle-eastern Muslim societies have little pornography *or* gender equality.[119]

Yet it is a mistake to conclude, as do many civil libertarians, that there is *no* demonstrable link between sexual expression, sexual attitudes, and sexual violence. In a nation that spends some $130 billion each year in advertising, it should not be necessary to belabor the point that images matter. A quarter-century's research leaves no doubt that aggression is in large part learned behavior, and that at least part of the learning process involves words and images. In short, the real question is not whether there is *some* link between pornography and social harms, but whether it is strong enough to justify the risks of regulation.[120]

Opponents of such regulation fall into two camps: those who object to any form of government censorship and those who object to prohibitions on sexual expression. The first position builds on a sharp distinction between public and private power and assumes that silencing by the government is qualitatively different from other forms of repression. As legal scholar Kathleen Sullivan puts it, "If Simon and Schuster rejects [your novel], you can go to Random House. If the government bans your novel, you may have to move to France."[121]

An alternative view is that whatever other forms of speech regulation we may tolerate, censorship based on content should never be acceptable. According to the federal court in the Indiana case, the central flaw in the disputed antipornography ordinance was that it punished a particular kind of expression—sexually graphic subordination. This, in the court's view, was "thought control."[122]

Yet the ordinance punished acts, not thoughts, and an unqualified antiregulatory position has never commanded a majority on the Supreme Court or among the American people. Free expression is not the only value that we value, and courts have long tolerated many content-based restrictions on speech. Obvious examples include prohibitions on libel, bribery, fraud, workplace harassment, and employers' threats concerning unions. The harms associated with some of this restricted speech are not self-evidently greater than those traceable to certain pornography, such as sexually violent material. Indeed, most civil libertarians support bans on child pornography despite their content basis.

Opponents of regulation usually respond that antipornography initiatives pose greater threats to First Amendment values than do other limitations on speech. As the Feminist Anti-Censorship Task Force argued in the Indiana case, prohibitions based on "subordination" and "degradation" have no fixed meaning. To some judges, jurors, and potential plaintiffs, any sexual images suggesting male dominance may seem subordinating, and any same-sex relations might qualify as degrading. Under laws like the Indianapolis ordinance, the most vulnerable materials are not likely to be the well-financed (and, to a largely male judiciary, unthreatening) men's magazines; rather, they may be radical feminist, lesbian, and gay publications. Experience in Canada bears this out. There, recently modified prohibitions authorize the suppression of sexually explicit material that is violent, degrading, or dehumanizing. Prominent targets of Canadian censorship have not been brutal misogynist works like the novel *American Psycho,* but gay and lesbian publications. These feminist-inspired changes may not have created the problem, but neither have they prevented it. Ironically enough, border patrols have seized two books by antipornography crusader Andrea Dworkin. Similar paradoxes could well emerge in the United States. To some decisionmakers, graphic descriptions by antipornography activists might fall within the prohibitions of their own proposed ordinances.[123]

A related concern is the absence of any logical limiting principle for legislation targeting subordination. Women are not the only, or necessarily the most, subordinate group in American society—and sexually explicit images are not necessarily the most harmful ones. As social science experts like Edward Donnerstein and Daniel Linz note, materials "outside of the pornographic or the X-rated market may in fact be of more concern, since they are imbued with a certain legitimacy, and tend to have much wider acceptance." So too, if the government can suppress sexually explicit expression that degrades women, what about hate speech that contributes to racial violence, or homophobic parodies that encourage gay-bashing? Though some restrictions may be justifiable, the risks of overly broad control are substantial. Once regulation starts down this road, logical stopping points might be hard to find.[124]

A further concern is that provisions distinguishing between "good" and "bad" forms of sexual pleasure will reinforce sexist stereotypes.

Some recent studies suggest that women rent 40 percent of hard-core videos, and almost half of surveyed women report watching pornographic films regularly. Many of these viewers find some images of female subordination arousing, as is obvious from any stroll into the world of romances discussed in Chapter 4. Even if such enjoyment is the product of sexist conditioning, it does not follow that women need more "sexual shame, guilt, and hypocrisy—this time served up as feminism."[125]

For those committed to gender equality, sexual relationships based on intimacy and mutual respect are generally the ultimate objective. But as legal scholars like Carlin Meyer note, it would be patronizing and disabling to deprive individuals of "the opportunity to operate on today's real (not tomorrow's ideal) sexual terrain." For many individuals, nonviolent erotica can provide a safe outlet for channeling sexual domination, treating sexual dysfunctions, and fantasizing about practices that they would not attempt in real life. In that sense, pornography provides some of the "safest sex" available.[126]

Even if our society's ultimate goal is to reduce the prevalence of pornographic material, censorship has never been adequate to the task. Suppression generally increases the appeal of sexually arousing materials. For many individuals, transgressing taboos enhances the erotic experience. Attempts to regulate "cybersmut" are particularly likely to be ineffective. Current computer software is unable to filter out only material that meets legal, much less feminist, definitions of pornography. Institutions that have attempted to block access to entire computer networks have learned what sophisticated users already know: "for every roadblock, there is a detour." Wherever we draw our legal lines, the temptation to cross over will remain inescapable.[127]

Yet it does not follow that all line drawing is futile, or that all antipornography regulation would carry the same risks as recent initiatives. For example, some First Amendment scholars propose banning only sexually explicit visual portrayals of force or violence that lack redeeming literary, artistic, political, or scientific value. Such a standard would sweep far less broadly than either prevailing obscenity laws or alternatives focused on subordination, and would target only material that is most clearly harmful. While such narrow prohibitions will be difficult to enforce, our experience with child pornography legislation suggests that limited restrictions can somewhat reduce the availability and acceptability of targeted material. At the very least, a narrowly drawn prohibition would make an important symbolic statement with relatively little cost to core First Amendment values. Films like "Dorothy: Slave to Pain" and "Pussy on a Stick" are not cornerstones of democratic discourse.[128]

Yet neither should we overstate the importance of such pornography prohibitions or place them at the top of women's agenda. Given the limited reach and barriers to enforcement of proposed legislation, any effect on cultural norms is likely to be quite small. Moreover, while censorship strategies may look like the "cheapest items on [women's] shopping list," they carry hidden costs. Suppression requires political coalitions that strengthen antifeminist organizations and deflect energy from strategies that are less sexy but ultimately more critical. According to the sponsor of one recent antipornography ordinance, his goal was to "restore [ladies] to what ladies used to be." In view of what most "ladies" experienced under earlier sexual double standards, this would not be a step in the right direction.[129]

Neither is antipornography regulation a quick-fix substitute for the structural changes in work, family, and reproductive policies that are necessary to secure gender equality. Censorship is also an inadequate alternative to education. If much of the sexually explicit material now available degrades women, the most promising long-term strategy is not repression. Rather, it is to offer alternative images and to encourage discussion of what is wrong with existing ones. Recent research suggests that carefully designed educational programs can counteract pornography's impact on attitudes toward sexual violence. So too, the evolution of computer technology creates new opportunities for safe spaces where individuals can not only exchange but also confront and challenge pornographic images. Yet the priorities in recent antipornography initiatives have been precisely the opposite. Education is what everyone endorses and almost no one funds.[130]

But although education is not the stated objective of the recent antipornography campaigns, it could be their most positive legacy. Yet this is a value that both sides often deny. Neither critics nor proponents of regulation find much "redeeming social value" in each other's campaigns. According to MacKinnon, "for those who seek to end pornography's harms to women, nothing short of stopping the industry will be sufficient." In her view, the continued pervasiveness of such materials serves to silence as well as subordinate women—to prevent them from expressing their true sexual identity. So long as pornography exists as it does, claims MacKinnon, "there will not be more speech by women."[131]

Yet the history of her own campaign suggests the contrary. In the course of a decade, a small number of feminists have challenged some of the nation's most entrenched constitutional principles and most successful entertainment industries. The pornography industry has increased, but so too has our capacity to counter its adverse effects. We *have* gained more speech by women. And it is heard differently by men. That in itself is no small accomplishment, and it is a useful foundation for a broader struggle.

Harassment, battery, rape, and pornography all raise common questions. What makes sexual abuse sexy? What accounts for its pervasiveness and persistence? Why have we managed to accomplish so much in changing consciousness and changing law, but so little in changing cultural practices? Answering these questions requires us to look more deeply not only at the dynamics of sexual abuse but also at the structures of social power.

American culture eroticizes male violence and objectifies female bodies. These practices are so omnipresent that it is difficult even to imagine a sexual ideology that excludes them. Yet part of our challenge is to make such an alternative realistic and appealing. As feminist theorist Carol Vance notes, it is "not enough to move women away from danger and oppression." We must also move women "toward something: toward pleasure, agency, self-definition." Not only must we promote a more egalitarian vision of sexuality; we must create the conditions that will make it possible. Women are trapped both by the social construction of sexuality and the social constraints on choice. As long as their status and economic security depend so much on relationships with men, the conditions for sexual abuse will persist. Social inequality increases physical vulnerability. To change the dynamics of men's aggression, we also must increase women's capacities for resistance.[132]

Pointing this out, of course, often gives feminism a bad press. Whining about "whiners" is in fashion; it is less threatening to dismiss all those victim-mongering messengers than to hear their messages. And so the denials persist. We refuse to believe that sexual abuse is common, that victims aren't somehow responsible, and that we could do more about it. Nor will we admit that whatever happens in our workplace, in our family, and in our relationships is part of the problem. Until we recognize how our denials perpetuate abuse, there will be plenty of abuse to deny.

6

Women's Work

At a recent discussion of diversity in the legal profession, a prominent law school dean expressed skepticism that the "woman problem" remained a problem. Although he was well aware of persistent issues involving racial and ethnic bias, he was surprised to hear that some of those present also viewed gender inequality as a significant concern. I was equally surprised by his surprise. Law, I noted, is no different from other elite professional settings. Women are substantially underrepresented at the top and substantially overrepresented at the bottom of status and reward structures. "Really?" he asked. "Are you sure?"

The facts, and his perception of those facts, illustrate a broader problem. In law as in other traditionally male-dominated occupations, women have made dramatic progress. Since the 1960s, female representation among new entrants to the bar has increased from about 3 percent to 45 percent. However, women still account for only about 16 percent of full professors in law schools, 13 percent of the partners in the nation's 250 largest law firms, and 8 percent of judges in the federal courts. Disparities in the pool of eligible candidates cannot explain the extent of this underrepresentation. Female lawyers are less than half as likely as similarly qualified male colleagues to become partners, and pay gaps range from 10 to 35 percent between men and women in comparable positions. The disparities are even greater for women of color.[1]

Law is not atypical. Nor is it the worst example of occupational inequality. Women now account for about a third of all corporate managerial positions, but account for only 5 percent of senior management in Fortune 1,000 and Fortune 500 companies. Only 5 percent of these senior women are women of color. At current rates of progress, it would take four centuries for women to achieve equal representation in executive suites.[2]

Similarly, although the wage gap between full-time male and female workers has narrowed significantly since passage of equal-pay legislation in the 1960s, pay scales remain far from equal. The statistics are familiar. After more than twenty-five years of equal-opportunity laws, the salaries of women still lag about 25 percent behind those of men. Women of color average less than two-thirds of the salaries of white men, and Hispanic female college graduates earn less than white males with high school diplomas. Moreover, these comparisons involve full-time workers. The gender gap in annual earnings is considerably higher, because women are more likely than men to remain trapped in part-time positions with low pay and few benefits.[3]

Inequalities in the workplace reflect and reinforce inequalities in the home. Although husbands have increased their share of household tasks, recent surveys find that wives still assume at least two-thirds of domestic obligations. When paid and unpaid labor are combined, women work longer and have less income than men. This pattern begins early. As a 1995 *Wall Street Journal* account noted, elementary school girls receive smaller allowances and more chores than boys do. The pattern is also self-perpetuating. If, as is typically the case, a wife has lower earning potential than her husband, it is economically rational for the couple to give priority to his career and assign her a greater share of family responsibilities. Women's disproportionate domestic burdens are, in turn, a major obstacle to career advancement.[4]

This cycle persists partly because we deny or rationalize its injustice. Such denials take two major forms. Some individuals simply cannot see a significant problem; they don't believe that a substantial gender gap persists, or they assume that it reflects men's and women's different choices and capabilities. Other individuals acknowledge inequalities but deny responsibility for causing or remedying them. In principle, the vast majority of both groups support gender equality in the workplace. But in practice, they view equal-employment reform strategies as unnecessary, unworkable, unaffordable, or someone else's obligation.

Myths of Meritocracy and Myths of Choice

To most men and most policymakers, women's recent history in American workplaces looks like a triumphant tale. Once upon a time, sex discrimination sometimes happened, but those days are gone. The early villains in this saga usually remain anonymous and not particularly villainous. Just misguided. (As in "People used to think that women's place was in the home.") But along came the women's movement, consciousness was raised, legislation was enacted, and doors were opened. Now women are everywhere, running corporations and driving buses, while men are toting tots and cooking casseroles. Or at least reheating them. From this perspective, women rarely encounter sex discrimination, but they often benefit from preferential treatment. Widely publicized commentators like Rene Denfeld assure us that the "good old boys" are retiring and "the glass ceiling [is] cracking." About three-fourths of male chief executives are convinced that no such ceiling even exists.[5]

Many female workers tell different stories. Theirs sound less like *Pilgrim's Progress* and more like the myth of Sisyphus. Despite recent equal-opportunity initiatives, women find themselves still pushing the same rocks up the same hills—working longer hours than men for less pay in less prestigious occupations. More than 90 percent of senior female managers believe that men's and women's opportunities remain unequal and that the pace of change is too slow. As a NOW vice-president puts it, "Women have been climbing the corporate ladder for thirty years now. We're well groomed for the executive suites, but too often we find we're all dressed up with no place to go." Increasing numbers of women at all job levels also report bumping up against biases that their male colleagues fail to recognize. Forty to 50 percent of female workers believe they are not paid what their jobs are worth, that an old-boy network persists, and that they would have higher salaries or positions if they were men. Yet most women also have difficulty identifying specific jobs or promotions that they have lost because of their sex. In recent studies, only 15 to 25 percent of women reported experiencing such discrimination, and only about a third perceived it as a major factor holding women workers back.[6]

What prevents women from seeing the significance of bias and prevents men from seeing it at all? Part of the problem involves widely prevailing myths of meritocracy and myths of choice. Where a gender gap persists, many Americans assume that it is because female workers do not have either the same capabilities or the same priorities as their more successful male colleagues.

A recent television parody of affirmative action opened with a top male official explaining the absence of women in upper-level government positions. "If women were qualified, they would be here. Since they aren't here, they obviously aren't qualified." A more sophisticated variation of the argument, put forward by conservative economists, is that gender discrimination cannot survive in a competitive market. By this logic, it is inefficient to exclude competent workers because of their sex; it follows that if women are excluded, they must not be competent.[7]

This argument has multiple problems, beginning with its failure to explain how competitive markets and overt sex discrimination both managed to flourish throughout most of American history. Any adequate explanation of that history has to acknowledge what other economists describe as "tastes for discrimination." If customers, clients, and coworkers prefer male employees, it can be profitable for employers to accommodate that preference. Of course, they can no longer afford to do so explicitly, at least where equal-opportunity laws apply. But subtle biases remain common in workplace cultures and standards.[8]

Take for example, the findings announced in a 1991 *Wall Street Journal* headline: "Women as Colleagues Can Turn Men Off." This was the less-than-startling conclusion of a new study on male employees' attitudes. It found that men in predominantly male workplaces are more motivated and less interested in leaving their jobs than men who work in comparable but more gender-integrated settings. Apparently, many male employees' sense of status and comfort is still linked to the absence of women. Related findings appeared in the 1995 report of the Department of Labor's Glass Ceiling Commission. As one participant in its research noted, "What's important [in organizations] is comfort, chemistry . . . and collaborations." Many white men "don't like the competition and they don't like the tension" of working with colleagues who are "different." The result is that women often remain outside the informal networks of advice, cooperation, and contacts that can be crucial for advancement.[9]

Of course, few individuals are as explicit about their preferences as the Air Force chief of staff who, in 1991, informed an incredulous

Senate panel that he would rather put a less qualified male pilot in a combat position than a top-notch female one. "I admit it does not make much sense." he conceded. "But that is the way I feel about it." These same prejudices, expressed in more subtle ways, continue to shape workplace cultures. Where an employee's effectiveness depends partly on an ability to attract men's support and business, women are at a decided disadvantage. The standards for evaluation may be gender-neutral in form, but they don't work out that way in fact. Yet pointing this out can compound the problem. One African American member of a corporate committee on equal opportunity made the mistake of identifying biases in her own department's hiring practices. This, she later learned, was viewed as "poor judgment." She had made her supervisors "uncomfortable," and it was easier to fault her than to fix the problem.[10]

Unconscious gender stereotypes work in similar ways to prevent women from breaking through the glass ceiling and to prevent men from seeing that any ceiling exists. The Glass Ceiling Commission and its consultants compiled a list of common assumptions: women are too emotional, indecisive, deficient in quantitative skills, and lacking in career commitment; African American women are incompetent, lazy, and hostile; Hispanic women are overly passive and undereducated; and Asian women are inflexible, unassertive, and ineffective in interpersonal communications. Yet while most employers acknowledge that these stereotypes may influence other people's views, they usually are sure that their own decisions are strictly "on the merits."[11]

The difficulty, however, is that at an unconscious level, race and gender biases affect assessments of the merits. People retain and interpret information to support preconceived beliefs about group characteristics. For example, many studies find that when people are asked to evaluate work performance or a résumé, they will rate it lower if they think it belongs to a woman rather than a man. Females' achievements also are more likely than males' to be attributed to luck rather than ability, and to be overlooked or undervalued in the evaluation process. A *Punch* cartoon aptly illustrates these dynamics in its caricature of a conference involving five men and one woman. The chair of the gathering looks out at the female participant and observes, "That's an excellent point, Miss Trigg. Perhaps one of the men here would like to make it."[12]

The consequences of such unconscious bias emerged clearly in a mid-1990s ABC documentary. Producers used hidden cameras to accompany a young man and woman with essentially the same qualifications as they applied for the same advertised jobs. The man got offers for managerial positions paying up to $500 per week. The woman got typing tests and information about receptionist and secretarial positions paying about $240. When asked whether they treated male and female applicants differently, the male employers insisted that they did not. When confronted with the films of their interviews, these men retreated only slightly. It's not that they were prejudiced. They had just tried to determine what positions would be "better" for the applicant. In their view, women just didn't "do well" as field managers. And men just didn't belong answering phones. Similar research involving race makes clear that women of color face bias on two fronts. Analysis of some ninety studies leaves no doubt that whites typically rate other whites higher than they rate similarly qualified people of color.[13]

The more subjective the standards for assessing qualifications, the harder it is to detect such biases. Which job candidates have the most impressive leadership skills, artistic creativity, or intellectual promise often is open to dispute. Because subjective criteria are particularly significant in allocating upper-level positions, women are particularly likely to be underrepresented at the top. But even lower-level employment decisions that ostensibly rely on "objective" standards may reflect sex-based prejudices.

An example is *Johnson v. Transportation Agency of Santa Clara County,* the first affirmative action case concerning gender to reach the United States Supreme Court. At issue was a program allowing agency decisionmakers to consider the sex of qualified applicants for positions where women historically had been underrepresented. Under that program, the plaintiff, Paul Johnson, had lost a promotion for a job as road dispatcher to Diane Joyce. Johnson objected to the decision because Joyce, while rated "well qualified" for the job, had scored two points below Johnson on a written exam and ranked lower in an oral interview. At the time of the decision, the agency employed no women in any of some 200 skilled craft positions and had never hired a female road dispatcher.[14]

Diane Joyce's experience suggests that this absence of women was partly attributable to gender biases in the agency's evaluation process and working conditions. One of Joyce's three interviewers had openly resisted her presence in a previous roadworking position; he had even refused to issue her work overalls until she filed a union grievance. Another interviewer had referred to her as "rebel-rousing skirt-wearing person." These men's evaluations of Joyce's performance partly determined her "objective" numerical ranking. Their prejudices also reflected a broader pattern of hazing and harassment that both the Court and the agency discreetly overlooked. The prevailing attitude in Joyce's workplace was, as one coworker put it, "Don't get me wrong, I love women. But the road is no place for females."[15]

Although a majority of Justices voted to uphold the affirmative action program, they failed to acknowledge the biases that made the program necessary. By characterizing Joyce as the "less qualified" applicant, the Court's description and the media's portrayal of the case contributed to a misleading myth of meritocracy. Here was a woman who had compiled an outstanding performance record, almost equivalent to that of her chief male rival, under far more difficult conditions and biased evaluation processes.[16]

Experiences like Joyce's prompt the common quip about gender stereotypes: "A woman has to be twice as good as a man in order to be thought half as qualified. But fortunately, that's no problem." Unfortunately, the punchline understates the challenge. For many women, outperforming men in unsupportive workplaces *is* a problem. Exceptional individuals may be able to manage. But the average female applicant still has difficulty getting the same opportunities as the average male.

Unconscious bias affects not only the options for individual women, but also the pay scales available to women as a group. Controlled studies find that people think jobs in female-dominated occupations require less ability and deserve less compensation than identical work performed in male-dominated occupations.

Gender biases are particularly noticeable in compensation for domestic work—for example, in pay scales that rank female childcare attendants below male parking-lot attendants. But gender inequalities even show up within the same job categories; for example, women who are nurses' aides, computer programmers, elementary school teachers, and waitresses earn 15 to 25 cents less for every dollar earned by men in these occupations. A recent cartoon captures what in real life is far less amusing: it shows a sign over a sewer entrance reading "Caution: Men Working." Several feet away appears another sign: "Women Working for Less Pay."[17]

The sequels to our myths of meritocracy are myths of choice. To many Americans, women's inequalities in the workplace are not a problem because they reflect women's different priorities. One version of this claim builds on the sociobiological assumptions discussed in Chapter 2. From this perspective, "It is nature, not patriarchal society, that puts motherhood and career on a collision course." Other theorists draw comparable conclusions based on "human capital" theories of labor force participation. These frameworks assume that women choose to invest less than men in preparing for careers because women expect to have greater domestic responsibilities. By this logic, sex-based differences in employment status simply reflect sex-based preferences regarding family roles.[18]

A related claim is that because most women are secondary wage earners, they can afford to accept lower pay in exchange for more pleasant working conditions. According to Warren Farrell's *Myth of Male Power*, it is men, not women, who are stuck in the "glass cellar" of American workplaces. Female workers opt out of the most dirty, dangerous, and stressful occupations, and avoid positions with extended or inconvenient hours.[19]

Although such accounts have some factual basis, they exaggerate the gender difference on which their conclusions depend. It is true that women are more likely than men to take extended leaves, work part time, and complete fewer years of postcollege training in order to accommodate family responsibilities. Female workers also tend not to look for positions in traditionally male-dominated blue-collar occupations. But these "choices" are a response to, as well as a cause of, gender inequality in the workplace, and they cannot account for its current magnitude.

Women with significant domestic obligations are not more likely to choose low-paying, traditionally female occupations. Nor do differences in career investment explain the extent of occupational segregation and stratification. Some studies find that factors such as experience, education, and hours worked account for no more than 50 to 60 percent of all sex-based disparities. Other research puts the figure higher, but respected experts generally agree that qualifications related to merit or choice cannot explain all of the current gender gap in employment. Women who make comparable career choices simply do not advance as far or as fast as their male counterparts. Neither do similar choices necessarily result in similar employment conditions. The sexual harassment and old-boy networks that prevail in many workplaces do not make for woman-friendly environments.[20]

Reliance on women's choices to explain occupational inequalities also diverts attention from the forces that limit the choices available. For many individuals, career decisions are not the product of some fully informed and independent preference. Rather, they reflect preconceptions about "women's work" that have been shaped by media portrayals, family attitudes, peer pressures, and restrictive job recruitment patterns. Gender segregation in the labor force is even more pronounced than racial segregation: about 80 percent of female workers remain in traditionally female occupations like teaching, sales, waitressing, and clerical assistance.[21]

Gender stereotypes affect not only employees' choice of occupation, but also the way in which they balance job and family responsibilities. The home still is not "an equal-opportunity employer." Employed women spend about twice as much time on family matters as employed men do, and women average two to three fewer hours of leisure per day. It is no accident that "working mothers" is a familiar description but the term "working fathers" seems redundant. One consequence of such implicit gender stereotypes emerges clearly in an observation by federal judge Patricia Wald: "It may be that the conscientious parent of a young child cannot simultaneously be in high-powered litigation. There are trade-offs in life and . . . women need to accept that." But men apparently don't. Fathers who devote all their energy to their careers are viewed as "good providers." Women who do so are viewed as selfish.[22]

Lillian Rubin's and Kathleen Gerson's surveys of men's attitudes toward family obligations underscore the persistent gap in cultural expectations. The following comments are typical:

"What do I know about doing stuff around the house? . . . Besides, I work my ass off every day. Isn't that enough?"

"I really think the children benefit from the absence of their father. If the father's not inclined [toward childcare], then what's the point?

People shouldn't do what they don't want to do . . . And I don't want to do it."

"I guess I could have done a little more with [my children] if I wasn't working all the time, but I've never hit my kids. I paid my daughter's tuition. I take them on vacations. Am I a good father? Yes, I would say so."

"Changing diapers is not my great ambition in life . . . [When the baby comes], I'm hoping I can just get the pleasure aspect and not too much of the dirty work."[23]

Can we imagine women feeling entitled to make those claims? What would we think of mothers who did? In recent surveys, about two-thirds of employed women felt guilty about not spending more time with their families. Such concerns are conspicuously absent among men. Although a few husbands in Rubin's and Gerson's studies felt pangs about their wife's disproportionate burdens, they preferred coping with some guilt to changing their behavior. As one man candidly acknowledged, "I know I should do more, but I'm not going to . . . because she's not forcing me." Yet as Rhona Mahony points out in her study of bargaining behavior in marriage, a major reason that wives don't face the issue is that they lack the necessary economic security. A woman may "choose" an unequal share of household tasks because she sees no realistic alternative.[24]

Many men who refuse to assume family responsibilities deny the unfairness of their behavior. Eighty-five percent of surveyed husbands do not think that they have a choice about how many hours they spend on the job. Many of these men believe that they work hard enough as it is without adding domestic chores, or that if one parent's career has to suffer it shouldn't be theirs. As husbands in Rubin's and Gerson's studies note, they earned more money than their wives. Other men were convinced that women had the cushier lives: "It's a jungle out here, and [the home] is not a jungle. It might be depressing to change sheets or whatever . . . but I see no problems in running a house today with microwaves and ovens. So it has to be easier on [women]."[25]

If domestic work appears "easier" to some men, it may be because they have never had to do much of it. As one corporate executive recalls, family problems in his household always ended up as his wife's problems. "My awareness of childcare was that you picked up the baby sitter, you took the baby sitter home, and sometimes you couldn't get a baby sitter."[26]

Although awareness is now considerably greater, changes in day-to-day behavior have come more slowly. As the discussion in Chapter 1 indicated, men's "learned helplessness" around the house remains a time-honored way of avoiding scutwork. Wives then "choose" to do the tasks that their husbands otherwise ignore or mess up. Of course, many women also occasionally fall back on deliberate incompetence. I personally have invoked centuries of sexist oppression as a rationale for making my husband program the VCR. But women's evasive strategies often serve as self-protection from any further increase in already un-equal household burdens. Given the traditional allocation of domestic roles, wives usually lose out in any "helplessness" sweepstakes.

Other couples agree in principle to divide tasks equally, but in practice some tasks remain more equal than others. For example, one of the dual-career families in sociologist Arlie Hochschild's study settled on an "equal" geographic division for their household: the wife took re-sponsibility for chores connected with the upstairs and the husband for the downstairs. In their split-level home, the downstairs was the garage. Yet such results do not appear unreasonable if, as many men assume, women are just "naturally" better with small children and housework.[27]

These patterns are, of course, far less pervasive today than in earlier eras. A growing number of men are involved fathers, and some get enormous personal satisfaction and public credit from accepting that role. William Galston, President Clinton's former domestic-policy ad-viser, received considerable public acclaim after resigning his position in order to spend more time with his son. In *It Takes a Village,* Hillary Clinton joins the chorus of approval for Galston's widely quoted expla-nation to the president. "You can replace me, but my son can't." Yet women routinely make such career sacrifices, and no one finds it par-ticularly noteworthy.[28]

The problem is not only that many men are unwilling to limit their worklives, but also that some who attempt to do so encounter so much resistance. Employers who are reluctant to accommodate mothers often see even less reason to make adjustments for fathers. Yet managers generally deny that *they* are responsible for discouraging equal parental roles. In their view, the fault lies with male workers, who place relatively low priority on such family-related benefits. Even where parental leave is available, only between 1 and 7 percent of eligible men typically take it.[29]

Yet this reluctance is at least partly attributable to prevailing workplace attitudes. Although female colleagues often are highly supportive, male coworkers and supervisors generally are not. As one Wall Street broker put it, "What is this [family] leave crap? *I* never had [parental] leave." Of course, some men also exaggerate the resistance they face. As a member of the Work/Family Directions consulting firm notes, a husband may find it easier to say that he can't take on major domestic burdens because the family "can't afford it," or "it will hurt my career," than to say "housework is beneath me, dear." But some resistance is quite real. A notorious example involved the Houston Oilers' response when lineman David Williams missed an important game to be with his wife during childbirth. In the coach's view, Williams "let the [team] down" and deserved a suspension and a $125,000 fine. Only a "public relations disaster in the making" caused reversal of the suspension. In countless other less publicized and more subtle cases, male employees hear that extended absences for "household" matters are unacceptable.[30]

Such discrimination against men with family commitments also discriminates against women. It encourages the unequal division of family responsibilities that limits a woman's workplace options, decreases her bargaining leverage within the family, and increases her economic vulnerability if the couple separate.

Those who invoke personal choice as a rationalization for workplace inequality often lose sight of the limited choices available and the permanent penalty that they may impose. Most female employees do not have options for flexible schedules, extended leaves, or decently paying part-time work. Even options that are available in theory are penalized in fact. About 85 percent of women believe that reducing hours or taking substantial time away from work will hurt their careers. About 70 percent "choose" to make that sacrifice.[31]

Those who remain on the fast track pay another kind of price. My own exposure to those costs first occurred almost two decades ago, when I was interviewing for a summer job. From one distinguished Chicago lawyer, I learned that there was no "woman problem" at his firm. The only female attorney among his forty partners had no difficulties reconciling her personal and professional life. Why, just the previous fall she had given birth to her first child. It happened on a Friday and she was back at the office the following Monday. Any "problem" that this might have presented apparently escaped his notice.

Our consciousness of work/family dilemmas obviously is greater now, but these faster-than-a-speeding-bullet maternity leaves persist. A leading example of how to reconcile personal and professional rhythms involves a lawyer who finished drafting documents while timing her contractions during labor. If your firm is billing at five-minute intervals, why waste a moment?

Nor do the pressures necessarily diminish after childbirth. Recent glass ceiling reports describe in deadening detail the sweatshop hours for full-time employees in male-dominated professions and the second-class status that accompanies part-time work. Many of these professions are in what social scientists term "greedy institutions." In workplace cultures, "face time" in the office commonly serves as a proxy for other qualities, such as dedication, loyalty, and commitment. The result is that all work and no play is the norm rather than the exception. Mothers talk of not seeing their children awake for a week and of negotiating with a "very understanding" supervisor who allows them to leave "early" at 6 P.M. if they come in at 6 A.M. As one woman summarized the situation, "This is not a life."[32]

Yet the prevailing advice in professional journals and mentoring programs is that "women on the road to success" can afford no detours from standard workplace obligations. Female employees should never make an issue out of being female, or "shirk late hours or weekend projects." Nor should they cook and tell; if they leave early to prepare dinner for their family, they should avoid letting anyone know about it. As one article advises, a woman should never present herself as "anything but a hard-driving capable [professional]." With no apparent irony, the author concludes, "Be yourself."[33]

Many women, particularly those who cannot afford outside help, face conflicting cultural signals and unsatisfying personal choices. Our society is extremely judgmental about "selfish career-driven" mothers who neglect their families. Yet women who make families a priority also hear that they are not sufficiently "committed" to their careers. "Choice" on such terms is not the answer; it's part of the problem.

Partial Policies

Another way of minimizing gender inequality as a problem is to discount the need for a response. A common assumption is that our society has done just about all that is possible at the policy level. We now have laws requiring equal employment opportunities, equal pay, family leaves, and tax-subsidized childcare assistance. We may not quite have reached the promised land, but many Americans assume that we are well on the way—that gender roles are breaking down and women are moving up. This is a comforting myth, but it confuses promise and performance in law reform efforts. Legal requirements have changed considerably, but gender hierarchies remain pervasive. The reason lies partly in our failure to enact and enforce comprehensive remedies.

One such failure involves the incomplete coverage of benefit policies. For example, the 1993 Family and Medical Leave Act still leaves more than half the workforce unprotected. It provides job security only for those who can afford to take unpaid leave, and excludes individuals who work for small employers or in temporary or part-time positions. Because women are overrepresented in such jobs, they are less likely than men to be eligible for family leave, even though they are far more likely to want it. They are also short-changed by policies that provide only full-time workers with other benefits like unemployment insurance and health care coverage.[34]

A similar example of such partial policies involves childcare. On this issue, those most directly involved often have a stake in denying a problem. Good care is expensive, and parents who can't afford it do not want to believe that they have settled for an inadequate alternative. Nor do political or business leaders want to take responsibility for costly assistance. Childcare providers are similarly reluctant to acknowledge inadequacies that might result in burdensome regulatory responses.

The result is a patchwork of policies that virtually every major study finds woefully deficient. One recent, comprehensive review points up the extent of our denial. Experts in the 1995 Cost, Quality and Child Outcome Study investigated a hundred randomly selected facilities and found that most programs provided poor to mediocre childcare. Almost half of the infants and toddlers were receiving less than minimal-quality care. Yet 90 percent of the parents relying on the surveyed centers rated these programs as very good.[35]

Such findings are consistent with those in other studies. But the problem is not, as some conservatives are fond of arguing, that most women with young children are working outside the home. A quarter-century's worth of research makes clear that such employment does not adversely affect child development, at least after the first several months following childbirth. What is relevant for children is the quality of care, not who provides it, together with the mother's satisfaction with her decision about paid employment.[36]

Our problem, rather, is that many working parents are unable to identify or to afford appropriate care and the unavailability of good programs adversely affects women as well as children. Most families now depend on unlicensed providers of uneven quality and continuity. Standards for licensed facilities are frequently lax, and parents have little systematic information on which to base comparisons. Even if families were better able to identify good care, millions could not afford it. Most governmental subsidies take the form of limited tax credits that primarily benefit middle- and upper-income consumers. Options for the working poor are grossly deficient in quality and quantity. Women as well as children pay a large price for these inadequacies. Childcare difficulties keep many women out of the workplace altogether, or in part-time positions with flexible hours but low pay, no benefits, and no possibilities for advancement. A third of all women who have "chosen" part-time work would prefer more hours if good childcare were available. Inadequacies in caretaking arrangements are a frequent cause of guilt, stress, and workplace absences, and help account for the fact that employed women report significantly greater dissatisfaction with their jobs and marriages than employed men report.[37]

Similar difficulties confront those who care for elderly relatives. A greatly disproportionate share of such responsibilities falls on women, and the burdens are expected to increase dramatically with the projected growth of the elderly population over the next decade.[38]

We do not lack alternative models. Many European countries have caretaking programs that are vastly superior in terms of access, quality, and government support. Reform initiatives in this country are in equally ample supply; we could do far more to provide financial assistance, information, and regulatory oversight concerning family care services. What stands in the way is our refusal to acknowledge the scope of our problem or the responsibility of anyone other than individual women to solve it.[39]

Another area in which current employment-related policies offer inadequate coverage involves discrimination on the basis of sexual orientation. Such discrimination is pervasive and, except in a few jurisdictions, still legal. Even in jurisdictions that prohibit such bias, noncompliance is widespread and sometimes quite explicit. A recent study of employers in Los Angeles, which bans discrimination against gays and lesbians, produced responses like, "Don't have any. Don't want any." Forty percent of survey participants reported witnessing or experiencing sexual-orientation bias. In another 1996 survey, a participant reported encountering similar prejudices in a company diversity-education program. When her boss said he "didn't know anyone who was gay and didn't want to," she didn't know whether "to throw up or stand up."[40]

Although many Americans deny that this is a "woman's issue," the linkage is obvious to those who look. Social science research confirms what social experience suggests. Hostility toward homosexuality is linked to support for traditional sex-based stereotypes. Workplace taboos against "effeminate" men and "unfeminine" women grow out of the same gender role assumptions that have limited opportunities for all individuals, irrespective of their sexual orientation. A male nursery school teacher fired for wearing an earring and a female accountant penalized for not wearing makeup have both violated similar gender boundaries. As long as those boundaries remain in place, equal opportunity will remain elusive.[41]

Barriers to Enforcement

Inadequate enforcement also compromises equal-opportunity policies. Some studies of laws governing parental leave and pregnancy discrimination reveal significant noncompliance. In one survey, two-thirds of workers reported problems obtaining full entitlements under the Family and Medical Leave Act—namely, twelve weeks of unpaid leave with all benefits and the right to return to the same or to a comparable job. Some supervisors' resistance has been disarmingly candid. One employer greeted a male employee's request for leave with "not in my lifetime." Other managers tell new parents who need time off that they have "an attitude problem."[42]

Other discrimination is more subtle. Employees who become pregnant or who return to work after a parental leave fail to receive raises and promotions, or find their jobs restructured into oblivion. Many employers believe that those who take time off are not sufficiently "committed" to their jobs and are likely to have future difficulties juggling work and family obligations. Such biases penalize even workers who take relatively brief leaves. One recent study found that women who were out of the paid labor force for less than a year still experienced a decline in earnings and promotion opportunities when they returned.[43]

Noncompliance with statutory requirements remains common because the costs of enforcement are so often prohibitive. Most employment discrimination never results in formal complaints. Women often are not sure whether their rights have been violated, whether they can prove a violation, or how to file a complaint. Nor can most women afford the costs of legal action or find lawyers willing to pursue their claims on a contingency fee basis. Unless liability is clear and damages are substantial, discrimination suits are simply too expensive to litigate. This is true even for government agencies, which lack sufficient resources to proceed except in a small fraction of cases. In the mid-1990s, the Equal Employment Opportunity Commission had a backlog of almost 100,000 grievances, and fewer than one-fifth of the complaints it received were litigated or settled.[44]

Employment discrimination claims that do result in legal action generally take two forms, and both are difficult to win. "Disparate-treatment" cases require proof that the employer intentionally treated similarly qualified women and men differently, and that the women otherwise would have obtained particular jobs or benefits. For example, a female manager might attempt to demonstrate that she was left out of informal business networks and that she lost a promotion to a male colleague with lower performance evaluations and sales records. "Disparate-impact" cases, the second type of employment discrimination claims, require proof that practices having an adverse effect on women are not job related and are not justified by business necessity. For example, a female applicant for a blue-collar position might show that qualifying tests disproportionately excluded women and demanded more physical strength than the position in fact required.

Proving such discrimination often requires expensive statistical studies or expert witnesses, and a pool of similarly qualified male and female applicants that is large enough to permit sex-based comparisons. Even where statistical evidence is compelling, courts are reluctant to find liability in the absence of some clearly identifiable villains. Given employers' increasing sensitivity to potential lawsuits, such individuals are in short supply.[45]

Many courts respond to claims of gender discrimination with the same patterns of denial that are common in the culture generally. One frequent reaction is that women's choices explain women's inequality. "Common sense" and "common knowledge" convince courts that female workers don't want to be welders, bakers, road workers, or educational administrators. A notorious example is the unsuccessful lawsuit by the Equal Employment Opportunity Commission against Sears, Roebuck and Company. To support its claim, the EEOC reviewed over 50,000 hiring decisions and offered extensive statistical evidence that women who applied for sales positions were less likely than men with similar qualifications to receive high-paying commission jobs. In defending its actions, Sears hired a female historian, Rosalind Rosenberg, who testified that such patterns were consistent with women's traditional preferences, including their reluctance to work irregular hours and their discomfort with competitive pay structures.[46]

The EEOC countered with historian Alice Kessler-Harris, who emphasized that female employees have been eager to take higher-paying nontraditional jobs when opportunities have been available. The court, however, credited Rosenberg's story and in the process overlooked other evidence that pointed to sexist stereotypes in the Sears workplace. For example, one witness explained that female employees weren't in higher-paid retail sales positions because they "didn't like going outside when it's snowing, raining, or whatever." To predict effectiveness in commission sales, Sears relied on tests that measured applicants' "vigor" by reference to their views on boxing, wrestling, and swearing. Despite the company's claimed commitment to affirmative action for women, its management failed to take steps that might have realized that goal:

flexible schedules and adequate recruitment, training, and support programs for women in nontraditional jobs.[47]

It is, however, such initiatives, rather than women's "natural" preferences, that account for much of our progress in reducing occupational segregation over the last decades. Female employees in historically male-dominated occupations often report that they did not initially "choose" those fields. Rather, they took advantage of opportunities available through affirmative action and related employer initiatives. Such efforts have been conspicuously absent in cases like that involving Sears.[48]

Problems in proving discrimination are still greater in contexts involving smaller workforces or upper-level positions, since such claims do not lend themselves to sex-based statistical comparisons. Winning such cases usually requires proof of fairly explicit bias, which is increasingly hard to come by. Colleagues who are aware of bias are frequently reluctant to expose it for fear of jeopardizing their own positions. And as courts and commentators note, employers of even "minimal sophistication will neither admit discriminatory . . . [conduct] nor leave a paper trail demonstrating it." Rarely are individuals as candid as the officers of one brokerage firm who, in the mid-1990s, were still explicitly instructing managers not to hire blacks or women. But even these officers had a largely effective strategy for getting away with it: "Give me fifteen minutes and I can find something not to like about anyone."[49]

In most cases of discrimination, however, employers simply announce what they don't "like," without acknowledging or sometimes even realizing their biases. To deter discrimination claims by workers who are terminated or denied promotions, management advisers recommend performance reviews that include discussion of employee weaknesses. As a recent article on such preventive strategies notes, "Nearly all employees have some room for improvement." When employers follow such advice, women generally have no way of identifying or proving discrimination. The female applicant in the ABC documentary described earlier never would have known that gender bias was at work if she had not been paired with a virtually identical male applicant who received far more favorable treatment.[50]

Even when plaintiffs can produce direct evidence of bias, courts often deny its significance. "Stray remarks" in the workplace are insufficient to establish liability if the defendant can demonstrate some legitimate reason for the unfavorable treatment. For example, both trial and appellate judges found no intentional discrimination against an African American woman despite comments like "[a bank teller position] is a big responsibility with a lot of money . . . for blacks to have to count." Courts were equally unpersuaded by a supervisor's announcement in another case: "Fucking women. I hate having fucking women in the office." According to the trial judge, this remark, although "inappropriate," seemed directed at "women in general" rather than the plaintiff in particular. Her claim failed because she could not prove that gender was the only reason that she did not receive promotion and training opportunities.[51]

Other courts view even explicit criticism of an employee's "femininity" as reflecting legitimate performance concerns rather than gender bias. For example, in an unsuccessful challenge to her tenure denial, a female professor introduced comments describing her as too "feminine"—that is, too "unassuming, unaggressive, unassertive, and not highly motivated for vigorous interpersonal competition." To both the lower and appellate courts, such comments related not to gender but simply to the effect of the professor's personality on graduate students.[52]

As these cases suggest, when gender prejudices are entwined with legitimate concerns, courts are often unable or unwilling to sort out their relative significance. Prevailing case law offers two general ways to establish unlawful disparate treatment. One is for plaintiffs to show that the employers' claimed reason for rejecting them was an "obvious pretext" and that gender was the real motive. The alternative is for plaintiffs to offer direct evidence that gender was a factor in the decision and to rebut any claims that the outcome would have been the same irrespective of gender. In essence, the law forces a choice between two simplistic stories. Courts must find that the basis for the employer's decision was real or phony, unbiased or biased. Yet in life, if not in law, a decision may reflect both legitimate concerns and group prejudices. Such prejudices may operate not at conscious levels at the time of the decision, but at unconscious levels throughout the evaluative process.[53]

Psychological research finds that when stereotypical images of women fail to fit the images associated with particular positions, female performance is likely to be devalued. So, for example, because the prototypical image of a corporate leader is an assertive white male, Asian American females face special burdens in establishing their competence. Ambiguous or conflicting information about their performance is also likely to be interpreted and recalled in ways that fit prevailing stereotypes. Supervisors will tend to remember these workers' mistakes and passivity more readily than their triumphs.[54]

As a result, decisionmakers who pass over a woman of color for promotion may not be consciously discriminating on the basis of race or gender. They may just perceive her as less qualified because of biases in their earlier evaluation processes. The complexity of such decision-making cannot be captured by a legal framework that insists on simple either/or explanations—on finding that race or gender bias did or did not "cause" a particular decision.

A classic illustration of the mixed-motive problem involves Ann Hopkins' lawsuit against Price Waterhouse for denial of an accounting partnership. Glass ceiling cases rarely are stronger than hers. In the mid-1980s, when Price Waterhouse withheld her promotion, all but seven of the firm's 662 partners were males. Hopkins had billed more hours and brought in more business than any other person nominated for partnership in the year of her rejection, and clients generally had given her high ratings. Opposition to her partnership was based not on objective performance measures, but rather on subjective assessments of her "interpersonal skills and social grace." Opponents found her "overbearing," "arrogant," and "abrasive." One male partner claimed that she needed a "course in charm school." Another thought that she "overcompensated" for being a woman. The most celebrated comment came from one of her supporters, who counseled her to "walk more femininely, talk more femininely, dress more femininely," and wear more makeup and jewelry. Yet several men who obtained partnerships that year were characterized as "abrasive," "overbearing," or "cocky." No one mentioned charm school for them. Although Hopkins eventually prevailed, it took seven years and five levels of judicial decisionmaking, with two trial and three appellate court rulings. And most of these judges found it a "close" case.[55]

If Hopkins' case was close, consider the chances of women in more typical circumstances. Many male employers may have views about the "femininity" of a particular applicant, but they usually have the good sense not to say so in personnel evaluations. Not all women who bump up against gender bias have the indisputably outstanding record of Ann Hopkins. And those who don't have little chance of prevailing. A sobering example involves Nancy Ezold, a lawyer who in 1990 unsuccessfully sued her Philadelphia firm for denial of a partnership. Many of the same gender stereotypes that worked against Ann Hopkins plagued Ezold. Male partners not only expressed concerns about her legal work, but also found her too "assertive" and too preoccupied with "women's issues." However, they promoted male associates with similar work evaluations. Although the trial court found sufficient evidence of discrimination, the court of appeals reversed. In its view, the partners' concerns about Ezold's performance were not so "obvious or manifest" a pretext as to justify liability.[56]

Nancy Ezold was not a superstar. Neither are most victims of discrimination. Nor do most women have the resources, personal and financial, to persevere in protracted litigation. Particularly in cases involving upper-level employment, individuals are putting their conduct, competence, and character at issue. Seldom will the portraits that emerge look entirely flattering. Plaintiffs like Ann Hopkins risk having their personal foibles aired not only in open court but also in newspaper accounts and gossip networks. Even when women win in court, they often pay the price outside it: lawsuits compromise reputations and sour relations with colleagues. Diane Joyce, the road dispatcher in the Supreme Court's first affirmative action case, was successful in litigation but she was punished on the worksite with hazing and hostility.[57]

Women who are unsuccessful in litigation are, of course, in far worse straits. They risk being blacklisted as incompetents or troublemakers and face crippling legal bills. Discrimination cases can drag on for years and can cost hundreds of thousands of dollars. Unsurprisingly, employment lawsuits are not most women's idea of a good time or a good investment. "Professional suicide" is a common description.[58]

Contrary to popular assumptions, employment law is not solving the problem of employment inequality. But neither have we reached the limit of what law could accomplish. One obvious reform strategy is to increase the enforcement resources of federal and state equal-opportunity commissions, and to make information about their complaint procedures more widely available. We could also ease the proof requirements for discrimination cases in ways that would bring legal doctrine more in line with social realities. One possibility would be to create two-tiered remedies closer to those applicable for other types of personal injuries. Under such a framework, in disparate-treatment cases, proof of *intentional* discrimination would entitle a plaintiff to full compensatory and punitive damages. Proof of *nonintentional* but negligent discrimination would result in more restricted remedies such as legal costs, back pay, and reinstatement. In effect, a negligence standard would require decisionmakers to take reasonable steps to identify and address subtle prejudices in their own decisionmaking process.[59]

Such a system would have advantages for all concerned. In cases involving mixed motives, plaintiffs and courts would face less pressure to read the minds of decisionmakers. Instead, the focus would be on improving the processes of decisionmaking. From defendants' perspective, a limited-liability option that removes the costs and stigma of intentional discrimination could reduce acrimonious disputes over personal integrity and encourage constructive settlements. Increased resources for governmental enforcement and informal complaint procedures would promote similar objectives.

Not only do we need such reforms in antidiscrimination law; we also need a clearer sense of the law's limitations. Equal-opportunity legislation can never guarantee equal opportunity in fact. Given the costs and difficulties of proving unlawful conduct, much gender and racial bias inevitably will escape judicial notice. To secure truly equal employment opportunities, more than lawsuits are necessary. Yet two of the most promising strategies, affirmative action and pay equity, provoke the greatest resistance.

Affirmative Action

Affirmative action, as courts and administrative agencies define it, is a temporary, flexible policy of limited preferences for qualified individuals in order to remedy serious gender and racial imbalances. Affirmative action, as conservative politicians and media leaders describe it, is something else again: a system of rigid quotas that incorporates the very biases society should be seeking to eliminate.[60]

During the early days of the Clinton administration, efforts to diversify presidential appointments raised lots of eyebrows. Caricatures of Clinton officials as "bean counters" ran in all the leading newspapers. One *Boston Globe* cartoon pictured an anxious president studying a spreadsheet of potential cabinet nominees with a few boxes checked ("Hispanic Males," "Black Females") but many left blank: "Icelandic Americans," "Gay Ambidextrous Americans," and "Lesbian Chess-Playing Beer-Drinking Americans." Yet these critics rarely challenged the asserted "meritocracy" of past administrations, when presidents parceled out cabinet positions to friends, brothers, and campaign contributors, or when politicians "balanced" party tickets with the right mix of Irish Catholics and Episcopalian WASPs. As a *Newsweek* article, aptly titled "White Male Paranoia," pointed out, conservatives often objected that the Clinton administration's "insistence on appointing the best female attorney general baldly and publicly violated the canons of fair play and equal opportunity. So, of course, does the ratio of male to female attorneys general in American history: counting Janet Reno, it now stands at seventy-seven to one. . . ." Clinton's widely criticized efforts put women in only three of fourteen cabinet seats, and almost no key White House advisory positions.[61]

Bean counting is not exactly new in American political life or in other employment and educational contexts. But some things *are* new: the type of beans, the willingness to count out loud, and the backlash that results. The handwringing over Clinton's commitment to diversity typifies our current dilemma. Given the persistence of racial and gender bias, many women and men of color would never even get auditions for desirable positions without affirmative action. But when these individuals receive more than walk-on opportunities, they pay a substantial price: their qualifications, credibility, and self-confidence are subject to continual challenge.

Such mixed results have much to do with affirmative action's practical successes and political failures. The most effective initiatives have also been the most controversial: those that incorporate temporary preferences for qualified individuals. Social science research generally finds that such affirmative action programs have been moderately successful in increasing opportunities for underrepresented groups. Yet public opinion polls indicate that most forms of preferential treatment provoke substantial resistance. Although results vary somewhat depending on how questions are asked, about three-fourths of white men, two-thirds of white women, and two-fifths of people of color oppose preferences on the basis of race or gender.[62]

Fueling this opposition is a range of concerns, some more explicit than others. Most critics claim a moral high ground; they maintain that sex- and race-based remedies subvert the premise of equal opportunity that they are seeking to establish. But underlying such objections are also less defensible assumptions and unstated anxieties. One widespread view is that women no longer need and seldom benefit from affirmative action. As participants in a recent survey put it, there may have been a problem "a hundred years ago." But that was then and this is now. Qualified women can make it without special help. "After all, I did." Or "she did." A related assumption is that white women have more to lose than to gain from affirmative action. Many of these women "stand by their man," and oppose preferential-treatment programs that might jeopardize opportunities for their husbands or sons.[63]

Self-interest is, of course, also part of the subtext for men's opposition. Among many Americans, preferential treatment has become a lightning rod for more general anxieties about stagnant incomes, job security, and educational opportunities. As commentator Michael Kinsley notes, affirmative action is one of the few policies that "gives white men whining rights in the victimization bazaar, just like minorities and women." Those who claim to be opposed "in principle" to gender or color consciousness obtain a "moral gloss for self-interest" and a socially acceptable way of expressing sexist or racist prejudices.[64]

Of course, not all opposition to preferential treatment is based on personal considerations or group biases. Many individuals, including some beneficiaries of affirmative action, believe that it is indefensible on both moral and practical grounds. The moral argument is that allocating educational and employment opportunities on the basis of sex or race compromises fundamental values of individual merit and responsibility. Preferential treatment based on involuntary group characteristics rather than on individual qualifications reinforces precisely the kind of gender and color consciousness that created problems in the first place.[65]

Whatever obligation society has to remedy the effects of discrimination, critics argue, the costs of that remedy should not fall on individual white males who are not personally responsible for injustice. Nor are affirmative action programs appropriate strategies for compensation, since they seldom reach individuals who have suffered most from discrimination. As one opponent of preferential treatment put it, "My parents were impoverished immigrants. Neither they nor we . . . oppressed anyone. Yet my sons are punished." And what's worse, they may be losing out to some upper-middle-class female or nonwhite applicant who looks anything but oppressed. To many commentators, the moral justification for favoritism toward white women is particularly weak because they have not endured the same socioeconomic disadvantages as people of color. From this perspective, the way to achieve gender blindness in society is not to enshrine it in law. As the title of an article by Supreme Court Justice Antonin Scalia suggests, the problem with affirmative action is that the "cure" is worse than the "disease."[66]

The problem with this argument, however, is that it understates both the lingering consequences of the disease and the limitations of other remedies. The claim that people should be treated on the basis of individual rather than group characteristics sounds right. But it comes several generations too early and several centuries too late. Group treatment has been a pervasive feature of America's social, economic, and political landscape and has exposed white women as well as minorities to systematic injustice. When defenders of affirmative action mention the historical roots and institutional practices that perpetuate inequality, "America yawns." Yet such discrimination has left a legacy of underrepresentation that neutral mandates have failed to correct. At this juncture, ignoring racial and gender differences will simply perpetuate them.[67]

We pay homage to equal opportunity and merit selection in principle, but in practice these principles are often not "even accepted, let alone realized." A delightfully ironic example involves a recent admissions controversy on a prominent Ivy League campus. One of its alumni wrote a letter to the school's newspaper claiming that his son had been passed over in the rush to admit less deserving women and minority applicants. It then emerged that while the overall odds of admission were one in seven, for children of alumni they were almost one in two. A recent study of the nation's ten most selective educational institutions found that they have admitted far more whites through alumni preferences than blacks and Hispanics through affirmative action.[68]

Contrary to opponents' claims, most ostensibly "meritocratic" decisions reflect some considerations unrelated to merit or to an individual's own efforts and talents. As is clear from the employment cases discussed earlier—such as those involving road workers, accountants, and ABC's televised job applicants—bias often creeps into the assessment of even "objective" qualifications. The American Society of Personnel Administration has acknowledged as much. In a brief supporting affirmative action before the Supreme Court, the society noted that rarely is there "a single 'best qualified' person for a job." Effective personnel systems will produce several "fully qualified" candidates with different strengths, and final selections will be "at best subjective." Moreover, considerations apart from merit, such as family background, economic resources, childhood environment, and societal stereotypes, all affect access to the educational and employment opportunities on which merit-based qualifications depend. Susan Faludi, the recipient of multiple journalistic awards, got her first press job through affirmative action. In an earlier era, she notes, the position would probably have gone to the son or nephew of a white male editor. No one would have called it "affirmative nepotism."[69]

So too, merit standards are highly imperfect predictors of academic or job performance. Law school admission is a representative example. Unsuccessful white applicants have sometimes successfully challenged admission systems that prefer nonwhite candidates with slightly lower grade point averages and LSAT test scores. But these qualifications are extremely inadequate measures of the talents that produce successful lawyers. Taken together, grades and test scores predict only about a quarter of the variation in grades among first-year law students. And we have no idea how well performance at the beginning of law school measures performance on the job.[70]

What we do know is that most surveyed practitioners think that law schools fail to teach or test many of the interpersonal skills most critical for professional success, such as interviewing and negotiating. As legal educators increasingly have recognized, part of their mission *should* be to teach potential lawyers how to collaborate and communicate with those who are "different." Such a mission requires students with varied backgrounds, experiences, and strengths. Diversity does not compete with educational quality—it enhances it.[71]

The moral case against affirmative action either denies the importance of these values or sidesteps the difficulties of realizing them under race- or gender-blind standards. Neutrality in formal policy cannot correct for bias in social practices. Estimates suggest that, without affirmative action programs, fewer than a fifth of African Americans who graduated from law school in the 1970s would have been admitted. Comparable underrepresentation would persist today. The same is true in a wide array of occupations. The most systematic studies find that affirmative action has significantly expanded employment and educational opportunities for white women and people of color from all socioeconomic backgrounds.[72]

We are, in short, unlikely to achieve a society without race or gender prejudices if we pretend that we are already there or that all preferences are equally objectionable. Disfavoring women stigmatizes, stereotypes, and subordinates; disfavoring white males does not. This is not to discount the economic injury or sense of unfairness that individual men may experience. But white males as a group suffer no implications of inferiority or systematic subordination as a result of affirmative action.

Of course, as opponents emphasize, preferential treatment does stigmatize some individuals: its beneficiaries. For this reason, critics often argue that affirmative action, even if morally acceptable, is socially counterproductive. Singling out women for special assistance risks reinforcing the very assumptions of inferiority that society should be trying to eliminate. Selecting those who might not succeed by conventional criteria also risks compromising organizational goals and entrenching negative stereotypes. In contexts involving affirmative action, even when white women or people of color perform effectively after affirmative action, their success is likely to be devalued. As long as they appear unable to advance without special favors, societal prejudices will persist.

In critics' view, the problem is not simply the inferiority that others attribute to affirmative action candidates. It is also the effect that favoritism has on the candidates themselves. Opponents claim that special treatment erodes recipients' incentives for excellence and their self-esteem when they achieve it. According to Shelby Steele, "affirmative action tells us that . . . preferences can do for us what we cannot do for ourselves." If individuals believe that they owe their positions to favoritism rather than their own achievements, why should they bother to achieve?[73]

The problem with these arguments is not that stigma is insignificant, but rather that critics mistake its causes and solutions. Social science research does indeed show that individuals rate a woman's performance lower when they believe that her selection is based at least partly on sex or race. Under these circumstances, women also devalue their own successes, and are less likely to be interested in continuing in their positions. But such assumptions of inferiority predate preferential treatment and would persist without it. Affirmative action is not responsible for adverse stereotypes. Racism and sexism are. White males who have long benefited from preferences by schools, jobs, and clubs have suffered no discernible loss of self-esteem. Nor have the children of alumni who get special treatment in school admissions; they certainly aren't clamoring for policy changes that would spare their own children such injuries.[74]

What, moreover, is the likely alternative to affirmative action programs? A return to the "neutral" policies that have perpetuated gender and racial hierarchies is hardly preferable. Women who benefit from preferential treatment may experience some stigma, but the absence of women is stigmatizing as well. Many members of underrepresented groups find it demeaning to lose affirmative action on the ground that they will experience it as demeaning. Barbara Babcock made a similar point while serving as an assistant attorney general in the Carter administration. When asked how she felt about gaining her position because she was a woman, Babcock responded, "It's better than not getting your job because you're a woman."

A final set of objections to affirmative action involves its cost not to recipients but to everyone else. Critics complain that race and gender preferences increase the risk of incompetent performance among beneficiaries and of resentment among their competitors. While there is no systematic evidence for the first claim, there is all too much for the second. Affirmative action programs target only those who are basically qualified, and researchers have found no declines in performance as a result of those programs. Nor have studies of employment grievances found significant evidence of overbroad preferences. One review of some 3,000 recent federal discrimination cases revealed fewer than 100 claims of reverse discrimination, and only six white male litigants prevailed.[75]

Researchers do, however, find plenty of male resentment, although affirmative action is often the scapegoat rather than the cause of the problem. Such misdirected misogyny figures in many of the "angry white male" cartoons that followed the 1994 elections. In one representative version, several men are venting their rage over drinks at a bar.

Corporations, they note, are laying them off or cutting their salaries. "So," fumes one of these men, "are we angry at corporations?" "No," comes the response. "At Hillary Clinton!"[76]

Affirmative action would be an even more plausible if somewhat less humorous target than the First Lady. It provides a socially acceptable way for unsuccessful white male applicants to rationalize their failures and vent their frustrations. It also gives employers and educators an acceptable excuse for rejecting those applicants. Yet the real reasons may have less to do with affirmative action than with the structure and competitiveness of the market or the relative qualifications of candidates.

A case in point involves academic hiring. Since the 1970s, white male Ph.D.'s, particularly in the humanities, have been complaining about the absence of equal opportunity for *them*. In their view, jobs and promotions are now going only to the "black lesbian with a nose ring studying literature by the disabled." But available research makes clear that any such mythical applicant isn't going to have a cushy experience either.[77]

Academic institutions have a long and shameful history of undervaluing work by and about members of subordinate groups. Although many departments are now trying to set a different course, their efforts are not the primary cause of hiring problems for white men. Those problems result from shrinking resources in higher education and overproduction of Ph.D. candidates for the limited faculty positions available. Some institutions receive more than 500 applications for a single opening. It makes little sense for those 499 disappointed applicants to blame white women and minority competitors. More appropriate targets would be the largely white male legislators who are cutting university budgets and the administrators who are admitting graduate students in numbers far beyond the projected faculty openings.[78]

Just as affirmative action is not the primary cause of employment problems for white men, it is not the primary solution for white women and people of color. Critics are right in claiming that limited preferential treatment can too readily pass for gender or racial justice on the cheap. Rather than address the root causes of underrepresentation, many decisionmakers have been willing to settle for token efforts at diversity. But if we simply hand out a few, usually entry-level positions to the "best black" or "best woman" and call it a day, we haven't solved the problem. We have only masked it.[79]

Although critics appropriately underscore the limits of affirmative action programs, it by no means follows that abolishing them would improve the situation. It is particularly galling to hear conservative political and business leaders condemn preferential treatment because it "diverts attention from the fundamental problems," such as inadequacies in early-education, job training, mentoring, work/family, and antidiscrimination initiatives. Whose attention? Theirs? Many of these opponents of affirmative action are also working to dismantle government programs aimed at the "fundamental" problems.

History suggests that decisionmakers are most likely to develop antidiscrimination strategies when white women and people of color are well represented in the decisionmaking process. Affirmative action is not the only means of promoting diversity among policy leaders. But it is a crucial one. Preferential programs have made an important difference in supplying underrepresented groups with role models, mentors, and spokespersons.

We should, of course, look for ways to reduce the need for affirmative action and the backlash that accompanies it. Tailoring programs carefully is part of the answer. Dismantling them entirely is not. President Clinton's commitment to effective administration of federal programs strikes a defensible political balance; it maintains some forms of preferential treatment but prohibits rigid quotas, assistance for unqualified applicants, or perpetuation of programs after their purposes have been achieved. So too, in other public- and private-sector contexts, the aim should be support for flexible goals that seek to attract and retain a critical mass of underrepresented groups. Managers and administrators should be accountable for achieving such objectives, minimizing backlash, and avoiding use of diversity as a "diplomatic" excuse for rejecting white males. Where there are unnecessary costs connected with affirmative action, we should, as Clinton maintains, "mend it, not end it."

To reduce gender consciousness in the long run, we cannot live without it in the short run. Some corrective action is essential to counteract the biases that remain. Without affirmative action, policies may be gender-blind but people are not.

Pay Equity

If affirmative action is the hot political issue on the employment agenda of the 1990s, pay equity is the cold-storage alternative. Its profile is curiously low, given that surveyed women identify increased earnings as their top reform priority. Despite such support, the most direct efforts to reduce male-female wage gaps seem frozen in place. The most prominent pay equity strategy, comparable worth, relies on job evaluation surveys to ensure that equivalent work receives equivalent compensation. During the 1980s, a series of lawsuits, legislative efforts, and union campaigns sought such pay equity reforms. But after some modest successes, largely in the public sector, and some major setbacks in the courts, the concept took early retirement. In the first four years of the Clinton administration, progress in this area was largely rhetorical. The president declared a National Pay Inequity Awareness Day and issued a proclamation urging all employers to see that their employees "are paid fairly for their work." More concrete federal proposals are going nowhere slowly, and most private-sector efforts are on perpetual hold. Now when the subject comes up at all, it is often in the form of a question: "Whatever happened to pay equity?"[80]

In part, the concept proved easier to attack than to justify, or even to explain. The most common approach uses job evaluation techniques to identify characteristics relevant to compensation (such as skill, responsibility, and working conditions). Evaluators then compare existing salary levels in light of those characteristics. This process frequently exposes the undervaluation of women's work: for example, nurses who earn less than tree trimmers, schoolteachers who earn less than state liquor store clerks, and librarians who earn less than street crossing guards. Similar patterns of undervaluation are apparent in job sectors dominated by employees of color. Antidiscrimination laws do not remedy such patterns, because they only prohibit unequal pay for work that is "substantially equal." Under prevailing judicial interpretations, the jobs must be essentially identical, not simply comparable, in their required skill, effort, responsibility, and working conditions.[81]

Efforts to institutionalize broader requirements of pay equity have unleashed widespread opposition. Attacks come from all points on the political spectrum. Critics from the right claim that replacing market mechanisms with bureaucratic salary determinations would invite economic chaos. From their perspective, comparable worth is "socialism in drag," and the "looniest idea since Looney Tunes." Increasing women's wages reportedly would increase inflation, worsen unemployment, and distort labor supply and demand. By contrast, critics from the left worry that management can manipulate job evaluation surveys to pit workers against one another and to produce only minor improvements. The result would be to rationalize pay disparities, reduce incentives for women to leave pink-collar ghettos, and increase divisiveness among workers across lines of class and race as well as gender. As a consequence, we would see slightly modified compensation structures in which the "haves" still came out far ahead, only with a few more women among them. To critics on the right, pay equity is a radical departure from tested market principles. To critics on the left, it is by no means radical enough.[82]

Although both sides in this debate have a point, neither is as damning as their rhetoric suggests. Conservatives correctly note that comparing the "worth" of particular jobs is an inherently difficult and ultimately subjective undertaking. Salaries do not depend solely on objective factors such as skill, responsibility, and working conditions, as the relative incomes of leading fashion models and public-health professionals suggest.

Since the nature of job evaluation is inevitably subjective, experts often disagree about how much weight they should give to particular abilities or working conditions, and how much skill a given position requires. Gender bias can enter such determinations at any point. For example, one salary evaluation study for New York public employees concluded that zoo keepers needed special skill to care for baby animals, but that caring for human infants and toddlers in daycare centers was essentially unskilled labor, justifying much lower salaries. Such recommendations run counter to those of child development experts, whose research consistently shows that caring *well* for small children in institutional settings often requires substantial education and training.[83]

Similar biases are apparent in a wide range of other occupations. Men in manual-labor occupations typically receive upward salary adjustments when their jobs involve "dirt." However, women caring for hospital and nursing-home patients often get no similar adjustments if their work involves blood and bedpans. As researchers Jerry Jacobs and Ronnie Steinberg note, "male dirt" is worth more.[84]

Criticisms of subjectivity in pay equity systems also ignore a related and ultimately more important question: What is the alternative? Gender stereotypes already distort our evaluations of "women's work." Case studies of the wage-setting process make clear that bias is what we have now; the fact that it is embedded in market structures does not make it morally just or economically productive. Nor has a decade's experience with pay equity reforms here and abroad led to the kind of inflation, unemployment, or inefficiency that conservative critics project. The typical cost of American comparable-worth initiatives has been no more than 5 to 10 percent of total wages, phased in over a number of years. The foundations of the free market are not shaking as a result.[85]

This, of course, is little consolation to critics from the left. And they clearly are correct that many pay equity reforms have fallen far short of achieving equity in fact, and that women who need help most have benefited least. But once again, what is the alternative? As one four-teen-state survey noted, women as a group are not worse off as a result of comparable-worth initiatives, and their wage rates in comparison to those of men typically have increased from 1 to 8 percent.[86]

Experience in states such as Minnesota and Washington suggests both the potential and the limitations of pay equity strategies. When these states required that public-sector employers reassess workforce compensation and remedy bias, managers sometimes used job evaluation surveys to create conflict among different groups of workers and to weaken unions that had to cope with such conflict. By claiming that certain minor salary adjustments reflected "objective" expert judgments, management was able to insulate wage hierarchies from more searching review. Yet despite those limitations, the gains for female workers were by no means trivial. Salary adjustments narrowed the gender pay gap in Minnesota by 6 to 8 percent and increased annual earnings for the lowest-paid Washington women by about 10 percent. The total cost in each state ran to less than 4 percent of payroll.[87]

Pay equity is not a complete cure for workplace inequities. But it pushes the reform process in the right direction. Focusing on comparable worth in union negotiations and political campaigns has helped raise women's expectations and strengthen their organizing skills. By directing public attention to wage disparities, the pay equity struggle can raise fundamental questions not just about gender equality but also about social priorities. How much difference across salary levels is essential to promote workplace efficiency? Does "efficiency" demand that American chief executive officers receive, on average, 160 times the take-home pay of an average worker? Are we comfortable with the fact that the United States has the widest income gaps of any industrialized nation? Do we want a society that pays more for gas station attendants than childcare attendants, whatever the male/female composition of those jobs?[88]

By making these questions visible and forcing them onto legislative and collective-bargaining agendas, pay equity campaigns can promote progress for all subordinate groups. Comparable worth could be a radical concept, but not in the sense critics usually claim. It need not imply a centrally planned economy, but it can address biases in our current structure.

In biblical times, women workers were valued at thirty pieces of silver and men at fifty. After some 2,500 years, this ratio has made only modest improvement. The difference is that, for the first time, many societies are trying to do something about it.[89]

America does not lack for promising proposals. Women's groups, policy experts, and governmental agencies all have lists. And while there is some disagreement about what belongs at the top, these policy agendas look strikingly similar. They center on two basic strategies.

First, we should promote greater gender equity in workplace opportunities and reward structures. This, in turn, requires more support for programs that recruit, train, and mentor women in nontraditional occupations. We also need more education and accountability on gender-related initiatives. Maintaining affirmative action programs, strengthening equal-opportunity laws, mandating pay equity, and increasing governmental enforcement resources are all critical.

Second, we should make it easier for both sexes to combine work and family responsibilities, while encouraging more equal distribution of those responsibilities. Adequate family leave, childcare, flexible schedules, and part-time work must become social priorities. This is more likely to happen if men bear more of the cost of their absence. As experience in other countries such as Sweden suggests, societies can promote greater sharing of family obligations through educational and media initiatives, as well as through financial incentives such as paid paternity leave.[90]

Such changes demand greater political commitment. Women must make their voices heard in voting booths, union campaigns, and work-place committees. For this to happen, we need to create a safer climate for raising "women's issues," and we need to emphasize that these issues affect not only women. They determine the productivity of our workforce and the future of our children. At stake is not only equality for women but the quality of life for all of us.

7

Family Values

The family, we are told, is in "crisis," and the women's movement is at least partly responsible. Feminism is blamed for free love, teen pregnancy, broken homes, and "baby killing." Commentators who trace the logical consequences of man-hating women and career-driven, neglectful mothers have even managed to find them at the root of the Los Angeles riots and the Oklahoma City bombing. To many Americans, the only remedy for our current social ills is a return to traditional family structures and the values that sustain them.[1]

Such accounts of the "crisis" misstate its dimensions, misdescribe its causes, and misjudge its solutions. All too often, our conventional wisdom on family issues denies the problem of gender inequality and the need for more adequate societal responses. On matters involving divorce, custody, welfare, and reproductive choice, Americans tend to hold individual women far too responsible for both the problem and the solution. We make family values central to our political rhetoric but not to our policy priorities. Of course, talk is cheap and effective social programs are not. But as long as we deny the true nature of our difficulties, we are destined to compound them.

Problems with the "Problem"

To many Americans, our nation's increasing numbers of divorces and unwed parents reflect a fundamental national crisis: a breakdown in the traditional family. Ironically enough, even when fatherlessness figures in descriptions of this crisis, most of the blame centers on mothers. Although "deadbeat dads" attract rhetorical abuse, they frequently escape practical consequences. Promiscuous teens and indolent welfare recipients are more vulnerable targets. In many such portrayals of family failure, women figure as the central villains, although they are also the primary victims.[2]

Perceptions of the current crisis build on several trends. Close to half of all marriages end in divorce, and most American children will spend some time living in a single-parent family. The United States also has the highest rate of adolescent pregnancy and childbirth among Western industrialized nations. These trends raise a variety of concerns. Half of all single-parent households are below the poverty line and many more are at the edge. Women head about 85 percent of these families, and the difficulties of combining primary-caretaker and primary-breadwinner roles take a heavy toll. Teenage mothers are particularly likely to have educational and employment difficulties. According to some studies, children growing up with only one biological parent also have disproportionate rates of delinquency, behavioral problems, school failure, and unemployment, even when race and family income are taken into account.[3]

Yet much conventional wisdom concerning our current "crisis" creates a distorted picture both of family life today and of its supposedly idyllic past. Even in the much romanticized 1950s, when "father knew best" and families "stayed together for the sake of the children," not everyone lived happily ever after. One-fourth of all Americans and one-third of all children were poor. Women of color seldom could afford to be full-time mothers, and neither they nor most white women workers could escape low-status, poorly paid occupations. Married women reported exceptionally high levels of dissatisfaction, and only about 10 percent of surveyed mothers wanted their daughters to have the same kind of lives that they had.[4]

Descriptions of our contemporary plight are equally distorted. Many Americans see poverty mainly as a problem of the urban underclass, perpetuated by "children having children" and by women of color with large families and little inclination to work. Other common diagnoses of the problem single out no-fault divorce, casual sex, and deviant (that is, nonheterosexual) lifestyles. For all of these patterns, the women's movement gets much of the blame. Radical feminists' "antifamily values," disdain for traditional homemaking, and demands for sexual liberation are held responsible for many of our current ills.[5]

Such popular images are out of touch with social realities. Contrary to widespread assumptions, most poverty remains outside the inner city, and many of the poor are divorced and separated white women. Mothers on welfare have smaller-than-average families, and most are in the labor force at least part time. Rates of childbearing among teenagers have declined, not increased, over the last decade, and the vast majority of these mothers are not children themselves; they are eighteen- and nineteen-year-olds, most of them white.[6]

Neither is there evidence for the common view that society's increasing acceptance of same-sex couples threatens traditional family structures and their underlying values. Countries that have legalized homosexual conduct do not experience an increase in such activity or a decline in heterosexual marriage. Nor are gay and lesbian parents disproportionately likely to raise children with same-sex orientations or behavioral problems. Millions of individuals live in committed same-sex relationships which provide the same love, support, and stability as marriage does. These relationships deserve the same recognition.[7]

This is not to imply that all is entirely well with American families. But it is to suggest that we are denying the true nature of our challenges. The root of our difficulties lies not in recent changes in family structures but in our refusal to address their underlying causes and accompanying hardships. As the following discussion also makes clear, the women's movement is not the source of the nation's problems. However, responding to the gender inequalities that it identifies is an essential part of the solution.

Divorce American Style

Popular perceptions of divorce law reflect comfortable myths. One family fantasy is that before "women's so-called liberation," marriages stayed together, homemakers stayed home, and almost everyone benefited, especially the kids. Then along came feminists, agitating for divorce on demand, sex-neutral statutes, and full-time careers, and look what happened: impoverished families, displaced homemakers, and fatherless kids with messed-up lives.

The women's movement is blamed for being both too hard on men and not hard enough. Contemporary champions of divorced home-makers claim that feminism has left them unprotected; the push for gender equality in formal law has ignored gender inequality in social fact. According to accounts like Nicholas Davidson's *The Failure of Feminism,* and Carolyn Graglia's "The Housewife as Pariah," the women's movement of the 1970s "forced through 'no-fault' divorce laws that trampled on homemakers' hard-earned rights to share in the fruit of [longstanding] marriages . . . The actions of [these] feminists led to real suffering for hundreds of thousands of women with little or no compensating benefit."[8]

By contrast, many divorced men and their increasingly vocal leader-ship insist that feminism has trampled *their* rights and that the justice system is biased against *them*. In principle, they claim, the law may promise equal treatment between the spouses. But in practice, it doesn't work out that way. According to fathers'-rights groups, ex-husbands are now experiencing the modern equivalent of "taxation without repre-sentation": they are denied visitation, impoverished by support pay-ments, and given no say in how their money is spent. Vindictive ex-wives reportedly keep fathers away from piano recitals and keep child support away from children. Funds that should go for kids' needs end up subsidizing mothers' lavish lifestyles. No wonder many men don't want to see or support their former families. From this perspective, "deadbeat dads" look like mainly "working-class men who must get by on very modest incomes to begin with." At the other end of the scale, affluent men allegedly pay through the nose upon divorce.[9]

Some judges hold similar views. As one Colorado court put it, "These women who stay home and cook and clean and do whatever it is they do, and think that they're entitled to the money that their husbands go out and work for, have another think coming." What such women need to learn, a California judge agreed, is that marriage "is not a ticket to a perpetual pension." These alimony drones should just shape up and get a real job. According to the chair of the American Bar Association Family Law Section, "A lot of judges are saying, 'You wanted to be equal, here you go.'"[10]

All that's missing from these indictments of women and the women's movement is evidence. Although feminists get much of the blame for the legacy of no-fault divorce, they were not prominent in most states' reform efforts. Few of the legislators, lawyers, and family law experts who *were* responsible for reform focused on equality for women. Rather, reformers' principal objective was to reduce the fraud, acrimony, and unnecessary expense that resulted from restrictive fault-based requirements. When gender equity surfaced in legislative debates, the concern usually was equity for men, who were supposedly staggering under excessive alimony payments.[11]

This problem turned out to be vastly overstated. Researchers estimate that even during the pre-reform era only about a fifth of women received regular spousal support. Since the 1970s, the number has declined still further. But until quite recently, the absence of systematic data allowed male judges and legislators to rely on misleading anecdotal experience. Although women's-rights advocates are now prominent in the campaign for divorce reform, their message meets resistance on several fronts.[12]

The problem is not a lack of evidence concerning gender inequality following divorce. Recent research consistently finds that the income of divorced women substantially falls and that of divorced men substantially rises. More than 40 percent of displaced homemakers are poor. Although the economic situation of most divorced women eventually improves, especially if they remarry, over half go through periods of considerable hardship and many older women remain in poverty.[13]

State divorce laws typically promise either "equality" or "equity" between the spouses, but in practice women receive neither. Part of the problem lies in contemporary approaches to marital property. Many courts mandate fifty-fifty splits of existing assets or give preference to the spouse who "earns" them. Yet as gender bias commissions often note, it is scarcely "equal" when the husband receives half of the marital property and the other half is shared by the wife and children. The inequity escalates when judges overestimate women's likelihood of remarriage and underestimate their career sacrifices. As Chapter 6 indicates, wives assume about 70 percent of household obligations in the typical marriage, and pay the price in lowered earning capacity. Yet many courts and legislatures are highly insensitive to the plight of older displaced homemakers with few marketable skills.[14]

Seldom are decisionmakers as candid as one Colorado judge who aired his disgust at the "Pekingese Problem"—a "generation of women bred for show," unwilling to leave the "gravy train" for a real job. But the same devaluation of women's domestic contributions underlies other rulings. For example, many courts refuse to award continuing financial assistance to homemakers who have made irreversible career sacrifices. Although four-fifths of women believe that they will get spousal support if they need it, only about a sixth of divorced wives actually receive such payments. Two-thirds of these awards are for brief periods, the amounts are usually modest, and only half are fully paid. A judicial survey involving hypothetical cases illustrates the problem. One question featured a nurse who had supported her husband through eight years of college, medical school, and residency, and then, after divorce, wanted to attend medical school herself. Less than a third of surveyed judges would have been willing to grant her four years of support; most thought it "unfair" to saddle her affluent ex-husband with such expenses when she was already self-sufficient.[15]

Courts' preference for a "clean break" rather than continuing spousal assistance institutionalizes gender disadvantages. Since more than half of divorcing couples have no significant property to divide at the time of divorce, many women end up with no compensation for career sacrifices. The problem is compounded by the inability of many wives to afford legal battles over settlements, and by the willingness of some husbands to use custody as a bargaining chip in financial negotiations. Although men's-rights activists deny that this occurs, surveyed attorneys suggest otherwise. They estimate that in more than a fifth of divorce cases, one parent, almost always the mother, experiences pressure to make financial concessions in order to prevent custody battles.[16]

Inadequate child support adds further difficulties. Much of the inequality of divorced women stems from one central fact: after most marriages end, men become single and women become single mothers. About four out of five divorces involve minor children, and women have physical custody in close to 90 percent of these cases. The result is that divorcing wives end up with greater needs and fewer resources than their husbands.[17]

Despite almost two decades of reform effort, America has made highly inadequate progress in increasing either the size or the reliability of child support. Some $30 billion in support awards remains unpaid. About 40 percent of single mothers receive no court-awarded assistance, and only half of the rest ultimately obtain full payment. The average amount of child support ordered is well below the actual costs of childrearing and a third to a half of what experts estimate that fathers could afford. Yet men are over fifteen times more likely to default on child support than on car payments. About half of all divorced fathers drop out physically as well as financially from their children's lives. Within a few years after divorce, fewer than a fourth of noncustodial fathers continue weekly visits.[18]

Of course, some mothers discourage contact, especially in circumstances presenting a high risk of conflict or abuse. But many fathers exit without such prompting. Men who avoided major childcare responsibilities during marriage often are even less willing to undertake them after divorce. More than 40 percent of surveyed women report that they would prefer more visitation and that their ex-husbands are not fulfilling even the minimal responsibilities specified in their custody agreements.[19]

Yet the most popular recent reform proposals mischaracterize both the problem and the remedy. According to a growing number of state legislators, the culprit is no-fault divorce law, and the appropriate response is to make it harder for couples to end a marriage if one partner objects. A majority of Americans support such reforms, and an increasing number of state legislatures are considering them. The most widely discussed proposals would deny divorce in cases involving children or one spouse's objection, unless the other spouse could prove fault, such as adultery, desertion, or extreme cruelty. Yet we have tried such initiatives before, and we should not yearn to relive the experience.[20]

Fault-based proposals rest on two assumptions. The first is that divorce brings a wide range of problems, particularly for children, who have disproportionate rates of poverty, delinquency, substance abuse, and educational difficulties. Although virtually no one denies the seriousness of these problems, the question is what to do about them. And there is no persuasive evidence for a second key assumption: that requiring proof of fault will discourage hasty, ill-considered divorces and promote children's well-being.

Some proponents of fault-based initiatives even deny that evidence is necessary. According to David Blankenhorn, president of the Institute for American Values, it is "intuitively obvious [that] . . . if you make it quicker and easier to break a marriage commitment . . . [then] more people will take that opportunity." Other proponents note that divorce rates have increased following no-fault reforms.[21]

Yet such arguments confuse cause and effect. As almost all experts in the field agree, changes in divorce law were a response to, not the trigger for, changes in public attitudes and behaviors. Divorce rates were rising even before no-fault legislation; the temporary increase following statutory reforms largely reflected legal formalization of separations that already had occurred. Careful cross-cultural research finds no significant causal relationship between the stringency of marital laws and the frequency of marital breakdowns. Making divorce harder does not keep couples together; it just makes the process of formal separation more costly and acrimonious. And according to the most systematic research, what harms children is high levels of conflict, low incomes, and poor-quality parenting, not divorce per se.[22]

Certainly this nation's experience with fault-based divorce statutes has little to recommend it. These statutes created wide disparities between the law in form and the law in fact, and between divorce for the rich and divorce for the poor. Individuals with sufficient resources could subvert their state's fault-based requirements by traveling to more permissive jurisdictions or by staging courtroom charades closer to home. The latter approach produced certain standard stories. In New York, for example, where adultery remained the only ground for divorce until 1966, court records revealed countless reenactments of the same carefully scripted melodrama, with the same supporting cast of paid "mistresses" rented for the occasion. As one judge noted, these women always seemed to be wearing a "sheer pink robe. It was never blue, always pink." Parties without funds for expensive courtroom dramas often resorted to self-help measures: domestic violence, desertion, or unenforceable mail-order divorce decrees.[23]

This is not an era we should strive to re-create. Nor would children's lives be better if we did. Most evidence indicates that a high-conflict marriage results in more problems for a child than a no-fault divorce. Of course, few would disagree with Hillary Clinton's much-publicized opinion in *It Takes a Village* that "people with children need to ask themselves whether they have given a marriage their best shot and what more they can do to make it work before they call it quits." But how often do parents fail to ask those questions now? For couples who do, what makes us think that fault-based divorce statutes would improve the situation?[24]

Proponents of such legislation claim that current law is too permissive. According to matrimonial lawyer George Stern, people can now say, "What the heck, we'll run down to the courthouse and we'll get a divorce." Since wives normally initiate most divorce proceedings, they attract special criticism for addressing their own "boredom" at the expense of their children's needs. Sponsors of fault-based statutes want to restrain these "walkaway wives" and end an era in which it is "easier to [escape] a marriage than . . . a contract for a household appliance." Yet researchers who have actually studied divorcing families paint a quite different picture of both divorce law and those who invoke it. Unlike contracts for appliances, divorce settlements must be approved by a judge, and their enforcement is no simple matter. Few mothers who choose to end their marriages do so casually. According to the divorced women in Demie Kurz's recent study *For Richer, For Poorer*, more than two-thirds of their former husbands were violent, a fifth were committing adultery, and about 15 percent had substance abuse or similar problems. With the benefit of hindsight, these women generally did not view their decisions as ill-considered. Five years after the divorce, only a fourth had negative feelings about the choice, and many of these reactions were connected only to its economic consequences.[25]

Of course, the vast majority of these women could probably have proven fault under recent reform proposals. But doing so would have been costly, acrimonious, and, for women in abusive marriages, potentially dangerous. Even if persuasive evidence suggested that too many divorces are impulsive, the most logical response would be waiting periods, not fault-based requirements. Given the already high costs of divorce, both emotional and economic, adding further legal hurdles is hardly the answer.

Reformers have identified real problems but tackled them at the wrong end. The way to prevent divorce is to prevent bad marriages. And when that fails, the way to minimize the costs of marital breakdowns is to ensure adequate economic support and social services for divorcing families. Recent proposals for mandatory waiting periods and counseling before marriage are promising strategies. So are proposals to increase resources for domestic-violence prevention and substance abuse treatment. But we also need to focus more directly on the gender inequalities accompanying divorce, and on society's responsibility to address them.[26]

As long as we continue denying that basic responsibility, we will end up with "cheap-fix" strategies like fault-based divorce. Such strategies are attractive because they do not involve substantial societal resources. But for divorcing couples, they will be neither cheap nor a fix. A better alternative is to change both the law and the attitudes of those applying it. Marital property and support law should promote more equal standards of living for divorced spouses. Where one partner has made irreversible career sacrifices, the couple's income should be shared for a period proportional to the length of their marriage or of their children's dependency. More legal assistance, more adequate child support awards, and more effective enforcement are also critical. Promising proposals include increased sanctions for noncompliance, expanded prosecutorial resources, and centralized collection authority in a federal agency. If we invested significant resources as well as rhetoric in our campaigns against deadbeat dads, we could greatly reduce the hardships for single moms.[27]

Yet it is naive to assume, as do most Americans, that we can solve all our child support problems through better enforcement. In many cases, fathers lack adequate assets or the costs of collection are prohibitive. Particularly when marriages end after a relatively short period or the couple lacks adequate income, ex-husbands cannot be expected to compensate for all the difficulties facing their former wives. Experts increasingly agree that, in the long run, we would be better off with a national "child assurance system" like the ones in Scandinavian countries. Under such a system, the government, rather than individual mothers, collects child support payments and provides supplemental subsidies where parental resources are insufficient.[28]

So too, we cannot address all the gender disadvantages associated with divorce simply by changing divorce law. Many of these disadvantages stem from deeper structural inadequacies in employment, welfare, health, and daycare policies. The stakes in addressing these problems involve fairness not just for women but also for their children.

Double Binds and Double Standards for Child Custody

Few issues arouse more conflict between the sexes than those involving child custody. And few legal policies have been more skewed by gender bias than those governing custody disputes. To be sure, the biases have shifted over time. Under early American law, fathers were entitled to sole custody of all minor children; mothers were entitled to "reverence and respect." During the latter part of the nineteenth century, courts' focus shifted from men's rights to children's interests. Under this new legal standard, judges became unwilling to "snatch" a child of "tender years" from the bosom of an affectionate mother and to place it in the "coarse hands of the father," except in cases of maternal unfitness.[29]

Not all women benefited from this maternal preference, however, because standards of fitness were exacting and double standards for parental behavior were common. Any evidence of female "impropriety"—abortion, infidelity, or careerism—could prove disqualifying. As one court noted, in the "eyes of the Lord" the sins of adulterous parents might be comparable, but "in the opinion of society it is otherwise." A mother "reduced to utter and irredeemable ruin" could not provide an acceptable home for her child.[30]

With the rise of the modern feminist movement came the decline of preferences for maternal custody and a weakening of double standards. Borrowing feminist rhetoric, a growing number of fathers'-rights groups joined forces with other constituencies seeking sex-neutral family laws. In an effort to promote more equal parental involvement, states gradually abolished gender preferences and some jurisdictions began favoring joint custody. These reforms, however, have not satisfied many fathers. Moreover, the incessant and insistent focus on unfairness to men obscures the injustices that persist for women.[31]

According to fathers'-rights activists, the women's movement has promoted a custody system that is "gender-biased, corrupt, and sexist." In their view, men cannot win a dispute unless the mother appears to be an "emotional cripple or a moral leper . . ., preferably both." Even in such cases, activists claim, some women still prevail by fabricating claims of child abuse. When men do obtain custody, they are less likely to receive child support, and their awards are lower. Many fathers see themselves restricted to the role of "Disney Dads," "Sunday Santas," or "activities directors" who can't even take their children to the movies without their ex-wife's permission. Although the government prosecutes men who withhold child support, critics charge that it does nothing about vindictive ex-wives who obstruct visitation.[32]

These grievances are deeply felt but also frequently exaggerated. Relatively few fathers fight for custody in court, and those who do have a good chance of winning. Reported success rates vary, but some research finds that fathers prevail as often as mothers. While child support awards for men are lower than for women, so are most men's economic needs. Contrary to assertions by fathers'-rights activists, women's allegations of child abuse are quite rare and false allegations are rarer still. The most systematic studies indicate that fewer than 2 percent of all contested custody and visitation cases involve claims of abuse. Only 5 to 8 percent of these claims are found to be fictitious, and judges who even suspect fabrication will severely penalize the offending party.[33]

So too, for every father who reports problems in exercising his visiting rights, researchers find other fathers who fail to show up or who make everyone's lives miserable when they do. Although state agencies do not actively assist men with visitation disputes, neither do they help women in such controversies. Nor do such agencies have adequate resources to enforce child support for mothers who are not on welfare.[34]

Fathers'-rights groups are on strongest ground in claiming that women sometimes benefit from sex-based stereotypes in custody disputes. Although family courts no longer talk in terms of a "maternal preference," some continue to apply one. "I do not care what the statute may say about sex neutrality," acknowledged one judge. "If the mother has been there and the children are small, I give custody to the mother." Yet such decisions rest not just on sexist stereotypes but also on social realities. Mothers as a group are far more likely than fathers to be the primary caretakers of their children. And when parents can't agree to share custody, courts often prefer the parent who has best demonstrated caregiving skills.[35]

To many men, however, this preferential treatment for primary caretakers still seems unfair. In their view, such decisions punish breadwinners who put their families' economic well-being first. Why penalize fathers who couldn't afford to take jobs that would permit greater family involvement? Yet never do these men explain why it would be *more* fair to penalize mothers who frequently sacrifice their own economic opportunities in order to put parenting first. Nor do fathers'-rights activists adequately acknowledge children's need for stability and continuity in primary-caretaker relationships.[36]

Although divorced men's claims of gender bias are not entirely without basis, they mask similar and in some ways more debilitating biases against women. Mothers continue to face double standards and double binds in custody disputes. Judges often hold women to a higher standard of parenting than men, while failing to award sufficient economic support for mothers' caretaking role. The result is that women risk losing custody either because they appear too involved in their jobs to provide good parenting or because they are not involved enough to provide adequate income.

Double standards are apparent in both sexual behavior and work/family priorities. "Promiscuity"—broadly defined to include any nonmarital sexual activity—often provides grounds for custody challenges. Judges are particularly critical of "loose" women and same-sex relationships. In one widely noted case, the Rhode Island Supreme Court affirmed a judgment prohibiting the custodial mother from having a male friend spend the night. Violation of the order would expose the woman to a one-year jail sentence. Commenting on that decision, columnist Ellen Goodman noted that at least the "rest of us can be grateful that Rhode Island is a very, very small state."[37]

Such attitudes are not, however, confined to small states, particularly where the relationship involves two women. To some judges, such "perversion" or "errant sexual behavior" is of itself sufficient reason to deny custody. In one particularly striking illustration of the double standard at work, a heterosexual father who admitted "adultery and fornication" with various women received custody in preference to a lesbian mother who had a stable relationship with one woman. In another 1996 case involving such a relationship, the trial court gave custody to a father convicted of murder in order to give the child "the option to live in a nonlesbian world." To reach such decisions, courts must deny, discount, or doggedly ignore a mounting array of research. It confirms that parents' sexual orientation has no effect on their children's sexual development, and does not adversely influence their social adjustment or emotional well-being.[38]

Double standards are equally apparent in judicial assessments of parents' work and family commitments. Recent cases bear out Goodman's concern that "mothers who do less caregiving than the judge's mother did are seen as neglectful. Fathers who do more are seen as heroic." When men participate actively in their children's lives, an "angelic halo typically descends." Fathers get "extra points" for care that is taken for granted when women provide it. Courts applaud a man who picks his children up from daycare or prepares their breakfast himself; by contrast, they sometimes penalize a mother who even uses daycare. Suing for sole or physical custody also works much more to a man's advantage than to a woman's. A father who seems willing to sacrifice other pursuits to raise his children alone appears exceptionally involved, committed, and above all selfless. By contrast, a mother fighting for sole custody may simply look selfish. In the view of many judges, if she were truly committed to her children's best interests, she would be eager to involve their father equally in parenting.[39]

A well-publicized example of such double standards involves Sharon Prost, counsel to Senator Orrin Hatch. A trial court denied her custody because she appeared overly "devoted to and absorbed by her work." The father got credit for participating in his sons' kindergarten class and no criticism for keeping them in daycare while he was unemployed for over two years. Yet Prost received criticism for relying on childcare help and no credit for her assistance with the same kindergarten class. Nor did the trial court make findings on the father's alleged domestic violence until after the case was reversed on appeal.[40]

A similar case offered a further, all-too-familiar twist: a working mother pitted against a full-time homemaker. In the controversy between Eileen Adams and Steve McCracken, which inspired a 1994 television movie, Adams lost custody to her remarried husband. The trial judge was particularly impressed that McCracken's new wife had no job and could be home with the child after school. The court was notably unimpressed that Adams was a teacher at the school that the child would attend if she had custody and that they would be together during the commute and part of the day.[41]

The attitudes underpinning these cases are by no means atypical. In a survey of Massachusetts judges, half agreed that a mother should be home when children return from school. If the mother could not be home, many judges were prepared to shift custody to the father. This was also the message of a widely reported custody trial involving Jennifer Ireland and her ex-boyfriend Steven Smith. On the surface, Ireland looked like the perfect redeemed heroine for the New Right. She was a single teenage mother who had pulled herself together without welfare and had obtained a scholarship to the University of Michigan. But her apparently unforgivable sin was to "commit daycare" along the way. While attending classes, she placed her three-year-old daughter in a childcare facility for thirty-five hours a week. After she sued for child support, the father sued for custody. She won $12 a week; he won custody.[42]

The sixty-nine-year-old trial judge had seven children and a firm commitment to "family values." Without benefit of any evidence, he declared that a single parent could not possibly "do justice to [her] studies and the raising of a small child." Under Ireland's proposed plan, her daughter would be "raised and supervised a great part of the time by strangers." By contrast, the child's father, also a college student, was able to have his mother care for the child at home. To the trial judge, it was self-evident which situation was preferable. No matter that the best available research indicates that the critical factor for children is the quality of care and that parents' relatives are no more likely to provide high-quality care than licensed providers.[43]

The double standard in the court's ruling is impossible to miss. The judge harshly criticized Ireland's prior sexual conduct (no "monument to morality and purity"), as well as her willingness to leave much of the child's early care to her own mother. The ex-boyfriend's extramarital activity prompted no such criticism, and his plan to have *his* mother care for the child appeared commendable. Such double standards place single mothers in an obvious double bind. Given the minimal child support available from the father, Jennifer Ireland had no good options. She could pursue her education and lose her child, or keep her child and go on welfare. If she took the latter option, she still could lose custody. All it would take would be a different court with a different set of "family values" and an active dislike of "idle" welfare moms. Ireland would scarcely have done better with another Michigan judge who, in another earlier case, gave custody to the father because he was most "financially able" to support the child.[44]

Mothers do not always lose these cases. Indeed, the Ireland case was eventually reversed on appeal. But the risk of a custody battle gives fathers considerable power to control their ex-wives' behavior or exact concessions regarding child support and visitation. Consider the case of Marcia Clark, chief prosecutor in the O. J. Simpson case. Partway through the proceedings, Clark sought an increase in child support because her financial circumstances had changed: she had new trial-related expenses, such as additional babysitters, clothes, and "hair-grooming." For a smart lawyer, this turned out to be not such a smart idea. Her ex-husband, who made a much lower salary, resisted paying for this "Hollywood makeover" and filed for temporary custody of their two sons. Clark, he claimed, was almost never home, and when she was there, she was always working. The boys were "starved for affection" and should be with him rather than babysitters.[45]

This controversy provided a diverting sideshow to the Simpson proceeding. Some commentators chortled at the plight of this uppity professional woman. Mothers were always whining about men who neglected their kids. Now, as one talk show critic put it, what's "good for the goose is good for the gander." Feminists were invited to weigh in against Clark, and some did. "Why shouldn't a high-powered professional woman be criticized for spending little time with her kids because of the demands of her job?"[46]

Why not indeed? Well, not to worry. Criticism was in ample supply. And some of it was fair enough. A father with a lower income should not bear the costs of his ex-wife's changing hairstyles—even if she is under pressure to adjust them weekly. Nor is it unreasonable for a parent with joint legal custody to provide more care himself rather than pay for additional babysitters. But what was unfair, both to Clark and her sons, was for her former husband to pick a custody fight in the middle of the most stressful and demanding professional experience imaginable. A trial in which it is major news if a female prosecutor "drops a verb or rips a stocking" does not provide an appropriate context for evaluating long-term custodial decisions.[47]

Even more unreasonable was the double standard implicit in the reaction of many Americans to Clark's circumstances. Almost no one seemed interested in how well the male litigators in the Simpson trial managed their family responsibilities. News that the lead defense attorney had long refused to pay child support barely raised an eyebrow.[48]

The controversies involving Clark, Ireland, Adams, and Prost epitomize the gender biases that continue to confront working mothers. Women are vulnerable to a crossfire of competing expectations and conflicting values. As the American Bar Association's first female president, Roberta Cooper Ramos, notes: "While we're telling welfare mothers to work, we're also telling professional women not to." We are promising to let women compete in men's worlds but punishing those who try. The prevailing wisdom is that working mothers cannot have it all. At least not all at the same time. But many working fathers can and do, which is why we rarely even use the term "working" to describe them.[49]

Child custody litigation is a poor forum for working out these cultural conflicts. All the current legal approaches to custody carry a price, and recent controversies have done little to clarify which costs are worth paying. The dominant legal standard, the "best interest of the child," looks highly appealing on the surface. Who could argue against putting children's welfare first? But in practice, the phrase is empty and indeterminate. Except in extreme cases, courts have no objective basis for accurate predictions; they cannot be sure what arrangements would best suit children's changing needs and parents' changing work and family situations.[50]

Nor is there any consensus among courts or the public generally about what constitutes the "best" outcome for children in sticky situations where parents' different strengths and weaknesses are at issue. Even experts are often mistaken. In one illuminating study, researchers attempted to predict which children were most likely to lead successful happy lives and which would become troubled adults. When these subjects turned thirty, the experts revisited their predictions and found that they had been wrong in two-thirds of the cases—a record worse than random guesses would have produced. Researchers' most systematic error involved underestimating children's ability to cope with stress and to gain strength from the experience.[51]

Not only does the "best-interest" standard fail to ensure reliable outcomes for children; it also imposes substantial costs on parents. The unpredictability of judicial decisionmaking encourages costly battles and subjects the more risk-averse parties, usually mothers, to custody blackmail.[52]

To minimize these problems, some experts have advocated, and some jurisdictions have adopted, a presumption favoring parents who have been the primary caretakers of their children. This standard is designed to discourage acrimonious litigation, reward past commitments, and deter extortionate threats of legal battles. In practice, however, it has fallen far short of those goals. Its main price is to reinforce traditional sex-based roles. Although gender-neutral in theory, the presumption is gender-biased in fact, since most primary caretakers are mothers. While that standard may benefit individual women in the short term, it also carries long-term costs. Privileging mothers' custodial rights perpetuates the assumption that parenting is largely the woman's responsibility.[53]

An alternative that some feminists and most fathers'-rights activists support is a presumption favoring joint custody. If, in an ideal world, we want men as well as women to be actively involved in childrearing, then shared responsibility among divorced parents seems an appropriate step along the way. In proponents' view, joint custody is necessary to combat gender stereotypes and to ensure that women do not end up with disproportionate family burdens and career sacrifices.[54]

We remain, however, at some distance from that ideal world. And according to most experts, we are unlikely to move closer by imposing joint custody on parents who do not mutually choose it. Past experience indicates that only a small proportion, probably less than a fourth, of divorcing couples are able to share physical custody and have children alternate between residences. The level of cooperation, consensus, and geographic proximity that joint residential arrangements require is simply beyond the capacity of most families.[55]

The more common choice is shared legal custody with physical custody given to the mother. Although this is the arrangement that most surveyed men prefer, it is for many women a poor substitute for more traditional arrangements in which mothers have sole custody and fathers have regular visits. Joint legal custody gives men equal rights without equal responsibilities. Fathers can intervene in their children's lives and their ex-wives' choices, while bearing few of the consequences. Contrary to the claims of some men's-rights activists, most research finds that joint legal custody does not increase the likelihood that fathers will pay child support or remain involved parents.[56]

Given the problems with all of these options, we would do well to experiment with further alternatives. One possibility, recently pioneered in the state of Washington, is to promote use of parenting plans. The Washington statute avoids the term "custody" and instead requires divorcing spouses to file a detailed agreement concerning future childrearing arrangements, including a method for resolving disputes. If a parent objects to mutual decisionmaking, the court must determine that such opposition is reasonable before granting one party sole control. Although this framework has the advantage of affirming parents' joint responsibilities, further experience is necessary to test whether such an approach can consistently reduce gender bias or provide sufficient guidance in difficult cases.[57]

Another proposal for parents who cannot agree is for courts to favor continuation of prior childrearing roles. Although similar to a primary-caretaker presumption, this approach can acknowledge comparable roles for both parents if both have been active caregivers. This framework has the additional advantage of minimizing opportunities for judicial bias and discouraging decrees that look good on paper but that are inconsistent with the parents' previously demonstrated caretaking priorities. The difficulty, however, is that childrearing patterns that worked best when parties lived together may not be desirable after they have separated, particularly if the divorce involves significant conflict. Continuity might work as a presumption, but not as an all-purpose solution for difficult cases.[58]

There are no ideal legal solutions for custody disputes because there are seldom ideal human ones. Asking couples to parent together after they have decided to live apart is often unrealistic. The needs of divorcing parties to disengage are often directly at odds with their children's needs to maintain relationships with both parents. Our legal system cannot solve such conflicts; it can only try to minimize their worst consequences. Yet while we cannot expect ideal solutions to custody dilemmas, we can improve our current framework. Whether we do so will depend in part on whether we stop denying the biases that disadvantage women as well as men. We need standards that affirm our commitment to equal parenting but also acknowledge our current distance from that goal.

Rhetoric and Reality in Social Welfare Policy

In his 1992 presidential campaign, Bill Clinton promised to "end welfare as we know it." During his administration, this aspiration was matched, then eclipsed, by promises of countless other politicians. As reform proposals grew increasingly punitive, the true nature of the challenge became increasingly apparent. The problem is not just welfare but what Americans "know"—or rather refuse to know—about it.

On few other policy issues are so many voters so insistently, and persistently, ignorant. The welfare reform campaign has proceeded on the battleground of symbolic politics, with women and children as the major casualties. The issue, as sociologist Nathan Glazer notes, is "what welfare symbolizes, not what it is." One particular program, Aid to Families with Dependent Children (AFDC), has become an all-purpose scapegoat for a host of social ills: crime, drugs, homelessness, delinquency, and promiscuity. Yet if we are serious about ending not just welfare but the human miseries that prompt it, we need a closer look at what most of us refuse to see. The problem is not, as the *Wall Street Journal* asserts, a "culture of malignant dependency," but rather a culture of malignant denial—of willful blindness to the true economic conditions, gender biases, racial prejudices, and policy tradeoffs at issue. Welfare is the "Teflon issue of the 1990s—the facts just never stick." Indeed, the myths have been "debunked so often it's amazing they have any bunk left." But as experts have long noted, the "evidence [about poverty] has remarkably little effect on what people think. Part of the reason is that conventional classifications of poor people serve such useful purposes. They offer a familiar and easy target for displacing rage, frustration, and fear."[59]

Moreover, it is convenient, both psychologically and financially, to assume that welfare dependence is a product of personal deficiencies, not societal failures. Such beliefs build on the just-world tendencies described in Chapter 1. People want to believe that individuals generally get what they deserve. *Losing Ground,* Charles Murray's influential indictment of liberal welfare policy, puts it baldly: "Some people are better than others. They deserve more of society's rewards." This view has obvious appeal, particularly for those who now receive the greatest share of those rewards and exercise the greatest political influence over their distribution.[60]

Yet missing from that account are the children, who presumably do not (at least yet) deserve their impoverished status. They account for two-thirds of AFDC beneficiaries. To justify policies that penalize children, many Americans fall back on a related form of denial. They refuse to believe that the problem is poverty; they insist, rather, that it is welfare and the perverse incentives that current programs have constructed. From this perspective, the best way to help children in the long run is to alter the parental behavior that puts them at risk. About two-thirds of Americans believe that poor people are poor because they choose not to work and that women have babies to stay on welfare. As policy analyst Robert Rector puts it, "In welfare you get what you pay for. We paid for nonwork and nonmarriage and we've gotten dramatic increases in both. The United States of America spends too much on welfare." Between half and two-thirds of the public agree, and a majority think the system has done more harm than good.[61]

Such views are prompting fundamental reform proposals. National welfare reform legislation passed in 1996 gives less money and more control to the states. It ends federal entitlements to assistance, requires recipients to find work within two years or lose benefits, generally limits aid to five years over the course of a lifetime, and largely excludes legal immigrants. States may impose further restrictions and many have, such as cutbacks in individual benefits, and denial of assistance either to all unwed mothers and their families or to additional children born while women are receiving welfare. To assist children denied coverage, several prominent reformers have proposed orphanages. Some of these policy initiatives at least claim to offer cost savings. Others are more clearly punitive. But all rest on distorted assumptions about the dynamics of welfare and the lives of its recipients.[62]

An obvious example involves many states' denial of assistance for children born to unwed mothers or to women already receiving welfare. The theory behind these "family caps" is, as conservative leaders like William Bennett put it, that "illegitimacy is the surest road to social decay and poverty . . . Welfare subsidizes and sustains illegitimacy. The most humane policy is to end it for those who have children out of wedlock." Humane for whom? Surely not for innocent children. If we take seriously the idea of replacing welfare with orphanages, the argument is irrational on its own terms. Taxpayers would hardly save money. Even assuming that large numbers of women modify their reproductive behavior, the average cost of institutionalizing a single child is almost $40,000 per year; the average benefit for an additional child on welfare is less than $70 per month.[63]

Moreover, women on welfare already have lower-than-average birthrates, and it is implausible to assume that cutting assistance will cause further reductions. A decade of research has found no such link between AFDC benefits and childbirth decisions. Birthrates among all unmarried women have increased dramatically at a time when government assistance has been declining. In many states with relatively generous benefit levels, recipients have smaller-than-average families, while some of the most tight-fisted states are at the opposite end of the spectrum. New Jersey's model "family cap" program has had no impact on birthrates.[64]

Some politicians dismiss such evidence on the ground that minor changes in welfare policies are not sufficient to change behavior. What we need, they claim, are massive cutbacks or total elimination of assistance for mothers who have children that they cannot support. "Cuts are compassionate: less is more," House Speaker Newt Gingrich assures his congressional colleagues. But centuries of experience in this and other nations suggests precisely the opposite. Less generally is less. Less aid means less food, medical care, education, and birth control, as well as less opportunity to break the cycle of poverty. The Western industrialized nations that have been most successful in reducing poverty have relatively generous social assistance, such as national health insurance, government-supported daycare, and guaranteed child support for single-parent families. If the opposite strategy worked—if the absence of aid were sufficient to keep impoverished people from having children—the world's poorest nations would not be struggling with such high birthrates.[65]

In the face of such facts, many politicians simply retreat into anecdote or rhetorical flourish. According to one Missouri state senator, "These breeding factories have got to stop." By this logic, eliminating financial "incentives" will eliminate childbirth. Yet surveys of low-income women point to no such conclusion. Welfare recipients do not view government assistance as an incentive; they overwhelmingly believe that additional children make their lives harder, not easier. This perception stands to reason, given the grossly inadequate monthly allowances—averaging only $67, and in some states less than $30—that an additional child obtains.[66]

Not only do Americans deny the ineffectiveness of a punitive welfare structure; they discount the hardships facing those with no adequate alternative. Our cultural callousness is most apparent in the rationalizations we offer for freezing or reducing benefits well below subsistence levels. A typical example is the comment of California governor Pete Wilson after his state cut benefits by 9 percent. Welfare recipients, he insisted, will still "be able to pay the rent, but they will have less for a six-pack of beer. I don't begrudge them a six-pack of beer, but it is not an urgent necessity."[67]

In fact, urgent necessities are precisely what many households do without. Hunger, malnutrition, inadequate medical treatment, unsafe housing, and insufficient childcare are chronic among the nation's poor. A lack of economic alternatives also traps many poor women and children in violent homes. During the mid-1990s, the average benefit, coupled with food stamps, gave families an income that was only three-quarters of the poverty level. A third of low-income women have no health insurance, and almost half of poor families spend up to 70 percent of their income on housing. The federal "poverty-line" budget contemplates no spending for books, magazines, movies, educational aids, paid babysitters, children's allowances, or emergencies—let alone "luxuries" like beer, cigarettes, or the ghetto Cadillacs that Ronald Reagan so often invoked.[68]

Another widespread assumption, that most welfare recipients prefer public assistance to paid employment, is equally removed from reality. To begin with, most welfare recipients are unable to work. Two-thirds are children, and another 10 percent are disabled. Almost three-fourths of adult beneficiaries work at least intermittently. Only about 10 percent of all AFDC recipients fall into the category that so many Americans associate with welfare—adults who are not working, not looking for work, or not finishing school. Even this group scarcely resembles the picture that politicians so often paint of "welfare moms" who lie around "feeding their faces with fudge as they watch the color TV." Rather, as a decade of research repeatedly demonstrates, most beneficiaries want to work but cannot find jobs that will pay enough to cover childcare, transportation, medical care, and subsistence needs.[69]

The economics of the situation are indisputable. Given the relatively low skills and education of the typical welfare recipient, the average job available pays only about $5 per hour. A single mother would need to make almost twice that much to cover her childcare expenses and to gain the same below-poverty income level that welfare benefits now provide. In all but a few states, full-time daycare for two children costs more than a mother's entire AFDC grant. Moreover, in most areas with high concentrations of poverty, low-skilled jobs are in extremely short supply; the average fast-food restaurant in Harlem has seventeen applicants for every opening. In other communities, inadequate public transportation leaves many poor women unable to reach jobs that might be available.[70]

As a result, programs imposing work requirements have proven impossible or highly expensive to implement, and seldom raise earnings enough to lift a family out of poverty. Part of the problem is that the necessary educational and training programs are costly, underfunded, sometimes poorly designed. They now reach only about 10 percent of the eligible population and disproportionately exclude the most unskilled groups. Providing childcare and creating public-work positions are equally expensive. The consequence is that states have failed to ensure jobs for about 50,000 of some 140,000 welfare recipients who already qualify for work. It is not self-evident how we expect to create the additional 2.5 million openings that recent legislation contemplates.[71]

"Just do it," says Michigan governor John Engler. But doing it turns out to be extremely expensive, and his own model policies have fallen far short of their goal. Federal proposals to provide the necessary employment, training, and childcare carry price tags on the order of $10 billion. This is almost ten times what we now spend on such services. Since fewer than 15 percent of Americans believe that we should increase our welfare budget, the prospects for such a resource commitment are hardly promising.[72]

Most voters simply will not come to grips with these economic realities. Nor are they willing to see welfare as a "women's issue." Some of the most intense opposition to increased welfare spending comes from working mothers like the woman who recently told a Republican pollster, "Let me get this right. Every day I have to pay for childcare, but people on welfare should get it for free?" Women with jobs or hours that they dislike often resist paying other mothers to do what they would prefer to do themselves, which is stay home with their kids.[73]

These are, of course, legitimate concerns. But it is a mistake to blame welfare mothers for the lack of choices that other women face, and to overstate the "special breaks" that the poor receive. The average middle-class family gets more public support in the form of direct government subsidies and tax relief than the average poor household. Couples with average incomes who confront major work/family conflicts should consider what it would be like to face the same difficulties as a single parent with no cash, no credit, and no car.[74]

Another mistake is to assume that the cost of assisting impoverished families must be absorbed by taxpayers who are none too well-off themselves. Other possibilities include reducing still-bloated defense budgets, cutting subsidies that provide "aid to dependent corpora-tions," and requiring wealthy Americans to pay their fair share. Surely the richest nation in the world can do better for its poorest citizens without crippling middle- and working-class taxpayers. America now has the greatest income inequalities in the industrialized world: the top 1 percent of our society has a greater net worth than the bottom 90 percent. Welfare accounts for only 1 percent of the federal budget, and American social assistance programs are far less effective in lifting fami-lies out of poverty than their European counterparts.[75]

We have accomplished little with our antipoverty initiatives over the last two decades because we have demanded little. And women have paid the highest price. Two-thirds of poor adults are female, and welfare policies reflect the same kind of double binds and double standards that perpetuate gender inequality in other contexts. Low-income single mothers often end up on welfare because of some crisis, such as divorce, domestic violence, layoffs, or disability. They then confront a no-win situation. Either they can accept government support, with all the societal stigma and economic deprivation that it involves—or they can seek a low-wage job that generates even less income and no housing or medical assistance.[76]

That double bind has much to do with double standards in our government policies. Men who can no longer support themselves typi-cally obtain comparatively generous benefits with comparatively little stigma, through Social Security, unemployment insurance, and worker's compensation programs. By contrast, women whose family obligations interfere with paid employment obtain far fewer benefits with far more demeaning conditions. That inequality rests on more fundamental gen-der biases—on the way we devalue "women's work."[77]

Welfare policies also devalue children. However much we wish to blame or punish single mothers for "irresponsible" choices, it makes no sense to impose the consequences on their families. Despite all of our breast beating about family values, our spending priorities make clear that we do not care very much or very long about "other people's children." Such indifference is shortsighted as well as mean-spirited. Whatever we save in the short term, we pay many times over in home-lessness, crime, unemployment, and health care costs.[78]

This, however, is a truth too unpleasant to acknowledge. It is more convenient to believe that poor people are responsible for their own impoverishment and that all they really need to do is get a job, a diploma, or a husband—preferably all of the above. With some effort, many Americans even manage to convince themselves that welfare cut-offs are good for impoverished children; as Congressman John Kasich told the Republican convention, the children "get to learn about the precious American work ethic." By overlooking the inadequacies in education, employment, health, and childcare, we absolve ourselves from responsibility for the misery that surrounds us.[79]

Alternatives are not in short supply, and the general direction of reform is obvious. If Americans are serious about "making work work" for welfare recipients, two strategies are crucial. Low-income women must have access to education, job-training programs, health insurance, and childcare. And they must be able to find jobs with sufficient pay and benefits to meet their families' basic needs. We also need to recognize that work cannot be the only feature of an effective antipoverty policy. Adequate assistance must be available for families headed by women who cannot function in the workforce due to physical and mental disabilities, substance abuse, and related problems. In essence, ending "welfare as we know it" requires changing what we "know" about it and addressing the social conditions that perpetuate it. Our target should be poverty, not the poor.[80]

America's most fundamental challenge lies not in identifying appropriate strategies, but in developing a political base that will make such initiatives plausible. Families at risk have insufficient leverage. Most poor adults lack resources to mobilize, and poor children lack votes and voices in the political process. Decentralizing control over welfare compounds these problems. States compete with one another to attract corporate investment, not impoverished families. Politicians score points by lowering taxes, not by helping the disadvantaged.[81]

The "race to the bottom" already is well underway; reversing its course must move to the top of our political agenda. The solutions are not cheap. But neither are our current misplaced priorities. Abandoning so many women and children to impoverished conditions compromises our humanity in this generation and our productivity in the next.

Reproductive Rights and Social Wrongs

In its landmark decision *Roe v. Wade,* the Supreme Court held that the Constitution protects a woman's fundamental right to choose whether or not to terminate her pregnancy. A quarter-century's experience with that ruling has taught us a bitter truth. What the Constitution protects, American society often does not. Under the banner of "family values," right-to-life activists are chipping away at reproductive rights. Legal restrictions, funding limitations, and clinic terrorism make family planning services inaccessible to the women who need them most.[82]

Several strategies of denial contribute to our current impasse. Although most Americans support a woman's right to reproductive choice, they underestimate the forces that constrain it. The public also denies its own responsibility to remove those constraints. Our prevailing assumption is that the battle for reproductive choice has largely been won. We cannot or will not see that limitations on reproductive choice remain substantial. And we too seldom hold men—whether as sexual partners or public policymakers—accountable for their contribution to the problem and its solution.

The illusion that reproductive freedom is already secure offers false comfort to women and additional difficulties for the pro-choice movement. As one of its leaders put it, "The majority of Americans don't even want to think about abortion." They want only to know that if their daughter gets pregnant, there is a place they can take her and "get in without a problem . . . But they don't want to . . . get involved with [the issue]." One result is that the minority of Americans who *are* willing to get involved wield disproportionate power over reproductive rights. Many of these activists oppose not only abortion but also the birth control programs that would make abortion less necessary.[83]

Part of the anti-choice campaign proceeds at the grassroots level against physicians, patients, and medical staff. In a single year, abortion clinics collectively experience more than 3,000 acts of harassment, violence, arson, stalking, blockades, chemical attacks, death threats, and murder. Anti-choice activists' "No Place to Hide" campaign targets the homes of patients and physicians, and subjects them to repeated abuse. Abortion opponents have vandalized doctors' homes, covered their driveways with nails, terrorized their families, and circulated their photos on "Killers Wanted" posters. One Texas physician had to obtain police escorts to accompany his family to church. Death threats are common and sometimes carried out. Although most anti-abortion leaders condemn clinic murderers as "deranged" extremists, some vocal leaders praise activists who are willing to "kill for life." Such praise is a predictable outgrowth of mainstream anti-choice rhetoric. After all, if abortions are murders and doctors who perform them are "hired assassins," then stopping the bloodshed can look like a "righteous deed."[84]

Clinic violence persists partly because many local law enforcement officials assign it low priority. Some of these officials openly oppose abortion; others are unwilling to venture into political minefields. Serious penalties for criminal conduct are accordingly rare. Although recent federal legislation promises modest improvement, many law enforcement agencies are still reluctant to invest the resources necessary for adequate protection. As one Justice Department official notes, "Abortion clinics have [averaged] fifteen bombings or arsons every year for a decade. If that had happened at churches or newspapers or federal office buildings, we would have called it terrorism." And we would have acted accordingly.[85]

Instead, we have tolerated an escalation of clinic violence and an erosion of abortion-related services. The number of doctors who are willing and able to provide such services is declining. Over four-fifths of medical programs do not require training in abortion techniques, and a third of obstetrics and gynecological residency programs do not even offer instruction in these procedures. Physicians who might otherwise plan on meeting all of women's reproductive needs get constant reminders of the personal costs of providing such care. One recent example is the failed nomination of Henry Foster for U.S. surgeon general—a man who delivered 10,000 babies but also performed about 600 abortions over the course of a thirty-eight-year career. The religious right's demonization of providers and disruption of clinics are having the desired effect. By the mid-1990s, about 85 percent of America's counties had no facility offering abortions. Two states had only one provider.[86]

Legal restrictions impose a further barrier to reproductive choice. They include mandatory waiting periods, expensive medical testing requirements, parental-consent obligations, and bans on the use of public funds, facilities, and insurance coverage for abortion-related services. Such regulations accomplish indirectly what the government may not do directly: deter women from terminating an unwanted pregnancy. Restrictive policies impose greatest hardships on teenagers and low-income women—the very individuals who are least able to bear the costs of an unwanted pregnancy. Some studies suggest that a fifth of the women who wish to obtain abortions are unable to do so because of legal and financial constraints. Many other pregnant women delay the procedure, which increases physical risks and psychological hardships. Even if nonsurgical abortion methods such as RU-486 become widely available, some of these barriers will remain. Although doctors can administer such procedures in an office, they are possible only for pregnancies that are in an early stage. Back-up surgical facilities are still necessary in case of complications, and the total costs for methods like RU-486 are likely to remain as high as for current techniques.[87]

In discounting barriers to reproductive choice, judges and legislators make several claims, none of them persuasive. Bans on funding typically are presented as trivial hardships for sexually irresponsible women, or as legitimate revenue-saving measures. Yet forcing women in poverty to pay for abortions is not a trifling matter; the average cost in some areas is more than an entire monthly welfare payment for a family of three. Nor are funding prohibitions a rational means of conserving scarce taxpayer dollars. Current welfare programs pay both for childbirth and for at least some of the living expenses of an additional child—an amount that is vastly greater than the cost of an abortion. Another claim, which surfaces in campaigns against insurance coverage for abortions, is that the procedure is a "voluntary" one, comparable to cosmetic surgery. Yet to equate the motivations for such procedures is absurd and offensive. Unwanted childbirth imposes a burden unparalleled in its combination of physical intrusiveness, psychological trauma, and life impairment.[88]

Other obstacles to reproductive choice are equally problematic. A case in point is parental-notification or parental-consent requirements for minors seeking abortion and contraceptive services. Many states, localities, and private medical facilities have adopted such requirements, and these policies command widespread support. Four-fifths of surveyed Americans favor mandatory notice or consent provisions, and such provisions generally have been upheld in court. States may, for example, require a minor to obtain approval from both parents before she can have an abortion, unless she establishes in court either that she is mature enough to make an independent decision or that, even if she is immature, the abortion would serve her best interest.[89]

On their face, parental-notice or -consent requirements for abortion and contraceptive services seem like a reasonable way of fostering family values. In practice, however, such policies fall short; they do not increase the likelihood that adolescents will restrict their sexual activity, consult their parents about birth control, or use contraceptives effectively. Minors who wish to avoid parental notification rely on over-the-counter products, go out of state, or petition courts for permission to obtain an abortion. Or they delay until it is too late.[90]

The petitioning option is a costly, traumatic, and unreasonably burdensome exercise. Courts almost never have defensible grounds for denying an abortion. It is virtually impossible to identify circumstances where a minor is too immature to make reproductive decisions for herself, but where her best interest nonetheless lies in having a child that she does not want. This does not, however, prevent some judges from subjecting teenagers to intrusive or punitive questions, such as "How will you feel about having a dead baby?" Nor does it prevent other trial courts from arbitrarily prohibiting abortions. One Toledo judge denied permission to a seventeen-year-old student who planned to attend college and who testified that she was not financially or emotionally prepared to have a child. In the court's view, this young woman had "not had enough hard knocks in her life." Even if such decisions are reversed on appeal, the expense, delay, and deterrent they impose remain substantial.[91]

No one doubts that many parents and children need to communicate better about sexual behavior. But virtually every major study agrees that parental-consent requirements do not effectively achieve that objective. Most teenagers planning an abortion, including three-quarters of those under sixteen, voluntarily consult at least one parent. Those who do not usually have a good reason—often fear of physical violence.[92]

This point came home dramatically during a 1996 National Public Radio discussion of consent requirements. One father called in to express outrage at the thought that his daughter might have been able to get an abortion without his knowledge. Two years earlier, this teenage "hussy" had "gotten herself knocked up." After learning about it from a neighbor, he "took her down to the woodshed and took care of the problem. She'll never get pregnant again." The somewhat stunned program host asked what exactly he meant. The father declined to provide details. But other guests on the show, including a prominent specialist in obstetrics and gynecology, had ample experience with comparable cases involving brutal retaliation and permanent injury. According to almost all experts, the best way to prevent such tragedies in dysfunctional families, while encouraging parental consultation in others, is through voluntary family-outreach programs.[93]

Contrary to anti-choice rhetoric, our society does not supply "abortion on demand," at least not for the women whose need is greatest. As constitutional law scholar Laurence Tribe notes, policymakers often discount the obstacles remaining because such barriers do not seriously affect people who are most influential in the policy process. Men who spearhead anti-abortion initiatives do not pay their price. And women of means can afford to travel to facilities that impose the fewest restrictions and the least risk of harassment. But one question still remains: Why are the majority of Americans who claim to support reproductive choice so unconcerned about constraints on access that affect others? Part of the answer is that it is easy to blame individual women for "immoral" choices. It is far harder to make adequate choices available.[94]

"Right-to-life" narratives frequently portray women seeking abortions as selfish, irresponsible, or both. One dominant image is the cold-hearted careerist willing to "kill [her] unborn children in order to succeed in a man's world." This is also the portrait that emerges in some judicial decisions. A frequently quoted example figures in the dissenting opinion of *Doe v. Bolton,* a companion case to *Roe v. Wade.* "At the heart of the controversy," claimed Justice Byron White, are pregnancies that do not threaten the life of the mother but are nonetheless unwanted for other reasons: "convenience, family planning, economics, dislike of children, the embarrassment of illegitimacy, etc." From this perspective, the *Roe* majority appeared to value "the convenience, whim, or caprice of [the pregnant woman] more than the potential life of the fetus."[95]

Such views of female selfishness and irresponsibility are widely shared. Even self-proclaimed feminists have joined the chorus of critics. Without any supporting evidence, Naomi Wolf asserts that "millions" of middle- and upper-middle-class women "have no excuse for their carelessness." Such estimates appear to be based on Wolf's personal knowledge of individuals who get carried away with "good Chardonnay," or who use abortions as ways of testing a relationship and as "rites of passage" during adolescence. Many Americans are equally critical of the assertedly common and similarly irresponsible "ghetto teenager, who couldn't bring herself to just say no to sex."[96]

Although most individuals report that they support women's right to choose an abortion, a majority also oppose making abortion available for the main reasons women give for making that choice. Less than half of surveyed Americans think abortion is appropriate in order to allow a woman to finish school, to pursue her career, or to avoid having a child that she cannot afford. Assumptions about such assertedly selfish and sexually irresponsible decisions provide the moral subtext for opposition to family planning services. As one congressional opponent put it, "Are we going to condone the self-indulgent conduct of the body of a woman who has already demonstrated, in most cases, [that she was] damned careless with it in the first place?"[97]

Similar views underpin grassroots anti-abortion campaigns. Studies of right-to-life activists make clear that struggles over reproductive policy are not only about unborn life. They are also about traditional gender roles. To abortion opponents, the stakes are marriage, motherhood, and morality. As one activist puts it, "abortion permits the woman to adopt the same sexual pattern as the male, although it is a pattern alien to her nature."[98]

The culprit in encouraging women to take this self-destructive path is, naturally, feminism. Indictments come from all points on the political spectrum. To critics from the right, abortion is simply the logical extension of feminists' insistence on sexual liberation and their disdain for homemaking roles. By contrast, the left and center blame pro-choice activists for relying on "confrontational" tactics and for minimizing the moral costs of terminating pregnancies. But it is not feminists who are turning the abortion debate into a terrorist crusade. When anti-choice vigilantes are using death threats and chemical assaults, it seems odd for critics like Rene Denfeld to denounce feminists for their "radical" bumper stickers and "militant" rhetoric. So too, when commentators like Wolf chide pro-choice leaders for their failure to engage in moral argument, a knowledgeable reader might wonder who exactly she has in mind. No such leaders are quoted or identified in her article.[99]

In fact, feminist defenses of abortion do not lack for moral foundation. Not only do pro-choice leaders justify a woman's right to choose on moral grounds of liberty, autonomy, and equality, but they also appeal to the same values of care and responsibility that their critics so often invoke. As legal scholar Robin West argues:

Women need the freedom to make reproductive decisions not merely to vindicate a right to be left alone but often to strengthen their ties to others; to plan responsibly and have a family for which they can provide . . . At other times, the decision to abort is necessitated not by a [callous] urge to end life, but by the harsh reality of a financially irresponsible partner . . . and a workplace incapable of accommodating or supporting the needs of working parents.

Women also have abortions because they are victims of rape or incest, their birth control method fails, their partner refuses to use contraceptives, or they discover a fetal abnormality. To describe these often agonizing decisions as "self-indulgent" or "mere lifestyle" preferences is itself morally irresponsible.[100]

The central question in the abortion debate should not be, as some would have it, "When does life begin?" Rather, it is "Who should decide this question?" On the latter point, we approach consensus. When opinion polls on abortion use phrases like "It's a matter between a woman, her doctor, her family, her conscience, and her God," almost three-fourths of Americans find that conclusion "about right."[101]

If the women's movement has failed to convey the essential moral stakes in the abortion campaign, it is not for lack of effort. This struggle must continue. The issue is not simply convenience or careerism, but social equality and individual identity—women's capacity to define the very terms of their existence. The right to abortion has been a foundation of the women's movement precisely because it challenges the assumption that "anatomy is destiny, that female biology dictates women's subordinate status." Women cannot afford either to relinquish that right or to deny the conditions that make it necessary. If, as most feminists hope, abortion is to become "safe and rare," we must eliminate the obstacles to alternative birth control services.[102]

Those obstacles are particularly great for adolescents and often have particularly tragic consequences. Teenagers account for a disproportionate number of abortions, and many of the reasons are attributable more to the irresponsibility of adult partners and policymakers than adolescent women. Not only do we misjudge the consequences of parental-consent requirements; we also mistake the causes of early pregnancy and the strategies most likely to prevent it.

Americans frequently oppose birth control education and assistance for adolescents on the ground that such programs will encourage sexual activity. According to congressional sponsors of abstinence-oriented provisions in the Adolescent and Family Life Act, "the most effective oral contraceptive yet devised is the word 'no.'" In denouncing contraceptive distribution in the schools, influential commentators like Rush Limbaugh claim that such programs sanction promiscuity and undercut what should be the "most important lesson": that "the only safe sex is no sex." For similar reasons, many sex education programs center on abstinence. Some offer "Reasons to Wait," with examples such as "God wants us to be pure" and "Pretend Jesus [is] on your date." An increasing number of communities rely on local ministers to set up "True Love Waits" chapters for students pledging virginity. And female chastity crusaders have been honored at presidential ceremonies on the White House lawn.[103]

But these approaches are not working, although many policymakers resist admitting it. As NOW president Patricia Ireland has suggested, the place where we most urgently need sex education is among legislators. Almost half of all female adolescents and about two-thirds of males have had intercourse by age eighteen. Researchers generally find no evidence that sex education programs increase such activity. Restricting access to birth control restricts birth control, not sex. And such restrictions carry a heavy cost. Every year three million adolescents contract sexually transmitted diseases, including AIDS. A million become pregnant, and almost half of these—roughly 20 percent of all female adolescents—give birth to a child. Four-fifths of these families are in poverty.[104]

These patterns are partly attributable to our irrational mix of permissive and prudish social signals. The media bombard teens with sexual images, but do little to promote responsible sexual behavior. In a single year, television airs about 20,000 messages discussing or portraying sex; almost none include references to contraception. Our culture links masculinity with sexual conquest and femininity with sexual attractiveness. Yet many schools preach chastity rather than responsibility in intimate relationships. Less than a fifth of public high schools and junior highs include instruction about birth control in sex education programs. In fact, some of these programs explicitly forbid teachers to discuss contraception before the tenth grade. For many students, that discussion comes too late. More than half of sexually active adolescents also have no access to reproductive services, and even schools with health programs rarely provide birth control assistance. Yet most national policymakers have supported funding cuts for family planning initiatives.[105]

These misplaced priorities help explain why America has the highest rate of adolescent pregnancy in the developed world. Many European countries have levels of sexual activity equivalent to those in the United States. However, birth control programs in these nations result in substantially lower rates of adolescent pregnancy. Other countries also do much more to prevent the disabling social conditions that encourage early childbirth in America.[106]

Much of our problem stems from our denial of its underlying causes. We are blaming young women who want "too much too soon" in sexual relationships, rather than blaming a society that offers too little too late: too little reason to stay in school, too little birth control assistance, and too little opportunity for health services, child support, vocational training, and decently paying jobs. Policymakers and school administrators focus too much on morality, too little on poverty. They want teens to "just say no" to sex and childbirth, but offer too few opportunities for saying yes to something else. Particularly for many low-income women of color, whose educational and employment options appear highly limited, motherhood offers status and meaning that are otherwise unavailable. But expanding those options is expensive. Denouncing promiscuity is cheap.[107]

Part of what prevents sensible policymaking is our tendency to overstate both the role of adolescent pregnancy in causing poverty and the significance of delayed childbirth in preventing it. Teenage mothers account for only about 4 percent of impoverished female-headed families. Many factors that Americans commonly assume to be the result of teenage pregnancy are also partial causes: educational difficulties, low income, and low self-esteem contribute both to the frequency of early childbirth and to the problems that accompany it. For example, most studies indicate that young mothers usually drop out of school before, not after, becoming pregnant. Women from disadvantaged backgrounds, particularly women of color, remain concentrated in low-paying occupations even if they delay parenting and finish high school. Indeed, some research comparing similar groups of disadvantaged adolescents has found that those who gave birth in their teens did not have significantly lower incomes or higher rates of welfare dependency later in life than those who waited to have children. In one 1995 study, teenage mothers actually did better.[108]

This is not, however, to understate the problems that do accompany adolescent pregnancy. Early childbirth increases the likelihood of medical difficulties for young mothers, as well as health, educational, and developmental problems for their children, regardless of the family's socioeconomic status. In short, while experts disagree about the extent to which early childbearing itself causes certain disadvantages, virtually no one disputes that an unwanted pregnancy poses some significant risks and that we need better strategies to prevent it.[109]

A critical first step is to improve reproductive instruction and assistance, as well as to expand educational and employment options for low-income adolescents. Particularly for young teens, making abstinence acceptable also can be an effective response, but not in the sanctimonious terms that current programs too often propose. Many young women report engaging in unwanted sex and having a child as a means to other ends—to gain status or to win approval from the child's father. Helping female adolescents to assess and assert their own best interests should be a more central objective.[110]

We must also direct more birth control and parenting initiatives toward males. Double standards of morality remain pervasive. No one is inviting boys who pledge chastity to sip tea at the White House. We can, however, support more practical strategies for reaching male adolescents, such as peer counseling, media campaigns, and free birth control assistance. We also need increased research on male contraceptives and more effective sanctions for older men who impose sexual relationships on adolescent women. Such coercive sex accounts for a substantial proportion of unplanned pregnancies. Encouraging greater reproductive responsibility among men is crucial to achieving greater social equality for women.[111]

Implicit in all of these proposals is a straightforward premise: if we want individuals to make responsible sexual choices, we must reduce the barriers to doing so. This will, in turn, require a greater sense of societal responsibility. No adequate concept of reproductive freedom can exclude the public initiatives necessary for its exercise.

Not only does American society impose undue barriers to reproductive choice; it has done little to improve the quality of choices available.

Just as some women are unable to choose safe abortion, others are unable to choose safe childbirth. Part of the reason involves grossly inadequate governmental support for prenatal care, for reduction of reproductive hazards, and for prevention of sexually transmitted diseases. Those who oppose funding for such health needs, as well as for family planning programs, are not "pro-life." The women's movement needs to reappropriate this label and to focus attention on all the conditions that must change before reproductive choices can be truly free.[112]

This strategy must also include challenging claims that greater access to birth control is some illusory "quick fix" which undercuts broader family initiatives. According to the president of Americans United for Life: "If abortion were not so readily available and accepted, there would be pressure on [employers] to accommodate . . . women who have children. Employers say, 'If you choose not to exercise this right, it's not our fault, it's not our problem' . . . [With legalized abortion] men are let off the hook." Such claims misread the history of American reproductive policy. In the days when abortion and birth control services were unavailable and unacceptable, neither men nor employers were "on the hook." Women were. Many pregnant employees lost their jobs; others lost their lives to backroom abortionists.[113]

We have come a considerable distance from those days, in part because more women have more control over their reproductive lives. The challenge now is to make better choices available to *all* women, especially those with the greatest economic vulnerability and the least powerful political voices.

Family values are in fashion. Truly valuing families is not. A wide gap persists between our political rhetoric and our public policies. We claim to support women's right to choice, but ignore the legal restrictions and terrorist tactics that obstruct it. We often pay homage to the sanctity of "innocent unborn life," but remain callously indifferent to the quality of life for the equally innocent children born in poverty. We claim to require gender equality in family laws, but institutionalize inequality in their enforcement. Double standards persist in our assignment of family roles and reproductive responsibilities. Divorced women end up with fewer resources and greater parental obligations than divorced men. Working mothers receive harsher treatment than working fathers in child custody decisions. Unplanned pregnancy appears as the fault of women who can't say no, not of men who insist on getting to yes.

These patterns reflect broader dynamics of denial. On such issues, many Americans neither recognize gender inequality as a serious problem nor accept responsibility for addressing it. A true commitment to family values requires translating our rhetorical concerns into social priorities.

8

Women's Movements, Men's Movements

Throughout the past quarter-century, commentators on feminism have been popping the same question. As *Time* put it to Gloria Steinem, "Since most women today embrace the goals of the women's movement, why are so many of them reluctant to embrace the feminist label?" Steinem responded: "Women have two problems with the label. The first is that people don't know what it means . . . The second is that people do know what it means."[1]

She is right on both counts. Many individuals who largely agree with the feminist agenda are alienated by its image. Others are uninformed, ambivalent, or unsympathetic concerning its objectives. Yet who is responsible for these attitudes remains open to dispute. According to many critics, the central problem lies with leaders of the women's movement. They are to blame for the refusal of most American women to consider themselves feminists.[2]

Leaders of the women's movement see the problem differently. Some fault the self-professed feminists who gain celebrity by sniping at their sisters, and who appear more interested in promoting themselves than a social movement. Others blame right-wing commentators who caricature the "feminazi position" and perpetuate the very image problem that they delight in criticizing. To most movement leaders, the real issue is not feminism's image but its objectives, and the threat that full gender equality poses to entrenched interests. When asked whether feminists should do more to tone down their message and counteract its negative stereotypes, Steinem responded, "This is a revolution, not a public relations movement."[3]

In fact, however, it is both. And that combination is inherently difficult to pull off. Until we gain a clearer sense of what drives resistance to the women's movement, we are unlikely to achieve its objectives.

The Women's Movement and Its Critics

A critical first step in understanding the challenges facing feminism is to put them in historical perspective. Women's willingness to identify themselves as feminists has bobbed up and down, partly in response to shifting media images. But public acceptance of feminist values has maintained a relatively steady upward climb. Since the 1960s, the proportion of women who perceive sex discrimination to be a serious problem has increased from less than 5 percent to more than 75 percent. The vast majority of Americans believe that the women's movement has improved women's lives, and all but a tiny percentage share its basic commitment to equal opportunity.[4]

Even people who reject the movement's label endorse many of its objectives. Polls find higher levels of agreement with statements about women's issues when the term "feminism" does not appear. Seventy to 80 percent of surveyed women agree with the objectives that dictionary definitions associate with "feminist": someone who supports political, economic, and social rights for women.[5]

Such polls should be a source of reassurance but not of rationalization. Rejection of the F-word is symptomatic of deeper difficulties. Most American women fail not only to identify themselves as feminists but also to provide active support for feminist causes. Although a majority of women see a need for a strong women's movement, they deny any responsibility for becoming involved with it personally. Three-fourths of those surveyed report paying no attention to feminism, and well under 10 percent belong to organizations that focus on women's issues. Despite some recent increases in funding, feminist causes and candidates still attract relatively little financial support. The National Organization for Women has about 280,000 members—fewer than the National Association of Garden Clubs.[6]

Moreover, most men remain at best ambivalent about feminist efforts. In principle, about 70 percent support efforts to improve women's social and economic status. In practice their response has been less enthusiastic. The majority of men appear even more resistant to the changes in their own roles and status that true equality for women would require.[7]

To understand the anxiety and animosity that feminism provokes, we need to look both beneath and beyond popular diagnoses. Most critics blame feminist leaders, although for inconsistent reasons. As the discussion below notes, activists are faulted for being too radical and not radical enough; for hating men and wanting to be just like them; for ignoring and romanticizing gender difference. This is, of course, a no-win situation, but almost no one talks about that. Nor do most critics focus on men—except to blame feminism for impersonating or demonizing them. The American public gets endless accounts of what is wrong with the women's movement. But rarely do we hear about what is wrong with the men's movement, or what might encourage more males to break free from traditional gender roles.

One of the most pervasive and persistent critiques of the women's movement inspired a *Ms.* cartoon from the early 1990s. It featured a man watching television coverage of feminist issues. "After more than two decades of advances," reports a woman newscaster, "the American female continues to occupy a position of inferiority . . ." "Manhater," he mutters. She continues: "Women workers still earn [substantially less than] men . . ." "Castrator," he responds. By the fourth frame, as she reports on women's underrepresentation in the legislature, he is on his feet, shouting "Shrew! Nag! Witch! Lesbo!" In the closing frame, while she calmly recites statistics on rape and domestic violence, he concludes: "That's what I hate about feminists—they're so hostile."[8]

This perception is widely shared. "Feminists hate men—that's the problem" is Jerry Falwell's widely accepted diagnosis. Many Americans believe that such hostility is at least partly responsible for our inadequate progress on gender issues. Commentators frequently charge that feminist fabrications of "sinister sexism" are poisoning male-female relationships, and that "male bashing" is a problem that Americans "constantly encounter." In their more intense versions, these critiques seem slightly unhinged, and considerably shriller than their targets. According to former presidential speechwriter Mary Matalin, the women's movement has alienated mainstream America—and no wonder, given its "sensationalized tales of endless, inescapable oppression at the hands of testosterone-mad, women-loathing, capitalist-pig, Cro-Magnon brutish men." And these are the folks telling feminists to get a grip. Even if the caricatures are meant to be tongue-in-cheek, their effect is not simply to amuse. It is also to taint the struggle for equality by millions of individuals who hold no such views.[9]

Programs in women's studies attract similar complaints. In one representative account, a female student analogized her classroom experience to a satirical skit from Monty Python. The skit had featured a quiz show where the answer to every question was "pork." And, the student recalled, "whatever the quiz show host asks—for example, 'What's the capital of Pennsylvania?'—the answer was 'pork.'" Similarly, in the student's class, "the answer was always 'men' . . . 'Who contributes to all the violence in the world?' 'Men.' 'Who's responsible for everything that we endure?' 'Men.'"[10]

Although these critics have a point, they vastly overstate it. Granted, some feminists paint with broad strokes, and a tiny but vocal minority do seem to hate men. But there also are men who hate women. Tarring either sex with the excesses of a vengeful faction makes little sense. To link all feminists with man-hating is no more reasonable than to link all men with misogyny.

Contrary to popular assertions, few feminists deny their debts to men, and prominent women's-studies texts feature no shortage of male heros. After all, many men have actively supported the women's-rights movement, and its legal foundations are the product of predominantly male legislatures and judiciaries. Judging from the introductions to feminist publications, most advocates of women's rights are deeply grateful for the contributions of male partners, colleagues, editors, and research assistants. Few of these women seem to believe that they are sleeping with the enemy, metaphorically or otherwise.

What they do believe, however, is that American society institutionalizes gender inequality. This is also the claim that critics consistently misrepresent. To point out that men as a group are advantaged by sex-based hierarchies is not to claim that all men oppress women. And to note that male dominance often yields male sexual violence is not to imply that men in general are "Cro-Magnon brutes." Although feminist analysis often would be stronger without indiscriminate reliance on terms like "patriarchy," they do not carry the implications that critics denounce. Except in critics' caricatures, "patriarchal theory" does not present women as "powerless victims in every aspect of their lives." Nor does it cast men as the enemy. Its aim, like that of feminist analysis more generally, is to understand and challenge gender roles that systematically disadvantage women.[11]

The flip side of claims that feminists demonize men are claims that feminists act just like them, and encourage other women to do the same. In essence, this objection is that feminism preaches male values and male strategies; it has enabled more women to play by men's rules but not to live by their own. Versions of this complaint come from all points on the political spectrum. Critics from the right blame the women's movement for devaluing traditional feminine roles. According to one anti-abortion activist, "Women's lib is on the wrong track . . . Women have [always] been the superior people. They're more civilized, they're more unselfish by nature, but now they want to compete with men at being selfish."[12]

Critics from the left also fault feminism for encouraging selfishness, although for different reasons. In *Women Together, Women Alone,* Anita Shreve notes that "one of the ironies of the Women's Movement is that in preparing the ground for greater career opportunity for women, it sowed the seeds of its own demise . . . Women who combine career and family life simply don't have any time left to devote to . . . activist issues." Moreover, "supposedly liberated progressive *feminist* women [now exploit] other women" by delegating childcare and housework to them. "It's as though the fruits of liberation were only for a certain class of women."[13]

Other commentators join in the claim that feminism's preoccupation with success measured by men's standards has sabotaged the movement's broader objectives. In a cover article for the *New York Times Magazine,* "When Feminism Failed," former newspaper editor Mary Ann Dolan describes her disillusionment with women's workplace conduct. At her own paper, when her female colleagues achieved equal representation on the masthead, their "power grab" began. Rather than working to transform the newsroom into a "warm" and "nurturing" environment, they courted male superiors in order to pursue their own advancement. In generalizing from this experience, Dolan quotes a prominent Los Angeles executive who lambastes the new breed of female MBAs for similar reasons: these women reportedly have lost touch with their "instinctive skills." They have been "trained like men" and they act accordingly.[14]

Indictments of "honorary males" or "male-identified" women are increasingly common. Variations on the theme appear in books like *A Lesser Life, Prisoners of Men's Dreams,* and *Feminism Is Not the Story of My Life.* In these accounts, "equal-opportunity feminism" has left women compromised and coopted by male values. Leaders of the women's movement, in their "ideological effort to free women from families," have lost touch with the movement's original goals. According to these critics, feminists have betrayed feminism by failing to demand balanced work and family lives for both sexes and by failing to secure the public policies that would make it all possible. As one beleaguered woman put it, "Before the women's movement we did the housework and the men took out the trash. But since we were liberated they don't take out the trash anymore."[15]

Such claims tend to overstate women's "difference," as well as understate the barriers to preserving it. Many indictments of feminism build on a romanticized view of female virtue and an inattentiveness to its cultural underpinnings. As the research in Chapter 2 makes clear, we have no convincing basis for believing that women are by nature significantly more unselfish, cooperative, or nurturing than men. To the extent that American women are especially likely to have these characteristics, it is because cultural forces reinforce such gender patterns. Where the reward structures for male and female workers are similar, it is naive not to expect similarities in their behavior.

It is even more naive to blame feminism when women adapt to current workplace values. Well before the rise of the contemporary women's movement, American culture produced its share of "Queen Bees"—female leaders who made it under male rules and failed to see why others couldn't do the same. So too, only historical amnesia permits claims that feminism is responsible for women's difficulties in balancing work and family or for their reliance on poorer women to provide domestic help. It is not feminists who have opposed paid parental leave, flexible schedules, and subsidized childcare. Yet as one reviewer noted, books like *Women Together, Women Alone* "end up blaming feminism for the faults of the system feminism is trying to change."[16]

This tendency to shoot the messenger has deeper roots. For well over a century, critics have presented the women's movement as an assault on traditional homemaking roles. Unsurprisingly, these attacks strike responsive chords in women whose primary sense of status and identity depends on family relationships. Feminist critiques of the restrictive and unequal aspects of traditional gender roles have left some women feeling embattled and embittered. Blaming the movement has been a way to vent their frustration and affirm their sense of importance in a changing social order. Once family and feminism were fixed as the symbolic poles of debate, many women rallied around the values by which they ordered their own priorities. The popularity of books like *The Rules*, with mid-Victorian courtship advice, suggests the continuing appeal of traditional scripts. If women have had trouble luring men to the altar, the problem, according to author Sherrie Schneider, is that "feminism was inadvertently applied to dating."[17]

Of course, scapegoating feminists, individually or collectively, has other advantages. As Chapter 4 notes, the media always love a catfight, and it is more diverting to hear women snarling at each other than droning on about sexist oppression. So too, if feminists are to blame, that lets men off the hook. This is no small virtue, particularly when males control all major media channels. A simplistic diagnosis of the problem also produces conveniently simplistic solutions. If women only would get their act together politically and personally, everyone could live happily ever after without any costly social adjustments.

Similar advantages are available from a second pair of complaints: that the contemporary women's movement is either too radical or not radical enough. The first of these complaints is that feminism has surrendered to extremist factions and has lost touch with the needs and values of the average woman: the "feminist fringe . . . [has become] the feminist mainstream." Some indictments of this sort, which inveigh against "cultural crackpots," are not without their own crackpot qualities. In 1992, presidential candidate Pat Robertson attracted considerable attention for his account of the Equal Rights Amendment campaign in Iowa: "[This fight] is about a socialist, anti-family political movement that encourages women to leave their husbands, kill their children, practice witchcraft, destroy capitalism and become lesbians." Anti-abortion leader Randall Terry similarly warns that the women's movement has been captured by "radical feminism," which has "vowed to destroy the traditional family unit, hates children for the most part, and promotes lesbian activity." No names are named.[18]

These caricatures do not come only from conservative men. Camille Paglia has received substantial airtime for her snarling denunciations of "crazed" and "clingy sob sisters" who control the women's movement. Mary Matalin, Katie Roiphe, Christina Hoff Sommers, Naomi Wolf, and even Betty Friedan also have weighed in against extremist feminists whose victim mythologies misrepresent the facts, exaggerate sexual oppression, and disempower women. By encouraging whiners to wallow in their subordination, contemporary feminism reportedly "burdens women with . . . the [very] status they have been struggling to escape." Rene Denfeld's *The New Victorians* offers a comprehensive catalogue of feminists' looniest theories on witchcraft, goddess worship, and matriarchal utopias. Generalizing from these examples, she sees a women's movement "bogged down in an extremist . . . crusade that has little to do with women's lives." It's a world that speaks to the very few, while alienating the many.[19]

To most of these critics, the solution is a more mainstream movement that is open to all who care about gender equality. But not too openly open. Otherwise, feminism would remain identified with what Betty Friedan once labeled the "lavender menace." The trump card in many contemporary critiques of the women's movement is still lesbianism. "I don't want to make too much of this," claims Rush Limbaugh (who obviously does), but an estimated "30 percent to 40 percent of NOW's membership is lesbian or bisexual." According to the editor of the most popular men's-movement newspaper, feminism is "largely driven by lesbians and that is why most women aren't feminists." For other critics, the issue is one of priorities: the women's movement "first and foremost" should be fighting gender discrimination, and in their view, discrimination on the basis of sexual orientation is something quite different.[20]

Of course, not all critics of feminist extremism explicitly target lesbians. But the label frequently lurks in the subtext, reminding women of the consequences of falling in with the feminist fringe. And some self-identified feminists indirectly underscore that point by taking pains to establish their own heterosexual credentials. "Male sexual attention is the sun in which I bloom," Wolf informs her readers. In the mid 1990s, *Esquire* ran an entire cover story on "do me" feminists, who similarly basked in such attention.[21]

The most obvious difficulty with the extremism critique is that it compounds the problems it claims only to describe. When critics project an image of feminists as delusional, whiny, and sexually "deviant" crusaders, many women understandably will keep their distance. Yet these caricatures that pass for critique hardly represent significant feminist constituencies. Not every sloppy use of statistics or exaggerated claim in women's-conference flyers reflects a position attributable to the movement as a whole. Moreover, in any enterprise with so many self-proclaimed followers, someone occasionally will get some facts wrong. So will their critics. Indeed, commentators like Christina Hoff Sommers, who gleefully chronicles feminists' faux pas, commit similar evidentiary indiscretions. Sommers' assertions about the frequency of rape do not correspond to the findings of respected experts.[22]

Feminism, of course, needs thoughtful criticism and factual correction. What it does not need are potshot polemics strung together as evidence of some radical conspiracy to capture the women's movement. Nor does it benefit from proposals to broaden its appeal by marginalizing those who most need public support.

For every claim that feminism has lost touch with mainstream middle-class women comes a counterclaim that it has instead placed the concerns of these women over the concerns of other, less privileged constituencies. From this perspective, the women's movement looks too preoccupied with the needs of white middle-class heterosexuals and too disconnected from its original transformative vision. Unlike many other criticisms, this one rests on solid factual footing. The women's movement has a history of inadequate attention to issues of race, ethnicity, class, and sexual orientation. Despite recent improvements, the most popular contemporary feminist publications generally do not focus on the most vulnerable women. Commentators fault author-activists like Susan Faludi for "staying up late trying to figure out why women aren't anchoring the CBS Evening News" while ignoring the plight of single mothers coping with "rats in the hamper." Naomi Wolf's preoccupation with beauty rituals and eating disorders among relatively well-off women has sparked similar concerns.[23]

Yet while it is fair to ask feminists to give more attention to those who suffer most from gender inequalities, it surely is unfair to dismiss the problems that Faludi and Wolf identify. The underrepresentation of women in prominent media positions and America's unhealthy standards of female attractiveness do not affect only privileged groups. Nor is it reasonable to fault prominent feminists because their work attracts wider audiences than the growing number of less celebrated authors who focus on needs of low-income women, women of color, disabled women, older women, and other particularly disadvantaged groups. It is the mainstream public that is leaving those books off its shopping list.

Lesbians raise similar concerns about the marginalization of their needs, and with similar justification. Despite—and partly because of— the identification of feminism with lesbianism, movement leaders generally do not place high priority on policy initiatives involving sexual orientation. Nor have some grassroots service providers, such as battered-women's shelters, been attentive enough to the particular needs of lesbian women. Ironically enough, when gay- and lesbian-rights organizations emerge to fill the vacuum left by other groups, some women's associations respond as if they have been let off the hook. Now someone else is officially responsible for these "other" women.[24]

Yet failure to recognize the linkages between discrimination based on sex and discrimination based on sexual orientation undermines our ability to challenge either. Both forms of bias rest on similar stereotypes about effeminate men and unfeminine women. As Chapter 7 notes, researchers consistently find that hostility toward homosexuals is usually linked with traditional attitudes toward gender roles. So too, women who raise "women's issues" risk being labeled as sexually "deviant," and that prospect serves to deter and discredit antidiscrimination efforts. Critics who advocate avoiding issues of sexual orientation compound the problem. The only way to make the label "feminist" safe for all women is to affirm the legitimacy of same-sex relationships, and to make challenging homophobia a crucial part of the feminist agenda.[25]

What is most frustrating about all these critiques is not only that they leave feminists in a double bind but also that critics seem so oblivious to that fact. The women's movement has multiple constituencies and multiple agendas, and any response to the problems that commentators identify involves tradeoffs. Feminism cannot be all things to all women, at least not at the same time. Organizations that spread their resources too thin, or that cannot reconcile different factions with competing priorities, compromise their effectiveness on goals that are widely shared.[26]

As commentators like Susan Estrich note, feminists put mainstream support at risk if they constantly climb the barricades on behalf of seemingly "extreme" positions or particularly vulnerable groups. In Estrich's view, leaders of the women's movement too often "fall into the trap of trying to defend the marginal case and end up being marginalized." But the trick lies in determining which cases really are peripheral. The commitment to equal rights and respect that underpins the feminist agenda demands alliance with other social movements. We cannot realize equality of opportunity for all women without addressing other barriers apart from gender, including those based on race, class, ethnicity, age, disability, and sexual orientation.[27]

Other diagnoses of feminist failures also rest on competing premises. For example, some commentators fault women's-studies scholars for being overly intellectual; others blame them for not being intellectual enough. According to critics like Denfeld, feminist researchers and teachers have "climbed out on a limb of academic theory that is all but inaccessible to the uninitiated." In their haste to "intellectualize the hell out of everything" and publish yet another unreadable tome, these theorists fail "to check in with reality" as most women experience it. Camille Paglia, herself the author of a 700-page, jargon-laden account of "sexual personae," has similarly condemned the "muddy maze-makers of soggy, foggy poststructuralism."[28]

Yet at the same time, Paglia, like other critics, also lambastes women's-studies scholars for being "anti-intellectual," and for pursuing political agendas rather than mastering the great works. Summarizing widespread views, journalist Karen Lehrman complains that in "many" feminist courses, "discussion alternates between the personal and po-litical, with mere pit stops at the academic."[29]

Yet while criticisms of some women's-studies work are not without basis, they both overstate the problem and overlook the complex forces that produce it. Publications that appear to outside observers as irrele-vant and unintelligible often appear to insiders as essential for academic credibility and tenure. In many fields, women's-studies scholars are much more likely to ensure their institutional survival by publishing murky poststructuralist monographs than by issuing lucid accounts of gender bias.

Moreover, both those who fault women's studies for being too dis-engaged from real-world issues and those who find it far too engaged with such issues are frequently casual in their methodology and highly selective in their targets. Virtually all of the prominent critiques have relied on anecdotal observation or a tiny number of surveyed courses. Rarely do critics of feminist teaching and scholarship acknowledge that the same faults crop up in many other fields. Much of the work in neoclassical economics is neither accessible to the uninitiated nor apolitical in its premises. Problems of shoddy scholarship and intolerant classrooms cut across all disciplines, and none of the recent indictments of women's studies demonstrate that its weaknesses justify unique concern.

Similar points apply to a final set of double binds facing the women's movement. Feminist leaders are faulted for both undervaluing and overstating gender differences, and also for focusing too much or too little on formal equality. Commentators from the right complain that the movement has strayed too far from its original commitment to equal rights. Commentators from the left maintain that activists have pursued individual rights at the expense of societal responsibilities, and have neglected the socioeconomic conditions that prevent women from exercising rights which are theoretically available.[30]

Throughout its history, the American women's movement has confronted what law professor Martha Minow labels "dilemmas of difference." Insisting on equality in formal treatment for men and women will not yield equality in actual experience as long as they face different social expectations and constraints. Yet recognizing women's "differences" risks perpetuating the stereotypes that perpetuate injustice. So too, an emphasis on achieving equal rights often diverts attention from the socioeconomic structure that limits their effectiveness. As preceding chapters have indicated, a wide gap persists between what the law promises and what it delivers regarding reproductive choice, workplace opportunities, and freedom from sexual violence.[31]

These gaps and tradeoffs are not, however, news to feminist leaders. The problem is less that the women's movement has placed too much faith in formal rights than that it has been unable to marshal sufficient societal support for their exercise. Nor have feminist efforts been insensitive to the difference dilemma. For example, the women's movement has long sought workplace policies that accommodate family responsibilities, which women still disproportionately shoulder. But activists also have worked to make such policies equally available to men, not just in theory but in practice. To understand why these efforts have had such limited success, we need to focus on more than feminist failings. We need also to confront the deeper sources of popular resistance.

Cutting across all these varied, often opposing critiques is one common tendency: to magnify feminist faults and to overlook the less visible roots of antifeminist attitudes. Many commentators assume that women's unwillingness to identify themselves as feminists is itself a central problem, and is attributable to the movement's radical agenda and man-hating image. Implicit in this claim is the further assumption that individuals who are sympathetic to feminist objectives but are put off by the label would enlist in the struggle if only activists would clean up their act.

Yet most in-depth research challenges these assumptions. Negative attitudes toward feminists are likely to be more a result than a cause of negative attitudes toward feminist objectives. Those who are uncomfortable with changes in traditional gender roles tend to project unfavorable traits and radical positions onto supporters of the women's movement. By invoking extremist images, opponents of change then discourage potential sympathizers. Men of color can increase the stakes by adding race to the equation. As bell hooks notes, young black women repeatedly hear that feminism "only serves white women and that 'dissin' it will win them points with just about anybody, particularly sexist black men."[32]

To understand these deeper sources of resistance, we need to reach more broadly and more deeply than popular criticisms suggest. Opposition to feminism involves the same selective perceptions that enable Americans to deny gender inequality as a serious problem: a reluctance to see ourselves as victims or perpetrators of injustice; our desire for roles that provide power, status, security, and a comfortable way of life; and our anxiety about alternatives. For many of us, feminism seems to put too many issues up for renegotiation.

Feminists should, of course, remain open to criticism about the way they are packaging their message. But critics, and the public generally, need to pay more attention to the other forces that encourage potshots at the wrong target. If, as both common sense and recent research suggest, most of the resistance comes from men, why aren't critics paying more attention to men's attitudes? On other issues of social inequality, we do not focus solely on the failure of the subordinate group to make change happen. When the subject is race, few commentators let white Americans off the hook. Yet in popular diagnoses of gender issues, the men's movement is nowhere to be found.

Conventional accounts of the "feminist mistake" mirror a classic vaudeville act. It features a drunk searching futilely for his lost change under a lamppost. As he acknowledges to a passerby, that isn't where he dropped the money, but it's the only place with any light. So too, when questions of gender move center stage, it is feminist fumbles that catch all the glare. But if we're truly hoping to find solutions, or even to get an accurate picture of the problem, we need better lighting.

The Men's Movement and Its Critics

O, the trouble, the trouble with women,
I repeat it again and again
From Kalamazoo to Kamchatka
The trouble with women is—men.

—Ogden Nash and Kurt Weill[33]

In one of Nicole Hollander's "Sylvia" cartoons, the heroine listens to a television report on the men's movement: "During the Seventies women bonded with each other, explored their feelings . . . Now men are getting a chance to have those things." "So," muses Sylvia, "now can we have the stuff they have?"[34]

The men's movement lends itself to this kind of parody. "Ain't they still running the world?" asks one piece in a women's humor collection. "What [do] they need a movement for?" "White men don't need a support group because they already have one," claims civil-rights leader Julian Bond. "It's called the United States of America."[35]

The most popular texts by male activists, Robert Bly's *Iron John* and Sam Keen's *Fire in the Belly*, have inspired caricatures of their own. The parodies in Alfred Gingold's *Fire in the John* don't need to depart much from the originals to produce the desired comic effect. These texts have, after all, lured mostly middle-class, middle-aged men to wilderness campfires, where they beat on tom-toms and search for the Wild Man within. Yet seldom do Americans acknowledge that underlying these seemingly eccentric rituals is a message that we urgently need to hear.[36]

It is, to be sure, misleading even to speak of *a* men's movement. No shared objectives or prominent national organizations unite the groups focusing on men's issues. Rather, there are multiple factions, often with competing concerns. Although relatively few American men are participants in these groups or knowledgeable about their agendas, activists' ideas are gaining a toehold in the culture.

One wing of the men's movement is an outgrowth and ally of feminist struggles. Its aim is to transform masculinity—to eliminate sex-based stereotypes that perpetuate sex-based inequalities, encourage homophobia, and restrict men's opportunities. This part of the movement, which draws on an increasingly rich body of men's-studies scholarship, has the strongest theoretical foundations but the weakest political appeal. At last count, groups like the National Organization for Men against Sexism numbered well under a thousand members. A related and to some extent overlapping constituency includes gay-rights scholars and activists, who also seek to challenge traditional gender roles.[37]

By contrast, men's-rights organizations have a quite different political base and social agenda. Members of these organizations generally see themselves as victims rather than allies of feminists. Many male activists are embittered survivors of hostile divorces. Their objective, according to the Men's Rights Association (MRA) newsletter, is "to marshall manpower in defense of men, masculinity, and the family. Our definition of men's liberation is freedom to be (not from being) men." Where the women's movement fits in all this is equally clear. A riddle from one MRA newsletter asks: "What's the difference between a terrorist and women's lib?" The answer: "You can negotiate with a terrorist."[38]

These groups complain mainly about how men are penalized by courts, "sucked dry" by lawyers, and "nabbed" for sexual "abuses" that only radical libbers see as abusive. Activists often draw on a broad literature of victimization that makes feminist "whining" look mild by comparison. *Playboy* columnist Asa Babar complains that men have had "twenty-five years of sexists calling us sexists" and it's time to stop the "sexual inquisition." Efforts to do just that are creating a new constituency of aggrieved activists, "diligently rolling their ball of pain" from one media event to another.[39]

On one level, as men's-studies scholars Michael Kimmel and Michael Kaufman note, these claims of oppression seem grossly exaggerated. Most participants in such organizations are middle-class, middle-aged, white heterosexual men—"among the most privileged groups in the history of the world." But somehow the collective "power of that group does not translate into an individual sense of feeling empowered." Many men of color, who view themselves as targets of the greatest societal prejudice, have particular difficulty with white feminists' claims.[40]

While conceding that "some men run the world," movement leaders emphasize that "most men don't." As Warren Farrell puts it: What's so great about earning more money when wives are the ones who get to spend it? According to Aaron Kipnis, author of *Knights without Armor*, "the conventional notion that men are somehow more privileged than women is starting to look like a bad joke . . . Many of us have, at various times, felt victimized, scapegoated, manipulated, dominated, or abused by women."[41]

Andrew Kimbrell's *Masculine Mystique* offers a representative parade of horrors. Compared with women, men die sooner, commit suicide more often, die on the job more frequently, drop out of high school in greater numbers, abuse drugs and alcohol at higher rates, are more often victims of violent crime, receive longer criminal sentences, and have greater risks of lung, liver, and heart disease. More African American men are in jail than in college, and in higher education, African American women outnumber their male classmates by 40 percent.[42]

Although these are serious problems, men's-rights literature contributes little toward solutions. These publications read like entries in an oppression sweepstakes: the apparent aim is to put men's grievances on equal footing with those of women. Yet not only are most such descriptions of gender inequality highly selective—they also deny men's responsibility for their own disadvantages. For example, men die sooner in large part because they engage in more risky behavior. They are less likely to receive physical custody of children after divorce because they are less likely to be primary caretakers during marriage. Males not only account for most of the victims of violent crime, but they also account for 90 percent of the perpetrators. They serve longer prison sentences largely because they have longer criminal records and fewer mitigating circumstances. For most disadvantages that men experience, it is difficult to hold women responsible. A similar point cannot be made about many of the inequalities that women experience.[43]

Men's-rights activists also deny the deeper ideological and structural causes of the problems they describe. For example, understanding men's disproportionate rates of violence, substance abuse, and other risk-taking behavior requires a much more complicated analysis than is currently in vogue. Racism, poverty, and inadequate governmental policies deserve more than walk-on roles. So do conventional understandings of masculinity, which are part of men's problems, not their solutions.

Similar criticisms apply to another prominent branch of the men's movement, which uses "mythopoetic" literature, rituals, and retreats to assist spiritual healing. According to popular leaders like Robert Bly, American manhood confronts a crisis rooted in the structures of modern industrial society. In Bly's view, these structures deprive male children of strong father figures and encourage domination by overpowering mothers. The result is a "feminized masculinity" and the remedy is for men to relive their adolescent struggle. They need finally to break free from their mothers and to reclaim their absent fathers. Other activists broaden the number of women accountable for men's problems. The fault, they say, lies not only with domineering mothers but also with emasculating wives and partners.[44]

By contrast, leaders like Sam Keen place primary blame for men's problems on other societal structures, such as the "corporate industrial warfare system." However, these activists, like Bly, focus on individual growth rather than societal transformation—on self-help strategies rather than political struggle. Through retreats and workshop rituals, the American male should get in touch with his genetically programmed warrior instincts. This will, in turn, create a stronger masculine identity. The beating of drums, literally and symbolically, creates a safe space in which a man can "shout and say what he wants" in a society that has repressed those desires.[45]

The use of male bonding rituals is, of course, by no means unique. Many fraternal organizations and men's recovery groups rely on such strategies. Even an elite all-male association such as California's Bohemian Club sends its members—including cabinet officials and Fortune 500 executives—off on mythic retreats at "Cave Man Camp." What is, however, distinctive about men's-movement gatherings is the premise that they are the answer to the current crisis of masculinity.[46]

There are multiple problems with this solution, largely because male leaders deny the true dynamics of the crisis. Even if their causal diagnoses were correct, these activists have offered no evidence that weekend retreats and mythic rituals can compensate men for the prolonged absence of their fathers or produce sustained personality changes. Virtually all respected psychological research suggests the contrary. In any event, if, as Bly and other leaders maintain, the root of the difficulty lies in cultural values that minimize men's parental role or encourage destructive corporate priorities, then self-help approaches hardly supply an adequate response.[47]

This wing of the men's movement also offers no analysis of why women are left with the vast majority of child-rearing responsibilities, or why male decisionmakers perpetuate socially dysfunctional policies. Nor do activists make any effort to place men's restricted family role in the larger context of men's power. Male leaders present themselves as the tragic figures of paternal neglect and corporate greed, while ignoring the social transformation necessary to prevent those patterns from recurring.[48]

Not only does the men's movement offer an impoverished analysis of solutions, but it also denies the full dimensions of the problem. Issues of class and race are largely absent, and the omissions cause little concern among predominantly white and economically comfortable audiences. As feminist critics note, leaders like Bly never even "mention the epidemic of male violence against women." Strengthening masculinity so that men can "shout [out their] wants" is not a helpful prescription for reducing abuse. Ann Jones, an expert on domestic violence, makes that point directly: "Battered women, who could use some *ironing* Johns, report that . . . the bedrooms of the nation are already filled with hairy men shouting relentlessly about what they want."[49]

This is not to suggest that the impulse behind these bonding rituals is entirely misguided. Men need more opportunities to express emotion and to establish intimacy with other men. At least the participants in such retreats and workshops realize that something is missing from their lives. But as men's-studies experts point out, these individuals "are not looking in even the approximately right direction for the cause of their wounds." And the prescriptions that they are getting cannot begin to treat even their symptoms.[50]

The same is true of the solutions offered by religiously affiliated men's organizations. Male dominance and the legitimacy of gender hierarchy is a shared premise of groups ranging from the religious right's "Promise Keepers" and "Jocks for Jesus" to Louis Farrakhan's "Million-Man Marchers." The message to men is "take your role back," become "leaders" of your family, church, and community. The message to women is to accept being followers.[51]

Promise Keepers is the inspiration of Bill McCartney, a born-again Christian and former football coach. What began in 1970 as a prayer meeting with some 70 participants now holds mass rallies with an annual attendance of over 700,000. According to McCartney, the group speaks to "godly men" who "recognize that [they] have fumbled the ball." Promise Keeper rallies extend the metaphor. They offer a kind of evangelical sporting event in which fans on one side of the stadium challenge the other with chants like "I love Jesus—How about you?" Although heralded as "spiritual revivals," these gatherings are not without commercial appeal. Each event typically grosses several million dollars through sales of shirts, caps, jackets, and instructional material.[52]

At the core of Promise Keepers' religious mission are seven commitments. These include requirements that members honor Christ; support the church; practice spiritual, moral, ethical, and sexual purity; reach beyond racial and denominational barriers; and build strong families through love, protection, and traditional biblical values. It is this last mandate that gives feminists pause, along with other values that do not appear among the core commitments. *Seven Promises of a Promise Keeper* advises men to insist on asserting the leadership role in their family: "If you're going to lead, you must lead . . . Treat the lady gently and lovingly. But lead." Promise Keepers' leaders are virulently anti-gay (McCartney is on record describing homosexuality as an "abomination against almighty God"), and its magazines include vitriolic messages concerning abortion, AIDS, and the American Civil Liberties Union.[53]

Moreover, the right wing of the men's movement has no monopoly on prejudice. Louis Farrakhan has an extended record of sexist, racist, anti-Semitic, and homophobic pronouncements, and his initial plan for a Million-Man March in Washington offered more of the same. African American men were to come together to atone for past misconduct, and to chart their future "as responsible heads of [their] families . . . [and] neighborhoods." Women were to stay at home, care for children, organize teach-ins, and pray from the sidelines. Although other black leaders sought to distance the occasion from Farrakhan's agenda, they did not lift the ban on female marchers. And that ban assumed added significance in the context of women's longstanding exclusion from leadership positions in the African American community. Why, asked columnist Julianne Malveaux, should "I stand by my man when he's trying to step over me?"[54]

For many women, however, that question is not rhetorical, and the answer is not self-evident. As historian Ruth Rosen notes, the religious wing of the men's movement is offering variations on an "age-old bargain"—one that "promises support and loyalty in exchange for power and control." To women straining under the double burden of breadwinning and caretaking, it may not seem like an unreasonable trade, especially if they don't have all that much power and control to begin with. And in poor black communities, ravaged by crime, violence, drugs, and unemployment, any mobilization around family values holds obvious appeal. Not surprisingly, many women support events like the Million-Man March and Promise Keepers' rallies.[55]

But whether they are getting a fair bargain is another question entirely. As *Washington Post* editorialist Donna Britt asks: If the call went out for a march dedicated to "black women's spiritual growth and empowerment, would scores of black men raise funds, answer phones, and organize [support] as black women now are doing?" To Britt, the answer to *that* question seems self-evident. The religious wing of the men's movement speaks to real needs. But as the African American Agenda 2000 emphasizes, those needs are "not served by men declaring themselves the only 'rightful' leaders of our families, our communities, and our ongoing struggle for justice."[56]

At its most fundamental level, the problem for American men parallels the problem for American women: both groups face widespread denial that there *is* a serious problem. But the task of building a coherent men's movement also bumps up against unique obstacles, because even those who acknowledge the need for change are deeply divided about the direction it should take. And men themselves seem profoundly ambivalent about whether reviving traditional understandings of masculinity would address or merely amplify the problem.

Part of the difficulty is that the upheaval in gender roles since the 1970s has supplemented, but by no means supplanted, traditional values. The once-dominant ideal was elusive enough: few if any men felt confident that they were sufficiently powerful, strong, economically secure, and sexually attractive. But today's demands are even harder to meet because they are internally inconsistent.[57]

Competing ideals play out in media images and social expectations.

Americans vacillate: Do they want men to be ambitious breadwinners or involved fathers? "Macho seducers" or "sensitive new-age guys"? Traditional understandings of masculinity are no longer the norm, but nontraditional ones have yet to be accepted. American society tells working mothers they can "have it all," at least in theory. But the same message isn't going out to working fathers. Except in occasional Hollywood fantasies, Mr. Mom is not a cultural hero, and neither private employers nor government decisionmakers are doing much to accommodate his needs. If, as social theorist Lynn Segal argues, the men's movement is stuck in "slow motion," it is partly because we provide little institutional support for changes in men's roles.[58]

Our society's schizophrenia about masculine ideals comes at a price and it is one we can ill afford. Men are "being asked to take on roles and show care in ways that violate the traditional male code and require skills that they do not have." The result is confusion and frustration. Some men also feel "hung out to dry" by feminists, who blame them for a structure of inequality that isn't their fault and who seem to be after their jobs, status, power, and even their magazines. From this perspective, even sex is becoming a chore, now that assertive women are "trying to supervise all the time. 'Now do this. No, not like that, like this.'" Many men are deeply resentful and resent not feeling free to say so. The problems men experience in the home are compounded by the problems they face in the world outside it. Their recent losses in real income and job security have taken a toll. Many men end up "nostalgic about the past, embattled in the present, and worried about the future."[59]

The challenge remaining is to channel disaffection into constructive strategies for change. This is not a hopeless task, but the most popularized wings of the men's movement are pushing in the wrong direction. The problems these groups identify will not be solved by symbolic rallies or self-help retreats. Nor will we find answers in newer versions of older hierarchies, with kinder, gentler dominance repackaged as responsible leadership. What women need from the men's movement is a substantial revision in traditional ideals of masculinity. And in the long run, that is what men need as well.

Western industrialized societies conventionally define masculinity in opposition to femininity. The roles and characteristics that we value for women we devalue for men. Psychological research consistently finds that people give lower ratings to men who display traits or perform work that departs from gender stereotypes. One consequence is that many men lose access to crucial experiences, emotions, and relationships. Prevailing images of masculinity encourage toughness, aggression, competitiveness, sexual conquest, and workplace achievement. Other values, such as tenderness, intimacy, and nurturance, fall outside our conventional vision of the "manly" man.[60]

Gender stereotypes discourage many men from taking an equal part in child-rearing, from forming close personal friendships, from working in nontraditional occupations, from accepting homosexuality, and from adequately controlling aggression. In low-income communities, the celebration of male power, coupled with the absence of other opportunities for achievement and self-esteem, has fostered some particularly destructive patterns. The prevailing rigidity of gender roles imposes substantial costs on both sexes, and both have much to gain from change.[61]

Why, then, have so few men been active in the struggle to achieve it? During the early days of the feminist movement, it was common to hear that "women's liberation is men's liberation too." Long lists of male benefits emerged, such as the twenty-one itemized examples in Warren Farrell's *The Liberated Man*. Feminism was supposed to free men from some of the pressure of breadwinning and to expand their choices at home and in the workplace. Men also would have more control over their own lives once women had more opportunities in theirs.[62]

That message met with only partial acceptance. While many men were prepared, at least in principle, to support equal rights for women, they were more ambivalent about changes in their own roles, status, and self-image. Often their initial tendency was to "sit tight, keep their heads down and wait it out, hoping that when the storm passes and the sociological dust settles, nothing fundamental will have changed."[63]

Now, some three decades later, the dust is still unsettled but it is clear that fundamental transformations are inevitable. The structural foundations for traditional gender patterns are eroding. Recent employment patterns are curtailing men's opportunities for economic independence and domestic dominance. Most families depend on women's wages and most Americans share, at least in principle, some commitment to gender equality. That commitment is, in turn, altering cultural expectations about everything from sexual behavior to parental responsibility. These transformations cannot be readily reversed. Changes in women's lives necessarily imply changes in men's. What is less clear is how long that process will take, where it will end, and how much resistance it will meet along the way.

Battle lines are apparent on multiple fronts. Hypermasculinity thrives in gangsta rap, slasher movies, and National Rifle Association literature. These values spill over into political life, and have encouraged what Michael Kimmel describes as the "Great American Wimp Hunt" among national leaders. What George Bush once termed the "manhood thing" has been the not-so-subtle subtext in many presidential campaigns. Examples abound: "Mondale Eats Quiche" bumper stickers; photos of Michael Dukakis trying to look combat ready atop a "real man's" tank; Bush's media appearances in hunting gear and his boasts that he "kicked a little ass" after debating Geraldine Ferraro; and Republican Party caricatures of Bill Clinton as a henpecked husband, hiding behind the skirts of a conniving careerist wife. Similar themes recur in almost all aspects of American culture, even in religious settings. "Christ was no wimp," according to Jocks for Jesus.[64]

Yet defining masculinity in opposition to femininity remains problematic if gender equality is our goal. Historical and cross-cultural experience suggest that no culture is likely to provide equal respect for qualities associated with women as long as men devalue those qualities in themselves. That insight underlies an increasingly rich body of work in men's studies. One of its core objectives is to offer new visions of masculinity that better express the full range of human potential, including characteristics historically viewed as feminine.[65]

This work could, and should, form the basis of a more constructive men's movement. Part of its agenda should include the kind of personal-growth initiatives popularized by some men's groups. These organizations speak to many men's need for "safe spaces" where they can raise intensely private concerns. But men also need more public settings where they can challenge the social forces that construct and constrain gender roles. The most active wings of the current men's movement fail to provide such opportunities. Some groups, like those at Wild Man retreats and Promise Keepers' rallies, are determinedly apolitical. Others, like fathers'-rights organizations, are highly politicized but virulently antifeminist. We need activism of a different sort.[66]

In the short run, however, it is naive to expect that American males will flock to join any organized campaign against traditional gender roles. Mass movements depend on a sense of solidarity around shared interests, which is difficult to sustain in a group as diffuse and divided as men. Moreover, most men have something to lose as well as to gain from challenging sex-based inequalities, and that complicates the task of political mobilization. As theorists like R. W. Connell have argued, the most promising strategies for enlisting male support are likely to involve coalitions within and among groups that are organized around other issues.[67]

For example, more effort should center on gender-related initiatives within established professional, labor, political, and educational associations. Both women and men need to do more to recruit and reward male colleagues for joining such efforts, and for leading gender-bias programs. Other countries such as Sweden have made modest strides through media campaigns and paid parental leaves that encourage males' family involvement. So too, America's support groups for single and divorced fathers, "big-brother" programs for boys with absent fathers, and sexual-violence prevention initiatives with respected male leaders all have modeled constructive images of masculinity.

The precise shape that these images should assume is, of course, still open to debate. For some commentators, the goal is to dismantle all gender stereotypes. From this perspective, we should try to make a full spectrum of traits and roles equally available to both men and women. Implicit in this vision is a commitment to individual self-determination unconstrained by gender.[68]

For other commentators, such a homogenized vision seems neither plausible nor desirable. All societies institutionalize sex-appropriate roles and traits. Although what constitutes appropriate behavior varies over time and across cultures, it is questionable whether we can dispense with culturally constructed differences altogether. Many Americans believe it is unwise even to try.[69]

So too, prominent men's-studies theorists often reject any "androgynous blurring of masculinity and femininity into a melange of some vaguely defined human qualities." They prefer a vision that combines virtues traditionally associated with masculinity, such as strength, self-reliance, courage, and dependability, with other virtues that should also become associated with masculinity, such as compassion and nurturance.[70]

Each of these competing visions holds some appeal and, at this juncture, few Americans seem ready to choose between them. Most individuals want neither to relinquish all sense of sexual identity nor to restrict each sex to stereotypical patterns. Yet it is by no means clear that we can have it both ways. Most of what we know about personality development suggests that as long as sex-linked traits remain, the pressures for conformity will limit individual choice.

We need not, however, reach consensus about the role of gender in an ideal society before we can address problems in the one we have. Although there are obvious limits to the cultural changes that we can consciously direct, we have by no means tested the boundaries of what is possible. On issues of gender, the personal is the political, but it is not always political enough. The challenge remaining is to direct some of the energy that is fueling the men's self-help movement into strategies for broader social change.

The trashing and bashing that characterize much of contemporary gender politics make good reading but bad policy. The recent polarization around gender issues has done more to obscure than to address the most pressing concerns of both sexes. Our current stalemates on key policy questions should remind us of what we already know. Men and women really are all in this together, and the reconstruction of gender roles requires our shared commitment.

9

The Politics of Progress

"Women who want to be equal with men lack ambition." This is a familiar quip, but it captures a partial truth. The vast majority of American women want equality, but that is not all they want. They want equality in education, employment, physical safety, financial security, and political representation. But they also want to preserve values that are traditionally associated with women—values such as care and compassion—and to increase their influence in public policy.[1]

Of course, women disagree about how to realize that goal. The question remaining is how to bridge these disagreements in pursuit of common objectives. Which strategies are most likely to promote equal status and respect, as well as preserve what is unique and valuable in women's experience?

Americans cannot answer these questions without a clearer recognition of our distance from that goal and the obstacles standing in our way. Much of our current problem stems from denial of what the problem is. We are unwilling to acknowledge the extent of gender inequality, the complexity of its causes, and our personal and societal responsibility for its persistence. These patterns of denial obscure the need for fundamental change. We settle for equality in form rather than equality in fact, for commitment in legal mandates rather than in daily practice.

To make significant progress, we need to see more clearly the connections between public policies and private choices. Inequalities in workplace opportunities encourage inequalities in family roles. Women with lower earnings than their male partners are more likely to assume the bulk of household responsibilities. These disparities in the home limit women's opportunities in the world outside it.

Our ideological assumptions and social policies are similarly related. We will not achieve structural reforms without changes in our attitudes about gender issues. And these reforms, in turn, are essential to increase women's expectations and capacities for change. If, for example, we want to alter patterns of sexual violence, we need to alter popular assumptions about what perpetuates it. And we need legal institutions and social support structures that enable more women to resist abuse.

So too, we cannot effectively challenge sex-based inequality without also challenging the other patterns of subordination with which it intersects. Gender is only part of what constrains women's experience, and it is often less critical than other factors, such as race, class, and sexual orientation. The commitment to sex-based equality that gave birth to the women's movement is necessary but not sufficient to express its underlying principles. Ensuring that *all* women can meet their fundamental human needs requires alliances against multiple structures of injustice.

Except at the rhetorical level, this is not a simple task. Even framing the challenge in these terms risks sounding somewhat pat. It is all too easy to meet pressures for political correctness by ritualized references to the importance of diversity. It is all too difficult to make good on that commitment in practice, and to build sustained coalitions for change among individuals with quite different priorities. As columnist Ellen Willis notes, the contemporary women's movement has long been caught between "the need to preserve its political boundaries and the need to extend them." What defines feminism is its claim to speak for women as a group. What limits feminism are the practical challenges of doing so, of bridging the diversity in women's interests and experience.[2]

These challenges are more apparent because the differences in women's needs are more visible. At earlier stages in the women's movement, it was easier to find common ground. Gender bias often was overt and universal; women as a group had a shared interest in challenging sex-based restrictions on employment and educational opportunities, in prohibiting sexual harassment, in establishing domestic-violence and rape crisis services, and in removing criminal penalties for abortion. The barriers to achieving those objectives now look more subtle and contested, solutions appear more complicated and costly, and differences in priorities are more explicit across class, race, and sexual orientation. On issues like welfare, pornography, child custody, and affirmative action, women are themselves divided. All too often, when speaking of sex, Americans discount at the political level what they know at the personal level: there is no single "woman's point of view," even, or especially, on women's issues. In one recent *New Yorker* cartoon, a white, middle-aged and seemingly well-to-do wife informs her husband: "Yes, Harold, I do speak for *all* women." This is not a claim that leaders of the women's movement can comfortably make.[3]

But these leaders can speak for a vast number of women on a wide range of issues concerning gender equality. And activists can do more to acknowledge and bridge the points of dissent. As Audre Lorde once noted, women are divided less by their differences than by their "refusal to recognize those differences, and to examine the distortions which result."[4]

Only by acknowledging this diversity can we as Americans gain a fuller sense of the aspirations that we share. On most of the issues that this book has addressed, it seems reasonable to expect some broad-based consensus for change if we can break through our current patterns of denial. That, in turn, will require greater awareness of how prevailing understandings of gender institutionalize inequalities.

Principles and Priorities

Reform efforts are critical on two levels. Our nation needs strategies that will broaden public understanding of the dimensions and dynamics of gender inequality, as well as strategies that will prove more effective in challenging it.

To change attitudes about "women's issues," we must first change the way these issues appear—or disappear—in the popular media. News coverage is often sparse, superficial, and stereotypical. Women are underrepresented both as subjects and commentators, and caricatures of the women's movement compound the "image" problem that reporters incessantly describe. Many commentators like to cast complex debates as catfights, in which simplistic soundbites displace reflective analysis.

Media entertainment and advertising reinforce traditional roles and characteristics, particularly males' tendencies toward aggression, females' anxieties over appearance, and parents' unequal family responsibilities.

We have more leverage, both individually and collectively, than we exercise over these images. Those of us who care about gender equality can boycott sexist entertainment and the products of its corporate sponsors. We can give more support to educational programming and public service campaigns on gender-related issues, as well as to organizations that monitor coverage and organize protests. We also can teach our children to be critical viewers, and provide them with books, videos, and toys that challenge conventional gender stereotypes.

Similar efforts can focus on education. Elementary, secondary, and college programs could do much more to address gender bias in the curricula, as well as gender-related problems like sexual harassment, acquaintance rape, and teenage pregnancy. Educational initiatives in the workplace are equally critical, particularly for judges and managers who exercise decisionmaking authority.

By increasing public understanding of gender-related problems, these educational strategies also could point us toward more effective responses. One focus of reform efforts should be the legal system. We need changes in the substantive law, in the way that courts interpret it, and in the procedures for its enforcement.

For example, in cases of sexual harassment, rape, and domestic violence, our legal process should do more to prevent the victimization of victims and the trivialization of their injuries. When men abuse, it should not be women who are on trial. Nor should we rely so heavily on formal legal proceedings to address sexual violence and harassment. Since only a small number of abuses result in civil or criminal charges, other strategies are critical. We need increased funding for rape crisis centers and battered-women's services, more effective prevention policies, and improved treatment for offenders.

We also need more adequate responses to employment practices that have the effect, if not the intent, of disadvantaging women. For most workers, the costs and difficulties of proving conscious discrimination are prohibitive. Additional remedies should be available for negligent patterns of gender bias. Governmental and employer policies should also encourage more active measures, such as pay equity, affirmative action, and family-related assistance. Adequate parental leave, flexible schedules, and childcare assistance should be available for all employees, not just a privileged minority.

Reform efforts in family law need to focus on reducing gender bias, protecting reproductive rights, and preventing poverty. Too many divorced women end up with disproportionate child-rearing obligations and insufficient resources to fulfill them. We need fairer standards for setting child and spousal support and more effective systems for collecting it. Child custody decisionmaking should reinforce shared parental responsibilities, not double standards of parental fitness. The law also should extend its prohibitions against sex discrimination to include discrimination on the basis of sexual orientation. Both forms of bias rest on similar stereotypes and compromise similar principles of liberty and equality.

The same values are at stake in current struggles over reproductive rights. To make these rights meaningful, the government must assume greater responsibility for removing the barriers to reproductive choice and expanding the choices available. If, as many political leaders claim, our objective is to make abortion safe, available, and unnecessary, then the government must strengthen its commitment to that goal. More support for birth control education and services is critical, particularly for adolescent and low-income women.

These women also need greater opportunities for education, job training, childcare, and health insurance. Rather than scapegoating welfare mothers for their dependency, we should be establishing the minimum conditions necessary for their independence.

During the suffrage campaign in the early twentieth century, women's-rights activists popularized a slogan designed to counter concerns about their radicalism:

> For the safety of the nation, to
> Women give the vote;
> For the hand that rocks the cradle
> Will never rock the boat.

This prediction may have been prudent politically, but it has proven wrong empirically. Ours is not a modest agenda. And at a time of increasing skepticism about "big government," a call for major public initiatives may seem at best naive and at worst irrelevant. Yet to allow what now seems politically appealing to establish the movement's agenda is to doom it from the outset. Partial strategies reinforce public disillusionment. Often what is expedient neglects what is essential. Those who pay the greatest price are the individuals least able to afford it, especially low-income women of color who lack leverage in the current political process.[5]

Moreover, as theorists like Thomas Nagel point out, many goals that "would have seemed utopian in former centuries," including formal legal prohibitions on sex discrimination, "are now accomplished facts." The task remaining is to translate these legal mandates into social priorities.[6]

To make that happen, more individuals need to see their own connection to the problem and the solution. This means making gender-based equality a political priority. Although most Americans perceive some measure of sex discrimination, a majority of surveyed women and over two-thirds of men do not report that it bothers them personally. And only a small number of either sex see any need to join efforts for change. Yet the vast majority of Americans will never be able to solve gender-related problems individually unless more of us act collectively.[7]

Political Commitment

Bella Abzug is fond of chronicling America's recent increase in concern for women, at least at the level of symbolic politics. For a considerable period, she notes, the nation was content with just one day for women—Mother's Day. Then the federal government recognized a Women's Year, and the United Nations handed over an entire decade. "If we behave," Abzug wonders, "will they let us in on the whole thing?"[8]

"No time soon" looks like the short answer. Female politicians did, of course, make record gains in 1992, which earned that period unofficial recognition as yet another year of the woman. But at current rates of change, it still would take more than three centuries to achieve equality between the sexes in political representation. In the mid-1990s—a time when some politicians complained that the nation's legislative process had become "femcentric"—women accounted for a majority of registered voters, but occupied only about 10 percent of congressional seats and less than a quarter of state elective offices.

Women of color accounted for only 2 percent of federal legislative positions, and were similarly underrepresented at state and local levels.[9]

Gender inequality in governmental leadership denies women opportunities for power, status, and economic reward. It also denies the public a range of backgrounds and values that should be reflected in political office. So too, women's underrepresentation undermines progress on women's rights and family issues, because male legislators are less likely than their female colleagues to make such issues a priority.[10]

Many feminists also claim that greater gender equality in public office could promote broader changes in the policy process. As they note, female voters give more support than male voters to family, environmental, and welfare measures, and less support to the use of military force. Such gender gaps have increased since the 1980s, and some related differences have become apparent between male and female legislators. To feminists like Gloria Steinem, these trends suggest that more political leadership by women would result in a "kinder, gentler" political agenda.[11]

This is a familiar argument, but its history should give us pause. During the fight for women's suffrage, supporters often claimed that female participation would "purify politics": women's compassionate, nurturing values would point the way to ending war, poverty, and assorted social evils. After some seventy-five years of experience, perhaps reality should begin to set in. Although gender variations in voting and legislative behavior recently have increased, over time the similarities between men and women have been far greater than the differences. Race and education account for larger gaps than gender. Female voters have not, on the whole, cast ballots as a bloc on women's issues or women candidates. And on some matters of feminist concern, such as gay and lesbian rights and sex education, they have been less supportive than men.[12]

Although feminists often assume that female politicians need to reach higher positions or a greater critical mass before broader changes are possible, the evidence for this assumption is mixed. Some state and local bodies with high percentages of women have been exceptionally successful in passing feminist initiatives, such as bills involving daycare and pay equity. But other state legislatures (such as New Hampshire) with unusually large numbers of women rank near the bottom in support for family and welfare services. Female leaders around the world span the political spectrum, and relatively few have made women's issues a priority. As examples like Margaret Thatcher remind us, putting more women in power is not the same as empowering most women.[13]

This is not to claim, as have feminists like Steinem, that having someone who "looks like us but thinks like them is worse than having no one at all." To assume that women constitute some unitary "us" is to obscure important differences in backgrounds, perspectives, and concerns. Moreover, reducing gender barriers in the political process has independent value, regardless of what substantive agenda any individual politician pursues. Effective leadership by women of varied perspectives, including highly visible politicians like Thatcher, is helpful in breaking the stereotypes that have hindered all female candidates. Yet an obvious truth, too often discounted, is that to advance a feminist agenda, we need to elect feminists, not simply females. And we need to create a political base that will make such an agenda possible. Supporters of women's issues have long focused on how to influence powerful politicians; more attention needs to center on how to become those politicians.[14]

Grover Cleveland once claimed that politics would change women more than women would change politics. He was only partly right. The gender gap has increased, not diminished, over time. But the process clearly exacts a price from candidates. We cannot expect that most women who take the positions now necessary for political success and who gain a stake in current structures will want to promote a transformative vision. Even those who wish to do so will confront powerful countervailing influences of money, seniority, and old-boy networks. We are unlikely to establish gender equality as a political priority without substantial changes in the electoral process.[15]

Significant progress on "women's issues" will require an expanded understanding of what those issues are and an expanded constituency that considers them crucial. Of course, in some sense, even labeling issues by gender is misleading. Women are, after all, half the human race and almost any political question is bound to affect them to some degree. But if our objective is promoting equality between the sexes, then our priorities become clearer. We need to focus not only on the legal and policy reforms aimed at reducing women's disadvantages, but also on the structural conditions that will make such reforms possible.

As former congresswoman Pat Schroeder once noted, "There's no money in women's issues." That must change, and it must matter less. Securing campaign finance reform and reducing the influence of political action committees should be central priorities. Although some of these committees, like Emily's List, have given important assistance to women's issues and women candidates, such contributions have been relatively small. In the short run, we could and should do more to increase them. But in the long run, women's interests would be better served by a system that is less hostage to financial influence. The funds available from individuals who care about gender equality are unlikely ever to match those of corporate donors and wealthy conservatives with competing agendas. Women would benefit most from changing the rules of a game in which their concerns are unlikely to win.[16]

Women also stand to gain from strategies that increase voters' knowledge and reduce barriers to political participation. Many Americans are poorly informed, not only about gender-related problems and policies but also about candidates' positions on these issues. Political organizations must do more to make such information available, through telephone, computer, and media channels, as well as in public education and voter turnout campaigns. Organizations for women's interests need to devote more effort to spearheading such campaigns and to building coalitions with broadbased support. For example, Canada has a national Action Committee that serves as an effective representative for 650 women's groups.[17]

More effort also should center on helping men see their own stake in family, employment, and antiviolence initiatives. A 1995 advertisement by the Women's Campaign Research Fund points in the right direction. It pictures a man hugging his son under a caption asking, "Who Needs More Women in Government? Men Do." The text adds that 65 percent of men believe that "we'd have a better Congress if it had more women." This ad ran in small type near the end of a low-circulation magazine; the same message needs to reach wider audiences.[18]

In a recent celebration of seventy-five years of women's suffrage, organizers protested that no statues of women appear in the rotunda of our nation's Capitol. The building's only female busts, of suffragists Susan B. Anthony, Elizabeth Cady Stanton and Lucretia Mott, languished for a half-century in the basement, inconspicuously nestled among shops and restrooms. Although in 1996 the busts finally secured a first-floor location, there is plenty of progress yet to be made. Only

5 percent of the "Nation's Historic Landmarks" are dedicated to women. Those monuments are a reminder of all that needs to change before periodic "years of the woman" become unnecessary.[19]

As American women approach the twenty-first century, they have much to be grateful for. But in one paradoxical sense, perhaps too much. The progress toward gender equality over the last three decades rivals that of the three preceding millennia. Women's control over the terms of their own destiny has never been greater. Yet this transformation too often obscures the challenges that remain. On almost all measures of social, economic, and political status, significant gender inequality persists. What is worse, many Americans fail to perceive this inequality as a concern that they need to address. Calls to political action seem to require too much time and money, which is precisely what most women have too little of.

A step in the right direction is to encourage manageable levels of political involvement. In one recent guide for grassroots activists, Thalia Zepatos and Elizabeth Kaufman outline strategies for those who want to "change the world in an hour a week": writing letters, organizing a fundraiser, building women's networks among colleagues and friends, or sending a check.[20]

Such support is especially critical in an era of declining government subsidies and minimal charitable support for key gender-related concerns. Overall, America's foundations target less than 5 percent of their funding to the specific needs of women and girls. Some sixty women's funds are now struggling to fill the gap, but their endowments remain quite modest. The institutions that they underwrite—everything from rape crisis hotlines to research in reproductive health—can make a difference, but only if more women make their checkbooks match their values.[21]

Finally, those committed to gender equality must seize more opportunities to make their personal lives express their political principles. The concerns that we express in families, schools, and workplaces create the conditions for broader cultural change. I can still remember one of my own first consciously feminist acts. Some twenty years ago, on a visit to meet my future husband's family, I was struck by the gendered pattern of labor in an otherwise highly progressive household. For several days I watched as three college-age males managed to avoid any contact with a dirty dish, unmade bed, or soiled sock. On my fourth day of joining the ladies to cope with these domestic details, I finally popped the question to my soon to be significant other: "Do you believe in kitchen fairies? How *do* you think the dishes travel to and from the dining-room table?" It was the last time I needed to ask. Well, almost the last. Had I settled for a different answer, I would have had a different life, and a book like this would not have been part of it.

Now, two decades later, I am visiting the same family. The same three men are on kitchen detail and their wives are watching *My Fair Lady* on video. Henry Higgins has just finished warbling "Why Can't a Woman Be More Like a Man," while his parlor maid is clearing tea. Collette, my nine-year-old niece, is getting an impromptu lecture on class and gender bias in Victorian England, and what has and has not changed for women. There is plenty in both categories, but I am struck mainly by our progress. My options look vastly better than those of Eliza Doolittle, and my niece takes for granted most of what my generation has struggled to achieve. It has not yet occurred to her that she might ever face limitations because of her sex. She is in deep denial.

My hope is that by the time she might want to read this book, there will be far less to deny. Nor does that optimism seem unreasonable. Our nation's aspirations to gender equality are, after all, widely shared. The vast majority of Americans acknowledge, at least in principle, that men and women are entitled to equal status and opportunity. The challenge remaining is to recognize our distance from that ideal and to draw from common aspirations the basis for a common struggle.

Notes / Acknowledgments / Index

Notes

1. The "No Problem" Problem

1. Betty Friedan, *The Feminine Mystique* (New York: Norton, 1964), 15–32.
2. Federal Glass Ceiling Commission, *Good for Business: Making Full Use of the Nation's Human Capital,* Fact-Finding Report, Bureau of National Affairs, Daily Labor Report (17 March 1995), 528, 541, 634–639 (executives). See the sources cited in Chapter 5 (sexual violence); Chapter 7 (poverty, family responsibilities, reproductive freedom); Chapter 6 (employment, work/family conflicts); and Chapter 9 (elected officials).
3. Contributions to women's causes and candidates have dramatically increased in the last decade but still account for only a small percentage of charitable and political contributions. And just over 5 percent of foundation support goes to issues involving women and girls. See National Council for Research on Women, "Women and Philanthropy," *Issues Quarterly* 1 (1994): 13. For polls on women's concerns, see Roper Organization, *The 1990 Virginia Slims Opinion Poll,* 11, 22. For women's membership data, see Harris Associates, *Women's Equality Poll* (New York: Feminist Majority Foundation, April 1995), 9.
4. Paul Craig Roberts, "The Decline and Fall of the White Male," *San Francisco Examiner,* 9 January 1996, A13 (discussing "special privileges"); David Gates, "White Male Paranoia," *Newsweek,* 29 March 1993, 48 (citing poll on unfair penalties). For surveys on perceptions about discrimination, see Federal Glass Ceiling Commission, *Good for Business,* 528, 541, 634–639; sources cited in Deborah L. Rhode, "Gender and Professional Roles," *Fordham Law Review* 63 (1994): 39, 64; and Lisa Grunwald, "If Women Ruled America?" *Life,* April 1992, 44.
5. For the percentage of white males in positions of status and wealth, see Federal

Glass Ceiling Commission, *Good for Business,* 634–637; Gates, "White Male Paranoia," 48, 49. For sex-based disparities in pay and promotion, see American Bar Association [ABA] Commission on the Status of Women, *Unfinished Business: Overcoming the Sisyphus Factor* (Chicago: American Bar Association, 1995) (lawyers); Sarah Boxer, "Mr. and Ms. Doctor," *New York Times,* 14 April 1996, E2 (academics and physicians); Jane Frieson, "Alternative Economic Perspectives on the Use of Labor Market Policies to Redress the Gender Gap in Compensation," *Georgetown Law Journal* 82 (1993): 31, 41–42. See also the sources cited in Chapter 6. For male perceptions, see Gates, "White Male Paranoia," 49.

6. Sol Linowitz and Martin Mayer, *The Betrayed Profession* (New York: Scribner's, 1994), 6.

7. ABA Commission, *Unfinished Business.* For differing reports of male and female attorneys, see Ann J. Gellis, "Great Expectations: Women in the Legal Profession: A Commentary on State Studies," *Indiana Law Journal* 66 (1991): 941, 971; and Rhode, "Gender and Professional Roles," 826. For judicial perceptions, see *Preliminary Report of the Ninth-Circuit Gender Bias Task Force* (Seattle: United States District Court, Western District of Washington, 1992). For Texas survey results, see Diane F. Norwood and Arlette Molina, "Sex Discrimination in the Profession: 1990 Survey Results Reported," *Texas Bar Journal* (January 1992): 50, 51.

8. See sources cited in Rhode, "Gender and Professional Roles," 66 (antitrust example); American Bar Association Multicultural Women Attorneys' Network, *The Burdens of Both, the Privileges of Neither* (American Bar Association: Chicago, 1994), 1 (stenographer example); "Los Angeles County Bar Association Committee Report on Sexual Orientation Bias," reprinted in *Southern California Review of Law and Women's Studies* 4 (1995): 295, 441–449, 471 (sexual-orientation examples). See also Chapter 6.

9. Patricia J. Williams, *The Rooster's Egg* (Cambridge, Mass.: Harvard University Press, 1995), 97.

10. For partnership data, see ABA Commission, *Unfinished Business;* Rhode, "Gender and Professional Roles," 58–59; American Bar Association Young Lawyers Division, *The State of the Legal Profession, 1990* (1991), 54, 63–64. For barriers facing women of color, see American Bar Association Task Force on Minorities and the Justice System, *Achieving Justice in a Diverse America: Report of the ABA Task Force on Minorities and the Justice System* (1992); ABA Multicultural Women's Network, *Burdens of Both.*

11. For survey data, see Roberta A. Sigel, *Ambition and Accommodation: How Women View Gender Relations* (Chicago: University of Chicago Press, 1996), 145; and Sherrye Henry, *The Deep Divide: Why Women Resist Equality* (New York: Macmillan, 1994), 4. For the trivialization of sexual harassment, see *Sand v. Johnson,* 33 Fair Employment Practice Cases (BNA) 716 (E. D. Mich., 1982); cases cited in Chapter 5; cases cited in Deborah L. Rhode, "Sexual Harassment," *University of Southern California Law Review* 65 (1992): 1459,

1461; and Eliza G. C. Collins and Timothy B. Blodgett, "Sexual Harassment: Some See It . . . Some Won't," *Harvard Business Review* 59 (March–April 1981), 92. For attitudes on bias, see David Rothman, quoted in Ninth-Circuit Gender Bias Task Force, *Discussion Draft* (U.S. Court of Appeals for the Ninth Circuit, 1992), 171.

12. Ann Wilson Schaff, *Women's Reality* (New York: Harper and Row, 1981), 44.

13. *Price Waterhouse v. Hopkins,* 490 U.S. 228 (1989), discussed in Chapter 6.

14. Faye J. Crosby, Ann Pufall, Rebecca Claire Snyder, Marion O'Connell, and Peg Whalen, "The Denial of Personal Disadvantage among You, Me, and All the Other Ostriches," in Mary Crawford and Margaret Gentry, eds. *Gender and Thought: Psychological Perspectives* (New York: Springer Verlag, 1989), 79.

15. Ibid., 80, 94. See also Rhoda Unger and Mary Crawford, eds., *Women and Gender: A Feminist Psychology* (New York: McGraw-Hill, 1992), 182–184.

16. For the division of work, see Juliet B. Schor, *The Overworked American* (New York: Basic Books, 1991); Scott J. South and Glenna Spitze, "Housework in Marital and Nonmarital Households," *American Sociological Review* 59 (1994): 337; and Colleen O'Connor, "Women, If You Think You Have No Time to Relax, You're Probably Right," *San Jose Mercury News,* 8 August 1994, E1. For husbands' perceptions, see Michalene Busico and Lori Eickmann, "Families Searching for Fair Workloads," *San Jose Mercury News,* 24 February 1992, A8. See also the sources cited in note 17 below and in Chapter 6.

17. For men's attitudes and their wives' responses, see Arlie Hochschild with Ann Machung, *The Second Shift* (New York: Viking, 1989), 43, 259; and Lillian B. Rubin, *Families on the Fault Line* (New York: Harper Collins, 1994), 86–89. According to demographer Martha Farnsworthe Riche, "The great lesson of the past 15 to 20 years is that men don't care if the house is clean and neat, by and large"; quoted in Barbara Vobejda, "Children Help Less at Home, Dads Do More," *Washington Post,* 24 November 1991, A1. For further discussion of men's avoidance strategies, see Vobejda, "Children Help Less," A1; Linda C. Thompson, "Family Work: Women's Sense of Fairness," *Family Issues* 12 (1991): 181, 186.

18. For research on men's tasks and attitudes, see Janet Saltzman Chafetz, *Gender Equity: An Integrated Theory of Stability and Change* (Beverly Hills: Sage, 1990), 50; Rubin, *Families,* 86, 88; and Hochschild with Machung, *The Second Shift,* 90. For women's responsibilities, see Thompson, "Family Work," 190–191; O'Connor, "Women," 6E; Patricia Schroeder, Public lecture, Stanford University, 2 April 1992.

19. For responsibilities concerning sick children, see William T. Gormley, Jr., *Everybody's Children: Child Care as a Public Problem* (Washington, D.C.: Brookings Institute, 1995), 19, n. 12. For responsibilities following divorce, see Frank Furstenberg, Jr., "History and Current Status of Divorce in the United States," *The Future of Children* 4 (1994): 29, 37; Ross Thompson, "The Role of the Father after Divorce," *The Future of Children* 4 (1994): 210, 223.

20. For tendencies toward same-sex comparison, see Faye Crosby, *Relative Deprivation and Working Women* (New York: Oxford University Press, 1982), 94; Rubin, *Families,* 89; Jerry Suls, "Comparison Processes in Relative Deprivation: A Life-Span Analysis," in *Relative Deprivation and Social Comparison: The Ontario Symposium,* vol. 4, ed. James Olson, C. Herman, and Mark Zanna (Hillsdale, N.J.: Erlbaum, 1986), 95, 97. For men's comparisons concerning family tasks, see Hochschild and Machung, *The Second Shift,* 51; Thompson, "Family Work," 196.

21. For women's assessments of family burdens, see Alison Cowan, "Poll Finds Women's Gains Have Taken Personal Toll," *New York Times,* 21 August 1989, A1, A4; Judith Lorber, *Paradoxes of Gender* (New Haven: Yale University Press, 1991), 190; Anna Quindlen, "Abhors a Vacuum," *New York Times,* 9 September 1992, A21. For women's misperceptions of burdens, see Thompson, "Family Work," 184; O'Connor, "Women," A1; Lorber, *Paradoxes of Gender,* 189.

22. For women's perceptions of fairness, see Roper Starch Worldwide, Inc., *1995 Virginia Slims Opinion Poll* (Storrs, Conn.: Roper Center for Public Opinion Research), 80–81 (56 percent of employed women and 49 percent of nonemployed women resent how little their partner does around the house, and two-thirds of women feel that men are not doing their fair share of family labor); Carol Tavris, *The Mismeasure of Woman* (New York: Simon and Schuster, 1992), 33. For expectations of inequality and behaviors provoking conflict, see Thompson, "Family Work," 185–186; Kathleen Gerson, "Men's Influence on Women's Work and Family Choices," in Michael Kimmel, ed., *Changing Men* (Newbury Park, Calif.: Sage, 1987), 115, 120–122; See also Henry, *The Deep Divide,* 95.

23. For women's reluctance to view themselves as victims, see Crosby, *Relative Deprivation,* 13–18, 65–67, 94–115; Kristin Bumiller, *The Civil Rights Society: The Social Construction of Victims* (Baltimore: Johns Hopkins University Press, 1988), 81–95; Sigel, *Ambition and Accommodation,* 83–94; Jackson, "Relative Deprivation and the Gender Wage Gap," *Journal of Social Issues* 4 (1989): 117, 119–120; and Rita J. Simon and Jean M. Landis, "The Polls—A Report: Women's and Men's Attitudes about a Woman's Place and Role," *Public Opinion Quarterly* 53 (1989): 265. For claims that feminism encourages women to exaggerate their victimization, see Katie Roiphe, *The Morning After: Sex, Fear, and Feminism on Campus* (Boston: Little, Brown, 1993); Naomi Wolf, *Fire with Fire* (New York: Random House, 1993); and sources discussed in Chapters 5 and 8.

24. For discussion of the appeal of victim status, see Martha Minow, "Surviving Victim Talk," *University of California Law Review* 40 (1993): 1411. For women's desire to avoid victim status, see Bumiller, *The Civil Rights Society;* Crosby, *Relative Deprivation;* Crosby, Pufall, Snyder, O'Connell, and Whalen, "The Denial of Personal Disadvantage"; Hillary Clinton, quoted in Wolf, *Fire with Fire,* 304.

25. Isaac M. Lypkus, "A Heuristic Model to Explain Perceptions of Unjust Events," *Social Justice Research* 5 (1992): 359, 361–362. Melvin Lerner, *The Belief in a Just World: A Fundamental Delusion* (New York: Plenum, 1980), vii–viii.

26. President Bill Clinton, Proclamation 6883, National Pay Inequity Awareness Day, 1996, published in *Weekly Compilation of Presidential Documents* 32 (April 11, 1996): 651; Jocelyn C. Frye, "Affirmative Action: Understanding the Past and Present," in Cynthia Costello and Barbara Kivimae Krimgold, eds., *The American Woman, 1996–1997* (New York: Norton, 1996): 33, 38.

27. See "Women's Choices, Not Bias, Blamed for Lower Earnings," *Los Angeles Times,* 15 December 1995, A43; and sources cited in Chapter 6.

28. For the wage gap, see Chapter 6. For gender bias and the devaluation of female labor, see Crosby, *Relative Deprivation,* 3–5; Bumiller, *The Civil Rights Society,* 26–30; and note 29 below.

29. For summaries of research on undervaluation, see Barbara Reskin, "Bringing the Men Back In: Sex Differentiation and the Devaluation of Women's Work," *Gender and Society* 2 (1988): 58; Michele A. Wittig and Rosemary H. Lowe, "Comparable Worth Theory and Practice," *Journal of Social Issues* 45 (1989): 233; Brenda Major, "Gender Differences in Comparisons and Entitlement: Implications for Comparable Worth," *Journal of Social Issues* 45 (1989): 99–106. For studies finding lower ratings for female work and résumés, see Michele Paludi and Lisa Strayer, "What's in an Author's Name? Differential Evaluations of Performance as a Function of Author's Name," *Sex Roles* 12 (1985): 353; Richard F. Martell, "Sex Bias at Work: The Effects of Attentional and Memory Demands on Performance Ratings of Men and Women," *Journal of Applied Social Psychology* 21 (1991): 1939. For women's sense of fair pay scales, see Linda A. Jackson and Severin V. Grabski, "Perceptions of Fair Pay and the Gender Wage Gap," *Journal of Applied Social Psychology* 18 (1986): 606; Alice Eagly, *Sex Differences in Social Behavior: A Social-Role Interpretation* (Hillsdale, N.J.: Erlbaum, 1987), 111; Major, "Gender Differences," 105. For examples of biased salary structures, see sources cited in Deborah L. Rhode, *Justice and Gender* (Cambridge, Mass.: Harvard University Press, 1989), 193, 199; and the discussion in Chapter 6.

30. For statistics on rape, see National Victim Center and the Crime Victim Research and Treatment Center, *Rape in America: Report to the Nation* (Arlington, Va.: National Victim Center, 1992); Patricia A. Harney and Charlene Muehlenhard, "Rape," in *Sexual Coercion: A Sourcebook on Its Nature, Causes, and Prevention,* ed. Elizabeth Grauerholz and Mary A. Koralewski (Lexington, Mass.: Lexington Books, 1991), 3; Mary P. Koss and Mary R. Harvey, *The Rape Victim: Clinical and Community Interventions,* 2nd ed. (Newbury Park, Calif.: Sage, 1991), 27–29, 262–263; and Chapter 5, below. For statistics on domestic violence, see Committee on the Judiciary, United States Senate Majority Staff Report, *Violence against Women: A Week in the Life of America,* 102nd Congress, 2nd Session, October 1992; also sources cited

in "Developments: Legal Responses to Domestic Violence," *Harvard Law Review* 106 (1993): 1498, 1501; Antonio C. Novello, "From the Surgeon General: A Medical Response to Violence," *Journal of the American Medical Association* 267 (1992): 3132; and Chapter 5.

31. For critiques of feminists, see Roiphe, *The Morning After;* Warren Farrell, *The Myth of Male Power* (New York: Simon and Schuster, 1993), 329; Rene Denfeld, *The New Victorians: A Young Woman's Challenge to the Old Feminist Order* (New York: Warner, 1995), 61, 63. For perceptions of acquaintance rape, see Robin Warsaw, *I Never Called It Rape: The "Ms." Report on Recognizing, Fighting, and Surviving Date and Acquaintance Rape* (New York: Harper and Row, 1988); Koss and Harvey, *The Rape Victim.*

32. Lisa Maria Hogeland, "A Fear of Feminism," *Ms.* (November–December 1994): 18; Crosby, Pufall, Snyder, O'Connell, and Whalen, "The Denial of Personal Disadvantage," 82; Minow, "Surviving Victim Talk."

33. For exaggerations of victims' responsibility, see Melvin J. Lerner, *The Belief in a Just World* (New York: Plenum, 1980), 21, 109–110, 123; Robert Garcia, "Rape, Lies, and Videotape," *Loyola Law Review* 25 (1992): 711. For a landmark study, see Apsler and Friedman, "Chance Outcomes and the Just World: A Comparison of Observers and Recipients," *Journal of Personality and Social Psychology* 31 (1975): 887. For judicial and juror attitudes, see *Report of the Florida Supreme Court Gender Bias Study Commission,* March 1990, 140–141 (reporting widespread belief that sexual-molestation victims precipitate abuse); and sources cited in Chapter 5. For blame of children, see Lynn Hecht Schafran, "Documenting Gender Bias in the Courts: The Task Force Approach," *Judicature* 70 (1987): 280, 289 n. 17.

34. Jill Smolowe, "Sex with a Scorecard," *Time,* 5 April 1993, 41; Emily Yoffe, "Girls Who Go Too Far," *Newsweek,* 22 July 1991, 58.

35. Majority Staff Report, Committee on the Judiciary, U.S. Senate, 103rd Congress, 1st Session, *The Response to Rape: Detours on the Road to Equal Justice* (Washington, D.C.: Government Printing Office, 1993), 8, 12.

36. The judge is quoted in "Report of the New York Task Force on Women and the Courts," *Fordham Urban Law Journal* 15 (1986–1987): 32. For similar views, see Naomi R. Cahn and Liz Herman, "Prosecuting Woman Abuse," in Michael Steinman, ed., *Woman Battering: Policy Responses* (Highland Heights, Ky.: Academy of Criminal Justice Sciences, 1991), 95–96; Martha Mahoney, "Legal Images of Battered Women: Redefining the Issue of Separation," *Michigan Law Review* 90 (1991); and sources cited in Chapter 5. For statistics on assaults and homicide, see Mahoney, "Legal Images," 64–65; and Tamar Lewin, "The Terror of a Stalker's Threat," *New York Times,* 8 February 1993, A1.

37. For protection orders, see Peter Finn, "Civil Protection Orders: A Flawed Opportunity for Intervention," in *Woman Battering,* 80, 155–159; Ruthann Robson, "Lavender Bruises, Intra-Lesbian Violence, Law, and Lesbian Theory," *Golden Gate Law Review* 20 (1990): 567, 576–581. For other assistance,

see Margi Laird McCue, *Domestic Violence: A Reference Handbook* (Santa Barbara, Calif.: ABC-CLIO, 1995), 119; "Developments," 1510; Robson, "Lavender Bruises," 576–581; and Chapter 5.

38. O. J. Simpson, quoted in Barbara Vobejda, "Allegations Focus National Attention on Society's Response to Spouse Abuse," *Washington Post*, 19 June 1991, A18.

39. For the infrequency of serious sanctions, see sources cited in Chapter 5 and in "Developments," 1585–1586; Lisa Lerman, "Mediation of Wife Abuse Cases: The Adverse Impact of Informal Dispute Resolution on Women," *Harvard Women's Law Journal* 7 (1990): 57. For the costs of violence, see NOW Legal Defense Fund, *Stop Violence against Women: Strategies for Ending Violence against Women* (New York: NOW Legal Defense Fund, 1994); Novello, "Surgeon General." For the Massachusetts case, see Ellen Goodman, "Equal Rights Award," *Boston Globe*, 25 August 1982, A11.

40. Phyllis Schneider, "The Managerial Mother," *Working Woman*, December 1987, 117; Kevin Leman, *The Pleasers: Women Who Can't Say No and the Men Who Control Them* (New York: Dell, 1987); Ellen Fein and Sherrie Schneider, *The Rules: Time-Tested Secrets for Capturing the Heart of Mr. Right* (New York: Warner, 1996). For Americans' general tendency to see individual, not structural, causes of inequality, see James R. Kluegel and Eliot R. Smith, *Beliefs about Inequality* (New York: Aldine de Gruyter, 1986), 223–225.

41. For discussion of "exit visas," see Suzanne Gordon, *Prisoners of Men's Dreams: Striking Out for a New Feminine Future* (Boston: Little, Brown, 1991), 283.

42. Ruth Sidel, *On Her Own: Growing Up in the Shadow of the American Dream* (New York: Penguin, 1990).

43. Gordon, *Prisoners of Men's Dreams*, 108–111; Henry, *The Deep Divide*, 108; Sigel, *Ambition and Accommodation*, 53, 83–95.

44. For qualities associated with femininity, see Chapter 2. For the value placed on femininity, see Henry, *The Deep Divide*, 39, 55.

45. For research on the relative importance of appearance for males and females, see Gloria Steinem, *The Revolution from Within* (Boston: Little, Brown, 1992), 299; Jane E. Smith, V. Ann Waldorf, and David L. Trembath, "Single White Male Looking for Thin, Very Attractive . . .," *Sex Roles* 23 (1990): 675. For women's concerns and purchases, see Steinem, *Revolution from Within*, 299; and Naomi Wolf, *The Beauty Myth* (New York: William Morrow, 1991), 17.

46. Maureen Dowd, "Hillary Rodham Clinton Strikes a New Pose and Multiplies Her Images," *New York Times*, 12 December 1993, E3. See also the discussion of media coverage of Clinton in Chapter 4.

47. For discussion of exemptions in the Family and Medical Leave Act of 1993, 3 U.S.C. § 2601, 2631, 2651, see Commission on Family and Medical Leave, *A Workable Balance: Report to Congress on Family and Medical Leave Policies* (Washington, D.C.: Women's Bureau, U.S. Department of Labor, 1996), 61–65. For recommendations of child development experts, see "Recommendations of Yale-Bush Child Center, Advisory Committee on Infants," in *The*

Parental Leave Crisis: Toward a National Policy, ed. Edward F. Zigler and Meryl Frank (New Haven: Yale University Press, 1988), 343–346. For the inadequacies in childcare and work/family policies, see Gormley, *Everybody's Children* (1990): 431; Rhode, *Justice and Gender,* 172–173; and Chapter 6.

48. Commission on Family and Medical Leave, *A Workable Balance,* 11, 144–245; Rosalind Barnett and Caryl Rivers, *He Works / She Works* (New York: Harper Collins, 1996).

49. Hochschild with Machung, *Second Shift,* 113.

50. For the "undue burden" standard, see *Planned Parenthood of Southeastern Pennsylvania v. Casey,* 112 S. Ct., 2791, 2820–2821 (1992). For restrictions, see *Webster v. Reproductive Health Services,* 492 U.S. 490, 511, 520 (1989); *Harris v. McRae,* 448 U.S. 297, 326 (1980); Charlotte Rutherford, "Reproductive Freedom and Afro-American Women," *Yale Journal of Law and Feminism* 4 (1992): 255. For other barriers, harassment, and terrorism, see Chapter 7, below. For the lack of providers, see Gina Kolata, "RU 486: It Isn't Just Popping a Pill," *New York Times,* 28 July 1996, E14; Center for Reproductive Law and Policy, *Ensuring Reproductive Freedom* (New York: Center for Reproductive Law and Policy, 1993); and Chapter 7.

51. Catharine MacKinnon, "*Roe v. Wade:* A Study in Male Ideology," in *Abortion: Moral and Legal Perspectives,* ed. Jay L. Garfield and Patricia Hennessey (Amherst: University of Massachusetts Press, 1984), 43, 52.

52. Dave Barry, *Complete Guide to Guys* (New York: Random House, 1995), 36; and Chapter 2, below.

53. Angela Lau, "More Women Are Pilots, but They're Still in Minority," *San Diego Union Tribune,* 14 February 1994, B1; Avid Firestone, "While Barbie Talks Tough, G.I. Joe Goes Shopping," *New York Times,* 31 December 1993, A12.

54. For men and beds, see L. M. Boyd, "Grab Bag," *San Francisco Chronicle,* 8 March 1986. For parents and children, see Chapter 3, below.

55. William Allen White, quoted in Anna Quindlen, *Thinking Out Loud: On the Personal, the Political, the Public and the Private* (New York: Random House, 1993), epigraph.

2. The Ideology and Biology of Gender Difference

1. Margaret Mead, *Male and Female: A Study of the Sexes in a Changing World* (New York: William Morrow, 1949), 159–160; Sherry B. Ortner, *Making Gender* (Boston: Beacon, 1996), 23.

2. Aristotle, *Ethica Nicomochea, Books 8–9,* trans. Geoffrey Percival (Cambridge: Cambridge University Press, 1940), book 9, ch. 1; Susan A. Basow, *Gender Stereotypes and Roles,* 3rd ed. (Pacific Grove, Calif.: Brooks/Cole, 1992), 4–7. Matt Ridley, *The Red Queen: Sex and the Evolution of Human Nature* (New York: Macmillan, 1993), 259 and n. 21; Gallup Organization, *Gender and Society: Status and Stereotypes—An International Gallup Poll Report* (Prince-

ton, N.J.: Gallup Organization, 1996); Jonathan Burton, "What Makes Us Different," *Scholastic*, 19 March 1993, 20.

3. The quote is from Ann Moir and David Jessel, *Brain Sex* (New York: Delta, 1991), 10. See also Robert Wright, "Feminists Meet Mr. Darwin," *The New Republic*, 28 November 1994, 34. For survey data, see Roper Starch Worldwide, 1985 *Virginia Slims American Women's Opinion Poll: Female Sample* (Storrs, Conn.: Roper Center for Public Research, 1985), 27, 37–38. The documentary aired on ABC, *Prime Time Live* with John Stossell, "Men, Women and the Sex Difference," 2 February 1994.

4. Edward Clarke, *Sex in Education; or, A Fair Chance for the Girls* (Boston: J. R. Osgood, 1873), 104, 137; Carroll Smith-Rosenberg, *Disorderly Conduct: Visions of Gender in Victorian America* (New York: Knopf, 1985), 258–260.

5. Gail Vines, *Raging Hormones* (Berkeley: University of California Press, 1993), 104; Ellyn Kaschak, *Engendered Lives* (New York: Basic Books, 1992), 38.

6. Richard Dawkins, *The Selfish Gene* (New York: Oxford University Press, 1976), 152; See Edward O. Wilson, *Sociobiology* (Cambridge, Mass.: Harvard University Press, 1980), 156.

7. Wright, "Feminists," 40.

8. Richard Epstein, *Forbidden Grounds: The Case against Employment Discrimination* (Cambridge, Mass.: Harvard University Press, 1992), 272; Michael Levin, *Feminism and Freedom* (New Brunswick, N.J.: Transaction Books, 1987), 3. For survey responses, see Sherrye Henry, *The Deep Divide* (New York: Macmillan, 1994), 141.

9. The quote is from David Buss, *The Evolution of Desire* (New York: Basic Books, 1994), 212. For similar views, see the theorists discussed in Kingsley R. Browne, "Sex and Temperament in Modern Society: A Darwinian View of the Glass Ceiling and the Gender Gap," *Arizona Law Review* 37 (1995): 971, 1008–1009.

10. David Barash, *The Whisperings Within* (New York: Harper and Row, 1979), 114, quoted in Ruth Hubbard, "Social Effects of Some Contemporary Myths about Women," in *Woman's Nature: Rationalizations of Inequality,* ed. Marian Lowe and Ruth Hubbard (New York: Pergamon, 1983), 1, 6.

11. For sociobiologists' views, see, e.g., E. O. Wilson, quoted in Lynda Birke, *Women, Feminism and Biology* (Brighton, England: Harvester, 1986), 30. For critiques, see Richard C. Lewontin, Steven Rose, and Leon Kamin, *Not in Our Genes: Biology, Ideology, and Human Nature* (New York: Pantheon, 1984) 157; Frances Dahlberg, *Woman the Gatherer* (New Haven: Yale University Press, 1981), 2–4; Eleanor Leacock, "Ideologies of Male Dominance as Divide and Rule Politics: An Anthropologist's View," in Lowe and Hubbard, eds., *Woman's Nature*, 11, 115.

12. Natalie Angier, "Sexual Harassment: Why Even Bees Do It," *New York Times,* 10 October 1995, C1. For lemurs and monkeys, see Rhona Mahony, *Kidding Ourselves* (New York: Basic Books, 1995), 171. See also Ruth Bleier, *Science and Gender: A Critique of Biology and Its Theory on Women* (New York:

Pergamon, 1984), 29; Ruth Hubbard, "The Political Nature of 'Human Nature,'" in Deborah L. Rhode, ed., *Theoretical Perspectives on Sexual Difference* (New Haven: Yale University Press, 1990), 67; Sarah Hrdy, *The Woman That Never Evolved* (Cambridge, Mass.: Harvard University Press, 1981), 59–130.

13. For variations in nurturing roles, see Bleier, *Science and Gender,* 144; Marion Howe, "The Dialectic of Biology and Culture," in Lowe and Hubbard, eds., *Woman's Nature,* 42–45. See Marian Lepowsky, *Fruit of the Motherland: Gender in an Egalitarian Society* (New York: Columbia University Press, 1993); Carol MacCormack and Marilyn Strathern, eds., *Nature, Culture, and Gender* (Cambridge: Cambridge University Press, 1980). For American fathers' caretaking abilities, see Diane Ehrensaft, *Parenting Together: Men and Women Sharing the Care of Their Children* (New York: Free Press, 1987), 164; Barbara J. Risman, "Intimate Relationships from a Microstructural Perspective: Men Who Mother," *Gender and Society* 1 (1987): 6. For men's avoidance of disagreeable tasks, see Lynne Segal, *Slow Motion: Changing Masculinities, Changing Men* (New Brunswick, N.J.: Rutgers University Press, 1990), 35–41.

14. Robert Wright, *The Moral Animal* (New York: Pantheon, 1994), 137; Wright, "Feminists," 36–37; Hubbard, "Human Nature," 71.

15. For fallacies concerning brain size, see Lewontin, Rose, and Kanin, *Not in Our Genes,* 157; Stephen Jay Gould, *The Mismeasure of Man* (New York: Norton, 1981), 104–105. For shifting theories of brain hemispheres, see Carol Tavris, "The Mismeasure of Woman," *Feminism and Psychology* 3 (1993): 149, 156. For IQ tests, see C. A. Dwyer, "The Role of Tests and Their Construction in Producing Apparent Sex-Related Differences," in Michele Wittig and Anne Peterson, eds., *Sex-Related Differences in Cognitive Functioning* (New York: Academic Press, 1979), 342.

16. Sally P. Springer and Georg Deutsch, *Left Brain, Right Brain,* rev. ed. (New York: Freeman, 1985); Gina Kolata, "Math Genius May Have Hormonal Basis," *Science* 222 (23 December 1983): 1312; Tavris, "Mismeasure," 157; Ridley, *The Red Queen,* 250.

17. For assertions of female inferiority, see George Gilder, "The Myth of the Role Revolution," in Nicholas Davidson, ed., *Gender Sanity* (Lanham, Md.: University Press of America, 1989), 233; see also Yves Christian, "Sex Differences in the Human Brain," ibid. For males' lack of nurturing capabilities, see Moir and Jessel, *Brain Sex,* 147. For infants' resistance to feminist efforts, see ibid., 65, 128. See also Ridley, *The Red Queen,* 275.

18. For theories of sexual disqualification, see James McKean Cattell, quoted in Anne Fausto-Sterling, *Myths of Gender: Biological Theories about Women and Men,* rev. ed. (New York: Basic Books, 1992), 14. For discrimination against women in education, see Deborah L. Rhode, *Justice and Gender* (Cambridge, Mass.: Harvard University Press, 1989), 288–292; and Barbara Miller Solomon, *In the Company of Educated Women: A History of Women and Higher Education in America* (New Haven: Yale University Press, 1985).

19. For claims to certainty, see Moir and Jessel, *Brain Sex,* 11. For the media's

delight in trivial differences, see Stephen Sherill and Paul Tough, "What Men Can Do," *New York Times*, 3 March 1995, A15. For biases in media coverage, see Janet Shibley Hyde, "Should Psychologists Study Gender Differences? Yes, with Some Guidelines," *Feminism and Psychology* 4 (1994): 507, 508. For examples of skewed reporting, see Beryl Lieff Benderly, *Myth of Two Minds* (New York: Doubleday, 1987), 3; Hyde, "Gender Differences," 507.

20. ABC, "Men, Women, and the Sex Difference."

21. For ambiguities concerning the significance of brain structure, see Gisela Kaplan and Lesley J. Rodgers, "Race and Gender Fallacies: The Paucity of Biological Determinist Explanations of Difference," in Ethel Tobach and Betty Rosoff, eds., *Challenging Racism and Sexism* (New York: Feminist Press, 1994), 66, 84; Ruth Bleier, "Sex Differences as Research, Science or Belief?" in Bleier, *Feminist Approaches to Science* (New York: Pergamon, 1986). For the small size of differences, see Cynthia Epstein, *Deceptive Distinctions: Sex, Gender and the Social Order* (New Haven: Yale University Press, 1988), 185; Kay Deaux and Brenda Major, "A Social-Psychological Model of Gender," in Rhode, ed., *Theoretical Perspectives*, 89; Janet S. Hyde, "How Large Are Cognitive Differences?" *American Psychologist* 36 (1981): 892; Mary Crawford, "Agreeing to Differ: Feminist Epistemologies and Women's Ways of Knowing," in Mary Crawford and Margaret Gentry, eds., *Gender and Thought: Psychological Perspectives* (New York: Springer Verlag, 1989): 128, 132–133. For sweeping claims about difference, see Marvin Harris, *Our Kind* (New York: Harper and Row, 1989), 274; Robert Pool, *Eve's Rib: The Biological Roots of Sex Differences* (New York: Crown, 1994), 248; Doreen Kimura, "Sex Differences in the Brain," *Scientific American* (September 1992): 119, 125.

22. For cross-cultural research, see Benderly, *Myth of Two Minds*, 217. For the decline in math differences, see Feingold, "Cognitive Gender Differences Are Disappearing," *Psychologist* 43 (1988): 95; Janet S. Hyde, Elizabeth Fennema, and S. J. Laman, "Gender Differences in Mathematics Performance: A Meta-Analysis," *Psychological Bulletin* 107 (1990): 139. For failures to eliminate environmental influences, see Jerry E. Bishop, "Boys Outnumber Girls among Leaders in Mental Tests," *Wall Street Journal*, 7 July 1995, B3; Fausto-Sterling, *Myths of Gender*, 55–57; Harris, *Our Kind*, 273; Claude M. Steel, "A Threat in the Air," *American Psychologist* (forthcoming). For the guidance counselor's view, see Caryl Rivers, *Slick Spins and Fractured Facts* (New York: Columbia University Press, 1996), 24–25.

23. Edgar Berman, Letter to the editor, *New York Times*, 26 July 1970, 35 (discussing woman bank president); Lewontin, Kanin, and Rose, *Not in Our Genes*, 133 (discussing woman president).

24. For assertions about menstruation and PMS, see Carol Tavris, *The Mismeasure of Woman* (New York: Simon and Schuster, 1992), 135–136. For example, in studies of gender bias in the legal profession, female practitioners reported that male colleagues attribute assertiveness to premenstrual syndrome. See Deborah

R. Hensler, "Studying Gender Bias in the Courts: Stories and Statistics," *Stanford Law Review* 45 (1993): 2187, 2192.

25. For general assertions about combat as men's work, see Lt. General Clark, quoted in Jill L. Goodman, "Women, War, and Equality: An Examination of Sex Discrimination in the Military," *Women's Rights Law Reporter* 5 (1979): 243, 262–263. See also Adam G. Mersereau, "'Diversity' May Prove Deadly on the Battefield," *Wall Street Journal*, 14 November 1996, A22. James Webb, "Women Can't Fight," in Davidson, ed., *Gender Sanity*, 211. For psychological unfitness, see Levin, *Feminism and Freedom*, 239; Eric Schmitt, "Generals Oppose Combat by Women," *New York Times*, 17 June 1994, A1. For biological drives, see Newt Gingrich, quoted in Lois Romano, with Mary Alma Welch, "Big Strong Men on Campus," *Washington Post*, 18 January 1995, B3.

26. Alan Quist, quoted in Linda Hirshman, "Out of the GOP 'Big Tent,' Back to the Kitchen," *Los Angeles Times*, 12 July 1994, B7. George Gilder, "The Case against Women in Combat," *New York Times Magazine*, 28 January 1979, 44 (discussing "overwhelming" evidence). See also Barash, *Whisperings Within*, 170–171, 189–193.

27. For PMS estimates and links to cultural influences, see Tavris, *Mismeasure of Woman*, 136; and Fausto-Sterling, *Myths of Gender*, 95–99, 101–105, 117–120. For the absence of adverse effects on performance, see Sharon Golub, "A Developmental Perspective," in Leslie H. Gise, ed., *The Premenstrual Syndrome* (New York: Churchill Livingston, 1988), 118–119; Tavris, *Mismeasure of Woman*, 150–151.

28. Vines, *Hormones*, 42; Sharon Lerner, "Are the Treatment Options for PMS Leaving You Bloated, Irritable, and Crampy?" *Ms.* (July–August 1996): 39.

29. For sociobiologists' assertions, see Ben Greenstein, quoted in Vines, *Hormones*, 83; Wright, "Feminists," 40. For behaviors, see Fausto-Sterling, *Myths of Gender*, 125. For cultural variations in rape, see Peggy Reeves Sanday, "Rape and the Silencing of the Feminine," in Sylvana Tomaselli and Ray Porter, eds., *Rape* (London: Basil Blackwell, 1987).

30. For discussion of women's support for war, see Jean Bethke Elshtain, *Women and War* (New York: Basic Books, 1987), 67; Tavris, *Mismeasure of Woman*, 154. For discussion of women's effectiveness in combat and related positions, see sources cited in Rhode, *Justice and Gender*, 100; Janet Sayers, "Science, Sexual Difference, and Feminism," in Beth Hess and Myra Ferree, eds., *Analyzing Gender: A Handbook of Social Science Research* (Beverly Hills: Sage, 1987), 68, 85. For research on testosterone and aggression, see Natalie Angier, "Does Testosterone Equal Aggression? Maybe Not," *New York Times*, 20 June 1995, A1; Fausto-Sterling, *Myths of Gender*, 126–127; Charlotte M. Otter, "Genetic Effects on Development of the Sex Ratio," in Roberta Hall, ed., *Male-Female Differences: A Biocultural Perspective* (New York: Praeger, 1985): 155, 209.

31. Diane F. Halpern, "Stereotypes, Science, Censorship, and the Study of Sex Differences," *Feminism and Psychology* 4 (1994): 525.

32. For gender, aggression, and cultural influences, see Basow, *Gender Stereotypes and Roles*, 67–69. For hormonal-abnormality research, see Vines, *Hormones*, 98–99; Harris, *Our Kind*, 268.

33. Barbara Ehrenreich, quoted in Fausto-Sterling, *Myths of Gender*, 259. See Chapters 3 and 5, below.

34. Webber Borchers, quoted in Mike Royko, "Borchers Hip to Girl Power," *Chicago Daily News*, 26 March 1973, A12 (hip structure); Barbara Bush, quoted in Elaine Sciolino, "Battle Lines Are Shifting on Women in War," *New York Times*, 25 January 1990, A1, A15; Gingrich, quoted in Romano, "Big Strong Men," B3; Richard Posner, *Overcoming Law* (Cambridge, Mass.: Harvard University Press, 1995), 355.

35. Craig Hymowitz, "The Title IX Sledgehammer: Where Idea of Gender Equity in College Sports Has Led," *San Diego Union Tribune*, 24 September 1995, 63; Levin, *Feminism and Freedom*, 217.

36. For professional women, see *In re Goodell*, 39 Wisc. 232, 244–245 (1875); Cynthia Epstein, *Women's Place: Options and Limits in Professional Careers* (Berkeley: University Of California Press, 1971), 22; Deborah L. Rhode, "Perspectives on Professional Women," *Stanford Law Review* 40 (1988): 1163, 1166, 1167. For protective labor legislation, see Judith Baer, *The Chains of Protection: The Judicial Response to Women's Labor Legislation* (Westport, Conn.: Greenwood, 1978), 31–32; Rhode, *Justice and Gender*, 42, 43.

37. ABC, "Men, Women and the Sex Difference."

38. Rhode, *Justice and Gender*, 95; Christine Littleton, "Reconstructing Sexual Equality," *California Law Review* 75 (1987): 1279.

39. For cross-cultural variations, see Marion Lowe, "The Dialectic of Biology and Culture," in Lowe and Hubbard, eds., *Woman's Nature*, 42, 45. For declining differences among Americans, see Lewontin, Rose, and Kanin, *Not in Our Genes*, 138; Natalie Angier, "Two Experts Say Women Who Run May Overtake Men," *New York Times*, 7 January 1992, C3.

40. Roberta Hall, "The Question of Size," in *Male-Female Differences*, 127, 149; Hubbard, "The Political Nature of Human Nature," in Rhode, ed., *Theoretical Perspectives*, 69.

41. Ridley, *The Red Queen*, 287–288. See Chapters 3 and 4, below.

42. John Dewey, quoted in Rachel T. Hare Mustin and Jeanne Marecek, "Beyond Difference," in Mustin and Marecek, eds., *Making a Difference: Psychology and the Construction of Gender* (New Haven: Yale University Press, 1990), 184.

43. Katha Pollitt, "Are Women Morally Superior to Men?" *The Nation*, 28 November 1992, 799.

44. For language patterns, see Deborah Tannen, *You Just Don't Understand: Women and Men in Conversation* (New York: William Morrow, 1990); Deborah Tannen, *Talking from Nine to Five: How Women's and Men's Conversational*

Styles Affect Who Gets Heard, Who Gets Credit, and What Gets Done at Work (New York: William Morrow, 1994); John Gray, *Men Are from Mars, Women Are from Venus* (New York: Harper Collins, 1993). For psychological differences, see Sara Ruddick, "Maternal Thinking," *Feminist Studies* 6 (1980): 342; Carol Gilligan, *In a Different Voice* (Cambridge, Mass.: Harvard University Press, 1982); Joan Tronto, *Moral Boundaries: A Political Argument for an Ethic of Care* (New York: Routledge, 1993).

45. Nancy Chodorow, *The Reproduction of Mothering: Psychoanalytic Feminism and the Sociology of Gender* (Berkeley: University of California Press, 1978); Ruddick, "Maternal Thinking," 342 (mothering); "Feminist Discourse, Moral Values and the Law: A Conversation," *Buffalo Law Review* 4 (1985): 11, comments of Catharine MacKinnon (subordination).

46. Tannen, *You Just Don't Understand;* Tannen, *Talking from Nine to Five;* Gilligan, *In a Different Voice;* Mary Jeanne Larrabee, ed., *An Ethic of Care: Feminist and Interdisciplinary Perspectives* (New York: Routledge, 1993); Tronto, *Moral Boundaries.*

47. For managers, see Jean Lipman-Blumen, "Connective Leadership: Female Leadership Styles in the 21st-Century Workplace," *Social Perspectives* 35 (1992): 183, 200–201; Judith B. Roesner, "Ways Women Lead," *Harvard Business Review* (November–December 1990): 120. For lawyers, see Mona Harrington, *Women Lawyers: Rewriting the Rules* (New York: Knopf, 1994), 251; Rand Jack and Dana Crowley Jack, *Moral Vision and Professional Decisions: The Changing Values of Women and Men Lawyers* (New York: Cambridge University Press, 1989), 56–58; Deborah L. Rhode, "Gender and Professional Roles," *Fordham Law Review* 63 (1994); 40, 43. For medicine, see John M. Smith, *Women and Doctors* (New York: Atlantic Monthly Press, 1992), 146–148; Natalie Angier, "Bedside Manners Improve as More Women Enter Medicine," *New York Times,* 21 June 1992, section 4, 18. For political movements, see Alison Jaggar, ed., *Living with Contradictions: Controversies in Feminist Social Ethics* (Boulder, Colo.: Westview, 1994), 52–69.

48. For Tannen's theories, see *You Just Don't Understand,* 61–66.

49. Henry, *The Deep Divide,* 43.

50. For moral-reasoning research, see Cynthia Fuchs Epstein, *Deceptive Distinctions: Sex, Gender, and the Social Order* (New Haven: Yale University Press, 1988), 185; Catherine G. Greeno and Eleanor E. Maccoby, "How Different Is the 'Different Voice'?" *Signs* 11 (1986): 310, 312–316. For the role of power, see Rhoda Unger and Mary Crawford, *Women and Gender* (New York: McGraw-Hill, 1992), 159; Suzette Haden Elgin, *Genderspeak: Men, Women, and the Gentle Art of Verbal Self Defense* (New York: Wiley, 1993), 280; Mary Crawford, *Talking Difference: On Gender and Language* (Thousand Oaks, Calif.: Sage, 1995).

51. For altruism, see Alfie Kohn, *The Brighter Side of Human Nature: Altruism and Empathy in Everyday Life* (New York: Basic Books, 1990), 81–82, 124; Tavris, *Mismeasure of Woman,* 63–67; Alice H. Eagly, *Sex Differences in Social*

Behavior (Hillsdale, N.J.: Erlbaum, 1987), 65. For moral behavior, see Epstein, *Deceptive Distinctions*, 76–77; Greeno and Maccoby, "Different Voice," 315. For politics, see Keith T. Poole and L. Harmon Zeigler, *Women, Public Opinion and Politics* (New York: Longman, 1985), 4–7, 68–69; Janet S. Chafetz, *Gender Equity* (Newbury Park, Calif.: Sage, 1990), 170–171. See also Chapter 9, below.

52. For managerial styles, see Epstein, *Deceptive Distinctions*, 173–184; Barbara Forisha, "The Inside and the Outsider: Women in Organizations," in Barbara L. Forisha and Barbara H. Goldman, eds., *Outsiders on the Inside: Women and Organizations* (Englewood Cliffs, N.J.: Prentice-Hall, 1981), 9, 23; Rosabeth Moss Kanter, "The Impact of Hierarchical Structures on the Work Behavior of Women and Men," in Rachel Kahn-Hut, Arlene K. Daniels, and Richard Colvard, eds., *Women and Work: Problems and Perspectives* (New York: Oxford University Press, 1982). For the small size of psychological differences, see Linda D. Molm and Hark Hedley, "Gender, Power and Social Exchange," in Cecilia Ridgeway, ed., *Gender Interaction and Inequality* (New York: Springer Verlag, 1992), 1, 6; Kay Deaux, "From Individual Differences to Social Categories: Analysis of a Decade's Research on Gender," *American Psychologist* 39 (1984): 105, 110–111; Janet Shibley Hyde, "Meta-Analysis and the Psychology of Gender Differences," *Signs* 55 (1990): 64, 65–68. For Gray's view, see *Men Are from Mars,* 5, 16, 18.

53. The rhetorical question is from Pollitt, "Are Women Morally Superior?" 799. For suffragist claims, see Susan B. Anthony and Ida Husted Harper, eds., *History of Woman Suffrage,* vol. 4 (Indianapolis: Hollenback, 1902), 39, 308–309.

54. Elgin, *Genderspeak,* 280.

55. Gray, *Men Are from Mars,* 148.

56. "Excerpts from Pope John Paul II's Apostolic Letter," *New York Times,* 1 October 1988, A6.

57. Gilligan herself protested this appropriation of her work. For discussion, see Katherine J. Franke, "The Central Mistake of Sex Discrimination Law: The Disaggregation of Sex from Gender," *University of Pennsylvania Law Review* 144 (1995): 1, 84–85. For women's different priorities, see George Gilder, "The Myth of the Role Revolution," in Davidson, ed., *Gender Sanity,* 231. For separate career tracks for women, see Felice Schwartz, "Management, Women, and the Facts of Life," *Harvard Business Review* (January–February 1989): 65; for critical views, see Rhode, *Justice and Gender,* 122; "So Where's the Daddy Track?" *New York Times,* 25 August 1988, A14.

58. Pollitt, "Are Women Morally Superior?" 304.

59. Elizabeth Spellman, *Inessential Women: Problems and Exclusion in Feminist Thought* (Boston: Beacon, 1988), 114, 117.

60. Molm and Hedley, "Gender"; Deaux and Major, "A Social-Psychological Model of Gender," in Rhode, ed., *Theoretical Perspectives,* 89; Crawford, "Agreeing to Differ," 140.

3. Beginning at Birth

1. Quoted in Rhona Mahony, *Kidding Ourselves* (New York: Basic Books, 1995), 177.

2. Ann Moir and David Jessel, *Brain Sex* (New York: Delta, 1991), 66.

3. Susan A. Basow, *Gender Stereotypes and Roles*, 3rd ed. (Pacific Grove, Calif.: Brooks/Cole, 1992), 130–135; Rhoda Unger and Mary Crawford, *Women and Gender* (New York: McGraw-Hill, 1992), 237.

4. For conservatives' views, see Christina Hoff Sommers, "The Myth of School-girls' Lower Self-Esteem," *Wall Street Journal*, 3 October 1994; Suzanne Fields, "Of Feminist Pigs, Pork and the Gender Equity Act," *Washington Times*, 29 September 1994, A19; John Leo, "When 'Subtle Sexism' Is a Con," *U.S. News and World Report*, 7 February 1994, 23.

5. Myra Sadker and David Sadker, *Failing at Fairness: How America's Schools Cheat Girls* (New York: Scribner's, 1994), 84. See also "Teenagers and Sex Roles," *New York Times*, 11 July 1994, B10.

6. Sandra Bem, *The Lenses of Gender: Transforming the Debate on Gender Inequality* (New Haven: Yale University Press, 1993), 149.

7. Unger and Crawford, *Women and Gender*, 245; Marsha Weinraub and Lynda Brown, "The Development of Sex-Role Stereotypes in Children: Crushing Realities," in Violet Franks and Esther Rothblum, eds., *The Stereotyping of Women: Its Effects on Mental Health* (New York: Springer Verlag, 1983), 30.

8. Eleanor Maccoby, "Gender and Relationships," *American Psychologist* 45 (1990): 513; Barrie Thorne, *Gender Play: Girls and Boys in School* (New Brunswick, N.J: Rutgers University Press, 1993).

9. For physiological differences, see sources cited in Chapter 2; also Myriam Miedzian, *Boys Will Be Boys: Breaking the Link between Masculinity and Violence* (New York: Doubleday, 1991), 44–46, 73. For psychoanalytic theories, see Nancy Chodorow, *The Reproduction of Mothering* (Berkeley: University of California Press, 1978); Dorothy Dinnerstein, *The Mermaid and the Minotaur* (New York: Harper and Row, 1976).

10. For the "get ahead" messages, see Bruce Bower, "Gender Paths Wind toward Self-Esteem," *Science News* 143 (1993): 308.

11. Hugh Lytton and David M. Romney, "Parents' Differential Socialization of Boys and Girls: A Meta-Analysis," *Psychological Bulletin* 109 (1991): 267.

12. For parental influences, see sources cited in Mahony, *Kidding Ourselves*, 153; Basow, *Gender Stereotypes*, 131–132; and Ellyn Kaschak, *Engendered Lives* (New York: Basic Books, 1992), 45. For diets, see Michelle Stacey, "Let Them Eat Cake," *New York Times Magazine*, 17 December 1995, 50, 51–52.

13. For parents' stereotypical interpretations, see Unger and Crawford, *Women and Gender*, 231–241, 259–260; Judy Mann, *The Difference: Growing Up Female in America* (New York: Warner, 1994), 21–23, 75–76, 98–100; Miedzian, *Boys Will Be Boys*, 62. For views on toys, see Unger and Crawford, *Women and Gender*, 237–241; Mann, *The Difference*, 22; Basow, *Gender Stereotypes*, 131.

For fathers' pressures, see Unger and Crawford, *Women and Gender,* 230, 255; Mann, *The Difference,* 22. For tomboys and sissies, see Donald R. McCreary, "The Male Role and Avoiding Femininity," *Sex Roles* 31 (1994): 517.

14. For cross-racial patterns, see Basow, *Gender Stereotypes,* 132. For dolls and personal appearance, see Susan Baxter, "The Last Word on Gender Difference," *Psychology Today* (March–April 1994): 53; M. G. Lord, *Forever Barbie* (New York: Avon, 1994), 284.

15. Marylou Tousignant, "'Superwoman' Losing Hero Status," *Washington Post,* 3 January 1995, B1.

16. Mary Daly and Margo Wilson, *Sex, Evolution and Behavior* (Boston: Willard Grant, 1993), 273.

17. For parents' math and science support, see Mann, *The Difference,* 270–271.

18. Joseph Pereira, "In Toyland You Get More If You're Male," *Wall Street Journal,* 23 September 1994, B10; Megan Rosenfeld, "Games Girls Play: A Toy Chest Full of Stereotypes," *Washington Post,* 22 December 1995, A1.

19. Mark Morris quoted in Rosenfeld, "Toy Chest," A1.

20. Cathy Guiswite, "Cathy: Enlightened, Educational, Contemporary Toys," in Roz Warren, ed., *Women's Glibber* (Freedom, Calif.: Crossing Press, 1992), 181.

21. For boys' toys, see Miedzian, *Boys Will Be Boys,* 260–279; Nancy Carlsson Paige and Diane Levin, *Who's Calling the Shots? How to Respond Effectively to Children's Fascination with War Play and War Toys* (Philadelphia: New Society, 1990). For girls' toys, see Rosemary L. Bray, "Toys Aren't Us," *Redbook,* December 1994, 31.

22. Rita Rudner, "Home Box Office Special," 24 June 1995; Lord, *Forever Barbie,* 177.

23. John Leo, *Two Steps Ahead of the Thought Police* (New York: Simon and Schuster, 1994), 156–158. Nicole Hollander's "Sylvia" cartoon is reprinted in Lord, *Forever Barbie,* 278.

24. For Barbie's unhealthy proportions, see Mann, *The Difference,* 184; Anna Quindlen, "Barbie at Thirty-Five," *New York Times,* 10 September 1994, A9. For toy manufacturers' explanations, see Lord, *Forever Barbie,* 12. For Dave Barry's parody, see "Barbie Sparks a Scientific Investigation," *San Jose Mercury News: West Magazine,* 17 July 1994, 19.

25. For surveys, see Susan Bordo, *Unbearable Weight: Feminism, Western Culture and the Body* (Berkeley: University of California Press, 1993), 56. For a discussion of Barbie's role, see Lord, *Forever Barbie,* 235–239.

26. Leo, *Two Steps Ahead of the Thought Police,* 156–158; "Barbie (and Ken) Raised My Consciousness," Letter to the editor, *New York Times,* 16 September 1994, A30.

27. See generally Bordo, *Unbearable Weight;* Brett Silverstein and Deborah Perlior, *The Cost of Competence: Why Inequality Causes Depression, Eating Disorders and Illness in Women* (New York: Oxford University Press, 1995).

28. Women on Words and Images Society, *Dick and Jane as Victims: Sex Stereotyp-*

ing in Children's Readers (Princeton, N.J.: Women on Words and Images, 1975); Carole M. Kortenhaus and Jack Demarest, "Gender Role Stereotyping in Children's Literature: An Update," *Sex Roles* 28 (1993): 219. For *I Can* and *Me Too,* see Janus Adams, "Children's Books: Buyer Beware," *Ms.,* September–October 1994, 72. For employed mothers, see Kortenhaus and Demarest, "Gender Role Stereotyping," 230–231.

29. For the boys' market, see Norma Pecora, "Superman/Superboys/Supermen," in Steve Craig, ed., *Men, Masculinity and the Media* (Newbury Park, Calif.: Sage, 1992), 61. The examples of teen romances, published in 1990 and 1993, are part of Ann Martin's series, *The Babysitter's Club.* For other examples and publisher guidelines, see Elizabeth Debold, Marie Wilson, and Idelisses Malave, *Mother-Daughter Revolution: From Betrayal to Power* (Reading, Mass.: Addison-Wesley, 1993), 42, 69–70. For feminist critiques, see Harriet Fraad et al., "For Every Knight in Shining Armor There's a Castle Waiting To Be Cleaned: A Marxist Feminist Analysis of the Household," *Rethinking Marxism* 2 (1989): 10.

30. Adams, "Children's Books," 74.

31. "See Jim and Pat Cook: Jim Cooks First," *New York Times,* 13 March 1986, A26.

32. For violence and the exclusion of women, see Eugene F. Provenzo, Jr., *Video Kids: Making Sense of Nintendo* (Cambridge, Mass.: Harvard University Press, 1991), 109–127; Marsha Ginsburg, "Violence Backlash for Video: Rating Games Made for Kids Called Overdue," *San Francisco Examiner,* 22 May 1994, B1. For stalker games and comic books, see Irene Lacher, "Separated at Mirth," *Los Angeles Times,* 20 January 1995, E1, E4; Pecora, "Superman"; Sue Woodman, "How Super Are Heroes?" *Health* 23 (1991): 40; Fred J. Fejes, "Masculinity as a Fad: A Review of Empirical Mass Communication Research on Masculinity," in Craig, ed., *Men, Masculinity, and the Media,* 17.

33. For games, see Rosenfeld, "Games Girls Play," A1; Lisa DiMona and Constance Herndon, eds., *The "Information Please" Women's Sourcebook* (Boston: Houghton Mifflin, 1994), 152.

34. For the focus on appearance, see Kate Peirce, "A Feminist Theoretical Perspective on the Socialization of Teenage Girls through *Seventeen* Magazine," *Sex Roles* 23 (1990): 491. For the racial composition of ads and readership, see Caroline Miller, quoted in Anastasia Higgenbotham, "Teen Mags: How To Get a Guy, Drop Twenty Pounds, and Lose Your Self-Esteem," *Ms.,* March–April 1996, 84; and Audrey Edwards, "From Aunt Jemima to Anita Hill: Media's Split Image of Black Women," *Media Studies Journal* 7 (1993): 214. For body images, see Karin Winegar, "Body Image Is Colored by Race," *Star-Tribune* (Minneapolis–St. Paul), 1 June 1994, 1E; Aimee Pohl, "Teen Magazines' Message to Girls: You Can Be Anything . . . Except Yourself," *Extra! (Fairness and Accuracy in Reporting,* Special Issue, 1992): 28; Natalie Angier, "Your Best Chest: It's Time to Preen," *New York Times,* 2 April 1995, E6.

35. For experts' views, see Eric Stice, Erika Schupak-Neuberg, Heather E. Shaw,

and Richard I. Stein, "Relation of Media Exposure to Eating-Disorder Symptomatology: An Examination of Mediating Mechanisms," *Journal of Abnormal Psychology* 103 (1994): 836. For protests, see Ellen Goodman, "Anorexic Chic," *San Francisco Chronicle,* 11 June 1996, A23. For editors' defenses, see Tina Gadoin, "Body of Evidence," *Harper's Bazaar* (July 1993): 74; Victoria Collison and Catherine Murphy, quoted in Kaz Cooke, *Real Gorgeous* (New York: Norton, 1996), 148, 149; Cyndee Miller, "Give Them a Cheeseburger: Critics Assail Waif Look in Sprite, Calvin Klein Ads," *Marketing News,* 6 June 1994, 1.

36. Calvin Klein, quoted in James Kaplan, "The Triumph of Calvinism," *New York,* 18 September 1995, 52.

37. For models, see Michael Gross, *Model: The Ugly Business of Beautiful Women* (New York: William Morrow, 1995); Mary Taran, "Appearance: Counter Intelligence," *New York Times Magazine,* 11 February 1996, 58. For "Fastest Firmers," see *Shape,* July 1994. For *Seventeen* readers, see Pohl, "Message," 28.

38. For industry explanations, see Bill Carter, "Children's TV, Where Boys Are King," *New York Times,* 1 May 1991, A1; Megan Rosenfeld, "Girls' Take on TV Examined: Survey Aims to Promote Female Role Models," *Washington Post,* 20 September 1995, F6. For racial and gender biases, see Basow, *Gender Stereotypes,* 159; Mann, *The Difference,* 45; Jennifer Mangan, "Fine Tuning," *Chicago Tribune,* 26 May 1996, section 13, 1; Rosenfeld, "Girls' Take," F6. For *Sesame Street,* see Katha Pollitt, "Hers: The Smurfette Principle," *New York Times,* 7 April 1991, section 6, 22.

39. For violence in children's media, see Elizabeth Kolbert, "The Media Business: Television Gets Closer Look as a Factor in Real Violence," *New York Times,* 14 December 1994, A1; Stephen J. Kim, "Viewer Discretion Is Advised: A Structural Approach to the Issue of Television Violence," *University of Pennsylvania Law Review* 142 (1994): 1383, 1388. For media leaders' defense, see, for example, Wayne Walley, "NAPTE '94 Takes Aim at Violence," *Electronic Media,* 31 January 1994, A1.

For children's exposure to television violence, see Statement of the Surgeon General, Jocelyn Elders, Hearings before the Subcommittees on Telecommunications and Finance of the Committee on Energy and Commerce, House of Representatives, 103rd Congress, 15 September 1993, 371, 372. For research linking media violence to viewer attitudes and behavior, see Brandon S. Centerwall, "Television and Violence: The Scope of the Problem and Where To Go from Here," *Journal of the American Medical Association* 267 (10 June 1992): 3059; George Gerbener, "Television Violence: The Power and the Peril," in Gail Dines and Jean M. Humez, eds., *Gender, Race, and Class in the Media* (Thousand Oaks, Calif.: Sage, 1995), 547; University of California at Santa Barbara, University of North Carolina, University of Texas at Austin, University of Wisconsin at Madison, *National Television Violence Study* (Los Angeles: Media Scope, 1996).

40. For V-chip technology, see Newton N. Minow and Craig L. LaMay, *Aban-*

doned in the Wasteland (New York: Hill and Wang, 1995), 23–25; Kohlbert, "Media Business," A1. For rating systems, see Martin Shafer, quoted in Nadine Strossen, *Defending Pornography: Free Speech, Sex, and the Fight for Women's Rights* (New York: Scribner's, 1995), 21; Richard Zogelin, "Rating Wars," *Time,* 23 December 1966, 26.

41. For the limits of V-chips, see Richard Zoglin, "Chips Ahoy," *Time,* 19 February 1996, 58–59; Mark Landler, "TV Turns to an Era of Self-Control," *New York Times,* 17 March 1996, H38. For industry priorities, see Arnold Becker, quoted in Todd Gitlin, *Inside Prime Time* (New York: Pantheon, 1983), 31.

42. Miedzian, *Boys Will Be Boys,* 225–236; Minow and LaMay, *Abandoned in the Wasteland,* 152–173; National Institute for Dispute Resolution, "Symposium on Dispute Resolution, Youth, and Violence," *Forum* (Spring 1994); Aletha G. Huston et al., *Big World, Small Screen* (Lincoln: University of Nebraska Press, 1992), 141.

43. Kathleen Deveny, "Chart of Kindergarten Awards," *Wall Street Journal,* 5 December 1994, B1.

44. For inadequacies in enforcement and funding, see Leora Tanenbaum, "Hey Teach! Inequities in How Boys and Girls Are Treated at School," *The Nation,* 28 February 1994, 280.

45. Sadker and Sadker, *Failing at Fairness,* 7.

46. For an overview, see ibid. For the underrepresentation of women in standard texts, see Michael Marland, "School as a Sexist Amplifier," in Marland, ed., *Sex Differentiation and Schooling* (London: Heinemann, 1983), 1; Barbara Anne Murphy, "Education: An Illusion for Women," *Southern California Review of Law and Women's Studies* 3 (1993): 21, 31–32; Marilyn A. Hulme, "Mirror, Mirror on the Wall: Biased Reflections in Textbooks and Instructional Materials," in Anne O'Brien Cavelli, ed., *Sex Equity in Education: Readings and Strategies* (Springfield, Ill.: C. C. Thomas, 1988), 187; Millicent Lawton, "Schools' 'Glass Ceiling' Imperils Girls, Study Says," *Education Week,* 2 February 1992, 17. For history texts, see Hulme, "Mirror, Mirror," 193–194; Murphy, "Education," 34; Sadker and Sadker, *Failing at Fairness,* 72, 124–131. For Jane Austen's assessment, see *Northanger Abbey* (London: MacDonald, 1818), 108.

47. For conservative critiques, see "Sinister Campaign to Hurt Schools," *Philadelphia Daily News,* 23 May 1994; Sommers, *Who Stole Feminism?* 60–63. For assumptions about female teachers, see Sharon L. Sims, "Women's History and Public Schools," *Women's Rights Law Reporter* 14 (1992): 9, 19.

48. Sadker and Sadker, *Failing at Fairness,* 72.

49. For gender bias, see ibid.; and Basow, *Gender Stereotypes,* 151–152. For the cartoon, see Sadker and Sadker, *Failing at Fairness,* 49.

50. For gender bias in the classroom, see American Association of University Women [AAUW], *How Schools Shortchange Girls: A Study of Major Findings on Girls and Education* (Washington, D.C.: American Association of University Women, AAUW Educational Foundation, 1992), 68; Murphy, "Education,"

41; Bernice Resnick Sandler, Lisa Silverberg, and Roberta M. Hall, *The Chilly Classroom Climate* (Washington, D.C.: National Association for Women in Education, 1996). For racial and ethnic bias, see Linda Grant, "Race-Gender Status, Classroom Interaction and Children's Socialization in Elementary School," in Louise Cherry Wilkerson and Cora B. Marrett, eds., *Gender Influences in Classroom Interaction* (Orlando, Fla.: Academic Press, 1985), 57–75; Peggy Orenstein, *Schoolgirls* (New York: Doubleday, 1994), 199–200.

51. For the views of surveyed women, see Roper Starch, Inc., *1995 Virginia Slims Poll* (Storrs, Conn.: Roper Center for Public Opinion Research, 1995), 21.

52. For test scores, see AAUW, *How Schools Shortchange Girls;* Lawton, "Glass Ceiling," 17; Phyllis Teitelbaum, "Feminist Theory and Standardized Testing," in Alison Jaggar and Susan Bordo, eds., *Gender/Body/Knowledge: Feminist Reconstructions of Being and Knowing* (New Brunswick, N.J.: Rutgers University Press, 1989), 324. For self-esteem, see AAUW, *How Schools Shortchange Girls;* Basow, *Gender Stereotypes*, 142–178. For racial differences, see Debold, Wilson and Malave, *Mother-Daughter Revolution*, 14; Basow, *Gender Stereotypes*, 173.

53. For language patterns, see Deborah Tannen, *Talking from Nine to Five* (New York: William Morrow, 1994); and Chapter 2, above. For employment patterns, see Chapter 6.

54. Ellen Nakashima, "When It Comes to Top School Jobs, Women Learn It's Tough To Get Ahead," *Washington Post,* 21 April 1996, B1.

55. *United States v. Virginia Military Institute,* 116 S.Ct. 2264 (1996). See Jo Sanders, "Separate Classes for Girls Aren't the Answer," Letter to the editor, *New York Times,* 5 December 1993, E20.

56. Laura Stepp, "How Girls Learn Best," *Washington Post,* 28 May 1996, B5.

57. AAUW, *How Schools Shortchange Girls,* 75.

58. AAUW, *America's Hostile Hallways: The AAUW Survey on Sexual Harassment in America's Schools* (Washington, D.C.: American Association of University Women Educational Foundation, 1993).

59. Leo, *Two Steps Ahead*, 236; Katie Roiphe, *The Morning After: Sex, Fear and Feminism on Campus* (Boston: Little, Brown, 1992), 95, 99; Debbie M. Price, "Victims of Their Gender?" *San Francisco Daily Journal,* 24 March 1992, 4.

60. The principal, Peter Kendeall, is quoted in Karen Mellencamp Davis, "Reading, Writing, and Sexual Harassment: Finding a Constitutional Remedy When Schools Fail to Address Peer Abuse," *Indiana Law Journal* 69 (1994): 1123, 1163. For cases, penalties, and retaliation, see, e.g., *Bruneau v. South Kortright School District,* 94 CV-0864 (N.D.N.Y., 1996), where boys hit, kicked, and spit on girls and grabbed their breasts; Adam Nossiter, "Six-Year-Old's Sex Crime: Innocent Peck on Cheek," *New York Times,* 27 September 1996, A9; AAUW, *Hostile Hallways;* Leora Tanenbaum, "'Sluts' and Suits," *In These Times,* 12 May 1996, 23; Judy Mann, "What's Harassment? Ask a Girl," *Washington Post,* 23 June 1993, D26; Jane Gross, "Schools Are Newest Arenas for Sex-Harassment Issues," *New York Times,* 11 March 1992, B8.

61. Miedzian, *Boys Will Be Boys,* 190.

62. Susan K. Cahn, *Coming on Strong: Gender and Sexuality in Twentieth Century Women's Sport* (New York: Free Press, 1994), 259.

63. For disparities in high school, see Bob Rohwer, "Are Boys' and Girls' Athletic Programs Treated Equally at the High School Level?" *Los Angeles Times,* 1 November 1994, section V, 1; Joan O'Brien, "Twenty-Two Years of Title IX Has Some Utahans Questioning Slow Progress: Girls Getting Foot in Door of the Gym, but Only If Boy Players Aren't Using It," *Salt Lake Tribune,* 11 September 1994, A1. For disparities in college, see National Collegiate Athletic Association, Gender Equity Task Force, *Final Report* (National Collegiate Athletic Association, 1993); Kathleen Sharp, "Foul Play," *Ms.,* September–October 1993, 22; Debra E. Blum, "Slow Progress in Equity," *Chronicle of Higher Education,* 26 October 1994, A45; Linda Joplin, "Athletic Equity: Twenty-One Years and Counting," *National NOW Times,* June 1993, 6.

64. Mark Lorenz, "A Reality-Based Plan for Achieving Gender Equity in College Sports," *Chronicle of Higher Education,* 2 March 1994, B1; David Roach, "Compliance and Quotas Don't Mix," *New York Times,* 27 Sept. 1995, S11.

65. Mary Jo Festle, *Playing Nice* (New York: Columbia University Press, 1996), 279. Mariah Nelson, *The Stronger Women Get, the More Men Love Football: Sexism and the American Culture of Sport* (New York: Harcourt, Brace, 1994), 124.

66. Ibid., 66; Laura K. Keeton, "Rah! Rah! Cheerleading Is Hot! Hot! Hot!" *Wall Street Journal,* 30 December 1994, B1.

67. Festle, *Playing Nice,* 271; Susan Gilbert, "The Smallest Olympians Pay the Biggest Price," *New York Times,* 28 July 1996, E4.

68. Festle, *Playing Nice,* 266–267; Cahn, *Coming on Strong,* 261–267; Debra E. Blum, "College Sports' *L* Word," *Chronicle of Higher Education,* 9 March 1994, A35.

69. Michael A. Messner, *Power at Play: Sports and the Problem of Masculinity* (Boston: Beacon, 1992), 24.

70. Nelson, *The Stronger Women Get,* 202; Jeff Z. Klein, "How to Slash, Maul, and Jab Your Way to Stardom," *New York Times Magazine,* 21 January 1996, 34; Tie Domi, "Tough Tradition of Hockey Fights Should Be Preserved," *USA Today,* 27 October 1992, 12C.

71. For injuries, see Nelson, *The Stronger Women Get,* 77; Miedzian, *Boys Will Be Boys,* 182. For ridicule, see ibid., 198; Messner, *Power at Play,* 72–76; Don Sabo, "Pigskin, Patriarchy and Pain," in Michael A. Messner and Donald Sabo, eds., *Sex, Violence and Power in Sports: Rethinking Masculinity* (Freedom, Calif.: Crossing Press, 1994), 202. For challenges to athletes' masculinity, see Nelson, *The Stronger Women Get,* 87; Ira Berkow, "The High Priest of Hoop Hysteria," *New York Times,* 14 May 1988, Sports section, 53.

72. For surveys, see Alison Bass, "How Jocks View Women: An Old Issue Gets New Scrutiny," *Boston Globe,* 5 December 1994, 39; Robert Lipsyte, "Why Do Male Athletes Assault Women?" *New York Times,* 11 November 1994, B14; Todd W. Crosset, James Ptacek, Mark McDonald, and Jeffrey R. Benedict,

"Male Student Athletes and Violence against Women," *Violence against Women* 2 (1996): 163. For athletes' statements, see Ellen Goodman, "Tyson's 'Day of Redemption,'" *San Francisco Chronicle,* 27 June 1995, A19; "Johnson's Emotions," *New York Times,* 11 December 1991, B16; Nelson, *The Stronger Women Get,* 82.

73. "Wilkenson Arrested for Domestic Dispute," *New York Times,* 15 September 1995, B10 ("private matters"); NCAA official, Dave Carwood, quoted in Gerald Eskenazic, "The Male Athlete and Sexual Assault," *New York Times,* 3 June 1990, section 8, 1, 4 ("unfair to single out athletes"); Eskenazic, "The Male Athlete," 8 (quoting NFL official: "athlete's attitude"); Nelson, *The Stronger Women Get,* 127–158 (harassment, date rape). See also Chapter 5.

74. Derrick Z. Jackson, "Trifling Fines Speak Volumes," *Boston Globe,* 30 November 1990, 21; Bass, "Jocks," 39; Rick Telander, "Not a Shining Knight," *Sports Illustrated,* 9 May 1988, 122 (discussing Bobby Knight).

4. Media Images

1. For a fuller discussion of some issues in this chapter, see Deborah L. Rhode, "Media Images, Feminist Issues," *Signs* 20 (1995): 685, reprinted in Martha Albertson Fineman and Martha McCluskey, eds., *Feminism, Media, and the Law* (New York: Oxford University Press, 1997). For historical material on women in journalism, see Maurine H. Beasley and Sheila J. Gibbons, *Taking Their Place: A Documentary History of Women and Journalism* (Washington, D.C.: American University Press, 1993), 16; Kay Mills, "The Media and the Year of the Woman," *Media Studies Journal* 7 (1993): 19. For television commercials, see Susan J. Douglas, *Where the Girls Are* (New York: Random House, 1994), 200. For Aunt Jemima, see Carol Moog, *"Are They Selling Her Lips?" Advertising and Identity* (New York: William Morrow, 1990), 206–207.

2. For the entertainment media, see John Carmody, "Minorities Still Shut Out, Survey Reports," *Washington Post,* 16 June 1993, B12; Elaine Dutka, "Women and Hollywood: It's Still a Lousy Relationship," *Los Angeles Times,* 11 November 1990, 8; Donna Lopiano, "Don't Touch That Dial," *Women's Sports and Fitness* (July–August 1996): 42. For the news media, see M. Junior Bridge, *Slipping from the Scene: News Coverage of Females Drops* (New York: Center for Women, Men and Media, 1995); "Women, Men and Media," in *Marginalizing Women* (New York: Freedom Forum, Columbia University, 1996).

3. Kurt Anderson, "Big Mouths," *Time,* 1 November 1993, 60, 65; Pat Williams, *The Rooster's Egg* (Cambridge, Mass.: Harvard University Press, 1996), 44, 48.

4. Susan J. Douglas, "Missing Voices: Women and the U.S. News Media," Fairness and Accuracy in Reporting [FAIR], *Extra,* Special issue, 1992: 4; Bridge, *Slipping from The Scene,* 3–9; Jane O'Reilly, "The Pale Males of Punditry," *Media Studies Journal* 7 (1993): 125, 127; Jean Ward, "Talking (Fairly) about the World: A Reprieve on Journalistic Language," *Media Studies Journal* 7 (1993): 92 (cartoon).

5. Minnesota Advisory Committee to the United States Commission on Civil Rights, *Stereotyping of Minorities by the News Media in Minnesota* (Washington, D.C.: Government Printing Office, 1993), 5–7; Center for Women, Men and Media, "The News, as if All People Mattered" (New York: Center for Women, Men and Media, 1993); Audrey Edwards, "From Aunt Jemima to Anita Hill: Media's Split Image of Black Women," *Media Studies Journal* 7 (1993): 214; Beasley and Gibbons, *Taking Their Place*, 307, 317. For soap operas, see Gloria Abernathy-Lear, "'His Name Was Not on the List': The Soap Opera Updates of Ti-Rone as Resistance to Symbolic Annihilation," in Gail Dines and Jean M. Humez, eds., *Gender, Race and Class in Media* (Thousand Oaks, Calif.: Sage, 1995), 190, 191. See, generally, K. Sue Jewell, *From Mammy to Miss America and Beyond* (New York: Routledge, 1993).

6. Karen Lindsey, "Race, Sexuality and Class in Soapland," in Dines and Humez, eds., *Gender, Race and Class*, 332, 333.

7. Lucy A. Williams, "Race, Rat Bites and Unfit Mothers: How Media Discourse Informs Welfare Legislation Debate," *Stanford Law Review* 43 (1991): 1159; Marie Ashe, "'Bad' Mothers and Welfare Reform in Massachusetts: The Case of Claribel Ventura," in Fineman, ed., *Feminism and Law;* Caryl Rivers, *Slick Spins and Fractured Facts* (New York: Columbia University Press, 1996), 199.

8. Deb Schwartz, quoted in Marguerite Moritz, "Lesbian Chic: Our Fifteen Minutes of Celebrity?" in Angharad N. Valdiva, ed., *Feminism, Multiculturalism and the Media: Global Diversities* (Thousand Oaks, Calif.: Sage, 1995): 127, 142; Edward Alwood, *Straight News* (New York: Columbia University Press, 1996), 323–328. Bruce Bawer, "Why Can't Hollywood Get Gay Life Right?" *New York Times,* 10 March 1996, H15; Eric Gutierrez, "Opening Hollywood's Closet," *Los Angeles Times,* 10 March 1996, Calendar, 4, 81.

9. Anna Quindlen, "Women as Change Makers," in *The Scholar and the Feminist* (New York: Barnard Center for Research on Women, 1993), 12; O'Reilly, "Pale Males of Punditry," 125.

10. Christine Craft, *Too Old, Too Ugly, and Not Deferential to Men* (Rocklin, Calif.: Prima, 1988).

11. Jean Kilbourne, "Beauty and the Beast," in Dines and Humez, eds., *Gender, Race and Class*, 122; Kathleen H. Jamieson, *Beyond the Double Bind: Women and Leadership* (New York: Oxford University Press, 1995), 155–163; Moog, *Selling Her Lips*, 198–199, 62.

12. Guy Trebay, "Racism on the Runway: Not an Ethnic Moment," *Village Voice,* 9 May 1995, 23.

13. Fern Mallis, quoted in Trebay, "Racism," 23.

14. "Dream Girls," Traveling exhibit of the American Advertising Museum (Portland, Ore., 1995).

15. Douglas, *Where the Girls Are,* 200.

16. Betsy Morris, "If the Damsel Is in Distress, Make Sure It's Career-Related," *Wall Street Journal,* 17 February 1984, 1, 12; Ann Barr Snitow, "Mass Market Romance," in Dines and Humez, eds., *Gender, Race and Class*, 383, 384. For publisher guidelines, see Carol Thurston, *The Romance Revolution: Erotic*

Novels for Women and the Quest for a New Sexual Identity (Urbana, Ill.: University of Illinois Press, 1987), 16.

17. See Kevin Sack, "Quayle Insists Abortion Remarks Don't Signal Change in His View," *New York Times,* 24 July 1992, A1; Rita C. Hubbard, "Male Parent Images in Advertising," in Sammy R. Dahna, ed., *Advertising and Popular Culture: Studies in Variety and Versatility* (Ohio: Bowling Green, 1992), 142; *Marketing,* 19 January 1981, 4.

18. Elizabeth G. Traube, *Dreaming Identities: Class, Gender, and Generations in 1980's Hollywood Movies* (Boulder, Colo.: Westview, 1992), 145.

19. For the overrepresentation of professional women, see Richard Butsch, "'Ralph, Fred, Archie and Homer': Why Television Keeps Recreating the White Male Working-Class Buffoon," in Dines and Humez, eds., *Gender, Race and Class,* 403. For the absence of realistic constraints, see Karen Lindsay, "Race, Sexuality, and Class in Soapland," in Dines and Humez, eds., *Gender, Race and Class,* 332, 338–339.

20. For professional women and neglectful mothers, see Tania Modeleskj, *Loving with a Vengeance: Mass-Produced Fantasies for Women* (Hamden, Conn.: Anchor, 1982); Rogers, "Daze of Our Lives," 326; bell hooks, "Save Your Breath, Sisters," *New York Times,* 7 January 1996, E19. For lawyers, see Carole Shapiro, "Women Lawyers in Celluloid: Why Hollywood Skirts the Truth," *University of Toledo Law Review* 25 (1995): 955, 986–991. For the punishment of selfish careerists, see Traube, *Dreaming Identities,* 113.

21. Ward, "Talking (Fairly) about the World," 190; Jamieson, *Beyond the Double Bind,* 170 (Richards); Linda Witt, Karen M. Paget, and Glenna Mathews, *Running as a Woman* (New York: Free Press, 1994), 206 (Yeakel, Braun); Cath Jackson, "Trouble and Strife" (cartoon), in Caryl Rivers, "Bandwagons, Women and Cultural Mythology," *Media Studies Journal* 7 (1993): 4.

22. Mariah B. Nelson, *The Stronger Women Get, the More Men Love Football* (New York: Harcourt, 1994), 212 (gymnasts); Rivers, *Slick Spins,* 148 (skaters).

23. Maureen Dowd, "On Washington: The First Lady's New Clothes," *New York Times Magazine,* 10 July 1994, 15, 17; "Hillary Pillory," *People,* June 1994, 42.

24. Jeffrey Toobin, "True Grit: What Does O. J. Simpson's Defense 'Dream Team' Face in Marcia Clark? A Prosecutor Who Refused to Give Up Trial Work and Is Winning So Far," *New Yorker,* 9 January 1995, 28–30.

25. Janine Haines, "The Front Page vs. the Female Pol," *Ms.,* January 1993, 84.

26. Rush Limbaugh, quoted in Jody Rohlena, ed., *Sounds Like a New Woman* (New York: Penguin, 1993), 57; Christina Hoff Sommers, quoted in Anna Quindlen, "And Now, Babe Feminism," *New York Times,* 19 Jan. 1994, A21.

27. "Leading Feminist Puts Hairdo before Strike," *New York Times,* 27 August 1970, A30 (Friedan); Nancy Friday, *The Power of Beauty* (New York: Harper Collins, 1996), 331–335 (Steinem); Noemie Emery, "Gloria in False Excelsis," *Weekly Standard,* 23 October 1995, 40 (Steinem); Camille Paglia, "*Playboy* Interview: Camille Paglia," *Playboy,* May 1995, 51, 57 (Wolf).

28. For racial biases, see Audrey Edwards, "Aunt Jemima," 216; Ellen McCracken,

Decoding Women's Magazines (New York: Macmillan, 1993), 150; bell hooks, *Black Looks* (Boston: South End Press, 1992), 72. For false promises, see Diane Barthel, *Putting on Appearances: Gender and Advertising* (Philadelphia: Temple University Press, 1988), 48.

29. Leonard Horn, quoted in Roxanne Roberts, "The Cheesecake Ballot: Pageant Viewers to Decide Fate of Swimsuit Competition," *Washington Post,* 13 July, 1995, C1; Frank Rich, "There She Is," *New York Times,* 20 September 1995, A21; Sam Donaldson, *This Week With David Brinkley,* 17 July 1995.

30. George Will, *This Week with David Brinkley,* 17 September 1995; Pete Dexter, "Wrap Our Beauty Queens in Spandex, Not Causes," *Sacramento Bee,* 18 September, 1995, A2.

31. Naomi Wolf, *The Beauty Myth: How Images of Beauty Are Used against Women* (New York: Morrow, 1991), 17; Susan Sherwin, *No Longer Patient: Feminist Ethics and Health Care* (Philadelphia: Temple University Press, 1992), 188.

32. For effortless dieting, see Barthel, *Putting On Appearances,* 144–145. For diets and cosmetics, see Naomi Wolf, *The Beauty Myth,* 113; Kaz Cooke, *Real Gorgeous* (New York: Norton, 1996), 106–107. For cosmetic surgery, see Sara Halprin, *"Look at My Ugly Face!"* (New York: Penguin, 1995), 59; Philip J. Hilts, "Maker Is Depicted as Fighting Tests on Implant Safety," *New York Times,* 13 January 1992, A1; Wendy Kaminer, *True Love Waits* (Reading, Mass.: Addison-Wesley, 1996), 160.

33. For the costs of being overweight, see Katharine Bartlett, *Gender and Law* (Boston: Little, Brown, 1993), 144–145; Gina Kolata, "The Burdens of Being Overweight: Mistreatment and Misconceptions," *New York Times,* 22 November 1992, A1. For studies noting the effect of beauty on educational and employment opportunities, social status, and individual self-esteem, see Meg Gehrke, "Is Beauty the Beast?" *Southern California Review of Law and Women's Studies* 4 (1994): 221. For surveys on body image, see Rosalyn M. Meadow and Lillie Weiss, *Good Girls Don't Eat Dessert* (New York: Harmony, 1992), 34; and Jennifer Warren, "Living Large," *Los Angeles Times,* 27 December 1994, E1.

34. For the health risks of being overweight, see Jane E. Brody, "Moderate Weight Gain Risky for Women, a Study Warns," *New York Times,* 14 September 1995, A1. For the messages in women's magazines, see McCracken, *Women's Magazines,* 149.

35. *Mademoiselle,* May 1982, 118–119. See examples in Gloria Steinem, "Sex, Lies, and Advertising," in Steinem, *Moving Beyond Words* (New York: Simon and Schuster, 1994), 131, 156–157; McCracken, *Women's Magazines,* 151, 178, 183, 219.

36. Barbara Ehrenreich, "The Women's Movements: Feminist and Antifeminist," *Radical America* 93 (1981): 97.

37. Helen Benedict, "Covering Rape without Feminism," in Fineman and McCluskey, eds., *Feminism, Media, and the Law.*

38. Helen Benedict, *Virgin or Vamp: How the Press Covers Sex Crimes* (New York:

Oxford University Press, 1992), 9, 219; Don Terry, "In the Week of an Infamous Rape, Twenty-Eight Other Victims Suffer," in Kenneth Winston and Mary Jo Bane, eds., *Gender and Public Policy* (Boulder, Colo.: Westview, 1993), 160.

39. Orlando Patterson, "Race, Gender, and Liberal Fallacies," *New York Times,* 20 October 1991, E15.

40. "The Editorialists," *San Francisco Examiner,* 24 June 1994, A23; Ellen Goodman, "O.J. Isn't Dead, Nicole Is," *San Jose Mercury News,* 22 June 1994, 11B; Jacqueline Adams, "The White Wife," *New York Times Magazine,* 18 September 1994, 36.

41. Warren Farrell, "Spouse Abuse: A Two-Way Street," *USA Today,* 29 June 1994, A15; Judith Sherven and James Sniechowski, "Women Are Responsible Too," *Los Angeles Times,* 21 June 1994, B7; Letters to the editor, *People,* 13 March 1995; Max Boot, "Wild Bronco Chase: Pundits Squeeze O.J.," *Wall Street Journal,* 24 June 1994, A9; Elizabeth Kolbert, "Our New Participatory Tabloid Videocracy," *New York Times,* 17 July 1994, E3.

42. Katie Roiphe, *The Morning After: Sex, Fear, and Feminism on Campus* (Boston: Little, Brown, 1993); Faludi, "Whose Hype?" *Newsweek,* 25 October 1993, 61. See Donna Hill, "Rape Hype? The Fight for Ideological Control over the Meaning of Unwanted Sex," in Fineman and McCluskey, eds., *Feminism, Media, and the Law;* Martha McCluskey, "Fear of Feminism: Media Stories of Victimization, Privilege and Passivity in Debates about Group Violence," ibid.

43. MacKinnon, quoted in Roiphe, *The Morning After,* 81; and in Christina Hoff Sommers, "Hardline Feminists Guilty of Ms.-Representation," *Wall Street Journal,* 7 November 1991, A14. Andrea Dworkin, quoted in Sarah Creighton, "Sexual Correctness: Has It Gone Too Far?" *Newsweek,* 25 October 1993, 54. For belated acknowledgments, see, for example, Wendy Kaminer, "What Is This Thing Called Rape," *New York Times Book Review,* 19 September 1993, 1, critiquing Roiphe and MacKinnon, and noting on the third page of a three-page review that there are some feminists in between. For Roiphe's unsupported and inaccurate claims, see Faludi, "Whose Hype?" 61; Katha Pollitt, "Not Just Bad Sex," *New Yorker,* 4 October 1993, 22; Kathryn Abrams, "Songs of Innocence and Experience: Dominance Feminism in the University," *Yale Law Journal* 103 (1994): 1533. For the *Newsweek* caption, see Creighton, "Sexual Correctness," 54.

44. Mike Royko, "Money Can't Buy Him Love: Hugh Grant Finds Trouble in Looking for a Bargain," *Pittsburgh Post Gazette,* 19 July 1995, A15; David Kronke, "Four Talk Shows and a Premiere," *Los Angeles Times,* 15 July 1995, F4.

45. Kronke, "Four Talk Shows," F4; Michael Walker, "The Hughman Factor," *Los Angeles Times,* 10 July 1995, F8 (quoting studio spokesperson).

46. Leno, quoted in Kronke, "Four Talk Shows," F4.

47. Mike Newell, quoted in Bernard Weinraub, "What's the Hollywood Topic? Hugh Grant's Future, Mainly," *New York Times,* 29 June 1995, 16. For the

risks facing prostitutes, see sources cited in Dorchen Liedholdt, "Prostitution: A Violation of Women's Human Rights," *Cardozo Women's Law Journal* 1 (1993): 133, 136–141; Margaret Baldwin, "Split at the Root: Prostitution and Feminist Discourse of Law Reform," *Yale Journal of Law and Feminism* 5 (1993): 47.

48. "Legalised Prostitution" *The Economist,* 7 September 1991, 28; Vednita Nelson, "Prostitution: When Racism and Sexism Intersect," *Michigan Journal of Gender and Law* 1 (1993): 81, 85.

49. Julie Pearl, "The Highest-Paying Customers: America's Cities and the Costs of Prostitution Control," *Hastings Law Journal* 38 (1987): 797; San Francisco Task Force on Prostitution, *Final Report Submitted to the Board of Supervisors of the City and County of San Francisco* (San Francisco: Task Force on Prostitution, 1996), 21–25; Alan Dershowitz, appearing on *Larry King Live,* CNN, 12 July 1995.

50. "Westside Neighbors Plan for Gay Center," *Los Angeles Times,* 22 July 1995, B1. See Tracy M. Clements, "Prostitution and the American Health Care System: Denying Access to a Group of Women in Need," *Berkeley Women's Law Journal* 11 (1996): 49, 64–66; San Francisco Task Force, *Final Report,* 21–25.

51. Elayne Rapping, *Media-tions* (Boston: South End Press, 1994), 46; Betty Friedan, quoted in Jane Galbraith, "Indecent Debate Fuels Box Office Movies," *Los Angeles Times,* 1 May 1993, F1.

52. Mark Lorando, "Sitcoms Full of Harassment, Study Finds," *San Jose Mercury News,* 6 January 1995, 5; Katherine Green, quoted in Lorando, "Sitcoms," 5.

53. bell hooks, *Outlaw Culture: Resisting Representations* (New York; Routledge, 1994), 120.

54. Michael Paul, quoted in Rohlena, ed., *Sounds Like a New Woman,* 33; Deborah D. Rogers, "Daze of Our Lives: The Soap Opera as Feminist Text," *Journal of American Culture* 14 (Winter 1991): 29; Lisa M. Cuklanz, *Rape on Trial: How the Mass Media Construct Legal Reform and Social Change* (Philadelphia: University of Pennsylvania Press, 1996), 87–93.

55. Jean Dobrino, "The Cinderella Complex: Romance Fiction, Patriarchy, and Capitalism," *Journal of Popular Culture* (Winter 1993): 103, 108; Ann Mather, *Born Out of Love* (Toronto: Harlequin, 1977), 72–73.

56. Thurston, *Romance Revolution,* 55, 78, 192 (publishing guidelines); Sayre, quoted in Jayne Ann Krentz, "Introduction," in Krentz, ed., *Dangerous Men and Adventurous Women: Romance Writers on the Appeal of Romance* (Philadelphia: University of Pennsylvania Press, 1992), 11 ("the woman wins"). For the appeal of subordination, see Doreen Owens Malek, "Mad, Bad, and Dangerous to Know: The Hero as Challenge," ibid., 73, 75; Daphne Chair, "Sweet Subversions," ibid., 61, 71; and the discussion of pornography in Chapter 5, below.

57. Marilyn Lowry, *How to Write Romance Novels That Sell* (New York: Rawson, 1983).

58. Susan Faludi, *Backlash: The Undeclared War against American Women* (New York: Doubleday, 1991), 194; Moog, *Selling Her Lips,* 144, 148. The diamond ad ran in the *New York Times Magazine* during the winter of 1995.

59. Beasley and Gibbons, *Taking Their Place,* 7 (discussing NOW coverage); Gloria Steinem, quoted in Mary Thom, "The Personal Is Political, Publishable Too," *Media Studies Journal* 7 (1993): 223, 225 (discussing advice); Flora Davis, *Moving the Mountain* (New York: Simon and Schuster, 1991), 109 (quoting male editor); Senator Jennings Randolph, quoted in ABC coverage of women's marches. Rivers, *Slick Spins,* 103 (referring to bubbleheads).

60. Faludi, *Backlash,* 75–76; Betty Friedan, "Feminism's Next Step," *New York Times Magazine,* 5 July 1981, 14; Ellen Goodman, "Women's Movement Misses . . . Movement," *St. Louis Post-Dispatch,* 25 February 1992, D3.

61. Sally Quinn, "Feminists Have Killed Feminism," *Los Angeles Times,* 23 January 1992, B7.

62. Catharine R. Stimpson, "Women's Studies and Its Discontents," *Dissent* 43 (1996): 67. For these longstanding caricatures of feminists, see Aileen Kraditor, *The Ideas of the Woman Suffrage Movement, 1890–1920* (New York: Columbia University Press, 1965), 14–42; Nancy Cott, *The Grounding of Modern Feminism* (New Haven: Yale University Press, 1987), 13, 44–45, 272, 282. For the focus on fringes, see Todd Gitlin, *The Whole World Is Watching* (Berkeley: University of California Press, 1980), 283–284; Lance Bennett, *News: The Politics of Illusion* (New York: Longman, 1988), 26–44.

63. See also Clarence Page, "New GOP Weapon: The Feminist Threat," *Chicago Tribune,* 30 October 1991, C19.

64. See sources cited in Rhode, "Media Images"; Douglas, "Missing Voices," 4; Claudia Wallis, "Onward, Women," *Time,* 4 December 1989, 80; Susan Douglas, *Where the Girls Are: Growing Up Female With the Mass Media* (New York: Random House, 1994), 275.

65. Nancy Woodhull, quoted in Naomi Wolf, *Fire with Fire* (New York: Random House, 1993), 73.

66. Irving Kristol, "Sex Trumps Gender," *Wall Street Journal,* 16 March 1996, A18; Sommers, "Hard-Line Feminists," A14; Camille Paglia, "The Return of Carrie Nation: Feminists Catharine MacKinnon and Andrea Dworkin," *Playboy,* October 1992, 36.

67. Quinn, "Feminists Have Killed Feminism," B7; Quinn, quoted in Karin Schwartz, "Lesbian Invisibility in the Media," FAIR, *Extra* (1992): 21; see also William Safire, "Politics Is Showcasing the New Woman," *San Francisco Chronicle,* 28 January 1992, 17.

68. Catherine Manegold, "Shannon Faulkner," *New York Times Magazine,* 11 September 1994, 59; Patti Doten, "Clare Dalton Looks Back in Anger," *Boston Globe,* 25 October 1993, 36.

69. For publications, see David Brock, *The Seduction of Hillary Rodham* (New York: Free Press, 1996); Patricia Williams, "Bewitched: The Demonization of Hillary Clinton," *Village Voice,* 26 January 1993, 35. For media charac-

terization, and Clinton's response, see Maureen Dowd, "Hillary Clinton as Aspiring First Lady: Role Model or 'Hall Monitor' Type?" *New York Times,* 18 May 1992, A18; Pat Morrison, "Time for a Feminist First Lady?" *Los Angeles Times,* 14 July 1992, A1; Tim Rutten, "Since When Did Working Women Become the Enemy?" *Los Angeles Times,* 27 August 1992, E1.

70. Kenneth T. Walsh, "How Hillary Clinton Plans a Bold Recasting of the Job Description for a President's Spouse," *U.S. News and World Report,* 25 January 1993, 46; Laura Blumenfeld, "Ultimate Feminist, Hillary Rodham Clinton," *Cosmopolitan,* May 1994, 213 (quoting press secretary).

71. Dowd, "Hillary Clinton," A18 ("yuppie wife"); Hillary Clinton, quoted in Henry Louis Gates, Jr., "Hating Hillary," *New Yorker,* 26 February and 4 March 1996, 116; see James Stewart, *Blood Sport* (New York: Simon and Schuster, 1996).

72. Gates, "Hating Hillary," 119; Peggy Noonan, quoted ibid., 119; Joan Steinau Lester, "Women's Month: Celebration and Concern," *San Francisco Examiner,* 17 March 1996, B11.

73. Clinton, quoted in Dowd, "Hillary Clinton," A18; Julianne Malveaux, "Wise Up Hillary: Women Bake Cookies," *San Francisco Examiner,* March 1993, A13.

74. Anna Quindlen, "The Two Faces of Eve," in *Thinking Out Loud* (New York: Random House, 1993), 197–198; Margery Eagen, "America Is Not Ready for a His and Hers Presidency from the Clintons," *Boston Herald,* 19 March 1992, A8.

75. Blumenfeld, "Ultimate Feminist," 213; Maureen Dowd, "All about Hillary," *New York Times,* 7 January 1996, E19.

76. Blumenfeld, "Ultimate Feminist," 213; Jamieson, *Double Bind,* 41–51.

77. Richard Grenier, "Killer Bimbos," *Commentary,* September 1991, 50; John Leo, "Toxic Feminism in the Big Screen," *U.S. News and World Report,* 10 June 1991, 20; John Robinson, "The Great Debate Over Thelma and Louise: Is It Evil Man-Bashing or a Liberating Fantasy? He Hates It," *Boston Globe,* 14 June 1991, 29.

78. Julie D'Acci, *Defining Women: Television and the Case of Cagney and Lacey* (Chapel Hill: University of North Carolina Press, 1994), 30–35; Faludi, *Backlash,* 151.

79. John Fiske, *Media Matters* (Minneapolis: University of Minnesota Press, 1994), 87.

80. Joyce Millman, "Oscar Is Unforgiven for 'Year of the Woman' Sham," *San Francisco Examiner,* 30 March 1993, A1; Sophie Dembling, "This Tribute Played Like a Bad Movie," *Dallas Morning News,* 2 April 1993, 1C.

81. For Freedom Now and Hamburger Helper, see Douglas, *Where the Girls Are,* 246; Jean Kilbourne, quoted in Nina Burleigh, "Advertisers Still Lagging Behind the Times," *Chicago Tribune,* 7 April 1991, C8. For Nivea, see "Dream Girls," Traveling exhibit of the American Advertising Museum. For Michelob, see Moog, *Selling Her Lips,* 32.

82. Steinem, "Sex," 140, 156–157; see also McCracken, *Women's Magazines,* 38–57.

83. Gregory Cerio and Lucy Howard, "Sorry, One of You Had To Go," *Newsweek,* 21 March 1994, 14.

84. Bob Hohler, "Some See Seeds of Abuse in Culture," *Boston Globe,* 13 October 1992, 21.

85. See Jane L. Levere, "Advertising," *New York Times,* 12 July 1996, C5 (discussing survey). For example, Maidenform pulled an ad featuring a woman professional exposing her underwear in a medical setting under the caption "You Never Know Where She'll Turn Up!" See Moog, *Selling Her Lips,* 26. Calvin Klein discontinued ads that viewers protested as verging on child pornography. See Chapter 3.

5. Sex and Violence

1. David Brock, "The Real Anita Hill," *American Spectator* (March 1992): 18.

2. Steve Kelly, artist, reprinted in Charles Brooks, ed., *Best Editorial Cartoons of the Year: 1991* (New York: Pelican, 1991).

3. See *Code of Federal Regulations,* section 1604 (1981); and cases discussed in Gillian K. Hadfield, "Rational Women: A Test for Sex-Based Harassment," *California Law Review* 83 (1995): 1151, 1158–1166. For male-female complaint ratios, see Marion Crain, "Women, Labor Unions, and Hostile Work Environment Sexual Harassment: The Untold Story," *Texas Journal of Women and the Law* 4 (1995): 9, 18–21; "Man Wins $1 Million Sex-Harassment Suit," *New York Times,* 21 May 1993, A15.

4. Walter Christopher Arbery, "A Step Backward for Equality Principles: The 'Reasonable Woman' Standard in Title VII Hostile Work Environment Sexual Harassment Claims," *Georgia Law Review* 27 (1993): 503, 544 ("overzealous" and "hypersensitive"); Gretchen Morgenson, "May I Have the Pleasure . . . ," *National Review,* 18 November 1991, 36 (dirty joke and "hypersensitive"); Orlando Patterson, "Race, Gender and Liberal Fallacies," *New York Times,* 20 October 1991, 15 ("neopuritan"); Camille Paglia, *Vamps and Tramps* (New York: Vintage, 1994), 48 ("neurotics"); Warren Farrell, *The Myth of Male Power* (New York: Simon and Schuster, 1993), 287 ("liable for look"); John McLaughlin, quoted in Deborah Epstein, "Can a 'Dumb Ass Woman' Achieve Equality in the Workplace? Running the Gauntlet of Hostile Environment Harassing Speech," *Georgetown Law Journal* 84 (1996): 399, 408; John Leo, *Two Steps Ahead of the Thought Police* (New York: Simon and Schuster, 1994), 238 ("unwelcome gazing" and *Playboy*); Katherine Dowling, "Sexual Harassment Jackpot," *Los Angeles Times,* 7 September 1994, B7; Crain, "Sexual Harassment," 39 ("banter" and "horseplay"); John Leo, "An Empty Ruling on Harassment," *U.S. News and World Report,* 29 November 1993, 20 ("McCarthyism"); Christina Hoff Sommers, *Crossfire,* 4 July 1994 ("witch-

hunt"); Stuart Taylor, Jr., "*Real* Sexual Harassment," *Legal Times,* 6 May 1996, 23 ("PC paranoia").

5. Deborah Rhode, *Justice and Gender* (Cambridge, Mass.: Harvard Univ. Press, 1989), 235, n. 14 (cases); *Zabkowicz v. West Bend Co.,* 585 F.Supp. 635 (E. D. Wisc. 1984); *Lipsett v. Rive Mora,* 669 F.Supp. 1188 (D. C. Puerto Rico, 1987); *Rabidue v. Osceola Refining Co.,* 805 F.2d., 611, 620–621 (7th Cir., 1984); *Henson v. City of Dundee,* 682 F.2d 897, 900 n.2 (11th Cir., 1982).

6. For examples of overreaction, see Christina Hoff Sommers, *Who Stole Feminism?* (New York: Simon and Schuster, 1994), 270–271; Andrew Blum, "Profs Sue Schools on Suspensions," *National Law Journal,* 6 June 1994, A6, A7; Barry R. Gross, "Salem in Minnesota," *Academic Questions* (Spring 1992): 67, 70–71. For denials of claims, see *Foster v. Township of Hillside,* 780 F. Supp. 1026 (D. N.J. 1992), aff'd without op. *Foster v. Hillside Police Dep't.,* 977 F.2d 567 (3d Cir., 1992); *Scott v. Sears, Roebuck, & Co.,* 798 F.2d 210, 212 (7th Cir., 1986); *Rabidue v. Osceola Refining Co.,* 805 F.2d. 611 (7th Cir., 1984); *Reed v. Shepard,* 939 F.2d 484, 486–487 (7th Cir., 1991). For further examples, see Epstein, "'Dumb Ass Woman,'" 416.

7. Phyllis Schlafly, quoted in Nancy C. McGlen and Karen O'Connor, *Women's Rights: The Struggle for Equality in the Nineteenth and Twentieth Centuries* (New York: Praeger, 1983), 186. For the frequency of harassment, see Epstein, "'Dumb Ass Woman,'" 403–404; Mary P. Koss, Lisa Goodman, Angela Browne, Louise F. Fitzgerald, Gwendolyn Puryear Keita, and Nancy Felipe Russo, *No Safe Haven: Male Violence against Women at Home, at Work, and in the Community* (Washington, D.C.: American Psychological Association, 1994), 112, 124–126; Louise F. Fitzgerald and Alayne J. Omerod, "Breaking Silence: The Sexual Harassment of Women in Academia and the Workplace," in Florence L. Denmark and Michelle A. Paludi, eds., *Psychology of Women: A Handbook of Issues and Theories* (Westport, Conn.: Greenwood, 1993), 558. For women of color, see Kimberle Crenshaw, "Whose Story Is It Anyway? Feminist and Antiracist Appropriations of Anita Hill," in Toni Morrison, ed., *Raging Justice, En-Gendering Power: Essays on Anita Hill, Clarence Thomas, and the Construction of Social Reality* (New York: Pantheon, 1992): 402. For lesbians, Beth E. Schneider, "Put Up and Shut Up: Workplace Sexual Assaults," in Pauline B. Bart and Eileen Gail Moran, eds., *Violence against Women: The Bloody Footprints* (Newbury Park, Calif.: Sage, 1993), 57, 62–63. For immigrants and other especially vulnerable groups, see National Council for Research on Women, *Sexual Harassment: Research and Resources* (New York: National Council for Research on Women, 1995), 29–32. For lawyers, see ibid., 26–27; Kerry Segrave, *The Sexual Harassment of Women in the Workplace* (Jefferson, N.C.: McFarland, 1994), 204. For military personnel, see Timothy Egan, "A Battleground of Sexual Conflict," *New York Times,* 15 November 1996, A10; Eric Schmitt, "Study Says Sex Harassment Persists at Military Academies," *New York Times,* 5 April 1995, B8; Alison Bass, "Military Remains Lair of Sexual Harassment," *San Francisco Chronicle,* 5 May 1995, 3.

See Department of Defense News Briefing, *Results of the 1995 Sexual Harassment Study* (Washington, D.C.: Department of Defense, 1996).

8. For complaints, see Louise F. Fitzgerald, Suzanne Swan, and Karla Fischer, "Why Didn't She Just Report Him? The Psychological and Legal Implications of Women's Responses to Sexual Harassment," *Journal of Social Issues* 51 (1995): 117; Koss et al., *No Safe Haven*, 135; American Management Association, *Sexual Harassment: Policies and Procedures* (New York: American Management Association, 1996). For awards, see Fitzgerald, Swan, and Fischer, "Why Didn't She Just Report Him?" 123. For advice by critics, see Robert Grant, president of the American Freedom Coalition, quoted in Jane Gross, "Suffering in Silence No More, Women Fight Back on Sexual Harassment," *New York Times,* 14 July 1992.

9. For judges and arbitrators, see Koss et al., *No Safe Haven*, 154; Crain, "Sexual Harassment," 55. For comments on Hill, see Camille Paglia, quoted in "Think Tank with Ben Wattenberg," *Federal News Service,* 4 November 1994, 30.

10. Robert Packwood, quoted in Peter J. Boyer, "The Ogre's Tale," *New Yorker,* 4 April 1994, 37.

11. Barbara Gutek, *Sex and the Workplace* (San Francisco: Jossey-Bass, 1985), 19; Daniel Goleman, "Sexual Harassment: It's about Power, Not Lust," *New York Times,* 22 October 1991, C1; Robert S. Adler and Ellen R. Peirce, "The Legal, Ethical, and Social Implications of the 'Reasonable Woman' Standard in Sexual Harassment Cases," *Fordham Law Review* 61 (1993): 773, 776; Stephen Gillers, quoted in Ruth Rosen, "'Boys Will Be Boys' No Longer Cuts It," *Los Angeles Times,* 29 April 1993, B7 (quoting Gillers).

12. Jane Gross, "When the Biggest Firm Faces Sexual Harassment Suit," *New York Times,* 29 July 1994, B7. The trial court reduced the jury's award of $7.1 million in punitive damages to about $3.5 million. William Vogeler, "Record Verdict Cut," *American Bar Association Journal* (February 1995): 18.

13. Mark Maremont, "Abuse of Power," *Business Week,* 13 May 1996, 86, 89; Maria Shao, "*Mitsubishi* Case Puts Spotlight on Harassment," *Boston Globe,* 28 April 1996, 1.

14. See Rhode, *Justice and Gender,* 232; Koss et al., *No Safe Haven,* 137–138; Segrave, *Sexual Harassment,* 203.

15. For examples, see Susan Estrich, "Sex at Work," *Stanford Law Review* 43 (1991): 813, 833; Crain, "Sexual Harassment," 53–54.

16. Erich Schmitt, "Military Falters on Prosecution in Sex Scandal," *New York Times,* 21 August 1993, 1; Diana B. Henriques, "Sexual Harassment and a Chief Executive," *New York Times,* 30 March 1995, C1.

17. Draft Report of the Judicial Council Advisory Commission on Gender Bias in the Courts, in "Achieving Equal Justice in Litigation and Courtroom Interaction," *Achieving Equal Justice for Women and Men in the Courts* (San Francisco: Judicial Council of California, 1990), 41–42; Shao, "*Mitsubishi*"; *Robinson v. Jacksonville Shipyards,* 760 F.Supp. 1486, 1515–1516 (M.D. Fla. 1991); reporters quoted in Mariah Burton Nelson, *The Stronger Women Get, the More*

Men Love Football: Sexism and the American Culture of Sports (New York: Harcourt, Brace, 1993), 224–228, 240.

18. Alan Dershowitz, "Putting a Gender Bias on Free Speech," *Buffalo News,* 27 July 1993, 3; Nancy Gibbs, "Office Crimes," *Time,* 21 October 1991, 52.

19. For legal standards, see *Meritor Savings Bank v. Vinson,* 477 U.S. 5769 (1986); and cases discussed in Estrich, "Sex at Work," 833. For harassing tactics, see Segrave, *Sexual Harassment,* 221; Ellen E. Schulz and Junda Woo, "Plaintiff's Sex Lives Are Being Laid Bare in Harassment Cases," *Wall Street Journal,* 19 September 1994, A1; Andrea Bernstein, "Sex Harassment Suits: The Fight for Damages Gets Uglier," *Ms.,* July–August 1996, 18–19. For seemingly imperfect plaintiffs, see cases discussed in Rhode, *Justice and Gender,* 235, n. 14; Jane L. Dolkart, "Hostile Environment Harassment: Equality, Objectivity, and the Shaping of Legal Standards," *Emory Law Journal* 43 (1994): 151, 235.

20. Gross, "Biggest Firm," B7; Richard Dunleavy, quoted in John Lancaster, "Tailhook Probe Implicates 140 Officers," *Washington Post,* 24 April 1993, A1; Linda Bird Francke, "The Legacy of Tailhook," *Glamour,* November 1994, 250.

21. Anna Quindlen, "The Perfect Victim," in *Thinking Out Loud* (New York: Random House, 1993), 144; Rush Limbaugh, *The Way Things Ought To Be* (New York: Pocket Books, 1992), 126; Wesley Prouden, "Feminist Hysteria and Sex-Baiting," *Washington Times,* 9 October 1991, A4; Ellen Goodman, "The Justice as Victim," *San Francisco Chronicle,* 20 May 1993, A23. See also David Brock, *The Real Anita Hill: The Untold Story* (New York: Free Press, 1993), criticized in Jane Mayer and Jill Abramson, *Strange Justice: The Selling of Clarence Thomas* (Boston: Houghton Mifflin, 1994), 90–92, 310–315; Rene Denfeld, *The New Victorians* (New York: Warner, 1995), 104 (quoting political aide).

22. Don Lee, "System Is Overloaded by Sexual Harassment," *Los Angeles Times,* 14 June 1995, A1; Catherine Young, "Getting Justice Is No Easy Task," *Business Week,* 13 May 1996, 98.

23. For the risks of complaints, see Segrave, *Sexual Harassment,* 219; Schmitt, "Military Academies," A13; Fitzgerald, Swan, and Fischer, "Why Didn't She Just Report Him?" 9–11. For women's views, see Ronni Sandroff, "Sexual Harassment: The Inside Story," *Working Woman,* June 1992, 47, 50; Fitzgerald, Swan, and Fisher, "Why Didn't She Just Report Him?," 9–11. For the summary, see ibid., 9–11. For the litigant's assessment, see Melissa Clerkin, quoted in Segrave, *Sexual Harassment,* 221.

24. Alex Kozinski, "The False Protection of a Gilded Cage," *The Recorder,* 27 May 1992, 8, 10.

25. *Documents Related to the Investigation of Senator Robert Packwood, Senate Select Committee on Ethics* (Washington, D.C.: Government Printing Office, 1995), quoted in Julia Reed, "The Case of the Kissing Senator," *New York Review of Books,* 1 February 1996, 23.

26. Kozinski, "The False Protection," 10 (mentoring); Lloyd R. Cohen, "Sexual

Harassment and the Law," *Society* (May–June 1991): 8, 10 (dance floor); Farrell, *Male Power,* 293 (courtship).

27. For the survey, see Louise F. Fitzgerald, "Science vs. Myth," *Southern California Law Review* 65 (1992): 1399, 1404. For judicial responses, see *DeAngelis v. El Paso Municipal Officers Association,* 51 F.3rd 591 (5th Cir. 1995); also cases cited in Blum, "Profs Sue" and Gross, "Salem in Massachusetts." For the *Jones* case, see Anna Quindlen, "Public and Private: A Tale of Two Women," *New York Times,* 11 May 1994, A25.

28. J. Harvey Wilkinson, "The Promise and Problems of Sex Harassment Litigation," *Harvard Journal of Law and Social Policy* 18 (1995): 47.

29. *Vermett v. Hough,* 627 F.Supp. 587, 607 (W. D. Mich., 1986). See Drucilla Cornell, *The Imaginary Domain* (New York: Routledge, 1995), 17; Kathryn Abrams, "Sexual Harassment," *Dissent* (Winter 1995): 50–51.

30. 58 Fed. Reg. 1266–1269 (1993) withdrawn, 59 Fed. Reg. 51196 (1994). *Ellison v. Brady,* 924 F.2d. 872 (9th Cir., 1991). For an overview of courts' and commentators' views, as well as proposed but withdrawn EEOC guidelines, see Sarah E. Burns, "Evidence of a Sexually Hostile Workplace: What Is It and How Should It Be Assessed after *Harris v. Forklift Systems, Inc.*," *New York Review of Law and Social Change* 221 (1994): 357.

31. Martha Chamallas, "Feminist Constructions of Objectivity: Multiple Perspectives in Sexual and Racial Harassment Litigation," *Texas Journal of Women and the Law* 1 (1992): 95, 127; Kathryn Abrams, "Title VII and Complex Female Subject," *Michigan Law Review* 92 (1995): 2479. For Internet harassment, see Wayne T. Price, "Harassment Goes On Line: Low-Tech Problem Hits PC Network," *USA Today,* 6 August 1993, B1; Judy DeHaven, "Cyber Crime: High-Tech World Faces Low-Life Realities," *Detroit News,* 10 January 1996, D10.

Cases are divided about whether same-sex harassment constitutes sex discrimination within the prohibitions of federal statutes. See Herma Hill Kay and Martha West, *Sex-Based Discrimination* (St. Paul: West, 1996), 832–834. For the need to ban such harassment, see Kathe Franke, "What's Wrong with Sex Harassment?" *Stanford Law Review* (Forthcoming, 1997).

32. *Gender Bias in the Courts: Report of the Special Joint Committee on Gender Bias in the Courts* (Annapolis, Md.: Committee on Gender Bias in the Courts, 1989), 2–3.

33. For the frequency of domestic violence, see Antonio C. Novella, "A Medical Response to Domestic Violence," *Journal of the American Medical Association* 267 (1992): 3132; Koss et al., *No Safe Haven,* 42; Staff of Senate Committee on the Judiciary, 102nd Congress, 2nd Session, *Violence against Women: A Week in the Life of America* (Washington, D.C.: Government Printing Office, 1992), 3. For homicides, see United States Department of Justice, *Murder in Families* (Washington, D.C.: Government Printing Office, 1994). For costs, see NOW Legal Defense Fund, *Stop Violence against Women: Strategies for Ending Violence against Women* (New York: NOW Legal Defense Fund, 1994).

34. For critics, see Cathy Young, "Crime, the Constitution, and the 'Weaker Sex,'" *Wall Street Journal*, 21 August 1996, A15; Katherine Dunn, "Truth Abuse—The Media's Wife-Beating Hype: Media and the O. J. Simpson Case," *The New Republic*, 1 August 1994, 16; Sommers, *Who Stole Feminism?* 194; For the risks to women, see Don Colburn, "Domestic Violence: AMA President Decries 'A Major Public Health Problem,'" *Washington Post*, 28 June 1994, Z10; Robert Ronet Bachman, *Violence against Women: A National Crime Victimization Survey Report* (Washington, D.C.: Bureau of Justice Statistics Report, 1994); U.S. Department of Justice, *Criminal Victimization in the United States* (Washington, D.C.: Bureau of Justice Statistics Report, 1994); Novella, "Medical Response."

35. For skeptics' allegations, see R. L. McNeely and Gloria Robinson-Simpson, "The Truth about Domestic Violence: A Falsely Framed Issue," in Nicholas Davidson, ed., *Gender Sanity* (Lanham, Md.: University Press of America, 1989), 163, 168–170; "Anti-Male Views Distort Abuse Problems," *Buffalo News*, 18 November 1993, 2 (editorial page). For relevant research, see Ellis Cose, *A Man's World* (New York: Harper Collins, 1995), 226; Koss et al., *No Safe Haven*, 64–73; Russell P. Dobash, R. Emerson Dobash, Margo Wilson, and Martin Daly, "The Myth of Sexual Symmetry in Marital Violence," *Social Problems* 39 (1992): 71.

36. For assertions about comparable assault rates, see Dunn, "Truth Abuse," 16; Sommers, *Who Stole Feminism?* 194–195; Rita J. Simon and Cathy Young, Letter to the editor, *New York Times*, 4 February 1994, A22; Armin Brott, "When Women Abuse Men: It's Far More Widespread Than People Think," *Washington Post*, 28 December 1993, C5. For the National Family Violence Surveys, see Murray A. Straus, "Physical Assaults by Wives: A Major Social Problem," in Richard J. Gelles and Donileen R. Loseke, eds., *Current Controversies in Family Violence* (Newbury Park, Calif.: Sage, 1993), 67. For critiques, Cose, *A Man's World*, 226; Koss et al., *No Safe Haven*, 64–73; Dobash, Dobash, Wilson, and Daly, "The Myth of Sexual Symmetry."

37. James Ptacek, "Why Do Men Batter Their Wives?" in Kersti Yllo and Michele Bogard, eds., *Feminist Perspectives on Wife Abuse* (Newbury Park, Calif.: Sage, 1988): 133, 146; Jan Hoffman, "When Men Hit Women," *New York Times Magazine*, 16 February 1992, 23–24; Adam Jukes, *Why Men Hate Women* (London: Free Association Books, 1993), 274; David Olive, *GenderBabble* (New York: Putnam, 1993), 157.

38. O. J. Simpson, quoted in Frank Rich, "The Second Word," *New York Times*, 14 October 1995, A19; Johnnie Cochran, quoted in Ann Jones, "I Object, Mr. Cochran," *New York Times*, 11 October 1995, E13; Michael Knox, quoted in Katha Pollitt, "Subject to Debate," *The Nation*, 23 October 1995, 457.

39. For denials and devaluation, see *Maryland Report*, 2–3; "Report of the New York Task Force on Women in the Courts," *Fordham Urban Law Journal* 15 (1987): 11, 28–33; Karen Czapansky, "Domestic Violence, the Family, and the Lawyering Process: Lessons from Studies on Gender Bias in the Courts,"

Family Law Quarterly 27 (1993): 247, 252–255. For the survey, see California Judicial Council Advisory Committee on Gender Bias in the Courts, *Achieving Equal Justice for Women and Men in the Courts,* Draft Report (San Francisco: Judicial Council of California, 1990), 92–93. For euphemistic discussions, see Ptacek, "Why Do Men Batter?," 155; Martha Mahoney, "Victimization or Oppression? Women's Lives, Violence and Agency," in Martha Albertson Fineman and Roxanne Mykitiuk, eds., *The Public Nature of Private Violence: The Discovery of Domestic Abuse* (New York: Routledge, 1994), 78; *Blair v. Blair,* 154 Vt. 201, 203–204 (1990). For homicide sentences, see Elizabeth Rapaport, "The Death Penalty and the Domestic Discount," in Fineman and Mykitiuk, eds., *Public Nature,* 224, 230–233.

40. Lynn Hech Schafran, "There's No Accounting for Judges," *Albany Law Review* 58 (1995): 1063, 1066–1067.

41. Ibid.

42. Sheridan Lyons and Michael James, "Man Gets Eighteen-Month Term for Killing Unfaithful Wife," *Baltimore Sun,* 18 October 1994, 1A.

43. Supreme Court of the State of Florida, *Report of the Florida Supreme Court Gender Bias Study Commission* (Tallahassee: Florida Supreme Court, 1990), 14.

44. Schafran, "Judges," 1066–1067.

45. Joyce Purnick, "A Judge Is Called a Symptom of a Failed Law," *New York Times,* 26 February 1996, B10.

46. For police and prosecutors' views, see Lisa Frohmann and Elizabeth Mertz, "Legal Reform and Social Construction: Violence, Gender and the Law," *Law and Social Inquiry* 19 (1994): 829, 837; Eve S. Buzawa and Carl G. Buzawa, "The Scientific Evidence Is Not Conclusive: Arrest Is No Panacea," in Gelles and Loseke, eds., *Current Controversies,* 340. For racial bias, see Linda L. Ammons, "Mules, Madonnas, Babies, Bathwater, Racial Imagery and Stereotypes: The African-American Woman and the Battered Woman Syndrome," *Wisconsin Law Review* (1995): 1003; Kimberle Crenshaw, "Mapping the Margins: Intersectionality, Identity Politics, and Violence against Women of Color," *Stanford Law Review* 43 (1991): 1241. For lack of support from other officials and the resulting cycle of blame, see Pamela Jenkins and Barbara Davidson, "Battered Women in the Criminal Justice System: An Analysis of Gender Stereotypes," *Behavioral Sciences and the Law* 8 (1990): 161; Susan Sward, "O. J. Simpson Case Throws Spotlight on Domestic Violence," *San Francisco Chronicle,* 24 June 1994, A1, A6. Donald G. Dutton, with Susan K. Golant, *The Batterer* (New York: Basic Books, 1995), 11.

47. For prosecution rates, see Adele Harrell, *A Guide to Research on Family Violence, Prepared for Courts and Communities* (Washington, D.C.: Urban Institute, 1993), 41. For misdemeanor classification, see NOW Legal Defense Fund, *Stop Violence against Women,* 5. In some jurisdictions, 90 percent of family violence cases are filed as misdemeanors. Bettina Boxall and Frederick M. Muir, "Prosecutors Taking Harder Line toward Spouse Abuse," *Los Angeles*

Times, 11 July 1994, A1, A16. For jail time, see Ann Jones, *Next Time She'll Be Dead: Battering and How to Stop It* (Boston: Beacon, 1994), 143. In one study, *The American Lawyer* tracked all the domestic-violence arrests that occurred in eleven jurisdictions on Father's Day, 1995. Half the offenders were never prosecuted, and only 10 percent served jail time. Alison Frankel, "Domestic Disaster," *The American Lawyer* (June 1996): 55, 56.

48. For women's needs, see Lee H. Bowker, "A Battered Woman's Problems Are Social, Not Psychological," in Gelles and Loseke, eds., *Current Controversies,* 154, 158. For risks of poverty and homelessness, see Margie Laird McCue, *Domestic Violence: A Reference Handbook* (Santa Barbara, Calif.: ABC-CLIO, 1995), 106–107, 113; Gretchen P. Mullins, "The Battered Woman and Homelessness," *Journal of Law and Policy* 3 (1994): 237. For men's promises, see Dutton, *The Batterer,* 49–57; Raoul Felder and Barbara Victor, *Getting Away with Murder* (New York: Simon and Schuster, 1996), 256.

49. For women's aversion to stereotypical images, see Mahoney, "Women's Lives," 78, 84; Elizabeth Schneider, "The Violence of Privacy," *Connecticut Law Review* 23 (1991): 973, 984. For immigrant and Asian American women, see Leslye E. Orloff, Deeana Jang, and Catherine F. Klein, "With No Place to Turn: Improving Legal Advocacy for Battered Immigrant Women," *Family Law Quarterly* 29 (1995): 313; Kimberly A. Huisman, "Wife Battering in Asian American Communities," *Violence against Women* 2 (1996): 260. For lesbians, see Mary Eaton, "Abuse by Any Other Name: Feminism, Difference, and Intralesbian Violence," in Fineman and Mykitiuk, eds., *Public Nature,* 195; Ruthann Robson, "Lavender Bruises: Intralesbian Violence, Law, and Lesbian Legal Theory," *Golden Gate University Law Review* 20 (1990): 567. For disabled women, see Dick Sobsey, *Abuse in the Lives of People with Disabilities* (Baltimore: Paul H. Brookes, 1994), 163–166. For underreporting, see Buzawa and Buzawa, "Scientific Evidence," 345; Center for Women for Policy Studies, *Violence against Women: Fact Sheet* (Washington, D.C.: Center for Women for Policy Studies, 1994).

50. Jones, *Next Time She'll Be Dead,* 82, 86, 147; Carole Warshaw, "Limitations of the Medical Model in the Care of Battered Women," in Bart and Moran, eds., *Violence against Women,* 134, 139–140.

51. Dutton, *The Batterer,* 39–41; Felder and Victor, *Getting Away with Murder,* 210; Ptacek, "Why Do Men Batter?" 142–148 ("didn't seem motivated"); Jukes, *Why Men Hate Women,* 257, 304; James C. Overholser and Sara H. Moll, "Who's to Blame: Attributions Regarding Causality in Spouse Abuse," *Behavioral Sciences and the Law* 8 (1990): 107, 111; O. J. Simpson, *I Want to Tell You: My Response to Your Letters, Your Messages, Your Questions* (Boston: Little, Brown, 1995), 101–108.

52. Jones, *Next Time She'll Be Dead,* 14; David P. Celani, *The Illusion of Love: Why the Battered Woman Returns to Her Abuser* (New York: Columbia University Press, 1994), 13, 176–187. For Simpson, see sources cited in Sheryl McCarthy, "The Role of the Media in Domestic Violence Cases: A Journalist's Perspec-

tive," *Albany Law Review* 58 (1995): 1235, 1242 and nn. 53–54. For Paglia's views, see *Vamps and Tramps,* 43–44.

53. For women's need for distance, see Kathleen Waits, "Battered Women and Family Lawyers: The Need for an Identification Protocol," *Albany Law Review* 58 (1995): 1027, 1036. For the "just world" belief, see Chapter 1. For the African-American woman's observation, see Jones, *Next Time She'll Be Dead,* 137.

54. Mahoney, "Legal Images," 64–65; Dutton, *The Batterer,* 14–15, 45–46. For protective orders, see Peter Finn, "Civil Protection Orders: A Flawed Opportunity for Intervention," in Michael Steinman, ed., *Woman Battering* (1991), 155–157; *Domestic Violence: Not Just a Family Matter,* Hearing before the Subcommittee on Crime and Criminal Justice, Committee on the Judiciary, House of Representatives, 103rd Congress, 2nd Session, (30 June 1994); Adele Harrell et al., *Court Processing and the Effects of Restraining Orders for Domestic Violence Victims* (Washington, D.C.: Urban Institute, 1993), 49, 61.

55. Koss et al., *No Safe Haven,* 105. For women of color, see Crenshaw, "Mapping the Margins," 1245–1250; Huisman, "Wife Battering"; Orloff, Jang, and Klein, "With No Place to Turn."

56. Lenore E. Walker, *The Battered Woman* (New York: Harper and Row, 1979), 45–51.

57. Farrell, *Male Power,* 261–270. See Sonny Burmeister, quoted in Nancy Gibbs, "'Till Death Do Us Part," *Time,* 18 January 1993, 38; Lawrence S. Wrightsman, *Psychology and the Legal System* (Pacific Grove, Calif.: Brooks/Cole, 1994), 13. Only about 700 of the two to four million women who are abused each year kill their partners; "Figuratively Speaking," *American Bar Association Journal* (July 1996): 14. Between 70 percent and 90 percent of women who kill are being attacked or are being threatened with imminent attack. Holly Maguigan, "Battered Women and Self-Defense: Myths and Misconceptions in Current Reform Proposals," *University of Pennsylvania Law Review* 140 (1991): 379, 384, 397–400. Only about 25–30 percent are acquitted (ibid.).

58. For the adverse effects of stereotypes, see Anne M. Coughlin, "Excusing Women," *California Law Review* 82 (1994): 1, 6; Sharon Angella Allard, "Rethinking Battered-Woman Syndrome: A Black Feminist Perspective," *UCLA Women's Law Journal* 1 (1991): 191, 195. For women's survival strategies, see Bowker, "A Battered Woman's Problems." For the reasons women endure abuse, see ibid.; Mahoney, "Legal Images," 25; Elizabeth M. Schneider, "Feminism and the False Dichotomy of Victimization and Agency," *New York Law School Law Review* 38 (1994): 387, 390.

59. Jones, *Next Time She'll Be Dead,* 37–39; Felder and Victor, *Getting Away with Murder,* 13–17, 169–171.

60. James Smith, quoted in Jones, *Next Time She'll Be Dead,* 39.

61. Don Van Natta, Jr., "Judge under Challenge Is an Eccentric Idealist," *New York Times,* 20 February 1996, B15; Jones, *Next Time She'll Be Dead,* 74–76.

62. For the impact on men, see Richard A. Berk, "What the Scientific Evidence Shows: On the Average, We Can Do No Better Than Arrest," in Gelles and Loseke, eds., *Current Controversies*, 323, 327; Buzawa and Buzawa, "Scientific Evidence Is Not Conclusive"; Joan Zorza, "Must We Stop Arresting Batterers? Analysis and Policy Implications of New Police Domestic Violence Studies," *New England Law Review* 28 (1994): 929. For the risks to women, see Lorraine Dutsky, *Still Unequal* (New York: Crown, 1996), 361; John Johnson, "A New Side to Domestic Violence," *Los Angeles Times,* 27 April 1996, A1, A19.

63. Kathleen J. Ferraro, "Cops, Courts, and Woman Battering," in Bart and Moran, eds., *Violence against Women,* 165, 175; Frohmann and Mertz, "Legal Reform," 837.

64. See Dutton, *The Batterer,* 175–177.

65. Edward Gondolf, *Battered Women as Survivors* (Lexington, Mass.: Lexington Books, 1988), 65–66; Daniel Goleman, "Standard Therapies May Help Only Impulsive Spouse Abuse," *New York Times,* 22 June 1994, C11; Lynn Smith, "Change Is Slow in Therapy Group for Men Who Batter," *Los Angeles Times,* 11 August 1994, A1, A26.

66. See statements of Lawrence W. Sherman and Joan Zorza in *Domestic Violence: Not Just a Family Matter,* 48, 57.

67. Asian Women's Shelter, *The Lotus Project: Family Violence Prevention in the Asian Community* (San Francisco: Asian Women's Shelter, 1992); sources cited in note 49; Felder and Victor, *Getting Away with Murder,* 56, 90–101.

68. For arrest policies, see Ferraro, "Cops"; Frohmann and Mertz, "Legal Reform," 837. For inadequate protection, see Peter Margulies, "Representation of Domestic Violence Survivors as a New Paradigm of Poverty Law: In Search of Access, Connection, and Voice," *George Washington Law Review* 63 (1995): 1071, 1076–1078; Solomon Bialywlos, "Battered Around," *Los Angeles Reader,* 16 September 1994, 12. For G. K. Chesterton's observation, see "The Twelve Men," in *Tremendous Trifles* (New York: Dodd, Mead, 1929), 157–158.

69. Lisa Memoli and Gina Plotino, "Enforcement or Pretense? The Courts and the Domestic Violence Act," *Women's Rights Law Reporter* 15 (1993): 39, 48.

70. For cross-cultural comparisons, see United Nations Development Programme, *Human Development Report, 1993* (New York: Oxford University Press, 1993), 192, table 3. For acquaintance rape, see Joel Epstein and Stacia Langenbahn, *The Criminal Justice and Community Response to Rape* (Washington, D.C.: U.S. Department of Justice, Office of Justice Programs, 1994); National Victim Center and the Crime Victims Research and Treatment Center, *Rape in America: Report to the Nation* (Arlington, Va.: National Victim Center, 1992); *Crime Victimization Survey Report* (Rockville, Md.: Bureau of Justice Statistics Clearinghouse, 1995). For denials, see Paglia, *Vamps and Tramps,* 24; Katie Roiphe, *The Morning After: Sex, Fear, and Feminism on Campus* (Boston: Little, Brown, 1993), 52; Susan Faludi, "Whose Hype?" *Newsweek,* 25 Octo-

ber 1993, 61. For child sexual abuse, see Dean D. Knudsen, "Child Sexual Coercion," in Elizabeth Grauerholz and Mary A. Koralewski, eds., *Sexual Coercion: A Sourcebook on Its Nature, Causes and Prevention* (Lexington, Mass.: Lexington Books, 1991).

71. Paglia, *Vamps and Tramps*, 24, 32; Roiphe, *The Morning After;* John Leo, "Don't Oversimplify Date Rape," *U.S. News and World Report*, 11 February 1991, 17; Neil Gilbert, "Counterpoint: A Few Women Want to Speak for Both Sexes," *San Francisco Chronicle*, 26 June 1991, A17; Mary Matalin, "Stop Whining!" *Newsweek*, 25 October 1993, 63.

72. Rhode, *Justice and Gender*, 245; Susan Estrich, *Real Rape* (Cambridge, Mass.: Harvard University Press, 1987).

73. Lance Morrow, "Men: Are They Really That Bad?" *Time*, 14 February 1994, 52; Margaret D. Bonilla, "Cultural Assault: What Feminists Are Doing to Rape Ought to be a Crime," *Policy Review*, October 1993, 22; Paglia, *Vamps and Tramps*, 36–37.

74. For the frequency of rape and attempted rape, see National Victim Center, *Rape in America* (New York: Vintage, 1994); Patricia A. Harney and Charlene Muehlenhard, "Rape," in Grauerholz and Koralewski, eds., *Sexual Coercion*, 3; Mary P. Koss and Mary R. Harvey, *The Rape Victim: Clinical and Community Interventions*, 2nd ed. (Newbury Park, Calif.: Sage, 1991), 19–27, 262–263. For underreporting, see U. S. Senate, Committee on the Judiciary, Majority Staff Report, 103rd Congress, 1st Session, *The Response to Rape: Detours on the Road to Equal Justice* (Washington, D.C.: Government Printing Office, 1993), 8. For women of color, see Koss et al., *No Safe Haven*, 203; Patricia H. Collins, *Black Feminist Thought: Knowledge, Consciousness and the Politics of Empowerment* (New York: Routledge, 1991), 178.

75. For characteristics of the offense and offenders, see Laurie Bechhofer and Andrea Parrot, "What Is Acquaintance Rape?" in Bechhofer and Parrot, eds., *Acquaintance Rape: The Hidden Crime* (New York: Wiley, 1991), 9–11; Isla L. Lottes, "Sexual Socialization and Attitudes toward Rape," in Ann Wolbert Burgess, ed., *Rape and Sexual Assault, II* (New York: Garland, 1988), 195; Susan B. Sorenson and Jacquelyn W. White, "Adult Sexual Assault: Overview of Research," *Journal of Social Issues* 48 (1992): 1; Lynn H. Schafran, "Writing and Reading about Rape: A Primer," *St. John's Law Review* 66 (1993): 979, 1003; For surveys of men, see Lynne Henderson, "Rape and Responsibility," *Law and Philosophy* 11 (1993): 127, 170; Gregory Matoesian, *Reproducing Rape: Domination through Talk in the Courtroom* (Chicago: University of Chicago Press, 1993), 9; Robin Warshaw, *I Never Called It Rape: The Ms. Report on Recognizing, Fighting, and Surviving Date and Acquaintance Rape* (New York: Harper and Row, 1988), 11–14 (describing Mary Koss's research); Susan Basow, *Gender: Stereotypes and Roles* (Pacific Grove, Calif.: Brooks/Cole, 1992), 318.

76. For statements blurring the distinction between rape and sex see Chapter 4; also Morrow, "Men: Are They Really That Bad?" For the unwillingness to label

rapes, see Warshaw, *I Never Called It Rape;* Koss and Harvey, *The Rape Victim.* For the normalcy of offenders, see Judith Lewis Herman, "Considering Sex Offenders: A Model of Addiction," in Patricia Searles and Ronald J. Berger, *Rape and Society* (Boulder, Colo.: Westview, 1996), 74, 77–79.

77. Diana Scully, *Understanding Sexual Violence: A Study of Convicted Rapists* (Boston: Unwim Hyman, 1990); Eugene J. Kanin, "Date Rape: Unofficial Criminals and Victims," *Victimology: An International Journal* 9 (1984): 95; Barry Burkhart and Mary Ellen Fromuth, "Individual Psychological and Social Psychological Understandings of Sexual Coercion," in Grauerholz and Koralewski, eds., *Sexual Coercion,* 79–83; Julie A. Allison and Lawrence S. Wrightsman, *Rape: The Misunderstood Crime* (Newbury Park, Calif.: Sage, 1993), 29.

78. Peggy Reeves Sanday, *Female Power and Male Dominance: On the Origins of Sexual Inequality* (New York: Cambridge University Press, 1981); Matoesian, *Reproducing Rape,* 8–12.

79. For the spur posse, see Nelson, *The Stronger Women Get, the More Men Love Football,* 82; and Chapter 1. For the Glen Ridge rape, see Michael Querques, quoted in Karen Houppert, "Boystown," *Village Voice,* 10 November 1992, 11; Joseph Phalon, "It Happened—But Could She Consent?" *National Law Journal,* 28 December 1992, 8.

80. Lea Haller, quoted in Lynn Hecht Schafran, "The Importance of Voir Dire in Rape Trials," *Trial* (August 1992): 26. For research and examples, see ibid.; also Linda Fairstein, *Sexual Violence: Our War against Rape* (New York: William Morrow, 1993), 135.

81. Bobby Knight, quoted in Nelson, *The Stronger Women Get,* 87; Clayton Williams, quoted in *Ms.,* January–February 1991, 15; Missouri mayor quoted in Allison and Wrightsman, *Rape,* 2; Tyson, quoted in Don Bickley, "Agony and Ecstasy," *Chicago Sun-Times,* 27 December 1992, 20.

82. Epstein and Langenbahn, *The Criminal Justice and Community Response to Rape,* 66 (bruises); Nelson, *The Stronger Women Get,* 154 (hair); Massachusetts Supreme Court Justice Jerome Marks, quoted in Anthony M. DeStefano, "Judge Outlasts Outcry: Recertified Despite Feminist Protest," *Newsday,* 3 July 1989, A8 (torture); *New York v. Garay* (Sup. Ct., March 11, 1992), discussed in Lynn Schafran, "Maiming the Soul: Judges, Sentencing, and the Myth of the Nonviolent Rapist," *Fordham Urban Law Journal* 20 (1993): 439, 440 (violence).

83. Senate Judiciary Committee, *The Response to Rape,* 12; Schafran, "Primer," 1005–1006; Ray F. Herndon, "Race Tilts the Scales of Justice," *Dallas Times Herald,* 9 August 1990, A1.

84. Sheila James Kuehl, "Legal Remedies for Teen Dating Violence," in Barrie Levy, ed., *Dating Violence: Young Women in Danger* (Seattle: Seal Press, 1991), 209–222; Rachel Singer, "Journey to Justice," *Ms.,* November–December 1994; Epstein and Langenbahn, *The Criminal Justice Response,* 137.

85. Paglia, *Vamps and Tramps,* 25, 33; Peggy Reeves Sanday, *Fraternity Gang Rape* (New York: New York University Press, 1990), and Peggy Reeves Sanday, *A Woman Scorned: Acquaintance Rape on Trial* (New York: Doubleday, 1996).

86. Compare Marcia Pally, *Sex and Sensibility: Reflections on Forbidden Mirrors and the Will to Censor* (Hopewell, N.J.: Ecco, 1994), 151, with Henderson, "Rape and Responsibility," 165–166. See also Warshaw, *I Never Called It Rape;* Koss and Harvey, *The Rape Victim.*

87. Schafran, "Primer," 978–985; National Victim Center, *Rape in America* (70 percent of rapes involve no other physical injury); Bonnie L. Katz, "The Psychological Impact of Stranger Versus Nonstranger Rape on Victims' Recovery," in Bechhofer and Parrot, eds., *Acquaintance Rape,* 251–253; Christine A. Gidycz and Mary P. Koss, "The Effects of Acquaintance Rape on the Female Victim," ibid., 270.

88. Roiphe, *The Morning After,* 45; Meier, quoted in Dianne Herman, "The Rape Culture," in Jo Freeman, ed., *Women: A Feminist Perspective,* 2nd ed. (Palo Alto, Calif.: Mayfield, 1979), 41, 53.

89. Sommers, *Who Stole Feminism?* 120; Margaret T. Gordon and Stephanie Riger, *The Female Fear* (New York: Free Press, 1989).

90. Sanday, *A Woman Scorned,* 238; John Leo, *Two Steps Ahead of the Thought Police* (New York: Simon and Schuster, 1994), 247; Sanday, *A Woman Scorned,* 43–46, 223–227 (quoting juror).

91. John Leo, "Date Rape," 17; discussed in Sanday, *A Woman Scorned,* 48.

92. Alan Dershowitz, *The Abuse Excuse* (Boston: Little, Brown, 1994), 275.

93. For proof problems, see Estrich, *Real Rape;* Senate Judiciary Committee, *The Response to Rape,* 9; Schafran, "Primer," 1004. For false reports, see Helen Benedict, *Virgin or Vamp: How the Press Covers Sex Crime* (New York: Oxford University Press, 1992), 18; Candy Cooper, "Nowhere to Turn for Rape Victims," *San Francisco Examiner,* 1 February 1992, A1; Schafran, "Primer," 1013.

94. For the lack of incentives to file any rape claim, see Patricia Yancey Martin and R. Marlene Powell, "Accounting for the 'Second Assault': Legal Organizations' Framing of Rape Victims," *Law and Social Inquiry* 19 (1994): 853. For conviction rates, see Epstein and Langenbahn, *The Criminal Justice Response,* 12; Gary LaFree, *Rape and Criminal Justice* (Belmont, Calif.: Wadsworth, 1989), 218–228. For jury perceptions, see ibid., 95–107; Lynne Henderson, "Getting to Know: Honoring Women in Law and in Fact," *Texas Journal of Women and the Law* 2 (1993): 41.

95. Benedict, *Virgin or Vamp,* 13; *Time,* 3 June 1991, 50–51; John Dwight Ingram, "It's Time for 'NO' to Really Mean 'NO,'" *American Journal of Criminal Law* 21 (1993): 4, 7–11. See also Colleen A. Ward, *Attitudes toward Rape: Feminist and Social Psychological Perspectives* (Thousand Oaks, Calif.: Sage, 1995), 44–82; Steve Jackson, "The Social Context of Rape: Sexual Scripts and Motivation," in Searles and Berger, eds., *Rape and Society,* 21.

96. For examples, see *State v. Colbath,* 540 A2d 1212 (New Hampshire, 1988); LaFree, *Rape,* 218–228; Henderson, "Getting to Know," 60–64; John Ingram, "Date Rape," *American Journal of Criminal Law* 21 (1993): 3, 19–21. For warnings, see Ann Landers, "A Male Viewpoint on Date Rape," *St. Louis Post-Dispatch,* 4 August 1991, 11C; Henderson, "Rape and Responsibility," 131. For assumptions about Scrabble, see *State v. Rusk,* 424 A 2d 720, at 733–734 (Cole J., dissenting).

97. Elizabeth Kessler, "Pattern of Sexual Conduct Evidence and Present Consent: Limiting the Admissibility of Sexual History Evidence in Rape Prosecutions," *Women's Rights Law Reporter* 14 (1992): 79; Bob Wilson, quoted in Martin and Powell, "Second Assault," 854. For an example, see Peter Laufer, *A Question of Consent* (San Francisco: Mercury House, 1994), 64–70.

98. Katha Pollitt, "Media Goes Wilding in Palm Beach," *The Nation,* 24 June 1991, 833; Sanday, *A Woman Scorned,* 219.

99. For complaints and risks to complainants, see Crenshaw, "Whose Story Is It Anyway?" 413; Collins, *Black Feminist Thought,* 178–179; LaFree, *Rape,* 219–220; Nelson, *The Stronger Women Get,* 129–137. For the Tyson case, see Kevin Brown, "The Social Construction of a Rape Victim: Stories of African-American Males about the Rape of Desiree Washington," *University of Illinois Law Review* (1992): 997; Ammons, "Mules, Madonnas, Babies, Bathwater," 1003, 1007 n. 117. For the basketball case, see Nelson, *The Stronger Women Get,* 129, 137.

100. Schafran, "Maiming the Soul: Judges, Sentencing, and the Myth of the Nonviolent Rapist," 439, 447.

101. Ibid., 447–448. Sanday, *A Woman Scorned.*

102. Jacqueline D. Goodchilds, Gail L. Zellman, Paula B. Johnson, and Roseanne Giarrusso, "Adolescents and Their Perceptions of Sexual Interactions," in Ann W. Burgess, ed., *Rape and Sexual Assault,* vol. 2 (New York: Garland, 1984), 245.

103. Warshaw, *I Never Called It Rape,* 46; Charlotte Muehlenhard and I. Hollabaugh, "Do Women Sometimes Say No When They Mean Yes? The Prevalence and Correlates of Women's Token Resistance to Sex," *Journal of Personality and Social Psychology* 54 (1988): 872.

104. National Victim Center, *Rape in America,* 14; Py Bateman, "The Context of Date Rape," in Levy, ed., *Dating Violence,* 94, 95; Marybeth Roden, "A Model Secondary School Date Rape Prevention Program," ibid., 267; Nelson, *The Stronger Women Get,* 130–132; Dana Mack, "What the Sex Educators Teach," *Commentary* 96 (August 1993): 33.

105. Cassia Spahn and Julie Horney, *Rape Law Reform* (New York: Plenum, 1992), 153–175; Ronald J. Berger, Patricia Searles, and W. Lawrence Newman, "Rape Law Reform: Its Nature, Origins, and Impact," in Searles and Berger, eds., *Rape and Society,* 223–229.

106. National Victim Center, *Rape in America,* 13–14; Epstein and Langenbahn,

The Criminal Justice Response; Ingram, "It's Time for 'NO' to Really Mean 'NO.'"

107. For characterizations of antipornography activists, see Paglia, *Vamps and Tramps,* 108, 111; Dershowitz, *The Abuse Excuse,* 271–274; for characterizations of anticensorship activists, see Catharine MacKinnon, *Feminism Unmodified: Discourses on Life and Law* (Cambridge, Mass.: Harvard University Press, 1987), 205; Catharine MacKinnon, quoted in Lynn Chancer, "Pornography Debates Reconsidered," *New Politics* 2 (1988): 74.

108. Catharine MacKinnon, quoted in Paul Brest and Amy Vandenberg, "Politics, Feminism, and the Constitution: The Anti-Pornography Movement in Minneapolis," *Stanford Law Review* 39 (1987): 607, 623.

109. For a historical overview, see Paul S. Boyer, *Purity in Print: The Vice-Society Movement and Book Censorship in America* (New York: Scribner's, 1968); Rhode, *Justice and Gender,* 263–267. For the current standard, see *Miller v. California,* 413 U.S. 15 (1973).

110. Kathleen Sullivan, "The First Amendment Wars," *The New Republic,* 28 September 1992, 38. See Cass R. Sunstein, *Democracy and the Problem of Free Speech* (New York: Free Press, 1993), 211.

111. Laura Kipnis, *Bound and Gagged: Pornography and the Politics of Fantasy in America* (New York: Grove, 1996), 161; Ronald K. L. Collins and David M. Stover, "The Pornographic State," *Harvard Law Review* 107 (1994): 1374, 1382, 1383. For examples, see Diana E. H. Russell, "Introduction," in Russell, ed., *Making Violence Sexy: Feminist Views on Pornography* (New York: Teachers College Press, 1993), 16; Marty Rimm, "Marketing Pornography on the Information Superhighway: A Survey of 917,410 Images, Descriptions, Short Stories, and Animations Downloaded 8.5 Million Times by Consumers in 2,000 Cities in Forty Countries, Provinces, and Territories," *Georgetown Law Journal* 83 (1995): 1849, 1899–1902, 1919–1920.

112. Nadine Strossen, *Defending Pornography: Free Speech, Sex, and the Fight for Women's Rights* (New York: Scribner's, 1995), 21, 22, 26; Sunstein, *Democracy and the Problem of Free Speech,* 210–211; for other examples, see Marjorie Heins, *Sex, Sin, and Blasphemy: A Guide to America's Censorship Wars* (New York: New Press, 1993); Pally, *Sex and Sensibility,* 2–7; Karen DeCrow, "Being a Feminist Means You Are against Sexism, Not against Sex," *New York Law School Law Review* 38 (1993): 359, 360, 364–365.

113. *American Booksellers Assn., Inc., v. Hudnut,* 771 F.2d 323 (7th Circ. 1985), aff'd *Hudnut v. American Booksellers Assn., Inc.,* 475 U.S. 1132 (1986). The ordinance also prohibited using men, children or transsexuals in the place of women. For congressional initiatives, see *Communications Decency Act of 1996,* 18 U.S. Code Annotated section 1462 (1996); *Pornography Victims Compensation Act,* S. Rep. no. 1521, 102nd Congress, 2nd Session (1992).

114. Robin Morgan, *Going Too Far: The Personal Chronicle of a Feminist* (New York: Random House, 1977), 169; Russell, "Pornography and Rape:

A Causal Model," in Russell, ed., *Making Violence Sexy*, 150; Strossen, *Defending Pornography*, 251; Gore Vidal quoted in David Futrelle, "The Politics of Porn, Shameful Pleasures," *In These Times*, 7 March 1994, 17.

115. For examples of abuse, see Brest and Vandenberg, "Pornography"; Russell, ed., *Making Violence Sexy*, 23–62; U.S. Department of Justice, *Attorney General's Commission on Pornography: Final Report* (Washington D.C.: U.S. Department of Justice, 1986). For workers' claims, see Strossen, *Defending Pornography*, 182–188; "From the Floor," in Laurie Bell, ed., *Good Girls / Bad Girls: Feminists and Sex Trade Workers Face to Face* (Seattle: Seal Press, 1987). For the difficulties involved in suppressing pornography, see Richard A. Posner, *Overcoming Law* (Cambridge, Mass.: Harvard University Press, 1995), 361.

116. Strossen, *Defending Pornography*, 253–258; Pally, *Sex and Sensibility*, 99–108.

117. For male learning, see Jukes, *Why Men Hate Women*, 172; Russell, "Pornography and Rape," 132–133. For examples, see Alice Mayall and Diana Russell, "Racism in Pornography," in Russell, ed., *Making Violence Sexy*, 169–175; Rhode, *Justice and Gender*, 271; Gloria Cowan, "Racism and Sexism in Pornography," in Laura J. Lederer and Richard Delgado, eds., *The Price We Pay: The Case against Racist Speech, Hate Propaganda, and Pornography* (New York: Hill and Wang, 1995), 92. For the effect of these messages, see *American Booksellers Assn., Inc., v. Hudnut*, 771 F.2d at 328.

118. Mary R. Murrin and D. R. Laws, "The Influence of Pornography on Sex Crimes," in W. L. Marshall et al., eds., *Handbook on Sexual Assault: Issues, Theories, and Treatment of the Offender* (1990), 73; Russell, "Pornography and Rape," 133–138; Edward Donnerstein, Daniel Linz, and Steven Penrod, *The Question of Pornography: Research Findings and Policy Implications* (New York: Free Press, 1987); *Attorney General's Commission, Final Report*, 322–347; Edward Donnerstein, "Pornography: Its Effects on Violence against Women," in Neil M. Malamuth and Edward Donnerstein, eds., *Pornography and Sexual Aggression* (Orlando, Fla.: Academic Press, 1984), 53–81. For experts' claims about violence, see William A. Fisher and Guy Grenier, "Violent Pornography, Antiwoman Thoughts, and Antiwoman Acts: In Search of Reliable Effects," *Journal of Sex Research* 31 (1994): 23; Edward Donnerstein and Daniel Linz, Hearing before the Committee on the Judiciary, United States Senate, on *The Pornography Victims' Compensation Act of 1991 and the Pornography Victims' Protection Act of 1991*, 101st Congress, 2nd Session, 135–145; sources cited in Pally, *Sex and Sensibility*, 51–57. For the percent of the pornography market, see Carlin Meyer, "Sex, Sin, and Women's Liberation: Against Porn Suppression," *Texas Law Review* 72 (1994): 1097, 1185–1186, n. 424; Pally, *Sex and Sensibility*, 33. For offenders, see Richard Randall, *Freedom and Taboo* (Berkeley: University of California Press, 1989), 109; Strossen, *Defending Pornography*, 253.

119. Malamuth and Donnerstein, eds., *Pornography and Sexual Aggression*, 589–

602; Randall, *Freedom and Taboo,* 95–109; Larry Baron and Murray A. Straus, *Four Theories of Rape in American Society: A State-Level Analysis* (New Haven: Yale University Press, 1989), 186–187 (finding a correlation between circulation of pornography and rape but doubting that the relationship is causal).

120. National Television Violence Study, *Scientific Papers* (Santa Barbara: University of California, Mediascope, 1995); Brandon S. Centerwall, "Television and Violence: The Scale of the Problem and Where To Go from Here," *Journal of the American Medical Association* 267 (1992): 3059. See Ch. 3.

121. Sullivan, "First Amendment Wars," 39.

122. *American Booksellers Assn., Inc., v. Hudnut,* 771 F. 2d at 328.

123. Nan Hunter and Sylvia Law, "Brief Amici Curiae of Feminist Anti-Censorship Task Force et al., in *American Booksellers Assn., Inc., v. Hudnut*" (Fact brief), reprinted in *University of Michigan Journal of Law Reform* 69 (1987–1988): 108; *Butler v. Regina,* 1 S.C. R 452, 478–479 (Canada, 1992); Jeffrey Toobin, "X-Rated," *New Yorker,* 3 October 1994; Leanne Katz, "Introduction: Women, Censorship and Pornography," *New York Law School Law Review* 38 (1993): 12, 13.

124. Edward Donnerstein and Daniel Linz, "Debate on Pornography," *Film Comment* (December 1984): 35. For the absence of limiting principles, see Ronald Dworkin, "Women and Pornography," *New York Review of Books,* 21 October 1993, 36.

125. For surveys, see Collins and Stover, "Pornographic State," 1383–1384; and Ann McClentock, "Gonad the Barbarian and the Venus Flytrap," in Lynne Segal and Mary McIntosh, eds., *Sex Exposed: Sexuality and the Pornography Debate* (New Brunswick, N.J.: Rutgers University Press, 1993), 111, 130. For women's interests, see Ellen Willis, "Feminism, Moralism, and Pornography," in Ann Snitow, Christine Stansell, and Sharon Thompson, *Powers of Desire: The Politics of Sexuality* (New York: Monthly Review Press, 1983), 4.

126. The quotes are from Meyer, "Sex, Sin, and Women's Liberation," 1133; and Carlin Meyer, "Reclaiming Sex from the Pornographers: Cybersexual Possibilities," *Georgetown Law Journal* 83 (1995): 1969, 1974. See Strossen, "Defending Pornography," 163–165, 260–261; Randall, *Freedom and Taboo,* 129; Paul R. Abramson and Steven D. Pinkerton, *With Pleasure* (New York: Oxford University Press, 1995).

127. Kipnis, *Bound and Gagged,* 166–167, 203; Meyer, "Reclaiming Sex," 1989.

128. Sunstein, *Democracy and the Problem of Free Speech,* 225; Attorney General's Commission on Pornography, *Final Report, II* (Washington, D.C.: U.S. Department of Justice, 1986), 1505–1506, 1534, 1550–1557.

129. Lisa Steele, "A Capital Idea: Gendering in the Mass Media," in Varda Burstyn, ed., *Women against Censorship* (Vancouver: Douglas and McIntyre, 1985), 58, 61; Michael D'Andre, quoted in Lisa Duggan and Ann Snitow, "Pornography Is about Images, Not Power," *Newsday,* 26 September 1984, 65. See also Lisa Duggan, "Censorship in the Name of Feminism," in Lisa Duggan

and Nan D. Hunter, *Sex Wars: Sexual Dissent and Political Culture* (New York: Routledge, 1995), 30, 40.

130. Meyer, "Reclaiming Sex," 1989; Donnerstein, Linz, and Penrod, *The Question of Pornography*, 171–196; Margaret Jean Intons-Peterson, Beverly Roskos-Ewoldsen, Laura Thomas, Mary Shirley, and Dafna Blut, "Will Educational Materials Reduce Negative Effects of Exposure to Sexual Violence?" *Journal of Social and Clinical Psychology* 8 (1989): 256.

131. Catharine MacKinnon, Personal communication, January 18, 1997; idem, "Speech, Equality, and Harm: The Case against Pornography," in Leder and Delgado, eds., *The Price We Pay*, 301, 302–303; Catharine MacKinnon, "Pornography, Civil Rights, and Speech," *Harvard Civil Rights–Civil Liberties Law Review* 20 (1985): 1, 63.

132. Carole S. Vance, *Pleasure and Danger* (Boston: Routledge, 1984), 24.

6. Women's Work

1. American Bar Association [ABA] Commission on Women in the Profession, *Unfinished Business: Overcoming the Sisyphus Factor* (Chicago: American Bar Association, 1996), 10–13, 24; Cynthia Fuchs Epstein, Robert Saute, Bonnie Oglensky, and Martha Gever, "Glass Ceilings and Open Doors: Women's Advancement in the Legal Profession—A Report to the Committee on Women in the Profession of the Bar of the City of New York," reprinted in *Fordham Law Review* 64 (1995): 291; Chris Klein, "Women's Progress Slows at Top Firms," *National Law Journal*, 6 May 1996, 1; Deborah L. Rhode, "Gender and Professional Roles," *Fordham Law Review* (1994): 39, 57–58.

2. Federal Glass Ceiling Commission, *Good for Business: Making Full Use of the Nation's Human Capital*, Fact-Finding Report, Bureau of National Affairs, Daily Labor Report (17 March 1995), 528, 531; Deborah J. Swiss and Judith P. Walker, *Women and the Work/Family Dilemma* (New York: Joseph Wiley, 1993), 5 (citing Feminist Majority Foundation study); Judith H. Dobrzynski, "Somber News for Women on Corporate Ladder," *New York Times*, 6 November 1996, C1.

3. Equal Employment Opportunity Commission, *Federal and Private Sector Employment Data: Executive Summary* (Washington, D.C.: Equal Employment Opportunity Commission, Office of Communication and Legislative Affairs, March 1995), 4; Barbara Bergmann, *In Defense of Affirmative Action* (New York: Basic Books, 1996), 42. For involuntary underemployment and part-time work, see Chris Tilly, *Half a Job* (Philadelphia: Temple University Press, 1996), 1–12; Edward J. McCaffrey, *Taxing Women* (Chicago: University of Chicago Press, 1997); and idem, "Equality of the Right Sort," *University of California at Los Angeles Women's Law Review* 6 (1996): 289, 298–304.

4. Kathleen Gerson, *No Man's Land: Men's Changing Commitments to Family and Work* (New York: Basic Books, 1993), 5–6, 8; Susan A. Basow, *Gender Stereotypes and Roles* (Pacific Grove, Calif.: Brooks/Cole, 1992), 247; Asra

Q. Nomani, "A F ourth-Grader's Hard Lesson: Boys Earn More Money Than Girls," *Wall Street Journal,* 7 July 1995, B1. See also Chapter 3.

5. Rene Denfeld, *The New Victorians* (New York: Warner, 1995), 250. See also Laura A. Ingraham, "Enter, Women," *New York Times,* 19 April 1995, A17; Herbert Stein, "White Male Rage Sweeps America," *Wall Street Journal,* 9 February 1995, A14. For views of CEOs, see Federal Glass Ceiling Commission, *Good for Business,* 577, 634-635. See also Catalyst, *Women in Corporate Leadership: Progress and Prospects* (New York: Catalyst, 1996), 136 (finding that over 80 percent of male CEOs blamed female managers' lack of experience for their underrepresentation).

6. Federal Glass Ceiling Commission, *Good for Business,* 637; Korn/Ferry International, *Decade of the Executive Woman* (1993), discussed in Nancy Rivera Brooks, "Gender Pay Gap Found at Highest Corporate Levels," *Los Angeles Times,* 30 June 1993, A1, A20; Beth Corbin, "Women Go Center Stage in Affirmative Action Debate," *National NOW Times,* May-June 1995, 1, 3. For women's perceptions of bias, see U.S. Department of Labor, Women's Bureau, *Working Women Count: A Report to the Nation* (Washington, D.C.: U.S. Department of Labor, Women's Bureau, October 1994), 16, 21; "Gender Issues in the Workplace," *San Jose Mercury News,* 25 February 1992, A12. For women's experience of discrimination and sense of its importance, see Women's Bureau, *Working Women Count,* 35-36; Roper Starch Worldwide, *The 1995 Virginia Slims Opinion Poll* (Storrs, Conn.: Roper Center for Public Opinion Research, 1995), 24.

7. Richard A. Epstein, *Forbidden Grounds: The Case against Employment Discrimination Law* (Cambridge, Mass.: Harvard University Press, 1992), 41-42, 102; Katherine Post and Michael Lynch, "Free Markets, Free Choices: Women in the Workforce" (San Francisco: Pacific Research Institute, 1995), 5-19; George Gilder, "The Myth of the Role Reversal," in Nicholas Davidson, ed., *Gender Sanity* (Lanham, Md.: University Press of America, 1989), 227, 237.

8. Gary S. Becker, *The Economics of Discrimination,* 2nd ed. (Chicago: University of Chicago Press, 1971), 13-17; Ruth Milkman, *Gender at Work: The Dynamics of Job Segregation by Sex during World War II* (Urbana: University of Illinois Press, 1987), 2, 6, 123-125.

9. "Women as Colleagues Can Turn Men Off," *Wall Street Journal,* 29 October 1991, B1; Federal Glass Ceiling Commission, *Good for Business,* 552. See also Judith Lorber, *Paradoxes of Gender* (New Haven: Yale University Press, 1994), 237-238.

10. U.S. Congress, *Department of Defense Authorization for Appropriations for Fiscal Years 1992 and 1993: Hearings before the Subcommittee on Manpower and Personnel of the Senate Committee on Armed Services,* 102nd Congress, 1st Session (1991), 838 (statement of General Merril McPeak, chief of staff, Air Force).

11. "Greener Pastures," *Perspectives: American Bar Association Commission on the Status of Women Newsletter* (Summer 1995): 3; Federal Glass Ceiling Commis-

sion, *Good for Business,* 585–586, 609, 620–621, 635. See also Catalyst, *Cracking the Glass Ceiling: Strategies for Success* (New York: Catalyst, 1994), 15.

12. For stereotypes, see Kay Deaux and Mary Kite, "Gender Stereotypes," in Florence L. Denmark and Michele A. Paludi, eds., *Psychology of Women: A Handbook of Issues and Theories* (1993), 107, 111; Linda Krieger, "The Content of Our Categories: A Cognitive Bias Approach to Discrimination and Equal Employment Opportunity," *Stanford Law Review* 47 (1995): 1161. For evaluation biases, see Barbara F. Reskin, "Bringing the Men Back In: Sex Differentiation and the Devaluation of Women's Work," in Judith Lorber and Susan A. Farrell, eds., *The Social Construction of Gender* (Newbury Park, Calif.: Sage, 1991), 141, 145–146; Rhode, "Gender and Professional Roles," 66.

13. ABC News, *Prime Time Live,* "The Fairer Sex," 7 October 1993. Fletcher A. Blanchard, "Effective Affirmative Action Programs," in Blanchard and Faye Crosby, eds., *Affirmative Action in Perspective* (New York: Springer Verlag, 1989), 193, 198; Cecilia Conrad, "The Economic Cost of Affirmative Action," in Margaret Simms, ed., *Economic Perspectives on Affirmative Action* (Washington, D.C.: Joint Center for Political and Economic Studies, 1995), 41.

14. *Johnson v. Transportation Agency,* 480 U.S. 616, 623–625 (1987).

15. Susan Faludi, "I Paid a Price for Wanting to Earn a Living: You Always Pay a Price," *West,* 27 September 1987, 18.

16. Martha Minow, "Forward: Justice Engendered," *Harvard Law Review* 101 (1987): 10, 46–47; Faludi, "You Always Pay a Price."

17. For studies, see Brenda Major, "Gender Differences in Comparisons and Entitlement," *Journal of Social Issues* 45 (1989): 97–101; Michele Adrisin Wittig and Rosemary Hays Lowe, "Comparable Worth Theory and Practice," *Journal of Social Issues* 45 (1989): 1, 7. For pay scales, see Sherrye Henry, *The Deep Divide: Why American Women Resist Equality* (New York: Macmillan, 1994), 179; National Committee on Pay Equity, *The Wage Gap* (Washington, D.C.: National Committee on Pay Equity), 3.

18. For sociobiological assumptions, see Camille Paglia, *Vamps and Tramps* (New York: Vintage, 1994), 31; Richard Posner, "An Economic Analysis of Sex Discrimination Law," *Chicago Law Review* 56 (1989): 1311, 1315; Kingsley R. Browne, "Sex and Temperament in Modern Society: A Darwinian View of the Glass Ceiling and the Gender Gap," *Arizona Law Review* 37 (1995): 971. For human-capital theories, see Gary S. Becker, *A Treatise on the Family* (Cambridge, Mass.: Harvard University Press, 1981), 14–26; Diana Furchtgott-Roth and Christina Stolbo, *Women's Figures* (Washington, D.C.: American Enterprise Institute, 1996), 7–12; June O'Neal, "The Shrinking Pay Gap," *Wall Street Journal,* 7 October 1994, A12. See generally, Epstein, *Forbidden Grounds.*

19. Warren Farrell, *The Myth of Male Power* (New York: Simon and Schuster, 1993), 105–109, 117–119.

20. For women's choices, see Paula England, *Comparable Worth: Theories and Evidence* (New York: Aldine de Gruyter, 1992); Vicki Shultz, "Telling Stories about Women and Work: Judicial Interpretations of Sex Segregation in the

Workplace in Title VII Cases Raising the Lack of Interest Argument," *Harvard Law Review* 103B (1990): 1750. For gender gap studies, see Elaine Sorensen, *Comparable Worth: Is It a Worthy Policy?* (Princeton, N.J.: Princeton University Press, 1994), 114; Claudia Goldin, *Understanding the Gender Gap: An Economic History of American Women* (New York: Oxford University Press, 1990), 105; Gillian Hadfield, "Households at War: Beyond Labor Market Policies to Remedy the Gender Gap," *Georgetown Law Journal* 82 (1993): 89–91. For a critical review of this literature see Steven E. Rhoads, *Incomparable Worth* (Cambridge: Cambridge University Press, 1993), 11–19. For examples of different advancement patterns, see Federal Glass Ceiling Commission, *Good for Business;* ABA Young Lawyers Division, *The State of the Legal Profession* (Chicago: American Bar Association, 1992), 63. For networks and harassment, see Susan Antilla, "Young White Men Only, Please," *New York Times,* 26 April 1995, C1, C7; and Chapter 5, above.

21. Maud Lavin, "Waging War on Wages," *New Woman,* February 1995, 126–128; Bergmann, *Affirmative Action,* 42.

22. Cynthia Starnes, "Divorce and the Displaced Homemaker: A Discourse on Playing with Dolls, Partnership Buyouts, and Dissociation under No-Fault," *University of Chicago Law Review* 60 (1993): 67, 72; Gerson, *No Man's Land,* 5–6; Marilyn Kennedy Melia, "Who Does What around the House and Why?" *Chicago Tribune,* 7 May 1995, A1 (a survey of 4,500 dual-career couples with children finds that men report doing a median of about five hours of domestic work per week and women report a median of about twenty hours); Patricia Wald, quoted in Joan Williams, "Gender Wars: Selfless Women in the Republic of Choice," *New York University Law Review* 66B (1991): 1559, 1611.

23. The first quote is from Lillian B. Rubin, *Families on the Fault Line* (New York: Harper Collins, 1994), 89. The others are from Gerson, *No Man's Land,* 189, 184, 186, 104.

24. Roper, *1995 Virginia Slims Poll,* 50; Gerson, *No Man's Land,* 190, 197, 194; Rhona Mahony, *Kidding Ourselves* (New York: Basic Books, 1995).

25. For perceptions about hours, see Terri Apter, *Secret Paths: Women in the New Midlife* (New York: Norton, 1995), 119. For perceptions about work and career sacrifice, see Rubin, *Families,* 85; Roberta A. Sigel, *Ambition and Accommodation: How Women View Gender Relations* (Chicago: University of Chicago Press, 1996), 97. For assumptions about women's easier lives, see Gerson, *No Man's Land,* 190; Aaron Kipnis and Elizabeth Herron, *Gender War, Gender Peace* (New York: Morrow, 1994), 62–63.

26. Carol Lawson, "A New Spokesman (Yes, Man) for Childcare," *New York Times,* 30 April 1992, B5.

27. Arlie Hochschild with Ann Machung, *The Second Shift* (New York: Viking, 1989), 43.

28. William Galston, quoted in Hillary Rodham Clinton, *It Takes a Village* (New York: Simon and Schuster, 1996), 216.

29. For employers' reluctance, see Sue Shellenbarger, "Family-Friendly Firms Often Leave Fathers Out of the Picture," *Wall Street Journal,* 2 November

1994, B1; Martin H. Malin, "Fathers and Parental Leave," *Texas Law Review* 72 (1994): 1047, 1072–1079. For fathers' reluctance, see Shari Rudavsky, "New Fathers Reluctant to Take Time Out," *Washington Post,* 7 July 1992, A3; Paula Span, "A Man Can Take 'Maternity' Leave . . . and Love It," *Redbook,* May 1995, 54.

30. For colleagues' attitudes, see Anne B. Fisher, *Wall Street Women* (New York: Knopf, 1990), 13. See also Diane Eyer, *Motherguilt* (New York: Time Books, 1996), 172, 200. For men's excuses, see Span, "A Man Can Take 'Maternity' Leave," 56. For the Williams case, see Sam Howe Verhovek, "At Issue: Hold a Baby or Hold That Line," *New York Times,* 20 October 1993, A1.

31. Sue Shellenbarger, "If You Want a Firm That's Family Friendly, the List Is Very Short," *Wall Street Journal,* 6 Sept. 1995, B1; Williams, "Gender Wars," 1598–1600; Swiss and Walker, *Women and the Work/Family Dilemma,* 10, 26–28, 36, 91, 219–220. For women's views, see ibid., 10; Dobrzynski, "Somber News," C6.

32. Renee M. Landers, James B. Rebitzer, and Lowell J. Taylor, "Rat Race Redux: Adverse Selection in the Determination of Work Habits in Law Firms," *American Economic Review* 86 (1996): 329. Epstein et al., "Glass Ceilings," 385; See also Harvard Women's Law Association, *Presumed Equal: What America's Top Women Lawyers Really Think about Their Firms* (Cambridge, Mass.: Harvard Women's Law Association, 1995), 68; Catalyst, *Women in Corporate Leadership,* 58.

33. Nell B. Strachan, "A Map for Women on the Road to Success," *American Bar Association Journal* 70 (1984): 94, 96.

34. Commission on Family and Medical Leave, *A Workable Balance: Report to Congress on Family and Medical Leave Policies* (Washington, D.C.: Women's Bureau, U.S. Department of Labor, 1996), 61–65. For example, women disproportionately lack unemployment coverage because they do not earn enough income or work enough hours, or because they leave positions due to sexual harassment, family emergencies, or childcare problems. Diana Pearce, *When Harassment Happens: An Analysis of State Unemployment Insurance Coverage of Workers Who Leave Employment Because of Sexual Harassment* (Washington, D.C.: Wider Opportunities for Women, 1992).

35. Suzanne Helburn et al., *Cost, Quality, and Child Outcomes in Child Care Centers* (Denver, Colo.: University of Colorado at Denver, 1995), 2, 9.

36. For studies on care, see Ellen Galinsky, Carollee Howes, and Marybeth Shinn, *Public Policy Report: The Study of Children in Family Care and Relative Care: Key Policy Findings and Recommendations* (Washington, D.C.: National Association for the Education of Young Children, 1994). For representative claims about the "disasters" for children from the women's movement, see David Gerlenter, "Why Mothers Should Stay Home," *Commentary* 101 (1996): 25. For the effect on children, see research summarized in Carol Sanger, "Separating from Children," *Columbia Law Review* 96 (1996): 401, 506–507, 513; Eyer, *Motherguilt,* 196–197; Susan Chira, "Study Says Babies in Child Care Keep Secure Bonds to Mothers," *New York Times,* 21 April 1996, A1.

37. For inadequacies in licensing standards, unlicensed care, and parental informa-
    tion, see Helburn et al., *Cost, Quality, and Child Outcomes;* William T. Gorm-
    ley, Jr., *Everybody's Children: Child Care as a Public Problem* (Washington,
    D.C.: Brookings Institute, 1995), 4–29, 172. For inadequacies in financial
    assistance, see Eyer, *Motherguilt,* 178; Peter Pitegoff, "Child Care Enterprise
    Community Development and Work," *Georgetown Law Journal* 81 (1993):
    1897, 1905–1908; Gormley, *Everybody's Children,* 24–25, 46–48. Ellen Galin-
    sky and James T. Bond, "Work and Family: The Experiences of Mothers and
    Fathers in the U.S. Labor Force," in Cynthia Costello and Barbara Kivimae
    Krimgold, eds., *The American Woman, 1996–1997* (New York: Norton, 1996),
    79, 95. For stress and dissatisfaction, see ibid., 80, 85. For women's prefer-
    ences, see Tilly, *Half a Job,* 3.

38. Christine Himes, *Parental Caregiving by Adult Women: A Demographic Per-
    spective* (University Park, Pa.: Population Research Institute, 1994); Paula B.
    Doress-Worters, "Adding Elder Care to Women's Multiple Roles: A Critical
    Review of the Caregiver Stress and Multiple Roles Literature," *Sex Roles* 31
    (1994): 597, 601–603, 611–612.

39. See Eyer, *Motherguilt,* 203–227; Gormley, *Everybody's Children,* 81, 175–176;
    Ruth Sidel, *Keeping Women and Children Last* (New York: Penguin, 1996),
    181–189.

40. Urvashi Vaid, *Virtual Equality: The Mainstreaming of Gay and Lesbian Libera-
    tion* (New York: Anchor Books, Doubleday, 1995). Only nine states prohibit
    job discrimination on the basis of sexual orientation, and in 1996 the Senate
    defeated a measure that would have imposed federal prohibitions. Marcia
    Stepanek, "Anti-Gay Marriage Bill Passes Senate," *San Francisco Examiner,* 10
    September 1996, A1. "Los Angeles County Bar Association Report on Sexual
    Orientation Bias," reprinted in *Southern California Review of Law and
    Women's Studies* 4 (1995): 295, 297, 305; Kara Swisher, "Coming Out in
    Corporate America," *Working Woman* (July–August 1986): 80.

41. Gregory M. Herek, "Heterosexuals' Attitudes Toward Lesbians and Gay Men:
    Correlates and Gender Differences," *Journal of Sex Research* 25 (1988): 451,
    470–473; Andrew Koppelman, "Why Discrimination against Lesbians and Gay
    Men Is Sex Discrimination," *New York University Law Review* 69 (1994): 197,
    234–238. For examples, see *DeSantis v. Pacific Telephone and Telegraph Co.,*
    608 F.2d 327 (9th Cir., 1979); *Hopkins v. Price Waterhouse,* 618 F. Supp. 1109,
    1117 (D.D.C., 1985), rev'd in part and remanded, 490 U.S. 228 (1988); and
    sources cited in Deborah L. Rhode, "Sex-Based Discrimination: Common
    Legacies and Common Challenges," *University of Southern California Review
    of Law and Women's Studies* 5 (1996): 11.

42. Eyer, *Motherguilt,* 200; Sue Shellenbarger, "Many Employers Flout Family and
    Medical Leave Law," *Wall Street Journal,* 26 July 1994, B1.

43. Diane Harris, "You're Pregnant? You're Out," *Working Woman,* August 1992,
    48, 51; Deborah L. Jacobs, "Back from the Mommy Track," *New York Times,*
    9 October 1994, B1, B6.

44. For barriers of information and cost, see Sigel, *Ambition and Accommodation,* 107–110; Bergmann, *Affirmative Action,* 173–176; Jonathan S. Leonard, "Use of Enforcement Techniques in Eliminating Glass Ceiling Barriers," (Washington D.C.: United States Department of Labor, Glass Ceiling Commission, April 1994). For the backlog, see Nina Schuyler, "Discrimination Doldrums," *California Lawyer,* February 1995, 24. See also Harris, "You're Pregnant," 51; and Joan E. Rigdon, "Three Decades after the Equal Pay Act, Women's Wages Remain Far from Parity," *Wall Street Journal,* 9 June 1993, B1.

45. Krieger, "The Content of Our Categories." An example involves *EEOC v. Sears, Roebuck & Co.,* 628 F.Supp. 1264, (N.D. Ill., 1986).

46. See *Johnson v. Transportation Agency of Santa Clara County,* 480 U.S. 616, 657 (1987), (Scalia, J., dissenting); cases cited in Shultz, "Telling Stories," 1802–1803; *EEOC v. Sears,* 628 F.Supp. at 1294–1295, 1308–1315.

47. Ruth Milkman, "Women's History and the *Sears* Case," *Feminist Studies* 12 (1986): 375–386; see also Jon Wiener, "The Sears Case: Women's History on Trial," *The Nation,* 7 September 1985, 161, 178; John Wiener, "Exchange," *The Nation,* 26 October 1985, 410; Shultz, "Telling Stories," 1793.

48. For women's choices, see Molly Martin, ed., *Hard-Hatted Women: Stories of Struggle and Success in the Trades* (Seattle: Seal Press, 1988), 71–73, 150; Mary Lindenstein Walshok, *Blue-Collar Women: Pioneers on the Male Frontier* (Garden City, N.Y.: Doubleday, 1981), 120, 134–138. For Sears' inaction, see Milkman, "Women's History," 376, 380–381.

49. *Riordan v. Kempiners,* 831 F.2d (7th Cir., 1987), 690, 697; Antilla, "Young White Men Only, Please," C7.

50. Ralph Baxter, Jr., and Thomas Klein, "Protecting against Exposure," *National Law Journal,* 28 February 1994, 51.

51. *Price Waterhouse v. Hopkins,* 490 U.S. 228, 277 (1989) (O'Connor, J. concurring) ("stray remarks"); *Watson v. Fort Worth Bank & Trust,* 487 U.S. 977, 990 (1988) (bank teller); *Heim v. State of Utah,* 8 F.3d 1541, 1546 (10th Cir., 1993) ("fucking women"). See also *Cesaro v. Lakeville Community School,* 953 F.2d 252 (6th Cir., 1992) (although the defendant's superintendent announced that he did not want to promote a woman, the plaintiff could not prove she was the most qualified applicant).

52. *Zahorik v. Cornell University,* 729 F.2d 85, 89–90 (2nd Cir., 1984). See Mary Anne C. Case, "Disaggregating Gender from Sex and Sexual Orientation: The Effeminate Man in Law and Feminist Jurisprudence," *Yale Law Journal* 105 (1995): 1, 71 and n. 243.

53. Under the Civil Rights Act of 1991, if the plaintiff shows that sex was a motivating factor but the employer demonstrates that the same action would have been taken irrespective of the plaintiff's sex, remedies are limited to declaratory and injunctive relief and attorneys' fees. Damages or reinstatement are unavailable. For a discussion of the case law see Krieger, "The Content of Our Categories."

54. See Krieger, "The Content of Our Categories"; Basow, *Gender Stereotypes*, 277–293; Federal Glass Ceiling Commission, *Good for Business*, 531, 585–589; American Bar Association Multicultural Women Attorneys Network, *The Burdens of Both, the Privileges of Neither* (Chicago: American Bar Association, 1994).

55. *Price Waterhouse v. Hopkins*, 490 U.S. 228 (1989), on remand, 737 F.Supp. 1202 (D.D.C., 1990), aff'd 920 F.2d 967 (D.C. Cir. U.S. 1990); see Martha Chamallas, "Listening to Dr. Fiske: The Easy Case of *Price Waterhouse v. Hopkins*," *Vermont Law Review* 15 (1990): 89.

56. *Ezold v. Wolf, Block, Schorr & Solis-Cohen*, 983 F.2d 509 (3rd Cir., 1992), cert. denied, 114 S.Ct. 88 (1993).

57. Faludi, "You Always Pay a Price."

58. See cases discussed in Deborah L. Rhode, *Justice and Gender* (Cambridge, Mass.: Harvard University Press, 1989), 183; Bergmann, *Affirmative Action*, 170–173. For women's descriptions, see George R. LaNoue and Barbara A. Lee, *Academics in Court: The Consequences of Faculty Discrimination Litigation* (Ann Arbor: University of Michigan Press, 1987), 216; for the infrequency of employment discrimination litigation, see Kristin Bumiller, *The Civil Rights Society: The Social Construction of Victims* (Baltimore: Johns Hopkins University Press, 1988); American Bar Association, Consortium on Legal Services and the Public, *Legal Needs and Civil Justice: A Study of Americans—Major Findings of the Comprehensive Legal Needs Study* (1994), 13–19; Sigel, *Ambition and Accommodation*, 103–110.

59. See Krieger, "The Content of Our Categories"; David Benjamin Oppenheimer, "Negligent Discrimination," *University of Pennsylvania Law Review* 141 (1993): 899.

60. Equal Employment Opportunity Commission, *The EEOC and Affirmative Action* (Washington D.C.: Equal Employment Opportunity Commission, Office of Communications and Legislative Affairs, 1995); "EEOC Guidelines on Affirmative Action," *Code of Federal Register* 29, section 1608.

61. *Boston Globe*, 29 December 1992, 14; David Gates, "White Male Paranoia," *Newsweek*, 29 March 1995, 48; Bergmann, *Affirmative Action*, 1.

62. For research on effectiveness, see Gertrude Ezorsky, *Racism and Justice: The Case for Affirmative Action* (Ithaca, N.Y.: Cornell University Press, 1991), 4; Nicholas Lehmann, "Taking Affirmative Action Apart," *New York Times Magazine*, 11 June 1995, 36, 43; Jay Matheus, "Reevaluating Affirmative Action," *Washington Post*, 4 July 1995, E1. See, generally, Bergmann, *Affirmative Action;* Susan D. Clayton and Faye S. Crosby, *Justice, Gender and Affirmative Action* (Ann Arbor: University of Michigan Press, 1992). For polls, see Susan Sward, "Women Split on Affirmative Action," *San Francisco Chronicle*, 31 March 1995, A1, A4; Ellen Ladowsky, "That's No White Male," *Wall Street Journal*, 27 March 1995, A18; Philip Hagar, "Not in the Affirmative," *California Lawyer*, April 1995, 27, 29.

63. Bergmann, *Affirmative Action*, 32; Sward, "Women Split"; Elizabeth Larson,

"Through the Feminist Looking Glass," *The Defender,* 1995, 4. For family loyalty, see Steven A. Holmes, "Defending Affirmative Action," *New York Times,* 2 March 1995, B7. See Ladowsky, "That's No White Male"; and Sonya Jason, "That's My Son," *Wall Street Journal,* 27 March 1995, A18; Frederick R. Lynch, *Invisible Victims: White Males and the Crisis of Affirmative Action* (New York: Greenwood, 1989), 75.

64. Michael Kinsley, "The Spoils of Victimhood," *New Yorker,* 27 March 1995, 60. See also Michele Galen and Ann Therese Palmer, "White, Male, and Worried," *Business Week,* 31 January 1994, 50; John F. Dovidio, Jeffrey Mann, and Samuel L. Gaertner, "Resistance to Affirmative Action: The Implications of Aversive Racism," in Fletcher A. Blanchard and Faye S. Crosby, *Affirmative Action in Perspective* (New York: Springer Verlag, 1989), 83, 84–88.

65. *Adarand Constructors, Inc., v. Frederico Pena* 115 S.Ct. 2097, 2119 (1995) (Thomas, J., concurring).

66. Jason, "That's My Son." See also Stephen L. Carter, *Reflections of an Affirmative Action Baby* (New York: Basic Books, 1991), 71–80; Gates, "Paranoia," 48. For white women, see James Scanlan, "Affirmative Action for Women: New Twist on an Old Debate," *Legal Times,* 5 December 1988, 17. See, generally, Antonin Scalia, "The Disease as Cure: 'In Order to Get Beyond Racism, We Must First Take Account of Race,'" *Washington University Law Quarterly* (1979): 147.

67. Trey Ellis, "How Does It Feel To Be a Problem," in Don Belton, ed., *Speak My Name: Black Men on Masculinity and the American Dream* (Boston: Beacon, 1995): 9.

68. Kinsley, "Spoils of Victimhood," 63; Katha Pollitt, *Reasonable Creatures: Essays on Women and Feminism* (New York: Knopf, 1994), 83; Jocelyn C. Frye, "Affirmative Action: Understanding the Past and Present," in Costello and Krimgold, eds., *American Woman,* 33, 41.

69. American Society for Personnel Administration, amicus curiae brief, quoted in *Johnson v. Transportation Agency of Santa Clara County,* 480 U.S. 616, 641 (1987); Susan Faludi, Unpublished Address, Stanford University, Stanford, California, March, 1996.

70. See *Hopwood v. State of Texas,* 1996 U.S. App. LEXIS 9919 (5th Cir., 1996); Wallace D. Loh, "On a Path toward Cultural Diversity," *Seattle Times,* 12 March 1995, B5.

71. For surveys, see Frances Kahn Zemans and Victor G. Rosenblum, *The Making of a Public Profession* (Chicago: American Bar Foundation, 1981), 163–164. For law schools' responsibility, see Paul Brest and Miranda Oshige, "Affirmative Action for Whom?" *Stanford Law Review* 47 (1995): 855, 852, 862.

72. For law school, see Lehmann, "Affirmative Action," 52. For effectiveness, see Ezorsky, *Racism and Justice;* Jonathan S. Leonard, "Use of Enforcement Techniques in Eliminating Glass Ceiling Barriers" (Washington, D.C.: U.S. Department of Labor, Glass Ceiling Commission, 1994), 18–22.

73. Shelby Steele, *The Content of Our Character: A New Vision of Race in America* (New York: St. Martin's, 1990), 119.

74. For research, see Dovidio, Mann, and Gaertner, "Resistance to Affirmative Action," 84.

75. For the absence of declines in performance, see sources cited in Dovidio, Mann, and Gaertner, "Resistance to Affirmative Action," 98–102; Rhode, *Justice and Gender,* 187; Leonard, "Affirmative Action"; Cecilia A. Conrad, "The Economic Cost of Affirmative Action," in Margaret C. Simms, ed., *Economic Perspectives on Affirmative Action* (Washington, D.C.: Joint Center for Political and Economic Studies, 1995), 33, 39. For the absence of meritorious reverse discrimination claims, see Kevin Merida, "Reverse Discrimination Rejected: Study Finds Many Claims by White Men 'Without Merit,'" *Houston Chronicle,* 1 April 1995, A5.

76. Ellis Cose, *A Man's World* (New York: Harper Collins, 1995), 45; Lynch, *Invisible Victims,* 3, 79.

77. Robin Wilson, "Among White Males, Jokes and Anecdotes," *Chronicle of Higher Education,* 28 April 1995, A20; Kipnis and Herron, *Gender War, Gender Peace,* 64.

78. For the history, see LaNoue and Lee, *Academics in Court;* Susan L. Gabriel and Isaiah Smithson, eds., *Gender in the Classroom: Power and Pedagogy* Urbana: University of Illinois Press, 1990). For the current market, see Wilson, "Among White Males," A20.

79. Carter, *Affirmative Action Baby,* 72.

80. For polls, see Women's Bureau, *Working Women Count,* 7, 19, 21; Roper, *1995 Virginia Slims Opinion Poll,* 19. For an overview of initiatives, see Joan Acker, *Doing Comparable Worth: Gender, Class, and Pay Equity* (Philadelphia: Temple University Press, 1989); Rhode, *Justice and Gender,* 190–197; William J. Clinton, "Proclamation 6883, National Pay Inequity Awareness Day, 1996," *Weekly Compilation of Presidential Documents* 32 (1996): 651; Michael W. McCann, *Rights at Work* (Chicago: University of Chicago Press, 1994). For the lack of recent initiatives, see ibid., 27; Harry Bernstein, "Closing the Wage Gap—Job Equality: Despite Some Gains in Women's Pay, the Idea of 'Comparable Worth' Languishes," *Los Angeles Times,* 8 April 1993, B7.

81. See sources cited in Rhode, *Justice and Gender,* 191; and Ronnie J. Steinberg, "[The] Social Construction of Skill: Gender, Power, and Comparable Worth," *Work and Occupation* 17 (1990): 449; National Committee on Pay Equity, *Pay Equity: An Issue of Race, Ethnicity, and Sex* (Washington, D.C.: National Committee on Pay Equity, 1987), 76–104.

82. For conservative denunciations, see Joyce P. Jacobsen, "The Economics of Comparable Worth: Some Theoretical Considerations," in M. Anne Hill and Mark R. Killingsworth, eds., *Comparable Worth: Analyses and Evidence* (Ithaca, N.Y.: ILR Press, Cornell University, 1989): 36–50; Linda M. Blum, *Between Feminism and Labor: The Significance of Comparable Worth* (Berkeley: University of California Press, 1991), 52; Lawson, "Women in State Jobs Gain in Pay Equity," *New York Times,* 20 May 1985, C12 (quoting Clarence Pendleton, Jr.). For claims of adverse effects, see Ellen Frankel Paul, *Equity and Gender: The Comparable Worth Debate* (New Brunswick, N.J.: Transaction, 1989),

55–57, 118–126; Rhoads, *Incomparable Worth,* 16–40, 226–246. For critiques from the left, see Acker, *Doing Comparable Worth,* 100–101, 167–169, 200–212; Johanna Brenner, "Feminist Political Discourses: Radical Versus Liberal Approaches to the Feminization of Poverty and Comparable Worth," *Gender and Society* 1 (1987): 457, 458–461.

83. See David Lauter, "How to Factor the Value of Workers' Skills," *National Law Journal,* 2 January 1984, 24; Helburn et al., *Cost, Quality, and Child Outcomes,* 4, 10–12; Gormley, *Everybody's Children,* 166.

84. Jerry A. Jacobs and Ronnie J. Steinberg, "Further Evidence on Compensating Differentials and the Gender Gap in Wages," in Jerry A. Jacobs and Ronnie J. Steinberg, eds., *Gender Inequality at Work* (Thousand Oaks, Calif.: Sage, 1995).

85. Robert L. Nelson and William B. Bridges, "Legalizing Gender Inequality," Working manuscript, American Bar Foundation, Chicago, 1996; Judy Fudge and Patricia McDermott, "Pay Equity in a Declining Economy: The Challenge Ahead," in Fudge and McDermott, eds., *Just Wages: A Feminist Assessment of Pay Equity* (Toronto: University of Toronto Press, 1991), 281–288; Heidi I. Hartmann, "Comparable Worth and Women's Economic Independence," in Christine Bose and Glenna Spitze, eds., *Ingredients for Women's Employment Policy* (Albany: State University of New York Press, 1987), 251, 256.

86. For the inadequacy of reforms, see Acker, *Doing Comparable Worth;* Julianne Malveaux, "Comparable Worth and Its Impact on Black Women," in Peggy Kahn and Elizabeth Meehan, eds., *Equal Value / Comparable Worth in the UK and the USA* (New York: St. Martin's, 1992), 82–93. For the positive effects of reform, see Institute for Women's Policy Research, *Pay Equity and the Wage Gap: Success in the States* (Washington, D.C.: Institute for Women's Policy Research, 1995).

87. For the limits of reform in these states, see McCann, *Rights at Work,* 196–204; Acker, *Doing Comparable Worth,* 100–101, 167–169, 209–212; Brenner, "Feminist Political Discourses," 459. For salary adjustments and costs, see McCann, *Rights at Work,* 280; Institute for Women's Policy Research, *Pay Equity;* Elaine Joy Sorensen, *Comparable Worth: Is It a Worthy Policy?* (Princeton, N.J.: Princeton University Press), 114.

88. See McCann, *Rights at Work,* 230–280; Linda M. Blum, "Gender and Class in Comparable Worth," in Kahn and Meehan, eds., *Equal Value / Comparable Worth,* 95, 110–111. For income inequalities, see Keith Bradsher, "Gap in Wealth in U.S. Called Widest in West," *New York Times,* 17 April 1995; A1. For pay comparisons, see Sorensen, *Comparable Worth,* 8.

89. Leviticus, 27:3–4.

90. Susan Faludi, "Swedish Sojourn," *Ms.,* March–April 1996, 64–70.

7. Family Values

1. See William F. Buckley, "Blame Illegitimate Births, Too," *San Diego Union Tribune,* 15 May 1992, B14 (riots); Thomas B. Edsall, "Understanding Okla-

homa: Masculinity on the Run: From Workplace to Bedroom—to Timothy McVeigh," *Washington Post*, 30 April 1995, C1 (bombings).

2. See political leaders quoted in Martha Fineman, *The Neutered Mother, the Sexual Family, and Other Twentieth Century Tragedies* (New York: Routledge, 1995), 113–114; and Tamar Lewin, "Creating Fathers Out of Men with Children," *New York Times*, 18 June 1995, A10. For deadbeat dads, see Diane Eyer, *Motherguilt* (New York: Times Books, 1996), 146–153; and the discussion below.

3. Lewin, "Creating Fathers," A10; Terry Lugaila, *Households, Families and Children: A Thirty-Year Perspective*, Series P-23, no. 181 (Washington, D.C.: U.S. Department of Commerce, 1992), 8; Sara McLanahan and Gary Sandefur, *Growing Up with a Single Parent: What Hurts, What Helps* (Cambridge, Mass.: Harvard University Press, 1994); Deborah L. Rhode, "Adolescent Pregnancy and Public Policy," in Annette Lawson and Deborah L. Rhode, eds., *The Politics of Pregnancy: Adolescent Sexuality and Public Policy* (New Haven: Yale University Press, 1993), 301, 316. For poverty, see Steven A. Holmes, "More Families in Poverty; Out of Wedlock Births Reach Record Levels," *New York Times*, 24 July 1994, D2. For teenage mothers, see Elizabeth Mulroy and Marcy Pitt-Catsouphes, *Single Parents in the Workplace* (Boston: Boston University Center on Work and Family, 1994); Eyer, *Motherguilt*, 28; Rhode, "Adolescent Pregnancy," 312. For children of single parents, see McLanahan and Sandefur, *Single Parent*, 1–4; David Blankenhorn, *Fatherless America: Confronting Our Most Urgent Social Problem* (New York: Basic Books, 1995); David Popenoe, *Life without Father* (New York: Free Press, 1996), 9, 55–61; Nancy E. Dowd, "Stigmatizing Single Parents," *Harvard Women's Law Journal* 19 (1995): 19, 20–27, 35–41.

4. For poverty and women of color, see Evelyn Nakano Glenn, "Social Constructions of Mothering: A Thematic Overview," in Evelyn Nakano Glenn, Grace Chang, and Linda Rennie Forcey, eds., *Mothering: Ideology, Experience, and Agency* (New York: Routledge, 1994), 1, 5. For poverty and dissatisfaction, see Stephanie Coontz, *The Way We Never Were: American Families and the Nostalgia Trap* (New York: Basic Books, 1992), 29; and Deborah L. Rhode, *Justice and Gender* (Cambridge, Mass.: Harvard University Press, 1989), 53.

5. See the public opinion polls summarized in Nancy Gibbs, "The Vicious Cycle," *Time*, 20 June 1994, 24, 26; the politicians quoted in Mark Robert Rank, *Living on the Edge: The Realities of Welfare in America* (New York: Columbia University Press, 1994), 3; and the commentary noted in Diana Pearce, "'Children Having Children': Teenage Pregnancy and Public Policy from the Woman's Perspective," in Lawson and Rhode, eds., *Politics of Pregnancy*, 46.

6. Rank, *Living on the Edge*, 8–9 (estimating that only 7 percent of the poverty population lives in low-income large urban areas); Institute for Women's Policy Research, *Few Welfare Moms Fit the Stereotypes* (Washington, D.C.: Institute for Women's Policy Research, 1995), 1–3; Rhode, "Adolescent Pregnancy," 313; *Wider Opportunities for Women: Fact Sheet—Teen Pregnancy Welfare and Poverty* (Washington, D.C.: Wider Opportunities for Women, 1994); Barbara

Vobejda, "Birthrate among Teenage Girls Declines Slightly," *Washington Post,* 26 October 1994, A3.

7. See sources cited in Rhode, *Justice and Gender,* 146; Gregory M. Herek, "Myths about Sexual Orientation: A Lawyer's Guide to Social Science Research," *Law and Sexuality* 1 (1991): 133, 157–161; Nancy D. Polikoff, "This Child Does Have Two Mothers: Redefining Parenthood to Meet the Needs of Children in Lesbian-Mother and Other Nontraditional Families," *Georgetown Law Journal* 78 (1990): 157, 161. For same-sex marriages, see William N. Eskridge, *The Case for Same-Sex Marriage* (New York: Free Press, 1996).

8. For critiques of formal equality, see Lenore J. Weitzman, *The Divorce Revolution* (New York: Free Press, 1985), xi, 357–401; Martha Albertson Fineman, *The Illusion of Equality: The Rhetoric and Reality of Divorce Reform* (Chicago: University of Chicago Press, 1991), 53–75. For criticism of feminists, see Nicholas Davidson, *The Failure of Feminism* (Buffalo, N.Y.: Prometheus, 1988), 315. See F. Carolyn Graglia, "The Housewife as Pariah," *Harvard Journal of Law and Public Policy* 18 (1995): 509, 510.

9. For "taxation without representation," see Warren Farrell, *The Myth of Male Power* (New York: Simon and Schuster, 1993), 368. For other claims, see Randy Salzman, "Deadbeat Dad Divorces Fact from Fiction," *Wall Street Journal,* 3 February 1993, A14; Kathleen Gerson, *No Man's Land: Men's Changing Commitments to Family and Work* (New York: Basic Books, 1993), 130–131. For the economic plight of deadbeat dads, see Davidson, *Failure of Feminism,* 315. See also Thom Weidlich, "Divorce Turns Ex-Husbands into Crusaders," *National Law Journal,* 24 July 1995, A1, A22.

10. Colorado Supreme Court Task Force on Gender Bias in the Courts, *Final Report* (Denver, Colo., 1990), 18; California judge, quoted in Graglia, "Pariah," 511; Laura Mansnerus, "The Divorce Backlash," *Working Women,* February 1995, 42.

11. Herma Hill Kay, "Equality and Difference: A Perspective on No-Fault Divorce and Its Aftermath," *Cincinnati Law Review* 56 (1987): 1, 67; Deborah L. Rhode and Martha Minow, "Reforming the Questions: Questioning the Reforms: Feminist Perspectives on Divorce Law," in Steven D. Sugarman and Herma Hill Kay, eds., *Divorce Reform at the Crossroads* (New Haven: Yale University Press, 1990), 191, 195.

12. Weitzman, *Divorce Revolution,* 17–18, 32–33.

13. For income comparisons, see Katharine T. Bartlett, *Gender and Law: Theory, Doctrine, Commentary* (Boston: Little, Brown, 1993), 348–349. For poverty, see Demie Kurz, *For Richer, for Poorer: Mothers Confront Divorce* (New York: Routledge, 1996), 3; *Women Work, Poverty Persists: A Status Report on Displaced Homemakers and Single Mothers in the United States* (Washington, D.C.: Women Work, 1995), 16.

14. California State Senate, "Final Report of the California Senate Task Force on Family Equity," reprinted in *Hastings Women's Law Journal* 1 (1989): 9, 23;

Joan Williams, "Is Coverture Dead? Beyond a New Theory of Alimony," *Georgetown Law Journal* 82 (1994): 2227, 2232–2234, 2251.

15. For expectations, see Lynn A. Baker and Robert E. Emery, "When Every Relationship Is above Average: Perceptions and Expectations of Divorce at the Time of Marriage," *Law and Human Behavior* 17 (1993): 439, 443. For actual payments, see Rhode and Minow, "Reforming the Questions," 202. For the judicial survey, see Weitzman, *Divorce Revolution,* 35.

16. For inadequate compensation, see Lorraine Dutsky, *Still Unequal* (New York: Crown, 1996), 306–315; Fineman, *Illusion of Equality;* Williams, "Coverture," 2258–2266. For denials of custody blackmail, see Judith Bond Jennison, "The Search for Equality in a Woman's World: Fathers' Rights to Child Custody," *Rutgers Law Review* 43 (1991): 1141, 1180; Gerson, *No Man's Land,* 130. For surveys, see Scott Altman, "Lurking in the Shadow," *University of Southern California Law Review* 68 (1995): 493, 497–504; Nancy D. Polikoff, "Why Are Mothers Losing? A Brief Analysis of Criteria Used in Child Custody Determinations," *Women's Rights Law Reporter* 14 (1992): 175, 182–183. In Demie Kurz's study, one-third of women reported that they feared violence or retaliation for pressing legal claims. Kurz, *For Richer, for Poorer,* 137.

17. Richard E. Behrman and Linda Sandham Quinn, "Children and Divorce: Overview and Analysis," *The Future of Children* 4 (1994): 4, 6, 10.

18. Marcia Mobilia Boumil and Joel Friedman, *Deadbeat Dads* (Westport, Conn.: Praeger, 1996), 36–37, 119; Irwin Garfinkel, Marygold S. Melli, and John G. Robertson, "Child Support Orders: A Perspective on Reform," *The Future of Children* 4 (1994): 84, 85; Pat Wong, *Child Support and Welfare Reform* (New York: Garland, 1993), 4, 13; Paula G. Roberts, "Child Support Orders: Problems with Enforcement," *The Future of Children* 4 (1994): 101. For experts' estimates, see Sonia Nazario, "The Second Wife," *Los Angeles Times Magazine,* 3 December 1995, 24; Paul R. Amato, "Life-Span Adjustment of Children to Their Parents' Divorce," *The Future of Children* 4 (1994): 143, 151; Frank F. Furstenberg, Jr., "History and Current Status of Divorce in the United States," *The Future of Children* 4 (1994): 29, 37; Behrman and Quinn, "Children and Divorce," 12. For car payments, see Susan Estrich, "Marcia Clark Deserves Better," *USA Today,* 9 March 1995, 11A. For visits, see Furstenberg, "Divorce," 36.

19. Gerson, *No Man's Land,* 131; Kurz, *For Richer, for Poorer,* 163, 166–171.

20. John Leland with Steve Rhodes and Susan Miller, "Tightening the Knot," *Newsweek,* 19 February 1996, 72.

21. David Blankenhorn, quoted in Barbara Vobejda, "Critics, Seeking Change, Fault 'No Fault' Divorce Laws for High Rates," *Washington Post,* 7 March 1996, A3.

22. Leland, "Tightening the Knot," 72 (citing experts); Max Rheinstein, *Marriage Stability, Divorce and the Law* (Chicago: University of Chicago Press, 1972), 277–311, 406–408 (cross-cultural comparison); Caryl Rivers, *Slick Spins and Fractured Facts* (New York: Columbia University Press, 1996), 172–175.

23. Justice M. Steinbrink, testimony before the New York Legislative Committee on Matrimonial and Family Law, *New York Herald Tribune,* 1 October 1965, A19; Walter Gellhorn, *Children and Families in the Courts of New York* (New York: Dodd, Mead, 1954), 285–286.

24. Kurz, *For Richer, for Poorer,* 206; Leland, "Tightening the Knot," 72; Hillary R. Clinton, *It Takes a Village* (New York: Simon and Schuster, 1996), 43.

25. George Stern, on Joi Chen, *CNN News,* March 10, 1996; Maggie Gallagher, *The Abolition of Marriage* (Washington, D.C.: Regnery, 1996), 50, 207; John Paul Akers, "Walkaway Wives," *American Enterprise* 7 (May–June 1996): 35; Jesse Dalman, quoted in Ruaridh Nicholl, "America's Romance with Divorce Is Over," *The Observer,* 24 March 1996, A25; Kurz, *For Richer, for Poorer,* 52–56, 187–191.

26. Leland, "Tightening the Knot," 71; Nicholl, "Romance with Divorce," 25.

27. Susan Moller Okin, *Justice, Gender and the Family* (New York: Basic Books, 1989), 165, 183; Williams, "Coverture," 2258–2266; Paula G. Roberts, "Child Support Orders: Problems with Enforcement," *The Future of Children* 4 (1994): 101; Garfinkel, Melli, and Robertson, "Child Support Orders."

28. See Garfinkel, Melli, and Robertson, "Child Support Orders"; McLanahan and Sandefur, *Single Parent,* 150; Rhode and Minow, "Reforming the Questions," 208.

29. See William Blackstone, *Commentaries on the Laws of England,* Book 2, ed. St. George Tucker (South Hackensack, N.J.: Rothman Reprints, 1996; orig. pub. 1803), 435; *Helmes v. Franciscus,* 2 Bland 544, 20 Am. Dec. 402 (Maryland, 1830).

30. Michael Grossberg, *Governing the Hearth: Law and the Family in Nineteenth-Century America* (Chapel Hill: University of North Carolina Press, 1985), 248–250; Carol Brown, "Mothers, Fathers and Children: From Private to Public Patriarchy," in Lydia Sargent, ed., *Women and Revolution: A Discussion of the Unhappy Marriage of Marxism and Feminism* (Boston: South End Press, 1981), 239.

31. Jay Einhorn, "Child Custody in Historical Perspective: A Study of Changing Social Perceptions of Divorce and Child Custody in Anglo-American Law," *Behavioral Sciences and the Law* 4 (1986): 119, 128–134.

32. For custody, see Sonny Burmeister, quoted in Ellis Cose, *A Man's World* (New York: Harper Collins, 1995), 160–161 ("sexist"); Mel Roman and William Haddad, quoted in Jennison, "Search for Equality," 1141 ("leper"). For child abuse, see Weidlich, "Ex-Husbands," A22; Jennison, "Search for Equality," 1177. For child support, see Hugh Nations, "Let's Call Them the Gender Biased Task Forces," *Texas Lawyer,* 9 August 1993, 14; Stuart A. Miller, "The Myth of Deadbeat Dads," *Wall Street Journal,* 2 March 1995, A14. For fathers' role, see Miller, quoted in Jennison, "Search for Equality," 1176; Ross Thompson, "The Role of the Father after Divorce," *The Future of Children* 4 (1994): 210, 213. See also Blankenhorn, *Fatherless America,* 150–155. For enforcement biases see Nations, "Gender Biased," 14.

33. For custody, see Eleanor E. Maccoby and Robert H. Mnookin, *Dividing the Child: Social and Legal Dilemmas of Custody* (Cambridge, Mass.: Harvard University Press, 1992), 266–296; Polikoff, "Why Are Mothers Losing?" 177. For child support and abuse, see Fineman, *The Neutered Mother,* 120; Catherine Paquette, "Handling Sexual Abuse Allegations in Child Custody Cases," *New England Law Review* 25 (1991): 1415, 1417.

34. For visitation, see Karen Czapanskiy, "Volunteers and Draftees: The Struggle for Parental Equality," *UCLA Law Review* 38 (1991): 1415, 1448–1449; Tamar Lewin, "Father's Vanishing Act Called 'Common Drama,'" *New York Times,* 4 June 1990, A15. For child support, see Boumil and Friedman, *Deadbeat Dads,* 121–122; Roberts, "Child Support Orders," 110. And as Roberts notes, the system is underfunded even for welfare cases (ibid.).

35. Jessica Pearson and Maria A. Luchesi Ring, "Judicial Decision-Making in Contested Custody Cases," *Journal of Family Law* 21 (1982–1983): 703; Maccoby and Mnookin, *Dividing the Child,* 163, 268; Mary Becker, "Maternal Feelings: Myth, Taboo, and Child Custody," *University of Southern California Review of Law and Women's Studies* 1 (1992): 133.

36. For fathers' claims, see Cose, *A Man's World,* 160–163; Jennison, "The Search for Equality," 1178. For children's needs, see Maccoby and Mnookin, *Dividing the Child;* David L. Chambers, "Rethinking the Substantive Rules for Custody Disputes in Divorce," *Michigan Law Review* 83 (1984): 477, 561.

37. See sources cited in Becker, "Maternal Feelings"; Polikoff, "Two Mothers," 459; B. Drummond Ayres, Jr., "Judge's Decision in Custody Case Raises Concerns," *New York Times,* 9 September 1993, A16; *Parillo v. Parillo,* 554 A.2d 1043 (R.I., 1989); Ellen Goodman, *Making Sense* (New York: Atlantic Monthly Press, 1989), 220.

38. *Bottoms v. Bottoms,* 457 S.E.2d 102 (Va., 1995); *Chicoine v. Chicoine,* 479 N.W. 2d 891, 896 (S.D., 1992) (Henderson, J., dissenting); *White v. Thompson,* 569 S0.2d 1181 (Miss., 1990); *Roberts v. Roberts,* 489 N.E.2d 1067, 1070 (Ohio App., 1985); William A. Henry III, "Gay Parents: Under Fire and on the Rise," *Time,* 20 September 1993, 66. For the adultery case, see *Bennett v. O'Rourke* (Tenn. Ct. App., 1985), discussed in Polikoff, "Two Mothers," 560, n. 553. For the ex-murder ruling, see *Ward v. Ward,* discussed in Diane Hirth, "Appeal Court Hears Sides in Unusual Custody Case," *Orlando Sentinel,* 25 July 1996, C1. For the research, see Bartlett, *Gender and Law,* 470, Polikoff, "Two Mothers," 544–557, and Herek, "Myths about Sexual Orientation," 133, 157–161.

39. Ellen Goodman, "Guilty of Success," *Boston Globe,* 5 March 1995, B7; Dutsky, *Still Unequal,* 344–348; Judith Levine, *My Enemy, My Love: Men and the Dilemma of Gender* (New York: Doubleday, 1992), 123; Marlene Adler Marks, "Perspective in the Simpson Trial: Words No Woman Dares to Speak," *Los Angeles Times,* 28 February 1995, B7. For daycare, see cases cited in *Borchard v. Garary,* 742 P.2d 486, 494, nn. 5–6 (Cal. Sup. Ct., 1986); and cases discussed in Polikoff, "Why Are Mothers Losing?" 181; and in Carol Sanger,

"Separating from Children," *Columbia Law Review* 96 (1996): 406, 499. For custody fights, see Levine, *My Enemy, My Love,* 123.

40. *Prost v. Greene,* 652 A.2d 621, 630–32 (D.C. App., 1995) (reversing lower court's custody decision and remanding for findings on the husband's alleged domestic violence); D. Kelly Weisberg, "Professional Women and the Professionalization of Mothers: Marcia Clark's Double Bind," *Hastings Women's Law Journal* 6 (1995): 295.

41. "Because Mommy Works," NBC Broadcast, 21 November 1994, discussed in Cheri L. Wood, "Childless Mothers—The New Catch-22: You Can't Have Your Kids and Work for Them Too," *Loyola of Los Angeles Law Review* 29 (1995): 383, 385, n. 6.

42. Hancock, "Working Moms," 56; Susan A. Basow, *Gender Stereotypes and Roles* (Pacific Grove, Calif.: Brooks/Cole, 1992), 236–238; Anna Quindlen, "Done in by Day Care," *New York Times,* 30 July 1994, A19; Susan Jane Gilman, "A Michigan Judge's Ruling Punishes Single Mothers," *Ms.,* November–December 1994, 92–93.

43. Gilman, "Michigan Judge."

44. Ibid.; Quindlen, "Day Care"; *Dempsey v. Dempsey,* 292 N.W. 2d 813 (Mich. Ct. App., 1980). See also cases cited in Polikoff, "Why Are Mothers Losing?" 178–179.

45. "Who's Minding Maranda?" *American Bar Association Journal* (August 1996): 21; Tamar Lewin, "Demands of Simpson Case Land Prosecutor in Custody Fight," *New York Times,* 3 March 1995, B8; Lynnell Hancock, "Putting Working Moms in Custody," *Newsweek,* 13 March 1995, 54–55.

46. Bettina Boxall and Frank B. Williams, "Marcia Clark's Custody Case Stirs Opinions, Emotions," *Los Angeles Times,* 3 March 1995, A30; Suzanne Gordon, "Perspective on Child Custody: Equality Comes to the Career Trap," *Los Angeles Times,* 9 March 1995, B7.

47. Goodman, "Guilty of Success," B7.

48. Jane Mayer, "Motherhood Issue: Marcia Clark Isn't the Only One Who's Got Troubles," *New Yorker,* 20 March 1995, 9 (noting that claims for two decades of child support from Johnnie L. Cochran have attracted little notice).

49. Ramos, quoted in Hancock, "Working Moms," 55.

50. Chambers, "Rethinking the Rules"; Jon Elster, "Solomonic Judgments: Against the Best Interest of the Child," *University of Chicago Law Review* 54 (1987): 1, 3–4, 11–16.

51. Coontz, *The Way We Never Were,* 227–228.

52. Altman, "Lurking in the Shadow."

53. *Garska v. McCoy,* 278 SE.2d 357 (W. Va., 1981); Gary Crippen, "Stumbling beyond Best Interests of the Child: Reexamining Child Custody Standard Setting in the Wake of Minnesota's Four-Year Experiment with the Primary Caretaker Preference," *Minnesota Law Review* 75 (1990): 427; Katharine T. Bartlett and Carol B. Stack, "Joint Custody, Feminism and the Dependency Dilemma," *Berkeley Women's Law Journal* 2 (1986): 9.

54. Bartlett and Stack, "Joint Custody."

55. Maccoby and Mnookin, *Dividing the Child*, 247.

56. For fathers' preferences, see Carl Bertoia and Janice Drakich, "The Fathers' Rights Movement: Contradictions in Rhetoric and Practice," *Journal of Family Issues* 14 (1993): 592, 600–603, 612. For mothers' experience, see Czapanskiy, "Volunteers and Draftees." For effects on fathers' behavior, see Eyer, *Motherguilt*, 127; Jana B. Singer and William L. Reynolds, "A Dissent on Joint Custody," *Maryland Law Review* 47 (1988): 497, 506.

57. Jane W. Ellis, "Plans, Protections, and Professional Intervention: Innovations in Divorce Custody Reform and the Role of Legal Professionals," *Michigan Journal of Law Reform* 24 (1990): 65.

58. Elizabeth S. Scott, "Pluralism, Parental Preference, and Child Custody," *California Law Review* 80 (1992): 615.

59. Nathan Glazer, "Making Work Work: Welfare Reform in the 1990s," in Demetra Smith Nightingale and Robert H. Haveman, eds., *The Work Alternative: Welfare Reform and the Realities of the Job Market* (Washington, D.C.: The Urban Institute Press, 1995), 17, 21; "Replacing the Welfare State," *Wall Street Journal*, 16 February 1995, A14; Gayle Kirschenbaum, "Why All But One Woman Senator Voted Against Welfare," *Ms.*, March–April 1996, 16 (teflon); Katha Pollitt, "Just the Facts," *The Nation*, 24 June 1996, 9 (debunking); Michael B. Katz, *The Undeserving Poor: From the War on Poverty to the War on Welfare* (New York: Pantheon, 1989), 10 (useful target).

60. Charles Murray, *Losing Ground: American Social Policy, 1950–1980* (New York: Basic Books, 1984), 234.

61. Kaiser/Harvard Program on the Public and Health/Social Policy, *Survey on Welfare Reform: Basic Values and Beliefs—Support for Policy Approaches Knowledge about Key Programs* (Menlo Park, Calif.: Kaiser Family Foundation, 1995): 4; Richard Morin, "Welfare Mothers and Dole Babies," *Washington Post*, 24 April 1994, C5; Rector quoted in Celia Dugger, "Why Lump Sums Mean Some Lumps," *New York Times*, 28 May 1995, E6; R. Kent Weaver, Robert Y. Shapiro, and Lawrence Jacobs, "Public Opinion on Welfare Reform: A Mandate for What?" in R. Kent Weaver and William Dickens, eds., *Looking before We Leap: Social Science and Welfare Reform* (Washington, D.C.: Brookings Institution, 1995), 109, 112–113.

62. Public Law 104-193, 110 Statutes 2105 (1996); Joel F. Handler, *The Poverty of Welfare Reform* (New Haven: Yale University Press, 1995), 110–138; Nancy E. Rose, *Workfare or Fair Work: Women, Welfare and Government Work Programs* (New Brunswick, N.J.: Rutgers University Press, 1995), 180–182.

63. William J. Bennett, "The Best Welfare Reform: End It," *Washington Post*, 30 March 1994, A19. See also Murray, *Losing Ground*, 54–66. For costs, see Douglas J. Besharov, "Clinton and Congress: Orphanages Aren't Welfare Reform," *New York Times*, 20 December 1994, A23.

64. Center on Social Welfare Policy and Law, *Welfare Myths: Fact or Fiction* (New York: Center on Social Welfare Policy and Law, 1996), 29; Handler, *Welfare*

Reform, 106; Rank, *Living on the Edge,* 169; Rebecca M. Blank, "Unwed Mothers Need Role Models, Not Roll Backs," *Wall Street Journal,* 7 March 1995, A18; Barbara Vobejda, "N.J. Welfare 'Cap' Has No Effect on Births, Study Finds," *Washington Post,* 21 June 1995, A3.

65. Gingrich, quoted in Jason De Parle, "Less Is More: Faith and Facts in Welfare Reform," *New York Times,* 3 December 1995, E1; Katherine McFate, Timothy Smeeding, and Lee Rainwater, "Markets and States: Poverty Trends and Transfer System Effectiveness in the 1980s," in Katherine McFate, Roger Lawson, and William Julius Wilson, eds., *Poverty, Inequality, and the Future of Social Policy: Western States in the New World Order* (New York: Russell Sage Foundation, 1995), 31–39.

66. For political rhetoric, see Rank, *Living on the Edge,* 3 (quoting senator); Nancy Gibbs, "The Vicious Cycle," *Time,* 20 June 1994, 24, 29. For recipients' perceptions and benefit levels, see Rank, *Living on the Edge,* 73, 72–79; Rita Henley Jensen, "Welfare: Exploding the Stereotypes," *Ms.,* July–August 1995, 56, Eyer, *Motherguilt,* 17.

67. Wilson, quoted in Rank, *Living on the Edge,* 3.

68. For necessities, see Martha Minow, "The Welfare of Single Mothers and Their Children," *Connecticut Law Review* 26 (1994): 817; Carnegie Task Force on Meeting the Needs of Young Children, *Starting Points: Meeting the Needs of Our Youngest Children* (New York: Carnegie Corporation, 1994). For violence, see Martha F. Davis and Susan J. Kraham, "Protecting Women's Welfare in the Face of Violence," *Fordham Urban Law Journal* 22 (1995): 1141; Barbara Ehrenreich, "Battered Welfare Syndrome," *Time,* 3 April 1995, 82. For health and housing, see Valerie Polakow, *Lives on the Edge: Single Mothers and Their Children in the Other America* (Chicago: University of Chicago Press, 1993), 164; Polakow, "On a Tightrope without a Net," *The Nation,* 1 May 1995, 590. For budgets, see John E. Schwarz, *The Forgotten Americans: Thirty Million Working Poor in the Land of Opportunity* (New York: W. W. Norton, 1992), 43; Ruth Sidel, *Keeping Women and Children Last* (New York: Penguin, 1996), 74.

69. Roberta Spalter-Roth, Beverly Burr, Heidi Hartmann, and Lois Shaw, *Welfare That Works: The Working Lives of AFDC Recipients* (Washington, D.C.: Institute for Women Policy Research, 1995); Member of the Indiana House of Representatives, quoted in Rank, *Living on the Edge,* 3–4; Mary Jo Bane and David T. Ellwood, *Welfare Realities: From Rhetoric to Reform* (Cambridge, Mass.: Harvard University Press, 1994), 117–119; Rank, *Living on the Edge,* 176–184, 188–190; Handler, *Welfare Reform,* 85–88.

70. Robert Kuttner, "The Welfare Perplex," *New York Times,* 19 June 1994, E17 (salary and expenses); Christopher Jencks, "What's Wrong with Welfare Reform," *Harper's Magazine* (April 1994): 20 (daycare costs); Sidel, *Keeping Women and Children Last,* 108 (Harlem).

71. For earnings, see Gary Burtless, "Employment Prospects of Welfare Recipients," in Nightingale and Haveman, eds., *The Work Alternative,* 71, 99–100;

Spalter-Roth et al., *Welfare That Works*. For training programs, see U.S. General Accounting Office, *Welfare to Work: Current AFDC Not Significantly Focused on Employment* (Washington, D.C.: General Accounting Office, 1994); Douglas J. Besharov and Karen N. Gardiner, "Paternalism and Welfare Reform," *The Public Interest* 122 (Winter 1996): 70, 74; Evelyn Brodkin, "Administrative Capacity and Welfare Reform," in Weaver and Dickens, eds., *Looking before We Leap*, 97. For job creation, see Paul Offner, "Welfare: Are the States Up to the Jobs," *Washington Post*, 18 May 1995, A31; Rose, *Workfare*, 167–168.

72. Engler, quoted in Offner, "Welfare," A31; Ruth Conniff, "Welfare, Ground Zero: Michigan Tries to End It All," *The Nation*, 27 May 1996, 16. For federal proposals, see Kuttner, "Welfare Perplex," E17. For public opinion, see Kaiser/Harvard Program, *Welfare Survey*, 4; Jason DeParle, "Despising Welfare, Pitying Its Young," *New York Times*, 18 December 1994, E5.

73. Robin Toner, "No More Bleeding Hearts," *New York Times*, 16 July 1995, E1, E16.

74. Mimi Abramovitz and Fred Newton, *Women on Welfare: Myths and Realities* (New York: Women's Resource Center of New York, 1995); Coontz, *The Way We Never Were*, 272–285; Martha Fineman, "Masking Dependency: The Political Role of Family Rhetoric," *Virginia Law Review* 81 (1995): 2181.

75. Bradsher, "Gaps in Wealth in U.S. Called Widest in West," *New York Times*, 17 April 1995, A1; Fineman, "Masking Dependency," 2214–2215; Sidel, *Keeping Women and Children Last*, 180–184; Lynne M. Casper, Sara S. McLanahan, and Irwin Garfinkel, "The Gender Poverty Gap: What We Can Learn from Other Countries," *American Sociological Review* 59 (1994): 594, 602–603; Jill Quadagno, *The Color of Welfare* (New York: Oxford, 1994), 183.

76. Jill Duerr Berrick, *Faces of Poverty: Portraits of Women and Children on Welfare* (New York: Oxford University Press, 1995), 145; Rank, *Living on the Edge*; Davis and Kraham, "Protecting Women's Welfare in the Face of Violence," 1141, 1145.

77. For discussion of this dual structure, see Mimi Abramovitz, *Regulating the Lives of Women: Social Welfare Policy from the Colonial Times to the Present* (Boston: South End Press, 1988); Linda Gordon, "What Does Welfare Regulate?" *Social Research* 55 (1988): 609, 612–613.

78. John Demos, "Images of the American Family: Then and Now," in Virginia Tufte and Barbara Myerhoff, eds., *Changing Images of the Family* (New Haven: Yale University Press, 1979), 43.

79. Remarks of John Kasich at the Republican National Convention, Federal Document Clearing House, August 13, 1996.

80. Glazer, "Making Work Work."

81. Forrest P. Chisman, "Can the States Do Any Better?" *The Nation*, 1 May 1995, 600.

82. *Roe v. Wade*, 410 U.S. 113 (1973).

83. Verlyn Klinkenborg, "Violent Certainties: Abortion Politics in Milwaukee, Wisconsin," *Harper's Magazine* (January 1995): 37, 41.

84. National Abortion and Reproductive Rights Action League [NARAL], *Clinic Violence, Intimidation and Terror,* Fact sheet (Washington, D.C.: NARAL, November 1995), 1; Judith Warner, "The Assassination of Dr. Gunn: Scare Tactics Turn Deadly," *Ms.,* May–June 1993, 86; Lisa Belkin, "Kill for Life," *New York Times Magazine,* 30 October 1994, 47, 49; Rebecca Eisenberg, "Beyond *Bray:* Obtaining Federal Jurisdiction to Stop Antiabortion Violence," *Yale Journal of Law and Feminism* 6 (1994): 155, 172; Sandra G. Boodman, "A Tale of Two Dallas Abortion Doctors: One Surrendered, One Is Fighting On," *Washington Post,* 8 April 1993, A16. For anti-abortion rhetoric, see Theresa Donovan, Massachusetts Citizens for Life, quoted in Ellen Goodman, "Pro-Life's Death Squad," *San Jose Mercury News,* 5 January 1995, B11; Belkin, "Kill for Life"; Anna Quindlen, "At the Clinics," *New York Times,* 5 April 1992, A17.

85. Warner, "Assassination," 86; Klinkenborg, "Violent Certainties," 40; Frederick Clarkson, quoted in Frank Rich, "Connect the Dots," *New York Times,* 30 April 1995, D15.

86. Amy Goldstein, "U.S. Abortion Services Drop," *Washington Post,* 22 January 1995, A1; Tamar Lewin, "Abortions in U.S. Hit Thirteen-Year Low, a Study Reports," *New York Times,* 16 June 1994, A1, A11; Belkin, "Kill for Life"; NARAL, Clinic Violence, 4.

87. For legal restrictions, see *Planned Parenthood of Southeastern Pennsylvania v. Casey,* 112 S.Ct. 2791 (1992) (upholding Pennsylvania's informed-consent requirements, waiting periods, and parental-consent provisions); *Webster v. Reproductive Health Services,* 492 U.S. 490 (1989) (upholding ban on providing public resources for abortion); *Harris v. McRae,* 448 U.S. 297 (1980) (upholding ban on Medicaid's funding of abortions). For the effect of limitations, see studies cited in Susan Randall, "Health Care Reform and Abortion," *Berkeley Women's Law Journal* 9 (1994): 58, 67–69; Marlene Gerber Fried, "Reproductive Wrongs," *Women's Review of Books* 11 (July 1994): 6. For RU-486, see Stanley K. Henshaw, "Factors Hindering Access to Abortion Services," *Family Planning Perspectives* 27 (March–April 1995): 59.

88. Henshaw, "Factors Hindering Access to Abortion Services," 57–59 (discussing cost); Congressional Caucus for Women's Issues, *Update,* April–May 1994, 7 (discussing analogies for elective surgery).

89. E. J. Dionne, Jr., "Justices' Abortion Ruling Mirrors Public Opinion," *Washington Post,* 1 July 1992, A4; *Hodgson v. Minnesota,* 497 U.S. 417 (1990); *Ohio v. Akron Center for Reproductive Health,* 497 U.S. 502 (1990); *Bellotti v. Baird,* 443 U.S. 622 (1979).

90. See studies cited in Rhode, "Adolescent Pregnancy," 320, n. 52; Robert H. Mnookin, "*Bellotti v. Baird:* A Hard Case," in Mnookin, *In the Interest of Children: Advocacy Law Reform and Public Policy* (New York: Freeman, 1985), 149.

91. For the petition process, see Mnookin, *"Bellotti,"* 239–240; Virginia G. Cartoof and Lorraine V. Klerman, "Parental Consent for Abortion: Impact of the Massachusetts Law," *American Journal of Public Health* 76 (1986): 397. For the infrequency of grounds for denial, see *Hodgson v. Minnesota,* 497 U.S. 417, 461 (1990); (Marshall, J., dissenting in part); and Rhode, "Adolescent Pregnancy," 320. For judicial actions, see Patricia Donovan, "Judging Teenagers: How Minors Fare When They Seek Court-Authorized Abortions," *Family Planning Perspectives* 15 (1983): 259–260, 265 and "Your Parents or the Judge, Massachusetts' New Abortion Consent Law," *Family Planning Perspectives* 13 (1981): 224; Rhode, "Adolescent Pregnancy," 320; Tamar Lewin, "Parental Consent to Abortion: How Enforcement Can Vary," *New York Times,* 28 May 1992, A1. See also Suellyn Scarnecchia and Julie Kunce Field, "Judging Girls: Decision Making in Parental Consent to Abortion Cases," *Michigan Journal of Gender and Law* 3 (1995): 75, 90–93.

92. Stanley Henshaw and Kathryn Kost, "Parental Involvement in Minors' Abortion Decisions," *Family Planning Perspectives* 24 (September–October 1992): 200, table 3.

93. Dr. David Grimes, *Forum,* National Public Radio, 8 April 1996; sources cited in Rhode, "Adolescent Pregnancy," 321; Mnookin, *"Bellotti,"* 258.

94. Laurence H. Tribe, *Abortion: The Clash of Absolutes* (New York: Norton, 1990), 151–159.

95. Linda C. McClain, "Equality, Oppression, and Abortion: Women Who Oppose Abortion Rights in the Name of Feminism," in Susan Ostrov Weisser and Jennifer Fleischner, eds., *Feminist Nightmares, Women at Odds: Feminism and the Problem of Sisterhood* (New York: New York University Press, 1994), 159, 168; Faye D. Ginsburg, *Contested Lives: The Abortion Debate in an American Community* (Berkeley: University of California Press, 1989), 216–217; *Doe v. Bolton,* 410 U.S. 179, 221 (White, J., dissenting).

96. Naomi Wolf, "Our Bodies, Our Souls," *The New Republic,* 16 October 1995, 32, 35; Mary Gordon, "A Moral Choice," *The Atlantic,* April 1990, 78.

97. Joan Williams, "Gender Wars: Selfless Women in the Republic of Choice," *New York University Law Review* 66 (1991): 1559, 1583; Rep. Richard Armey, quoted in Congressional Caucus for Women's Issues, *Update,* 7.

98. Kristin Luker, *Abortion and the Politics of Motherhood* (Berkeley: University of California Press, 1984), 169, 171, 192; see also Ginsburg, *Contested Lives,* 216–217; McClain, "Equality."

99. For sexual liberation, see Elizabeth Fox-Genovese, *Feminism Is Not the Story of My Life* (New York: Doubleday, 1996), 94. For tactics and arguments, see Wolf, "Our Bodies, Our Souls," 26; Denfeld, *The New Victorians,* 195.

100. Robin West, "Foreword: Taking Freedom Seriously," *Harvard Law Review* 104 (1990): 43, 84–85. For anti-abortion descriptions, see sources cited in McClain, "Equality," 176; Williams, "Gender Wars," 1578–1579.

101. *Newsweek* poll, quoted in Wolf, "Our Bodies, Our Souls," 33.

102. Ellen Willis, *No More Nice Girls: Countercultural Essays* (Middletown, Conn.: Wesleyan University Press, 1992), 79.

103. Senators Jeremiah Denton and Orrin Hatch, quoted in Rosalind Pollack Petchesky, *Abortion and Woman's Choice: The State, Sexuality, and Reproductive Freedom* (Boston: Northeastern University Press, 1990), 270; Rush H. Limbaugh, *The Way Things Ought To Be* (New York: Pocket Books, 1992), 130, 133. For abstinence programs, see sources cited in Rhode, "Adolescent Pregnancy," 316–317, n. 44; National Abortion Rights Action League, *The Right Wing in the Classroom: The Rise of Fear-Based Sexuality Education* (Washington, D.C.: NARAL, November 1995); Michele Ingrassia, "Virgin Cool," *Newsweek,* 17 October 1994, 58, 62; Lisa Yungmann, "Mrs. Bush Praises Girls' Abstinence," *Washington Times,* 16 June 1992, B3.

104. Patricia Ireland, Unpublished remarks, Printer's Ink Bookstore, Palo Alto, Calif., 22 June 1996; Alan Guttmacher Institute, *Sex and America's Teenagers* (New York: Alan Guttmacher Institute, 1994), 68–69; Melody G. Embree and Tracy A. Dobson, "Parental Involvement in Adolescent Abortion Decisions: A Legal and Psychological Critique," *Law and Inequality* 10 (1991): 53, 58; Cheryl D. Hayes, ed., *Risking the Future: Adolescent Sexuality, Pregnancy, and Childbearing* (Washington, D.C.: National Academy Press, 1987), 3, 41–42. For disease and pregnancy rates, see ibid., 1, 15, 50–67, 123–128; Alan Guttmacher Institute, *Sex and America's Teenagers,* 38.

105. For media images, see Faye Wattleton and Marian Wright Edelman, "Teenage Pregnancy: The Case for National Action," *The Nation,* 24 July 1989, 138, 140; Laurie Becklund, "The '80s: Greenhouse for Teen Pregnancy," *Los Angeles Times,* 14 March 1993, E5. For the inadequacy of sex education programs and birth control services, see Kristin Luker, *Dubious Conceptions: The Politics of Teenage Pregnancy* (Cambridge, Mass.: Harvard University Press, 1996), 184–187; Rhode, "Adolescent Pregnancy," 301, 316–318; Maris A. Vinovskis, *An 'Epidemic' of Adolescent Pregnancy? Some Historical and Policy Considerations* (New York: Oxford University Press, 1988), 38, 63, 213–214; Peggy Orenstein, *Schoolgirls: Young Women, Self-Esteem, and the Confidence Gap* (New York: Doubleday, 1994) 59–60; Carol Jouzaitis, "Political Attacks on Abortion Also May Cut Family Planning," *Chicago Tribune,* 30 July 1995, A3.

106. Elise F. Jones et al., "Teenage Pregnancy in Developed Countries: Determinants and Policy Implications," *Family Planning Perspectives* 17 (1985): 57–58; Hayes, *Risking the Future,* 1, 15, 50, 52–67.

107. On this topic, see Sharon Thompson, "Search for Tomorrow: On Feminism and the Reconstruction of Teen Romance," in Carole S. Vance, ed., *Pleasure and Danger: Exploring Female Sexuality* (Boston: Routledge, 1984), 350; Rhode, "Adolescent Pregnancy," 323; Hayes, *Risking the Future,* 125–128; Jewelle Taylor Gibbs, "The Social Context of Teenage Pregnancy and Parenting in the Black Community: Implications for Public Policy," in Mar-

garet K. Rosenheim and Mark F. Testa, eds., *Early Parenthood and Coming of Age in the 1990s* (New Brunswick, N.J.: Rutgers University Press, 1992), 71.

108. For female-headed families, see Wider Opportunities for Women, *Teen Pregnancy, Welfare, and Poverty: Myths v. Facts* (Washington, D.C.: Wider Opportunities for Women, 1994) (4 percent). For interrelationships and causal ambiguities, see Luker, *Dubious Conceptions,* 113–137, 180–182; Frank F. Furstenberg, Jr., and Jeanne Brooks-Gunn, "Teenage Childbearing: Causes, Consequences, and Remedies," in Linda H. Aiken and David Mechanic, eds., *Applications of Social Science to Clinical Medicine and Health Policy* (New Brunswick, N.J.: Rutgers University Press, 1986), 307, 316–317. For school dropout findings, see Dawn M. Upchurch and James McCarthy, "The Timing of a First Birth and High School Completion," *American Sociological Review* 55 (1990): 224. For comparisons of disadvantaged teens, see V. Joseph Hotz, Susan Williams McElroy, and Seth G. Sanders, "The Costs and Consequences of Teenage Childbearing," Working paper, Harris School of Public Policy Studies, Chicago, 1995; Emory Thomas, Jr., "Is Pregnancy a Rational Choice for Poor Teenagers?" *Wall Street Journal,* 18 January 1996, B1; Arline T. Geronimus and Sanders Korenman, "The Socioeconomic Consequences of Teen Childbearing Reconsidered," Working paper 3701, National Bureau of Economic Research, Cambridge, Mass., 1991, 1.

109. Saul D. Hoffman, E. Michael Foster, and Frank F. Furstenberg, Jr., "Reevaluating the Costs of Teenage Childbearing," *Demography* 30 (1993): 1, 4–9; Gibbs, "Social Context," 71.

110. Programs encouraging abstinence need to be targeted to appropriate age groups and to be coupled with other initiatives for teens who are already sexually active. Douglas Kirby et al., "School-Based Programs to Reduce Sexual Risk Behaviors: A Review of Effectiveness," *Public Health Report* 109 (1994): 339. For discussion of teenage mothers' motivation and the need for better pregnancy prevention strategies, see the research summarized in Rhode, "Adolescent Pregnancy"; Judith S. Musick, *Young, Poor, and Pregnant: The Psychology of Teenage Motherhood* (New Haven: Yale University Press, 1993); Luker, *Dubious Conceptions,* 148–164.

111. Mireya Navarro, "Teen-Age Mothers Viewed as Abused Prey of Older Men," *New York Times,* 19 May 1996, 1, 11. On programs for male adolescents, see Eyer, *Motherguilt,* 234–235.

112. See Margaret Conway, David W. Ahern, and Gertrude A. Severnagel, *Women and Public Policy* (Washington, D.C.: Congressional Quarterly, 1995), 44, 50.

113. For anti-abortion arguments, see Edward Walsh, "Anomalies of the Abortion Fight," *Washington Post,* 22 May 1994, A3; McClain, "Equality," 168. For the history of abortion restrictions, see Rhode, *Justice and Gender,* 117–119, 205–208; Petchesky, *Abortion and Woman's Choice.*

8. Women's Movements, Men's Movements

1. Gloria Steinem, quoted in Nancy Gibbs and Jeanne McDowell Berkeley, "How to Revive a Revolution," *Time*, 9 March 1992, 56.

2. Nancy Gibbs, "The War against Feminists," *Time*, 9 March 1992, 50 (37 percent); Feminist Majority Foundation, *Women's Equality Poll*, Fact sheet (New York: Feminist Majority Foundation, April 1995) (30 percent); but see 1995 Harris Poll, cited in Susan Faludi, "Feminism Is Not the Story of My Life," *The Nation*, 15 January 1996, 28 (51 percent).

3. See Susan Faludi, "I'm Not a Feminist But I Play One on TV," *Ms.*, March–April 1995, 31; Anthony Flint, "New Breed of Feminist Challenges Old Guard," *Boston Globe*, 29 May 1994, 1; Gloria Steinem, quoted in Dierdre English, "Fear of Feminism," *Washington Post*, 4 September 1994, X7. For discussion of such conflicts, see Wendy Kaminer, *True Love Waits* (Reading, Mass.: Addison-Wesley, 1996), 39–42.

4. For perceptions of discrimination, see Faye Crosby, "Male Sympathy with the Situation of Women: Does Personal Experience Make a Difference?" *Journal of Social Issues* 42 (1986): 55; Judith H. Dobrzynski, "Women Less Optimistic about Work, Poll Says," *New York Times*, 12 September 1995, D5 (77 percent in 1995). For acknowledgments of improvement, see Susan Basow, *Gender Stereotypes and Roles* (Pacific Grove, Calif.: Brooks/Cole, 1992), 335 (85 percent); Naomi Wolf, *Fire with Fire* (New York: Random House, 1993), 58 (77 percent). For equality, see Rene Denfeld, *The New Victorians* (New York: Warner, 1995), 4 (between 90 and 98 percent of Americans believe that men and women should have the same education and employment opportunities).

5. Feminist Majority Foundation, *Women's Equality Poll*; 1995 Harris Poll, cited in Faludi, "Feminism," 28; Roper Starch Worldwide, *1995 Virginia Slims Opinion Poll* (Storrs, Conn.: Roper Center for Public Opinion Research, 1995), 9; Martha Burk and Heidi Hartmann, "Beyond the Gender Gap," *The Nation*, 10 June 1996, 19.

6. For support without responsibility, see Gibbs, "War," 52; Christina Hoff Sommers, *Who Stole Feminism?* (New York: Simon and Schuster, 1994), 18; Roberta A. Sigel, *Ambition and Accommodation: How Women View Gender Relations* (Chicago: University of Chicago Press, 1996), 75–82, 173–175. For lack of attention and membership, see Wolf, *Fire with Fire*, 58; Feminist Majority Foundation, *Women's Equality Poll*. For financial support, see Rick Wartzman, "Power of the Purse: Women Are Becoming Big Spenders in Politics and on Social Causes," *Wall Street Journal*, 17 October 1994, A1. For membership, see Dennis Boyles, *The Modern Man's Guide to Modern Women* (New York: Harper Collins, 1993), 128.

7. Roper, *1995 Virginia Slims Poll*, 9.

8. Marian Henley, *Ms.*, January 1992, 59.

9. Jerry Falwell, quoted in Jody L. Rohlena, ed., *Sounds Like a New Woman* (New

York: Penguin, 1993), 19; Karen Lehrman, "The Feminist Mystique," *The New Republic,* 16 March 1992, 30; Christina Hoff Sommers, "Hard-Line Feminists Guilty of Ms.-Representation," *Wall Street Journal,* 7 November 1991, A14; Denfeld, *The New Victorians,* 28; Mary Matalin, "Stop Whining!" *Newsweek,* 25 October 1993, 62.

10. Daphne Patai and Noretta Koertge, *Professing Feminism: Cautionary Tales from the Strange World of Women's Studies* (New York: Basic Books, 1994), 83. See also Lehrman, "The Feminist Mystique," 30; Sommers, "Hard-Line Feminists," A14.

11. Denfeld, *The New Victorians,* 162.

12. Kristin Luker, *Abortion and the Politics of Motherhood* (Berkeley: University of California Press, 1984), 163.

13. Anita Shreve, quoted in Gayle Greene Fawcett, "Women Together" (book review), *The Nation,* 29 April 1991, 564.

14. Mary Ann Dolan, "When Feminism Failed," *New York Times Magazine,* 26 June 1988, 20.

15. Lea Brilmayer, "Inclusive Feminism," *New York University Law Review* 38 (1993): 377, 378 (discussing "honorary males"); Sylvia Ann Hewlett, *A Lesser Life* (New York: William Morrow, 1986); Suzanne Gordon, *Prisoners of Men's Dreams* (Boston: Little, Brown, 1991); Elizabeth Fox-Genovese, *Feminism Is Not the Story of My Life* (New York: Doubleday, 1995), 204 ("ideological effort"); Burk and Hartmann, "Gender Gap," 21 (housework).

16. See Carolyn G. Heilbrun, *Reinventing Womanhood* (New York: Norton, 1979), 42 (discussing Queen Bees); Fawcett, "Women Together," 563 (book review).

17. For discussion of these themes in the context of the failed campaign for the Equal Rights Amendment, see Deborah L. Rhode, *Justice and Gender* (Cambridge, Mass.: Harvard University Press, 1989), 68–70. See also Ellen Fein and Sherrie Schneider, *The Rules: Time-Tested Secrets for Capturing the Heart of Mr. Right* (New York: Warner, 1996); Schneider, quoted in Mike Littwin, "Retro Feminism," *Pittsburgh Post-Gazette,* 18 September 1996, D5.

18. Denfeld, *The New Victorians,* 9 ("feminist fringe"); Matalin, "Stop Whining!" 62 ("crackpots"); Pat Robertson, quoted in "Robertson Letter Attacks Feminists," *New York Times,* 26 August 1992, A16; Randall Terry, quoted in Rohlena, ed., *Sounds Like a New Woman,* 53.

19. Camille Paglia, quoted in Daniel Harris, "Nietzsche Does Downtown," *The Nation,* 21 November 1994, 615; Matalin, "Stop Whining!" 62; Katie Roiphe, *The Morning After: Sex, Fear, and Feminism on Campus* (Boston: Little, Brown, 1993), 10; Wolf, *Fire with Fire,* 136; Kate Saunder, "Winning Not Whining," *Sunday Times* (London), 7 November 1993, 36; Sarah Chrichton, "Sexual Correctness," *Newsweek,* 25 October 1993, 52 (quoting Friedan's statement that she is "sick of women wallowing in the victim status"); Denfeld, *The New Victorians,* 5.

20. Wolf, *Fire with Fire,* 126 (advocating inclusive feminism); Rush Limbaugh, *The Way Things Ought To Be* (New York: Pocket Books, 1992), 192; Chris Harding, quoted in E. Anthony Rotundo, *American Manhood* (New York: Basic Books, 1993), 288; Denfeld, *The New Victorians,* 41.

21. Wolf, *Fire with Fire,* 185–186; Tad Friend, "The Rise of 'Do Me' Feminism," *Esquire,* February 1994, 47.

22. Paula Kamen, "Acquaintance Rape: Revolution and Reaction," in Nan Bauer Maglin and Donna Perry, eds., *"Bad Girls" / "Good Girls"* (New Brunswick, N.J.: Rutgers University Press, 1996), 142–143. See also Chapter 5, above.

23. See Nancie Caraway, *Segregated Sisterhood: Racism and the Politics of American Feminism* (Knoxville: University of Tennessee Press, 1991); bell hooks, "Black Students Who Reject Feminism," *Chronicle of Higher Education,* 13 July 1991; bell hooks, "All the Men Are White," in Marita Golden and Susan Richards Shreve, eds., *Skin Deep: Black Women and White Women Write about Race* (New York: Doubleday, 1995). For criticisms of Faludi, see Boyles, *The Modern Man's Guide to Modern Women,* 131. For criticisms of Wolf, see bell hooks, *Outlaw Culture: Resisting Representations* (New York: Routledge, 1994), 96, 102; Susan Vogel, "A Feminist Revisits Feminism," *The Recorder,* 8 March 1995, 7.

24. David Tuller, "Law Doesn't Take Problem Seriously When Gays Batter Their Partners," *San Francisco Chronicle,* 3 January 1994, A1. See also sources cited in Chapter 5, above.

25. Andrew Koppelman, "Why Discrimination against Lesbians and Gay Men Is Sex Discrimination," *New York University Law Review* 69 (1994): 197, 234–241; Patricia Ireland, *What Women Want* (New York: Dutton, 1996), 230–231; Suzanne Pharr, *Homophobia: A Weapon of Sexism* (Inverness, Calif.: Chardon, 1988), 47–49.

26. Janet Saltzman Chafetz, *Gender Equity: An Integrated Theory of Stability and Change* (Newbury Park, Calif.: Sage, 1990), 210–211.

27. Susan Estrich, "The Last Victim," *New York Times Magazine,* 18 December 1994, 59.

28. Denfeld, *The New Victorians,* 5; Vogel, "A Feminist Revisits Feminism," 7; Camille Paglia, *Sexual Personae* (New York: Vintage, 1991); Paglia, quoted in Harris, "Nietzsche Does Downtown," 615.

29. Camille Paglia, "The Return of Carrie Nation: Feminists Catharine MacKinnon and Andrea Dworkin," *Playboy,* October 1992, 36; Karen Lehrman, "Off Course," *Mother Jones,* September–October 1993, 49. See also Sommers, *Who Stole Feminism?* 90. Patai and Koertge, *Professing Feminism,* 28; Michelle Easton, "The Finishing School of the '90s," *Wall Street Journal,* 28 March 1996, A14.

30. For critiques from the right, see Denfeld, *The New Victorians,* 5–20; Sommers, *Who Stole Feminism?* 22–24; Sarah Bryan Miller, "Why I Quit NOW," *Wall Street Journal,* 10 August 1995, A8. For critiques from the left, see sources cited in Deborah L. Rhode, "Feminist Critical Theories," *Stanford Law Review*

42 (1990): 617, 633–635. For a general critique of the rights focus, see Mary Ann Glendon, *Rights Talk: The Impoverishment of Political Discourse* (New York: Free Press, 1991).

31. Martha Minow, *Making All the Difference: Inclusion, Exclusion and American Law* (Ithaca, N.Y.: Cornell University Press, 1990), 49.

32. For antifeminist attitudes, see Gloria Cowan, Monja Mestlin, and Julie Masek, "Predictors of Feminist Self-Labeling," *Sex Roles* 27 (1992): 321, 329; Jennifer Crocker and Riia Luhtanen, "Collective Self-Esteem and Ingroup Bias," *Journal of Personality and Social Psychology* 58 (1990): 60. For the use of extremist images, see Cynthia Cockburn, *In the Way of Women: Men's Resistance to Sex Equality in Organizations* (Ithaca, New York: ILR Press, 1991), 167; Greta Gaard, "Anti-Lesbian Intellectual Harassment in the Academy," in VeVe Clark, Shirley Nelson Garner, Margaret Higonnet, and Ketu H. Katrak, *Antifeminism in the Academy* (New York: Routledge, 1996), 115; hooks, "Black Students Who Reject Feminism," A44.

33. Reprinted in Matt Ridley, *The Red Queen: Sex and the Evolution of Human Nature* (New York: Macmillan, 1994), 245.

34. Nicole Hollander, "Sylvia," reprinted in Kay Leigh Hagan, ed., *Women Respond to the Men's Movement* (San Francisco: Harper Collins, 1992), 149.

35. Hattie Gossett, "Mins Movement?" in Ross Warren, ed., *The Best Contemporary Women's Humor* (New York: Crossing Press, 1994), 149; Julian Bond, quoted in Sally Jacobs, "The Put Upon Privileged Ones," *Boston Globe*, 22 November 1992, 1.

36. Robert Bly, *Iron John* (New York: Vintage, 1992); Sam Keen, *Fire in the Belly* (New York: Bantam, 1991); Alfred Gingold, *Fire in the John* (New York: St. Martin's, 1991).

37. Basow, *Gender Stereotypes*, 336 (describing organizations). For a fuller description of different wings of the men's movement, see William G. Doty, *Myths of Masculinity* (New York: Crossroad, 1993), 57–63.

38. *The Liberator*, quoted in Diane Mason, "National Men's Rights Group Has It All Wrong," *St. Petersburg Times*, 15 June 1990, 1D.

39. Ibid.; Asa Babar, quoted in Michael Kimmel, *Manhood in America: A Cultural History* (New York: Free Press, 1996), 302. See also James L. Wilks, "Fathers Have Rights, Too," *Essence*, June 1995, 134; Richard Doyle, *The Rape of the Male* (St. Paul: Poor Richard's Press, 1986). For the description of activists, see Jerry Adler, with Karen Springen, Daniel Glick, and Jeanne Gordon, "Drums, Sweat, and Tears," *Newsweek*, 24 June 1991, 46.

40. Michael S. Kimmel and Michael Kaufman, "Weekend Warriors: The New Men's Movement," in Michael S. Kimmel, ed., *The Politics of Manhood: Profeminist Men Respond to the Mythopoetic Men's Movement* (Philadelphia: Temple University Press, 1995), 15, 18; Christopher McLean, "The Politics of Men's Pain," in Christopher McLean, Maggie Carey, and Cheryl White, eds., *Men's Ways of Being* (Boulder, Colo.: Westview, 1996), 11. For men of color, see bell hooks, *Black Looks: Race and Representation* (Boston: South End Press, 1992), 99–113.

41. Mel Feit, quoted in Ellis Cose, *A Man's World: How Real Is Male Privilege and How High Is Its Price?* (New York: Harper Collins, 1995), 29; Warren Farrell, *The Myth of Male Power* (New York: Simon and Schuster, 1993), 33–34; Andrew Kipnis, quoted in Cose, *A Man's World,* 36.

42. Andrew Kimbrell, *The Masculine Mystique* (New York: Ballantine, 1995), 4–12; idem, "A Time for Men to Pull Together," *Utne Reader,* May–June 1991, 67.

43. For custody, see Chapter 7. For crime, see Myriam Miedzian, *Boys Will Be Boys* (New York: Doubleday, 1991), 11, 20–22; Kathleen Daly, *Gender, Crime and Punishment* (New Haven: Yale University Press, 1994).

44. Bly, *Iron John,* 189–190; Hans Sebald, *Momism: The Silent Disease of America* (Chicago: Nelson Hall, 1976); Herb Goldberg, *Inner Male* (New York: New American Library, 1987); Herb Goldberg, *What Men Really Want* (New York: Signet, 1991). For a critical review, see Fred Pfeil, *White Guys: Studies in Post-Modern Domination and Difference* (New York: Kerso, 1995), 171–172.

45. Keen, *Fire in the Belly,* 39–67, 233–246; Bly, *Iron John,* 8, 26. For critical discussion of assumptions, R. W. Connell, *Masculinities* (Berkeley, Calif.: University of California Press, 1995), 6.

46. Kimmel, *Manhood in America,* 315–316.

47. Ronald F. Levant, "Toward the Reconstruction of Masculinity," *Journal of Family Psychology* 5 (1992): 384.

48. Rosemary Radford Ruether, "Patriarchy and the Men's Movement: Part of the Problem or Part of the Solution," in Hagan, ed., *Women Respond to the Men's Movement,* 16; Myriam Miedzian, "'Father Hunger': Why 'Soup Kitchen' Fathers Are Not Good Enough," in Hagan, ed., *Women Respond to the Men's Movement,* 127.

49. Elizabeth Dodson Gray, "Beauty and the Beast: A Parable for Our Time," in Hagan, ed., *Women Respond to the Men's Movement,* 159, 165; Ann Jones, *Next Time She'll Be Dead: Battering and How to Stop It* (Boston: Beacon, 1994), 98.

50. Ken Clatterbaugh, "Mythopoetic Founders and New Age Patriarchy," in Kimmel, ed., *Politics of Manhood,* 44, 59; McLean, "Men's Pain," 16–19.

51. *Promise Keepers Handbook,* quoted in Ellen Goodman, "What Role Will Black Women Play in the 'New' Family?" *Chicago Tribune,* 24 October 1995, 17.

52. Richard Wolf, "Men at Work," *USA Today,* 8 August 1995, 9A; David Briggs, "The New Rugged Cross: The Burgeoning Christian Men's Movement," *Buffalo News,* 16 August 1995, B7.

53. Louis Sahagun, "For Men Only: Spiritual Drive Fills Stadiums—Group Targets Male Identity Crisis," *New Orleans Times-Picayune,* 9 July 1995, A2; Joe Conason, Alfred Ross, and Lee Cokorinos, "The Promise Keepers Are Coming: The Third Wave of the Religious Right," *The Nation,* 7 October 1996, 14; James D. Davis, "Rooted in Christianity: Movement Rallies Men to Pledge a New Approach to Family and Society," *Sun-Sentinel* (Fort Lauderdale), 30 July 1995, 1E.

54. Donna Britt, "Black Women, Loyalty, Pride and the March," *Washington Post,*

22 September 1995, B1; Julianne Malveaux, "A Woman's Place Is in the March: Why Should I Stand by My Man When He's Trying to Step Over Me?" *Washington Post*, 8 October 1995, C3. See also Kristal Brent Zook, "A Manifesto of Sorts for a Black Feminist Movement," *New York Times Magazine*, 12 November 1995, 86.

55. Ruth Rosen, "A Feminist Send-Off for a Million Men," *Los Angeles Times*, 12 October 1995, B9; Britt, "Black Women"; Briggs, "Christian Men's Movement."

56. Britt, "Black Women," B1; Theresa Moore, "March Inspires Emotional Debate for Black Women Left Behind," *San Francisco Chronicle*, 14 October 1995, A8.

57. Kimmell, *Manhood in America*, 7; McLean, "Men's Pain," 16.

58. Basow, *Gender Stereotypes*, 337; Lynn Segal, *Slow Motion: Changing Masculinities, Changing Men* (New Brunswick, N.J.: Rutgers University Press, 1990).

59. Levant, "Reconstruction of Masculinity," 381 ("male code"); Kimmel and Kaufman, "Weekend Warriors," 40–41 ("hung out to dry"); Eric Skjei and Richard Rabkin, *The Male Ordeal: Role Crisis in a Changing World* (New York: Putnam, 1981), 119 (sex); Kathleen Gerson, *No Man's Land* (New York: Basic Books, 1993), 277 ("embattled and nostalgic").

60. Rhoda Unger and Mary Crawford, *Women and Gender: A Feminist Psychology* (Philadelphia: Temple University Press, 1992), 137. For images, see Rotundo, *American Manhood*, 291; Miedzian, *Boys Will Be Boys*, 11, 101.

61. Robert A. Strikwerda and Larry May, "Male Friendship and Intimacy," in May and Strikwerda, eds., *Rethinking Masculinity* (Lanham, Md.: Rowman and Littlefield, 1992), 95; Larry May and Robert A. Strikwerda, "Fatherhood and Nurturance," ibid., 75; Patrick D. Hopkin, "Gender Treachery, Homophobia, Masculinity, and Threatened Identity," ibid., 111, 119; Michael S. Kimmel, "Rethinking Masculinity" in Kimmel, ed., *Changing Men: New Directions in Research on Men and Masculinity* (Newbury Park, Calif.: Sage, 1987), 9; Robert Staples, *Black Masculinity: The Black Male's Role in American Society* (San Francisco: Black Scholar Press, 1982).

62. Warren Farrell, *The Liberated Man* (New York: Random House, 1994), 182; Connell, *Masculinities*, 24.

63. Skjei and Rabkin, *The Male Ordeal*, 100.

64. Kimmel, *Manhood in America*, 292–298, 313.

65. For historical and cross-cultural experience, see ibid., 318; Peggy Sanday, *Female Power and Male Dominance: On the Origins of Sexual Inequality* (New York: Cambridge University Press, 1991). For men's studies, see Connell, *Masculinities*; David D. Gilmore, *Manhood in the Making: Cultural Concepts of Masculinity* (New Haven: Yale University Press, 1990); Kimmell, *Manhood in America*; Pfeil, *White Guys*; Nancy Levit, "Feminism for Men: Legal Ideology and the Construction of Maleness," *University of California Law Review* 43 (1996): 1038.

66. Pfeil, *White Guys*, 187–188, 227; Michael Schwalbe, "Mythopoetic Men's

Work as a Search for Communitas," in Kimmel, ed., *The Politics of Manhood,* 186, 201–202.

67. Connell, *Masculinities,* 237–238. See also Andrew Tolson, *The Limits of Masculinity* (London: Tavistock, 1977), 143.

68. For classic forms of the argument, see Carolyn Heilbrun, *Toward a Recognition of Androgyny* (New York: Knopf, 1973); Joyce Trebilcot, "Two Forms of Androgynism," in Mary Vetterling-Braggin, ed., *Femininity, Masculinity, and Androgyny: A Modern Philosophical Discussion* (Totowa, N.J.: Rowman and Littlefield, 1982).

69. Gilmore, *Manhood in the Making,* 9, 22–23, 230, 231.

70. Kimmel, *Manhood in America,* 333.

9. The Politics of Progress

1. See Sherrye Henry, *The Deep Divide* (New York: Macmillan, 1994).

2. Ellen Willis, *No More Nice Girls: Countercultural Essays* (Middletown, Conn.: Wesleyan University Press, 1992), 149.

3. *New Yorker,* 1 November 1993, 85 (Victoria Roberts, cartoonist), emphasis added.

4. Audre Lorde, *Sister Outsider* (Trumansburg, N.Y.: Crossing Press 1984), 115.

5. The slogan is reprinted in Gerda Lerner, *The Majority Finds Its Past* (New York: Oxford University Press, 1979), 34.

6. Thomas Nagel, *Equality and Partiality* (New York: Oxford University Press, 1991), 90.

7. Roberta S. Sigel, *Ambition and Accommodation: How Women View Gender Relations* (Chicago: University of Chicago Press, 1996), 75, 173–174, 121, 185.

8. Bella Abzug, Speech at the Women's Bicentennial Celebration of the United States Constitution, Atlanta, Ga., 1988.

9. Henry, *The Deep Divide,* 2 (three centuries); Dick Armey, quoted in Patricia Ireland, *What Women Want* (New York: Dutton, 1996), 298 ("femcentric"). For women's underrepresentation, see Thalia Zepatos and Elizabeth Kaufman, *Women for a Change: A Grassroots Guide to Activism and Politics* (New York: Facts on File, 1995), 3; Michael Janofsky, "Women Make Only Moderate Gains Despite the Many Contenders," *New York Times,* 7 November 1996, B2; Adam Nagourney, "More Women, Fewer Careers," *New York Times,* 28 April 1996, E4; sources cited in Deborah L. Rhode, "Feminism and the State," *Harvard Law Review* 107 (1994): 1181, 1206.

10. Henry, *The Deep Divide,* 2, 16; Sue Thomas, *How Women Legislate* (New York: Oxford University Press, 1994), 78–79, 88–104, 124–125; Ruth B. Mandel, "The Political Woman," in Sherri Matteo, ed., *American Women in the Nineties: Today's Critical Issues* (Boston: Northeastern University Press, 1993).

11. Kathleen Dolan and Lynne E. Ford, "Women in the State Legislatures: Feminist Identity and Legislative Behavior," *American Politics Quarterly* 23 (1995):

96; Thomas B. Edsall, "Pollsters View Gender Gap as Political Fixture," *Washington Post*, 15 August 1995, A10; Robin Toner, "With G.O.P. Congress the Issue, 'Gender Gap' Is Growing Wider," *New York Times*, 21 April 1996, A1; Gloria Steinem, quoted in Thomas, *How Women Legislate*, 11.

12. For suffragettes' claims, see Jane Addams, "The Modern City and the Municipal Franchise for Women," in Susan B. Anthony and Ida Husted Harper, eds., *History of Woman Suffrage*, vol. 4 (Indianapolis: Hallenback, 1902), 178; Aileen S. Kraditor, *Ideas of the Woman Suffrage Movement* (New York: Columbia University Press, 1965), 50–74. For similarities over time, see Keith T. Poole and L. Harmon Zeigler, *Women, Public Opinion and Politics: The Changing Political Attitudes of American Women* (New York: Longman, 1985), 4–7, 68–69; sources cited in Rhode, "Feminism and the State," 1206. For race and education, see Steven Stark, "Gap Politics," *Atlantic Monthly*, July 1996. For women's votes, see Nancy Woloch, *Women and the American Experience* (New York: Knopf, 1984), 534; Robert S. Erikson, Norman R. Luttbeg, and Kent L. Tedin, *American Political Opinion: Its Origins, Content and Impact* (New York: Wiley, 1980), 186–187; William J. Turnier, Pamela Johnston Conover, and David Lowery, "Redistributive Justice and Cultural Feminism," *American University Law Review* 45 (1996): 1275; Kate O'Beirne, "Bread and Circuses," *National Review*, 27 November 1995, 27.

13. Thomas, *How Women Legislate*, 89–90; Cathy Young, "The Sexist Subtext of the Year of the Woman," *Tallahassee Democrat*, 18 October 1992, B1, B4; Barbara Crossette, "Enthralled by Asia's Ruling Women? Look Again," *New York Times*, 11 November 1996, E3.

14. Gloria Steinem, quoted in Zepatos and Kaufman, *Women for a Change*, ix.

15. Grover Cleveland, quoted in David Olive, *GenderBabble* (New York: Putnam, 1993), 87.

16. Pat Schroeder, quoted in Margaret Carlson, "Hand Over the Cash," *Redbook*, September 1992, 29. For discussion of women's need for campaign financing reforms, see Marcia Lynn Whicker and Todd W. Areson, "The Maleness of the American Presidency," in Lois Lovelace Duke, *Women in Politics: Outsiders or Insiders?* (Englewood Cliffs, N.J.: Prentice-Hall, 1993): 165, 171.

17. For voters' lack of information, see Henry, *Deep Divide*, 323–328, 334, 339. For Canada's National Action Committee, see Martha Burk and Heidi Hartmann, "Beyond the Gender Gap," *The Nation*, 10 June 1996, 21.

18. Richard L. Berke, "In '94, 'Vote for Woman' Does Not Play So Well," *New York Times*, 3 October 1994, A1. The ad appeared in *The Nation*, 18 December 1995, 786.

19. James Brooke, "Three Suffragists (in Marble) Win Niche in the Capitol," *New York Times*, 27 September 1996, A12.

20. Zepatos and Kaufman, *Women for a Change*, 151–168.

21. National Council for Research on Women, "Do Universal Dollars Reach Women and Girls?" *Issues Quarterly* 1 (1994): 1.

Acknowledgments

Acknowledgments are a daunting art form. It seems impossible to express in any sufficiently graceful way the depth of gratitude that I feel toward those who have contributed so much to this book. Many students have provided invaluable research and editorial assistance, particularly Jeanine Becker, Betsy Facher, Edward Frueh, Linda Holmes, Sarah Killingsworth, Isabel Traugott, and Abigail Trillin. Their work, as well as my own, benefited immeasurably from the superb staff of the Stanford Law Library; to Andrea Eisenberg, Paul Lomio, and Erika Wayne I am especially indebted. My agent, Gerry McCauley, had the wisdom and experience to steer me to the ideal editor for this manuscript, Joyce Seltzer. She saw what the book could and should be, even before I did. Her insights, along with those of her assistant, Cherie Weitzner Acierno, supplied clarity and coherence to the analysis.

Many colleagues gave generously of their time and talents in commenting on early drafts: John Cavanagh, Jan Costello, Cynthia Epstein, William Eskridge, Catharine MacKinnon, Linda McClain, Carlin Meyer, Temma Kaplan, Michael Kimmel, David Richards, Carol Sanger, Kathleen Sullivan, and Michael Wald. To two colleagues, Barbara Babcock and Lawrence Friedman, I dedicate the book. Their vision, values, and judgment have not only enriched this project but supported me in all the efforts that laid its foundation. I owe similar debts to Carol Crane, who prepared this manuscript with painstaking care, exceptional patience, and unfailing good humor.

My deepest gratitude goes to Ralph Cavanagh. His support and insight has sustained my work for over two decades. This book could not have been written without him. For this, and for so much else in my life, I am grateful beyond what any acknowledgment can express.

Index